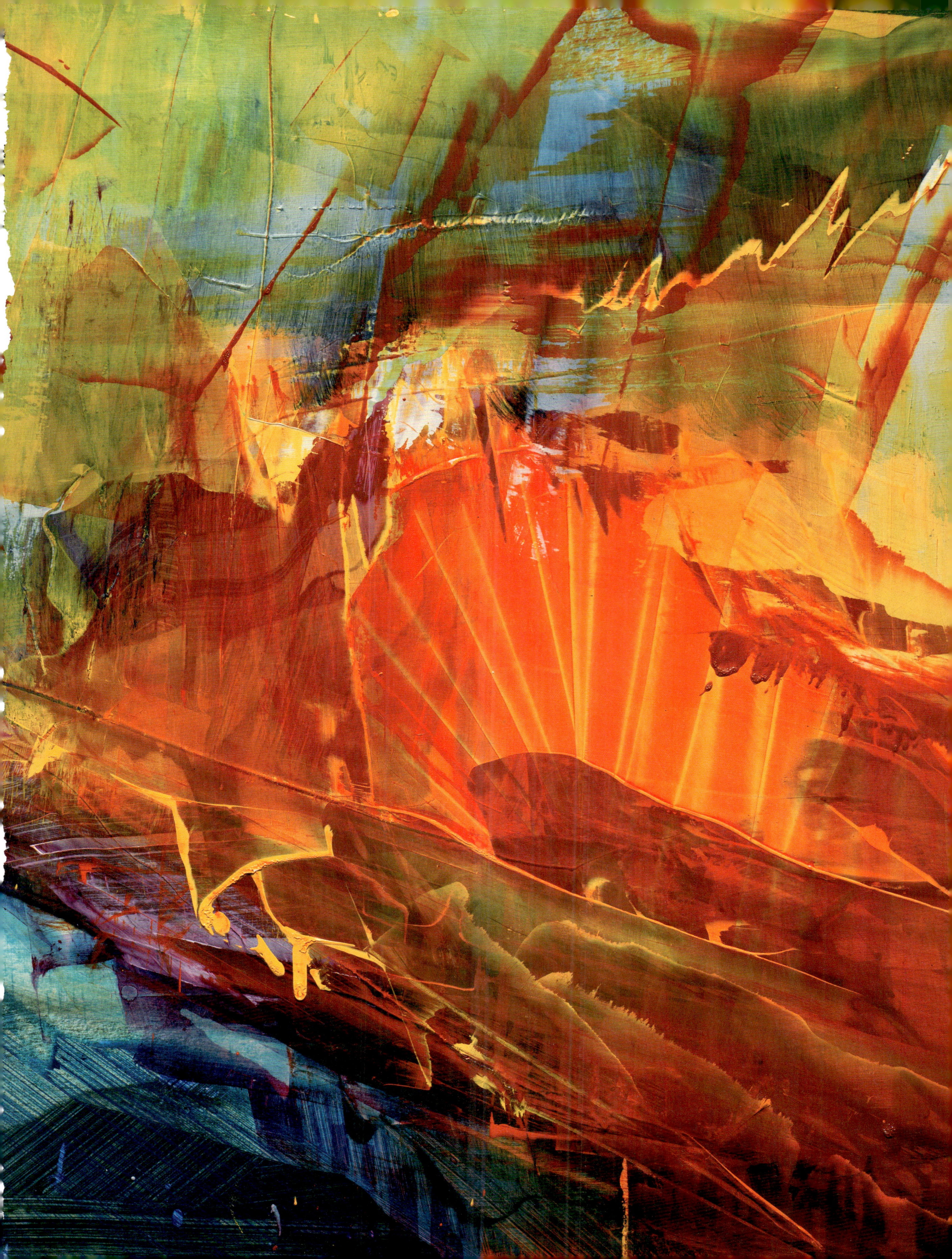

UNIVERSITY OF OREGON

Jordan Schnitzer Museum of Art
University of Oregon, Eugene, OR

Distributed by Oregon State University Press

JORDAN SCHNITZER
MUSEUM OF ART

Previous page: **Lucky Star** (detail), 2024. Oil on wood, 74 x 145 inches. Collection of the Jordan Schnitzer Family Foundation.

JAMES LAVADOUR | LAND OF ORIGIN

Jordan Schnitzer Museum of Art, University of Oregon
Eugene, OR
August 9, 2025 – January 11, 2026

Northwest Museum of Arts and Culture
Spokane, WA
January 31 - June 7, 2026

Boise Art Museum
Boise, ID
August 29, 2026 - February 28, 2027

Whatcom Museum
Bellingham, WA
March 20 - September 6, 2027

Heard Museum
Phoenix, AZ
March 31 - September 4, 2028

Missoula Art Museum
Missoula, MT
October 3, 2028 - March 31, 2029

Art Bridges

James Lavadour: Land of Origin national tour made possible by Art Bridges

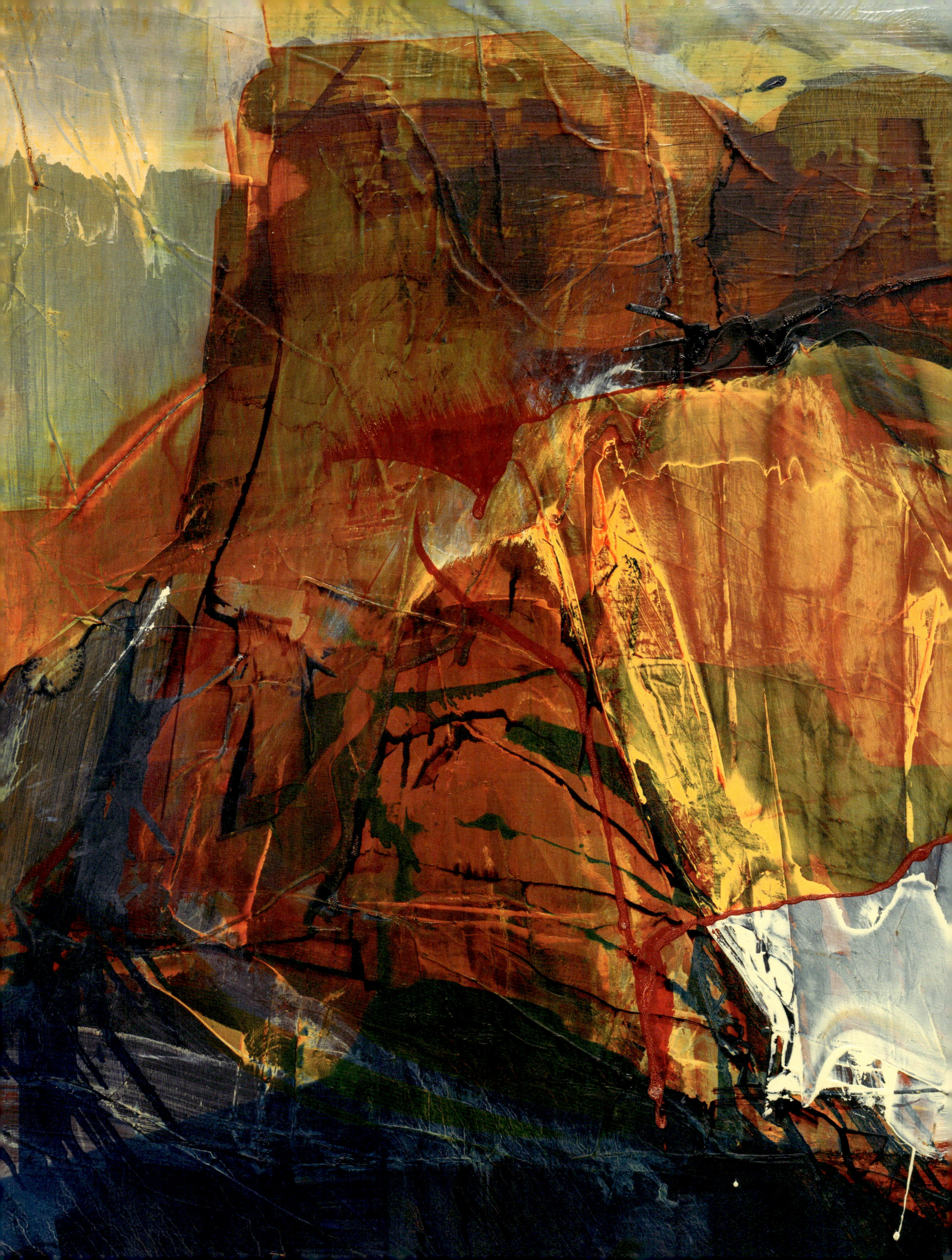

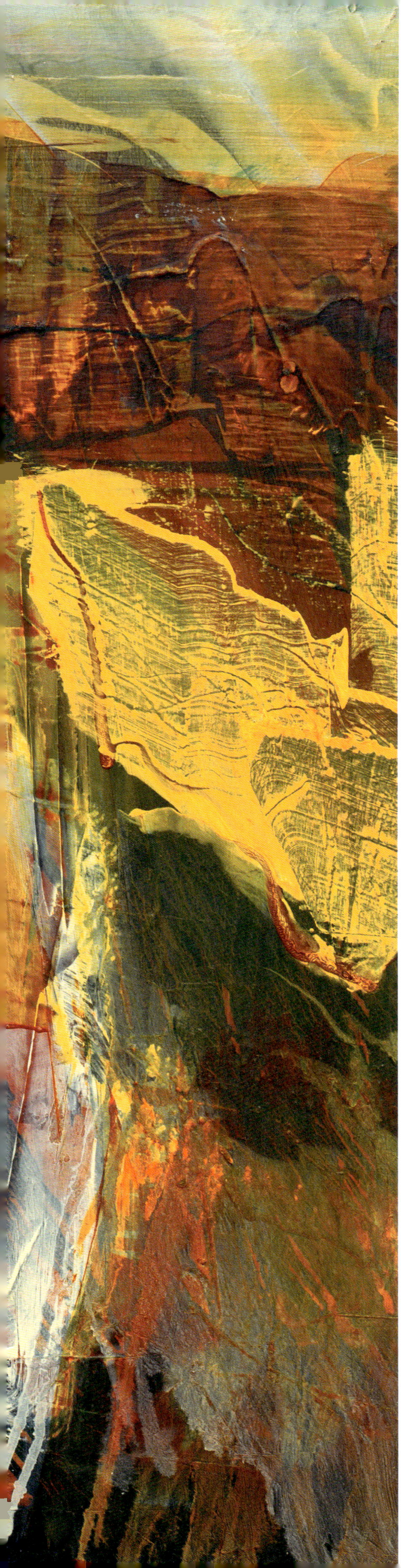

Contents

Lucky Star (detail), 2024. Oil on wood, 74 x 145 inches. Collection of the Jordan Schnitzer Family Foundation.

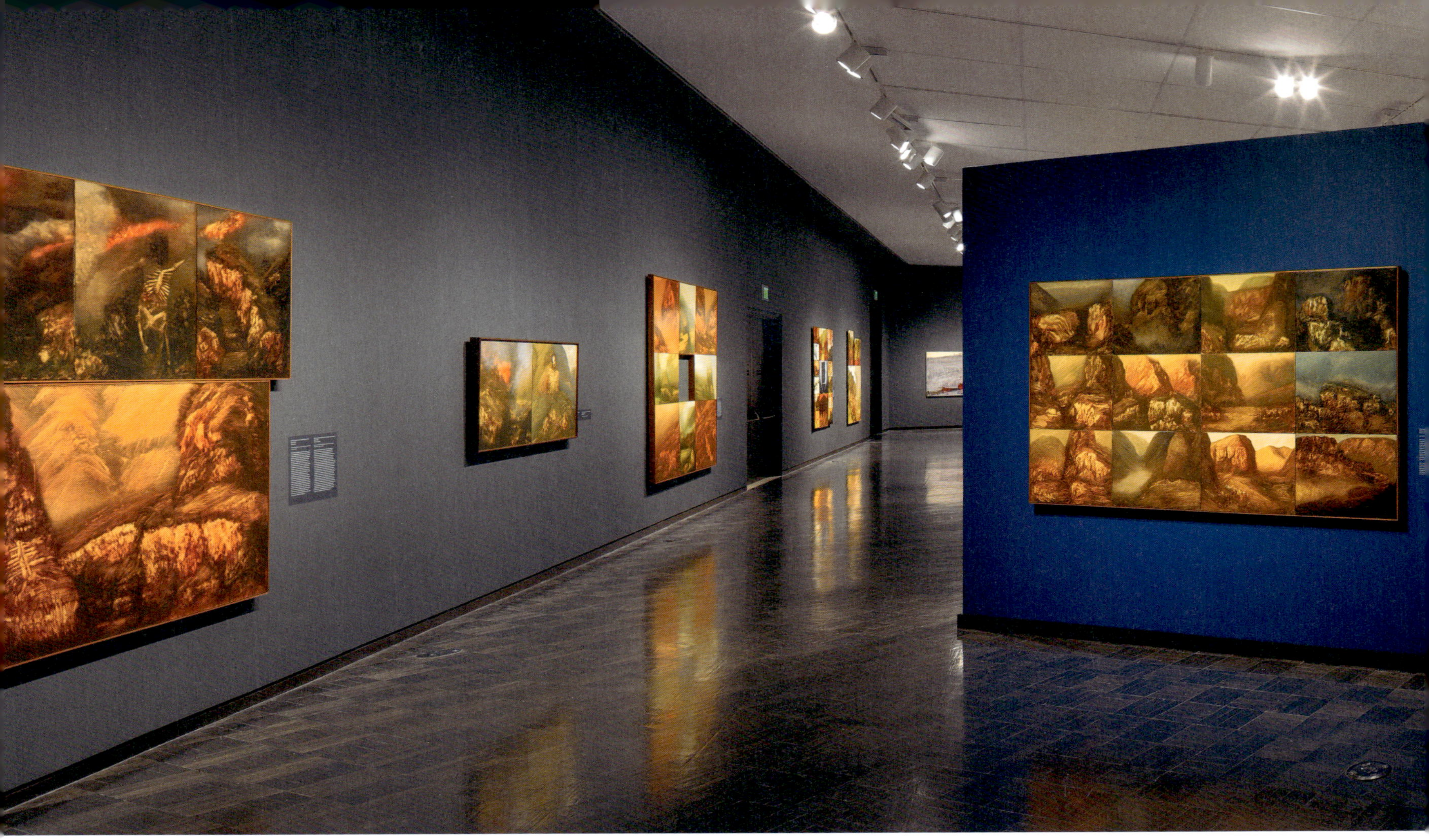

Director's Introduction and Acknowledgments

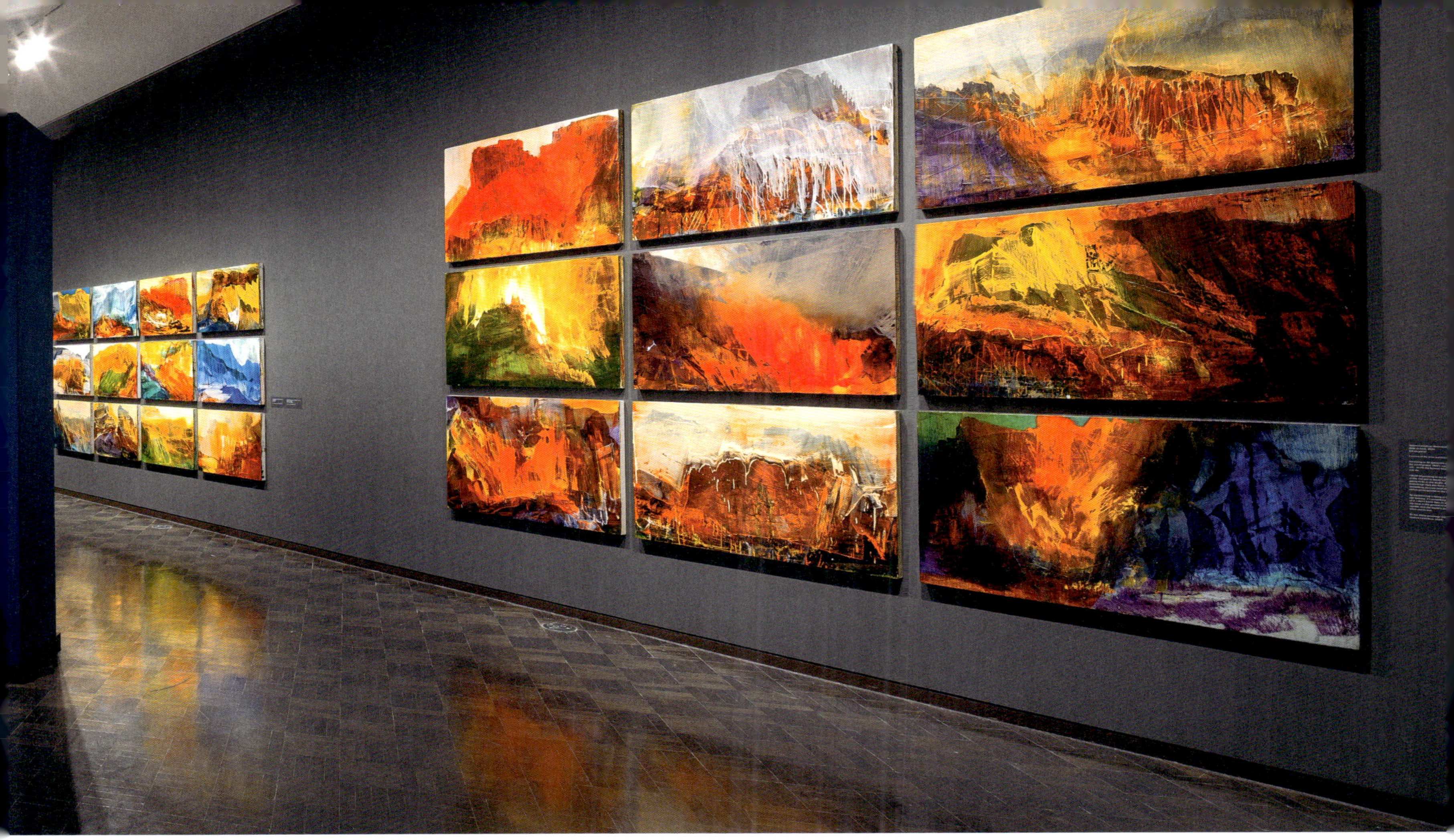

More than four years ago, Danielle Knapp and I asked ourselves what artists in Oregon and the Pacific Northwest had created a body of work so original, powerful, and sustained across time that it demanded a career retrospective exhibition, full catalogue, and national tour. Our response was identical and immediate: James Lavadour. We were both grateful and more than a little relieved when he agreed to our proposal to work together on what has become *James Lavadour: Land of Origin*, a survey of his work spanning five decades. Although it includes printmaking, the exhibition focuses on Lavadour's painting, particularly the multi-panel grids he began exhibiting in the late 1980s. Utterly original and viscerally convincing, those works have made a unique contribution to contemporary art, even as Lavadour's approach to painting itself underwent a major transition and evolution over the course of his long career. The nature of that artistic journey is the story this exhibition tells, and it is fully visible in the paintings themselves.

My own first experience of Lavadour's work was in Portland in the later 1980s, when he began showing in Oregon. His work from that time shared many aspects of his current paintings. Emotionally riveting and unlike anything else I'd seen, they often took the form of haunting landscape imagery shown in grouped panels, often in a grid layout. Dark, brooding, and at times incendiary and cataclysmic in feeling, Lavadour's first grid paintings were brushed on thinly in earthy tones of brown, orange, red, and muddy yellows, seemingly depicting ragged cliff faces, ravines, mountain ranges, and valleys. Areas of flaming red and glowing orange evoked forest fires. At times ghostly skeletons or skulls were visible, as if inscribed into the earth. Ominous and searingly beautiful, those paintings immediately established Lavadour as a force in Northwest art. They feel just as fresh and urgent today as they did when he painted them.

In the mid-2000s, Lavadour's approach to painting and to his process underwent a seismic shift. The result was a brilliant fusion of abstraction that joined and complicated the loosely pictorial landscape impulse underlying his earlier work. Essays in this catalogue explore how and why that evolution occurred in Lavadour's painting, as do his own words in the interview anthology. The result of that fusion has been an outpouring of painting and printmaking that continues to express powerfully Lavadour's experience of the land and his awareness that, as Lavadour has long said, "The land and I are one."

This catalogue documents the breadth and depth of Lavadour's singular achievement, bringing it to a national audience and registering his place in American art history. My thanks to catalogue essayists Meagan Atiyeh, Rebecca Dobkins, Danielle Knapp, and Marie Watt for sharing their insights on Lavadour's art, life, and impact. I am also grateful to James Lavadour for working with me on a new interview, and the interview anthology published here.

The exhibition, book, and tour have been a labor of love for all of us involved, and I thank James Lavadour for his collaboration with us on all facets of the exhibition. Many thanks as well to his longtime Portland gallerist, Jane Beebe of PDX CONTEMPORARY ART, and her son Sam Beebe and staff JM Fields and Nathan Anderson for their assistance with this project. I also acknowledge the important role played by Elizabeth Leach, who showed Lavadour's paintings in her Portland art gallery where many of us in Oregon first saw them.

I am deeply grateful to the exhibition's curator, Danielle Knapp, the museum's McCosh Curator responsible for American and regional art, for all she has done to bring this exhibition to fruition. She has been a skillful and dedicated shepherd of the project and a tireless advocate of Lavadour's work, its value, and importance. My thanks to our Head Registrar and Shared Visions Manager, Alexander Ellis, for overseeing initial shipping arrangements for the exhibition, and to Chris White, Collections Manager, and Melissa Dawn, Associate Registrar for continuing and completing that work so ably. My thanks to Danielle Knapp, Mackenzie Karp, Kurt Neugebauer, Rosemarie Oakman, and Chris White for their collaboration on grant applications and fundraising.

The exhibition was installed beautifully in our Barker Gallery and Focus Central Gallery by head preparator Joey Capadona, Mark O'Harra, Noah Greene, Anthony Edwards, and Beth Robinson from our installation staff. My thanks to Debbie Williamson Smith for her work on publicity and communications, and to Mike Bragg, the museum's designer, for the elegant production of this book and the design of all associated exhibition graphics and printed matter. Text editing was done with the assistance of Katie Loney and Susan Mannheimer, and we thank Irene Arce for her Spanish translations of the gallery texts.

James Lavadour: Land of Origin includes works from a wide range of museums and collectors. I am happy to thank Art Bridges, Bill Avery, the Boise Art Museum, Crystal Bridges Museum of American Art, the Denver Art Museum, the Hallie Ford Museum of Art, James Lavadour, Burton Lazar and Claire Stock, Sarah Dougher, the Northwest Museum of Arts and Culture, Jane Beebe and PDX CONTEMPORARY ART, the Regional Arts and Culture Council of greater Portland, Al Solheim, the Tacoma Art Museum, and the Whitney Museum of American Art for lending to this exhibition.

The museum gratefully acknowledges that the *James Lavadour: Land of Origin* exhibition, catalogue, and related programs are made possible with the generous support of The Ford Family Foundation in Oregon, the Coeta and Donald Barker Changing Exhibitions Endowment at the museum, and the JSMA's Hartz FUNd for Contemporary Art. Thank you also to Bill Cornog and, again, to Jane Beebe and PDX CONTEMPORARY ART for supporting this catalogue. I extend a particular thanks to Art Bridges, which is partnering with the museum to organize the national tour. Art Bridges has supported the project's organization costs, provided generous support for our education and audience development efforts, and offers significant assistance to other museums in the presentation of this exhibition.

I thank the members of the Jordan Schnitzer Museum of Art, our Patrons Circle, and our Leadership Council for supporting this project and all the work we do. We could not do it without you. I also gratefully acknowledge the support of the University of Oregon for the museum and all of our work.

Finally, and most of all, I thank James Lavadour for his work, his vision, his dedication, and for sharing so much of himself and where he comes from with the world.

John S. Weber
Executive Director, 2019 - 2025

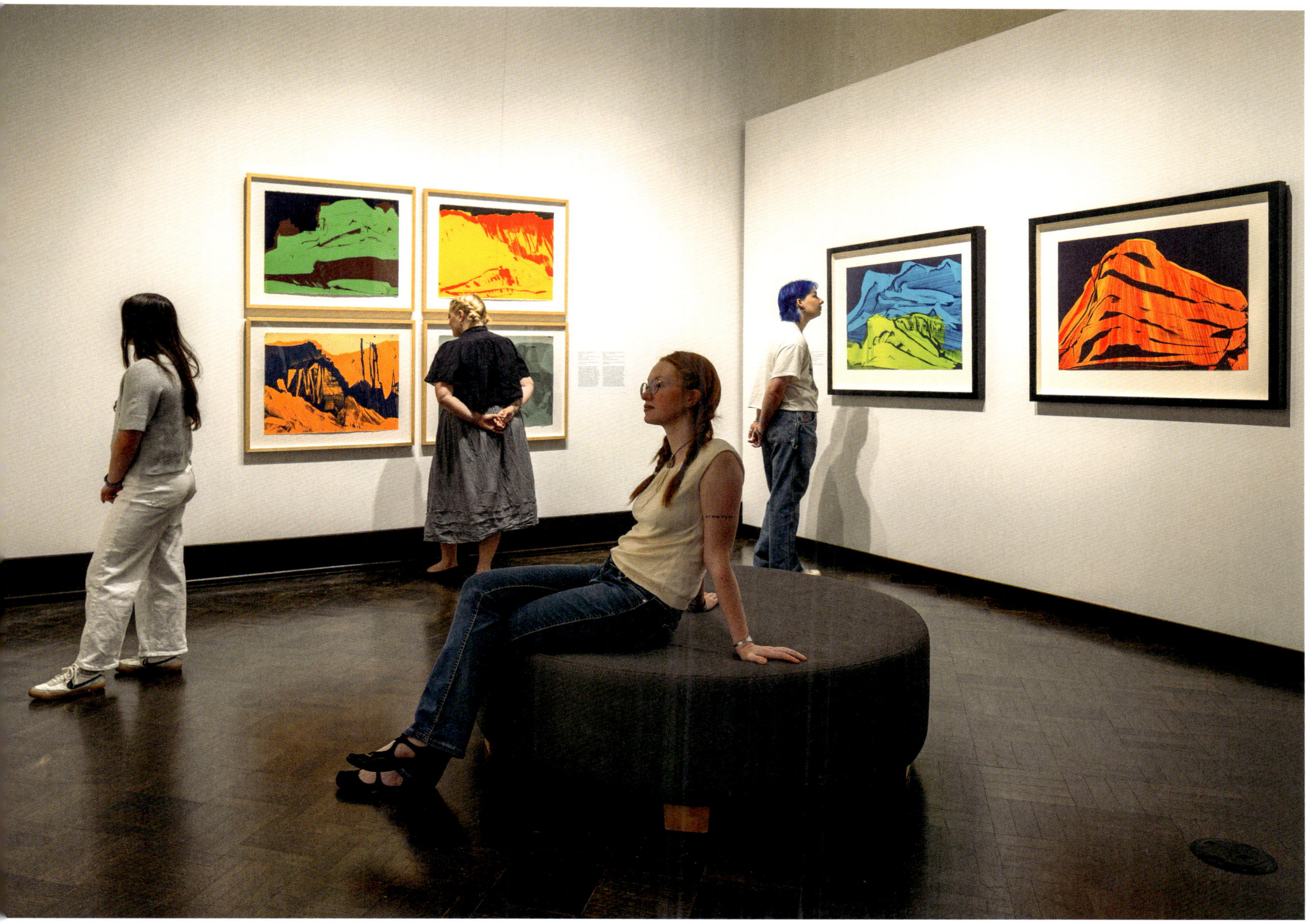

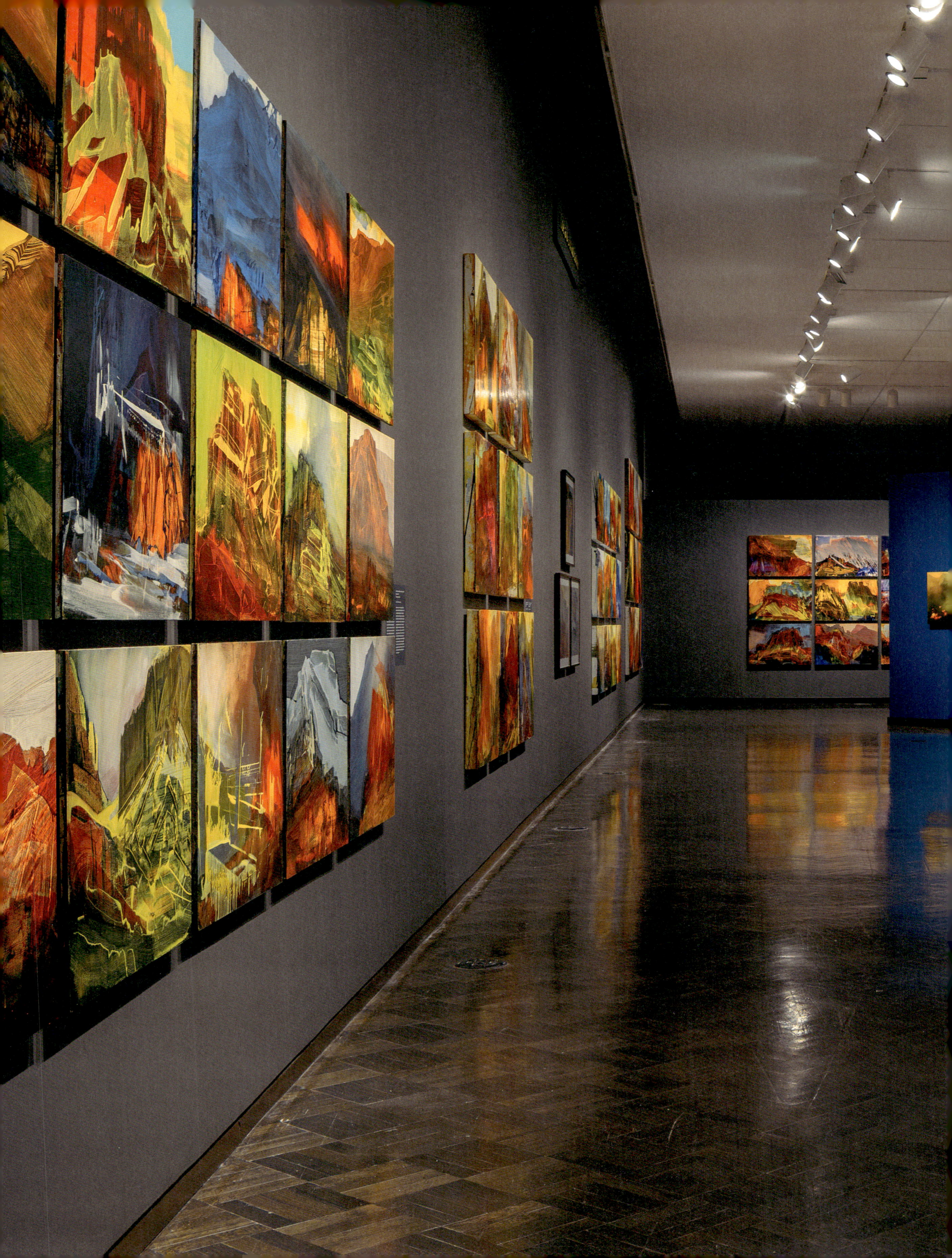

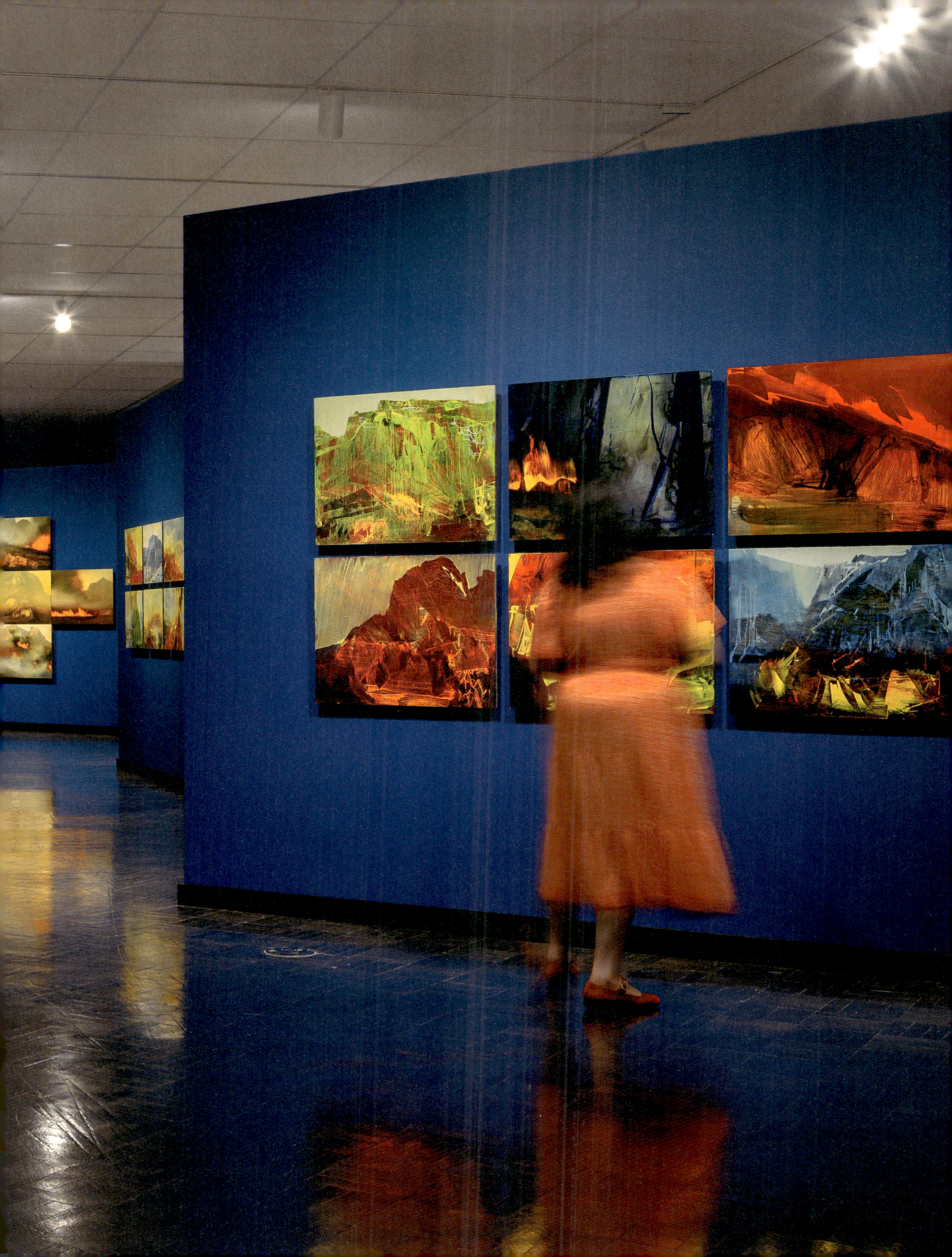

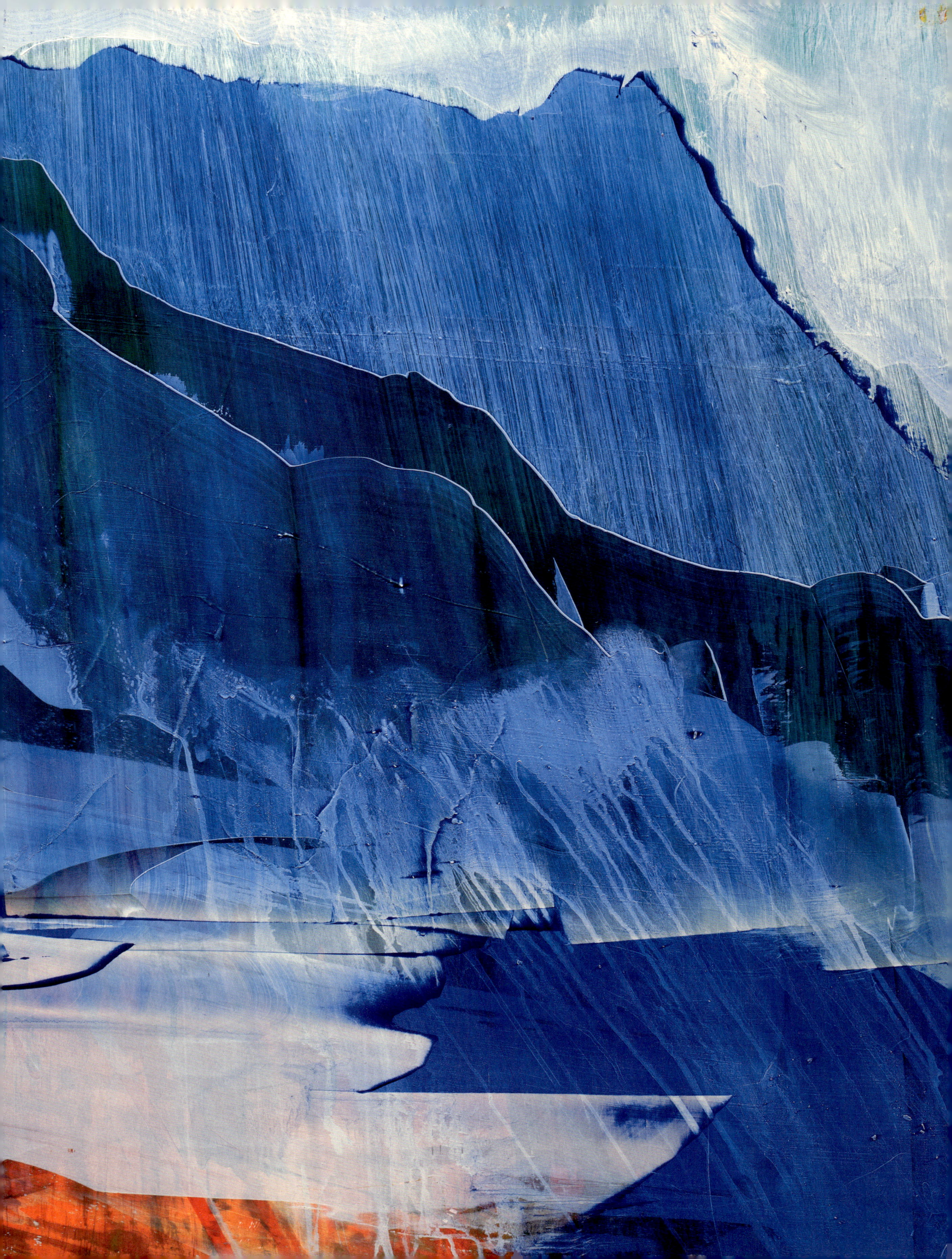

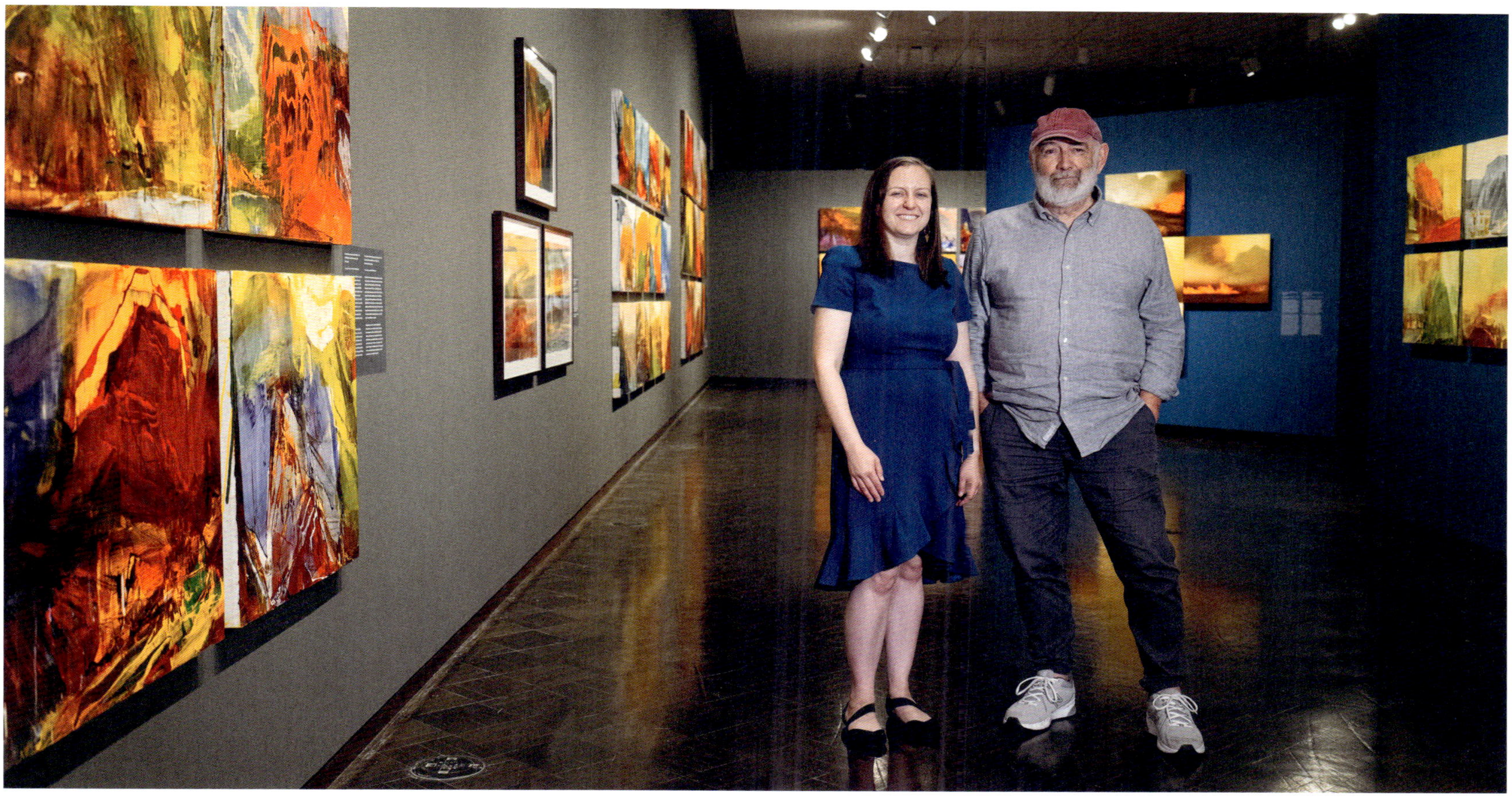

Curator's Acknowledgments

There is the version of an exhibition that is carefully researched, developed, and installed, and there's the version that comes to life once the gallery doors open and people are spending time with the works. I find that I only learn half of what an exhibition project has to teach me during its long planning phase. The other half of the lesson is revealed in the months and years after opening day, when new meanings are created through community engagement with the show, its artworks, and its artists. This has certainly been true of *James Lavadour: Land of Origin*. To see firsthand how visitors have responded to Jim's works, to hear personal stories about the many ways they felt connections with his paintings and prints, and to know Jim Lavadour—both through his powerful artmaking and through his wonderful partnership in planning this retrospective—has been a joy and an honor. Jim is as generous with his time and energy as he is talented with paint. It is impossible to express the level of gratitude I hold for his trust in me to organize this exhibition.

I am humbled by the incredible efforts of our team at JSMA and everyone who had a role in bringing forth *James Lavadour: Land of Origin*. In addition to recognizing the excellence of my museum colleagues, I want to say a special thanks to Jane Beebe and all at PDX CONTEMPORARY ART; Mario Gallucci; the remarkable staff at Art Bridges; JSMA's 2021-25 post-grad museum fellows in European & American Art, Zo Kambour and Alexis Garcia, and 2025 curatorial intern, Miranda Guppy, for their support during exhibition planning; Roberta Lavadour and an ever-expanding network of Jim's friends and supporters; faculty partners and community members at the University of Oregon; and the collaborators (especially Rachel Allen, Amy Chaloupka, Melanie Fales, and Tara Centybear) and lenders for *Land of Origin's* national tour. I am grateful for the invaluable scholarship of Kate Morris, Rebecca Dobkins, and Vicki Halper that helped me develop my own understanding of Jim's intertwined commitments to artmaking and community, and for the perspectives shared by Marie Watt and Meagan Atiyeh that illuminated how Jim inspires and supports other artists. The leadership of (now retired) JSMA executive director John Weber, who championed *James Lavadour: Land of Origin* at every step of the process, and current executive director Olivia Miller, whose excitement for Jim's work and this exhibition was palpable before she even arrived in Eugene, were instrumental in presenting this project at JSMA. As the traveling exhibition and this catalogue reaches even wider audiences, I know that there is still so much for us all to learn from Jim and his work.

Lucky Star (detail), 2024.

James Lavadour: Land of Origin was organized at the Jordan Schnitzer Museum of Art at the University of Oregon located on Kalapuya Ilihi, the traditional indigenous homeland of the Kalapuya people. Following treaties between 1851 and 1855, Kalapuya people were dispossessed of their indigenous homeland by the United States government and forcibly removed to the Coast Reservation in Western Oregon. Today, descendants are citizens of the Confederated Tribes of the Grand Ronde Community of Oregon and the Confederated Tribes of Siletz Indians of Oregon, and continue to make important contributions in their communities, at UO, and across the land we now refer to as Oregon.

We express our respect for all federally recognized tribal nations of Oregon. This includes the Burns Paiute Tribe; the Confederated Tribes of the Coos, Lower Umpqua and Siuslaw Indians; the Confederated Tribes of the Grand Ronde Community of Oregon; the Confederated Tribes of Siletz Indians of Oregon; the Confederated Tribes of the Umatilla Indian Reservation; the Confederated Tribes of Warm Springs; the Coquille Indian Tribe; the Cow Creek Band of Umpqua Tribe of Indians; and the Klamath Tribes. We also express our respect for all other displaced Indigenous peoples who call Oregon home.

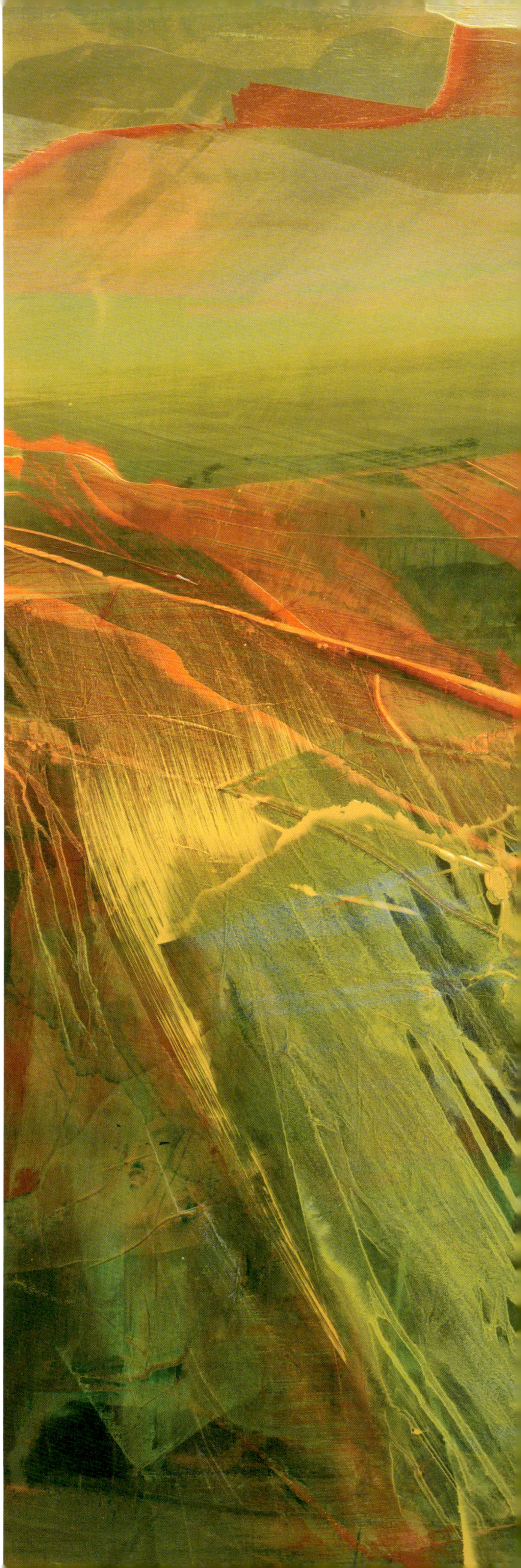

Lucky Star (detail), 2024.

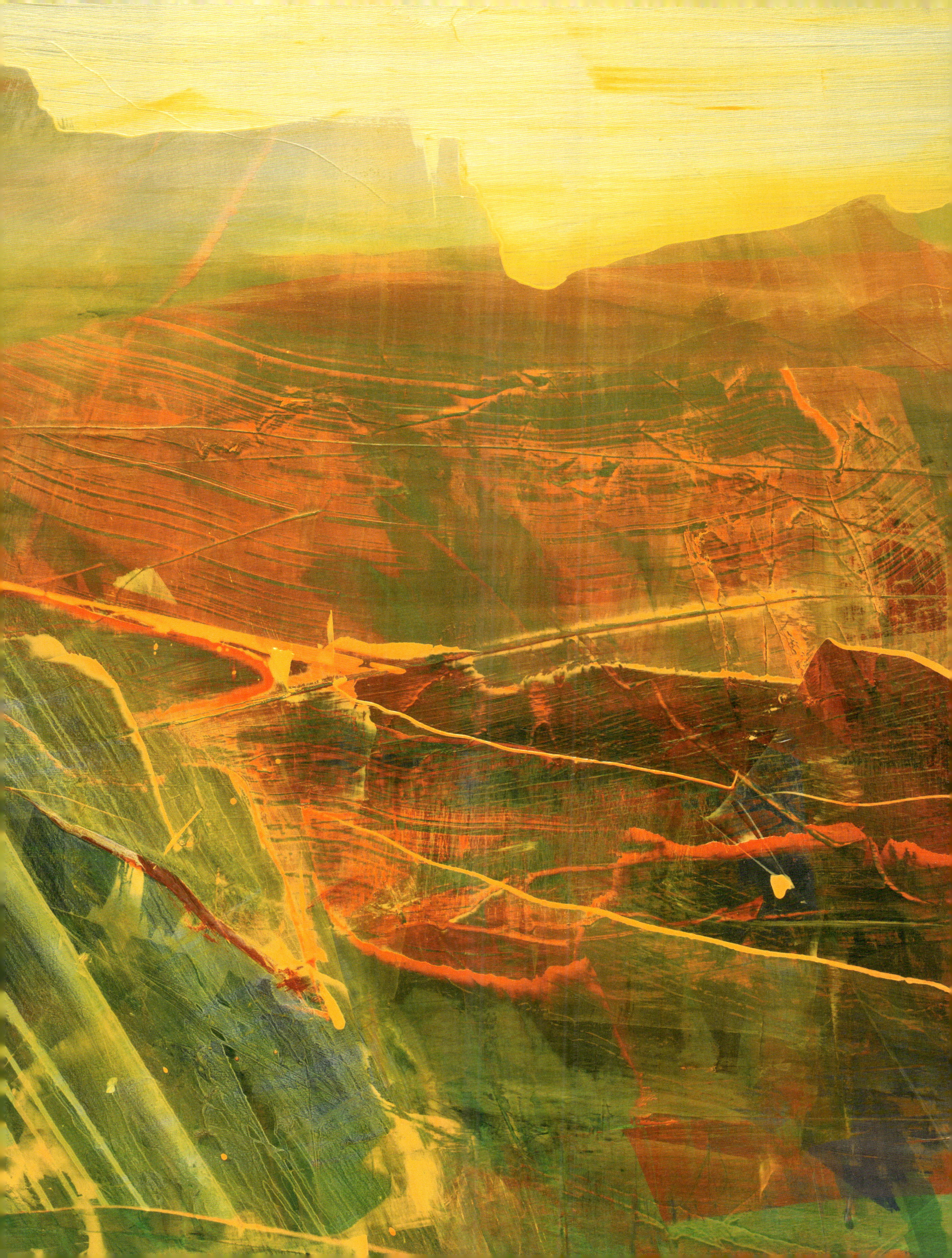

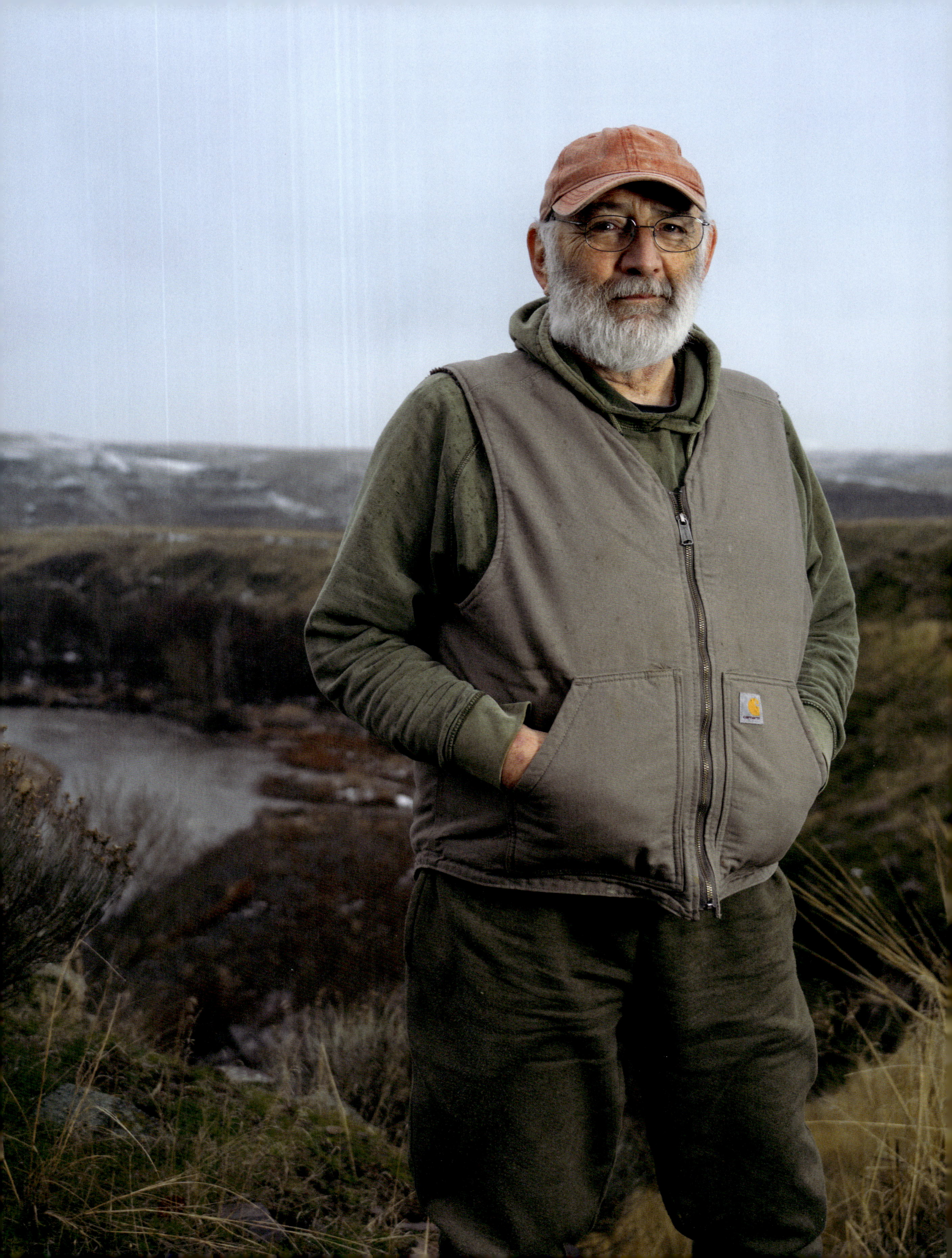

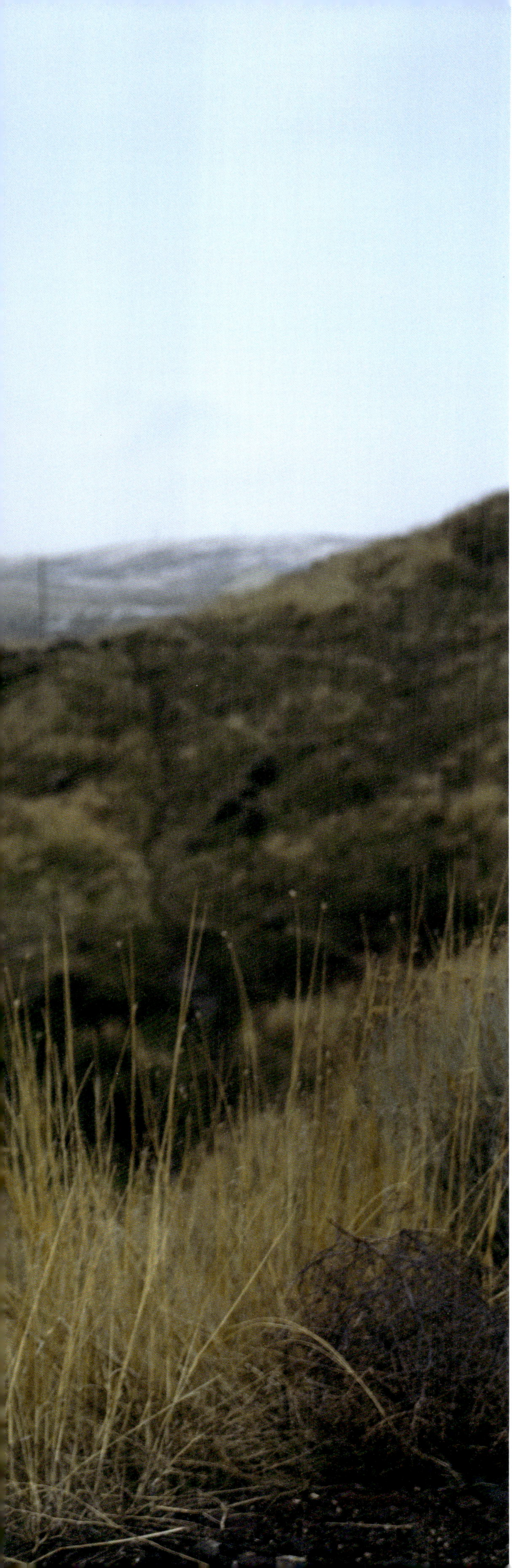

Knowing the Land, Lifting the Spirit

Danielle M. Knapp

The Umatilla Indian Reservation sits on 172,000 acres in the Umatilla and Union Counties of northeastern Oregon, just east of the city of Pendleton. The Blue Mountains, which contain some of the oldest rocks and the greatest geological diversity in the state, cradle this region for 190 miles along its southeast edge, extending from central Oregon to the southeastern corner of Washington state. Encompassing 15 000 square miles, this ancient range covers nearly one-sixth of Oregon's land area.[1] Its English name is grounded in the act of observation: smoke from forest fires and the burns set by Native communities for fire stewardship seemingly tints the mountains blue from afar. The combined effects of viewing the Blues' pine trees, dark basalt cliffs, and wide stretches of overhead sky enhance this coloration further. Rocky Mountain elk, deer, birds, small scurrying mammals, and coyotes abound. The Umatilla River runs from its headwaters in these mountains, winding northwest until it joins the Columbia in a reservoir at the John Day Dam. Painter James Lavadour has made his home here for nearly all of his life. His family history, which descends from Walla Walla, Chinook, Assiniboine Sioux, German, Irish, and French-Canadian heritage, reflects the myriad overlapping Indigenous and settler communities of the Columbia Basin. "Stories of people who existed in between all the 'History'—it's who people are, who I am," he has stated.[2] Tribal communities whose ancestors lived in the larger surrounding region for millennia came to the Blues for hunting and fishing long before Euro-American explorers and settlers arrived in the early 1800s. The Walla Walla, Cayuse, and Umatilla leaders ceded 6.4 million acres of their land in a treaty with the U.S. Government in 1855 and established the Confederated Tribes of the Umatilla Indian Reservation, in which Lavadour is an enrolled member.

Photo of James Lavadour, 2025, by Mario Gallucci.

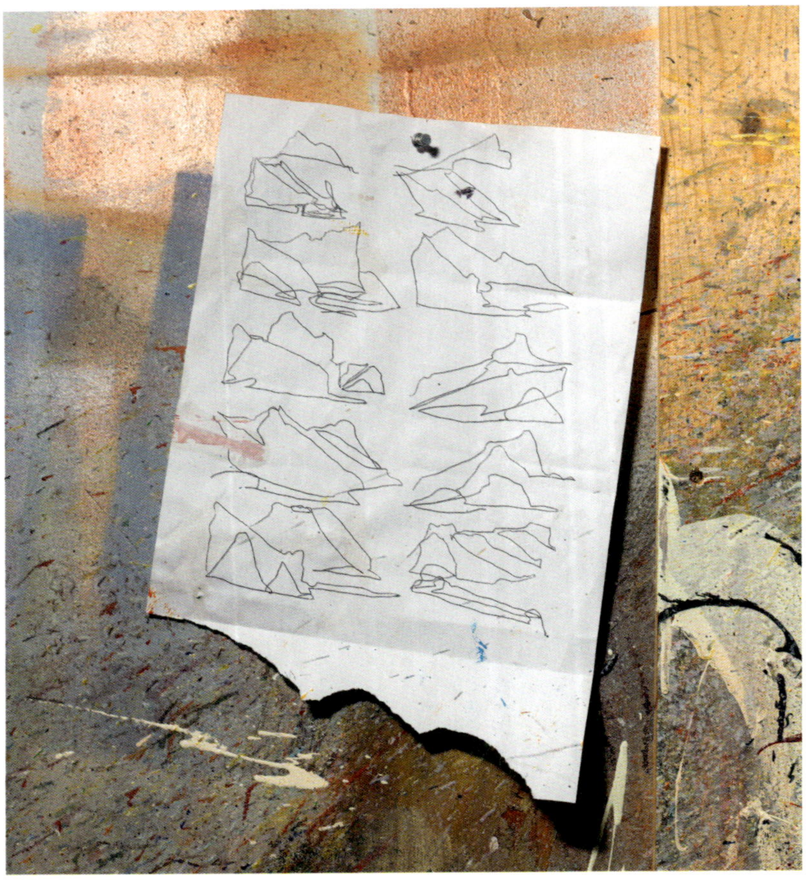

Many of Lavadour's earliest memories are about looking. As soon as he was old enough to walk, he accompanied his father, Joseph Lavadour, for excursions on the land. He learned to appreciate both its natural beauty and the significance of the traditional stories of its creation.[3] Seven decades later, according to his long-held practice, Lavadour rises before the sun and embarks on his daily routine of walking and looking upon this place, in community with the Earth and its nonhuman inhabitants.[4] For decades, this morning ritual was hiking; in more recent years, he has taken a long drive within a 60-mile radius. He pulls over when and where the mood strikes or when a particular view grabs his attention. This practice, and the art-making it informs, is Lavadour's kinetic way of acquiring knowledge. The looking and the learning are meaningful precisely because they have no end.

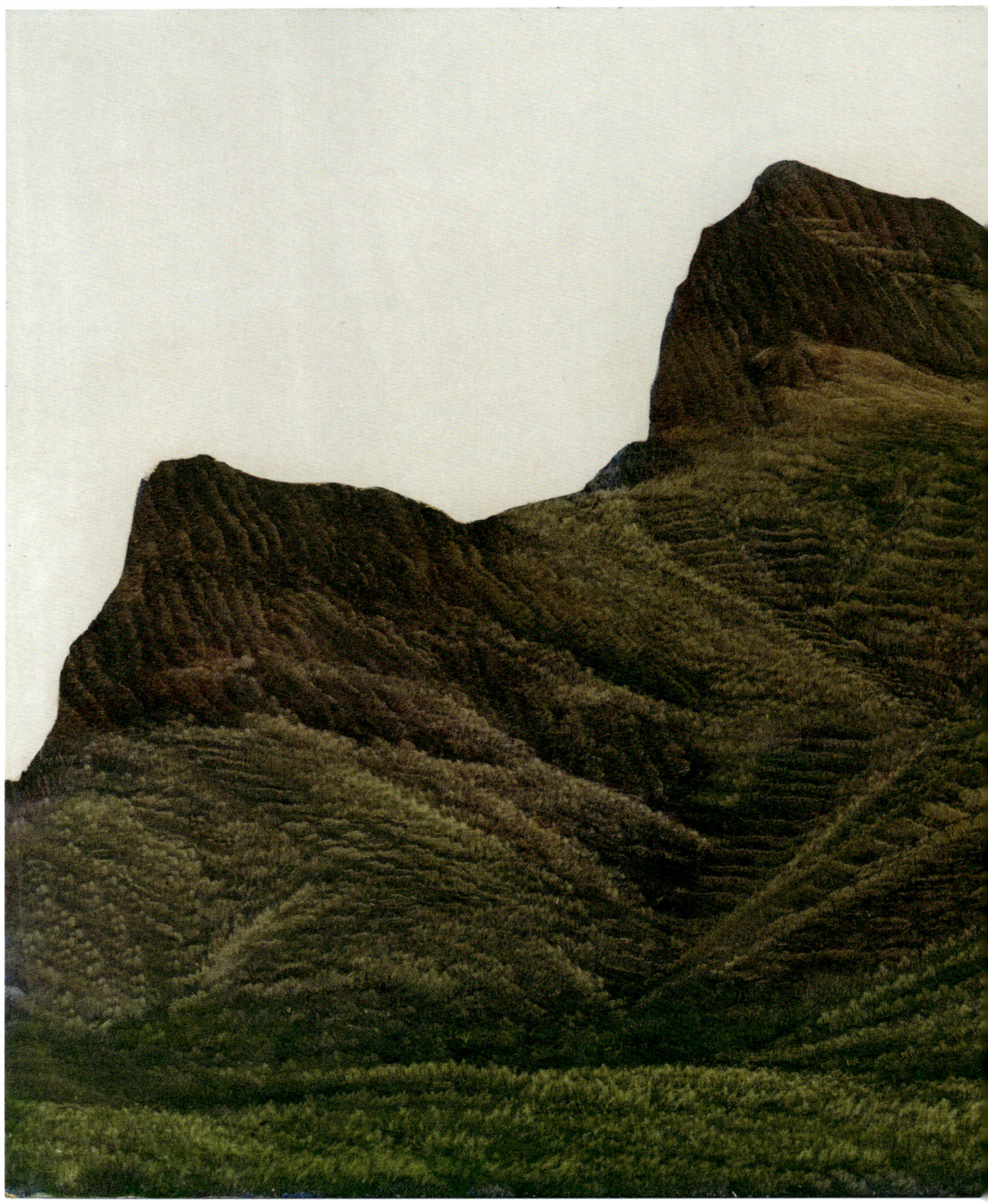

Fig 1: **Rock Healer**, 1980. Oil on hardboard, 30 x 66 inches. Courtesy of the artist.

Lavadour has playfully referred to his own past as "all myth and legend." The very nature of his painting practice pushes him forward in pursuit of deeper exploration, as do his Bahá'í beliefs, which situate art and creativity as acts of service equivalent to personal worship. Artists, as Lavadour explains, contribute to community and human good by dedicating their skills, discipline, and talent, no different than doctors, scientists, engineers, and other experts working for the betterment of one's society. His work has evolved dramatically over his career, yet there is a clear continuum in his painting from the earliest period of serious art-making in the 1970s to the powerful, emotionally-charged paintings of the present day. As Vicki Halper identified at a mid-career moment in 2001, "before [Lavadour was] twenty years old, as a very raw painter, he had established two of his still-dominant working techniques: a subtractive method of depiction, and an exploration of the physical properties of his materials."[5] A third component that is core to Lavadour's work over the last twenty-five years is his nuanced understanding of how the dynamic elements of a landscape (geological and emotional, rather than representational) and the structural components of a painting coincide. Natural phenomena—water and fire, emergence, and erosion—coexist within the dimensional framework provided by controlled abstractions: height and depth, construction, and deconstruction.

During a visit to Lavadour's studio in March 2023, I arrived to find a characteristically large number of colorful paintings arranged throughout his workspace. Each rectangular panel had all the elements for which Lavadour is best known: bold strikes of color, expertly balanced, with the suggestions of horizon lines and craggy rock features and a physical texture akin to the natural landforms just

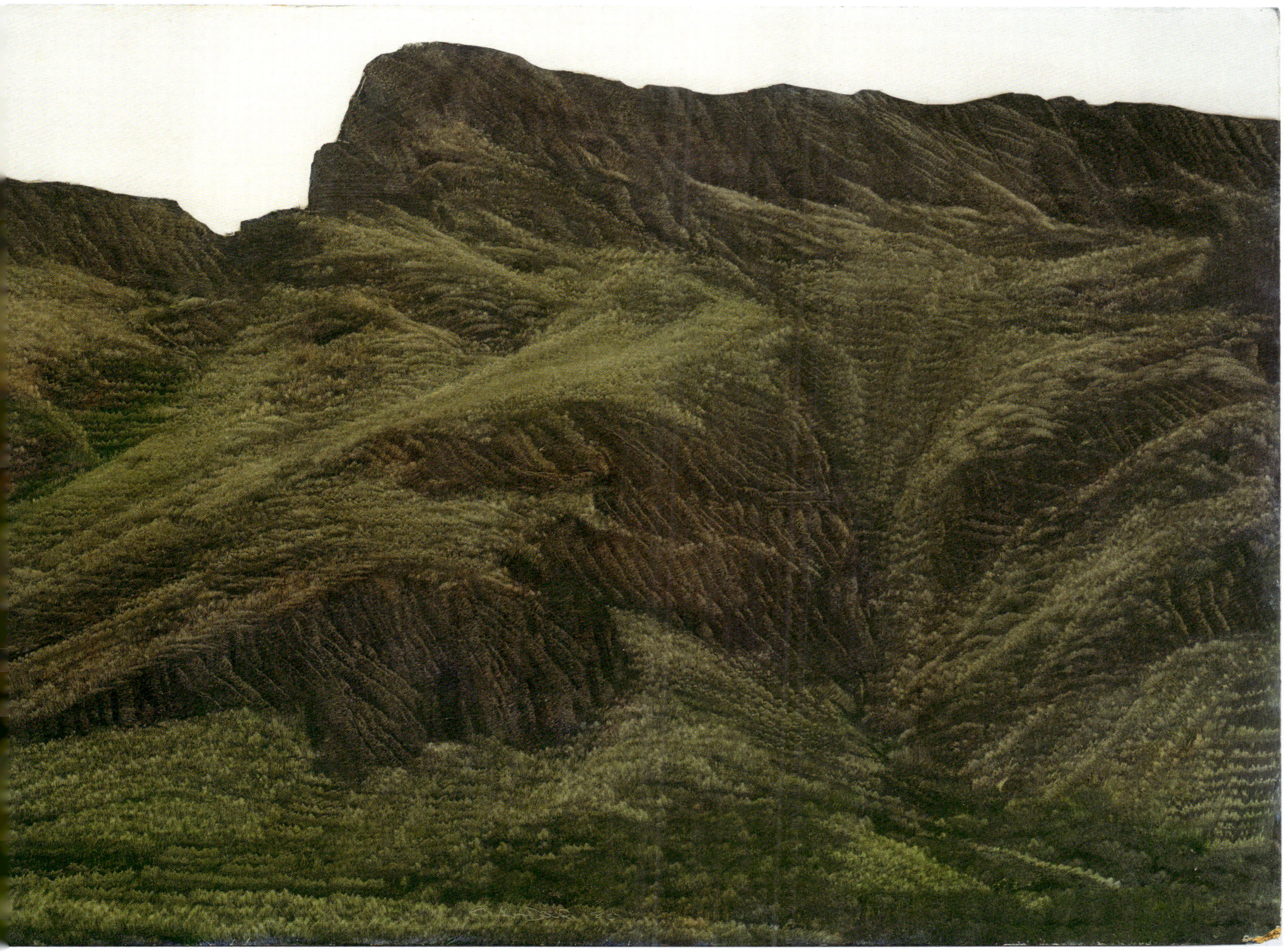

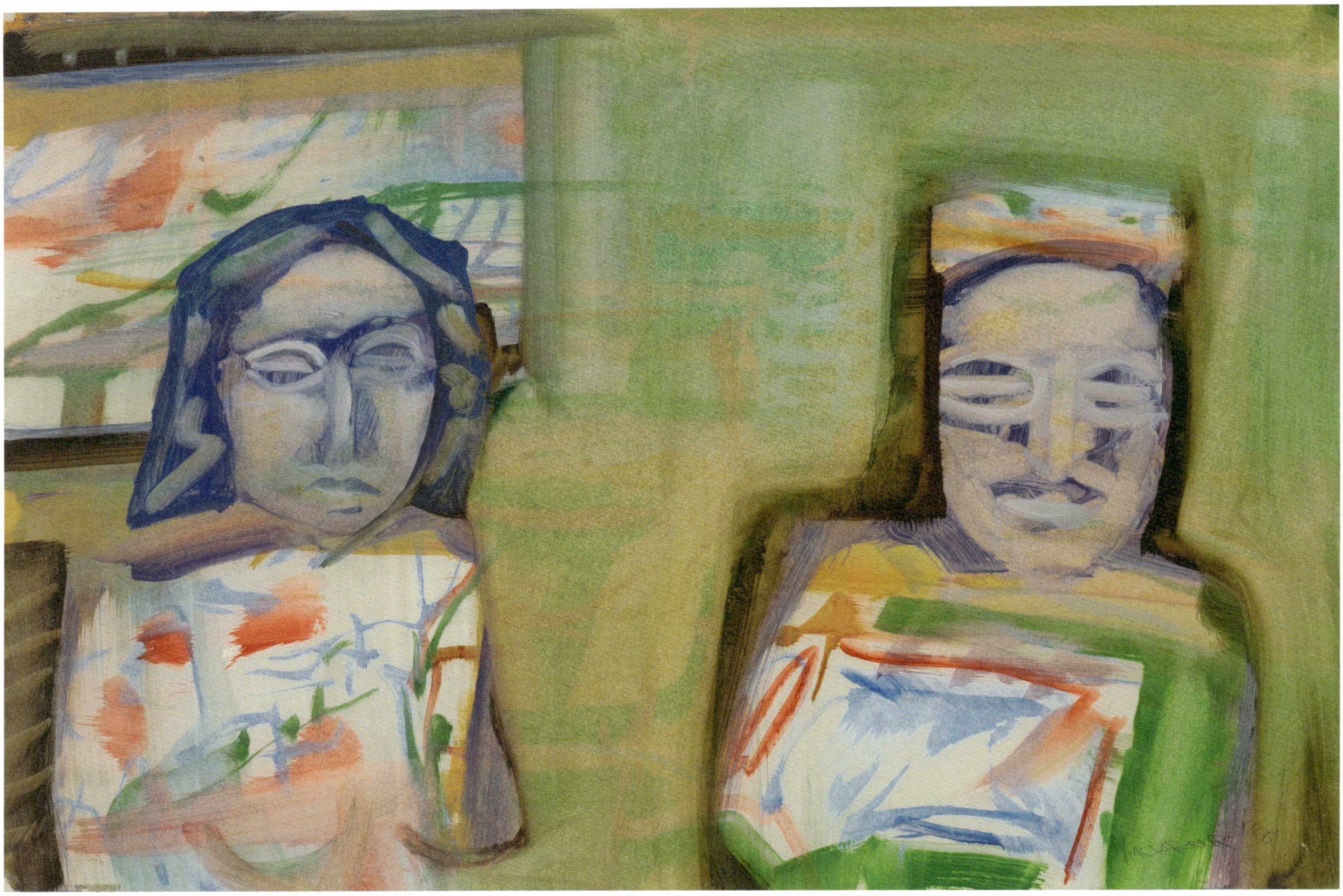

Fig. 2: **Man and Woman**, 1981. Oil on paper, 24 ¼ x 31 inches. Courtesy of the artist.

beyond his studio door. Combined into the artist's signature grid arrangements of as many as 9, 12, or even 24 images, these works take on an excitement and life force beyond what a single panel might express. Torn strips of white paper with jagged edges that mirror the crests of mountain ridges are folded over some works in progress, Lavadour's exercise in imagining where a horizon line might fall. He has used this compositional tool since the 1990s. Many of the panels in his studio were older paintings: perhaps previously shown at his gallery and returned home unsold, or pieces that he had worked to a natural stopping point years ago and then tucked away for future consideration. Lavadour draws from this endless pool of possibilities. He frequently revisits earlier works as he composes new grids, just as one might return to a once-familiar place and suddenly see it anew. The energies of the earth replenish and cycle through.

Associations with Abstract Expressionism have followed Lavadour's work for most of his professional career, but his approach to painting as an event remains grounded in his deep knowledge of the land and his commitment to the spiritual awakening that painting provokes. He rejects an iconographic or narrative reading of his works and he does not assign meaning to particular colors: the balance between moments of high contrast and perfect harmony is more important. As Lavadour has stated, "painting and color are two different things." His palette is just one of many tools Lavadour employs to make visible extraordinary events, allowing new understandings to be revealed to him. Writing in 2005, W. Jackson Rushing likened the "glistening" effect of Lavadour's works to Old Master paintings, a quality immediately apparent to any viewer upon close inspection of Lavadour's sumptuous, vibrating surfaces.[6]

Lavadour spent several of his boyhood years living with his grandmother. He recalled in a 2005 interview, "I developed my whole aesthetic very young, as a child actually. [...] When I discovered paint—that was it."[7] His early memories of curiously examining the peeling, stained wallpaper and ceiling cracks at her house, and the ways that this experience ignited his young imagination, translated to a similar admiration of the surrounding natural landscape. Lavadour never attended a formal painting program, yet his self-led education was no less robust or rigorous, propelled by his own deeply-held motivation. He was surrounded by traditional artforms of the confederated tribes, including beadwork and basketry ("stuff you could hold in your hand," he explains). As a high schooler, he voraciously sought inspiration in art books, favoring the work of J.M.W.

Turner, Pierre Bonnard, and Richard Diebenkorn, and absorbing images by popular western artists like Charles M. Russell. Perhaps most significantly, he was encouraged and guided by the celebrated ceramicist Betty Feves, who grew up in a rural community just over the Washington border. Feves had studied with Clyfford Still, Alexander Archipenko, and at the Art Students League in New York City prior to relocating to Pendleton for her husband. Dr. Lou Feves served the tribal community as a physician, even delivering a newborn Lavadour at the local hospital in 1951. Betty encouraged the aspiring artist's creativity and self-confidence and advocated for an appreciation of his earliest works among her peers. Lavadour recalls his mentor putting his paintings on view around her home when members of the Oregon Arts Commission visited.

As a young man, while working in tribal government, land management, and educational, janitorial, and social services for the Umatilla Indian Reservation, Lavadour maintained an artistic practice. He would later call the watercolor paintings of this era "his first love."[8] His earliest works were typically painted with a mix of food coloring. These were followed by monochromatic studies of geological forms and landscapes. Watercolor on paper behaved like water in the outside world: its fluidity was dynamic and unpredictable, yet Lavadour learned he could exert a certain amount of control. Tipping the paper moved the pigments like a stream. Holding it still captured the paint in its own puddle. The finished works carried the emotional weight of Lavadour's deep appreciation for these views. For a brief period, Lavadour moved away from making landscape paintings in an effort to avoid being categorized as a regional painter. His gallery representation at Sacred Circle, Seattle, urged him to focus on marketable, "Indian" imagery, which Lavadour interpreted through brightly patterned scenes of reservation life painted in oil. Despite these works receiving museum and collector attention,[9] Lavadour soon tired of this subject matter. The University of Oregon was an early organizer of his land-based works, arranging for a selection of his oil paintings to travel throughout the region between 1981 and 1984 and a solo show titled *James Lavadour: Landscapes & Interiors* to be presented at the University of Oregon Museum of Art (now the Jordan Schnitzer Museum of Art) at the tour's conclusion. "I see my artistic diversity as a spectrum that ranges from landscapes to abstraction," Lavadour wrote at the time. "My paintings are like music, full of rhythms, contrasts, movement ... They are orchestrations of visual elements which cause me to reflect upon my inner self."[10]

Prior to Betty Feves' passing in 1985, she coordinated fundraising efforts with local gallerist Lorie Baxter to establish The Pendleton Artist Advocate Project. They gathered donations from over twenty community members to support Lavadour's work, providing a financial boost that positioned him to focus on full-time artmaking for the first time in his life. Lavadour had recently turned his full attention to oil paint. Its materiality and slow drying time empowered him to shape the physical surface beyond what watercolors could provide. "I thought I had perfected monochromes," Lavadour recalled, "and then I started thinking about color." He switched to red underpainting and experimented with synthetic resin in his paints to increase their textural possibilities.[11] "Paint has all the complexity of reality," Lavadour has said, reflecting on how oils allow a more direct translation of the physical sensations of the land. This ranges from the immediate (sticking one's hand in flowing water or scraping against dirt) to the long span of geological time (dynamic forces shaping the Blue Mountains or the Umatilla River carving through the landscape).

Lavadour's travels in the 1980s developed his understanding of what painting could achieve. He recalls singular moments that sparked his thinking: encountering Albert Pinkham Ryder's *The Flying Dutchman* in an exhibition at the Seattle Art Museum; peering down into the Grand Canyon during a flight and marveling at its emergent shapes. In more recent years, he has referred to the significance of sighting a meteor streaking over the Blue Mountains on one of his morning walks, and how the sudden blast of light inspired terror, wonder, and extreme clarity. Combined with these pivotal experiences, his daily immersion in the land keeps him and his studio practice trained on a steady pursuit of a fundamental knowledge.

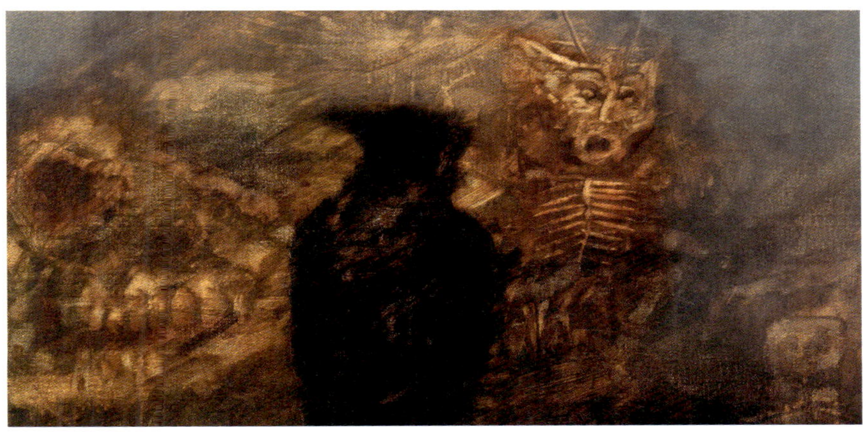

Crow's Shadow (detail), 1987. Oil on canvas, 48 ¾ x 34 ¾ inches. Lazar-Stock Collection.

By the time he painted *Crow's Shadow* (plate 1) in 1987, Lavadour had completely abandoned reservation motifs and bright colors. The skulls and bones in his new, anthropomorphized rock-scapes seem to suggest the coyote story of the land's creation. "The land," Lavadour explains, "looks like flesh," in which one's eyes can naturally find a face emerging from basalt cliffs or the curve of a body along a hillside. Present, too, are a place's embedded memories and the energies of its former inhabitants. *Crow's Shadow,* a reference to his beloved Weimaraner named Crow, and a companion two-paneled painting titled *Seed* were among his first Portland sales through Elizabeth Leach Gallery. The large, four-segment *Boom!* (plate 3) of the same year demonstrates how these elements could work together in a composition that engaged the physical boundaries of each of its canvases, creating an overall shape that deviates from the rectangle.

Scale became one more tool in Lavadour's approach to inciting the grandeur of his experiences with nature. The magnificent 12-canvas grid *The Seven Valleys and The Five Valleys* (plate 2) takes its title from the Bahá'í poetic book *The Seven Valleys* (1857-58; English translation 1906) and the corresponding valleys of search, love, knowledge, unity, contentment, wonderment, and true poverty and absolute nothingness. Its imagery expands beyond the dark, smoky palette to give recognizable form to horizon lines, offering a stronger suggestion of places where the sublime can be wholly felt. At this point, Lavadour's practice was to complete one painting at a time. He moved each finished canvas into position, assembling a grid that sought to give visual expression to his personal understanding.

The 1990s were hugely prolific yet challenging for Lavadour. Prudence Roberts organized a major show of his work, presenting *Northwest Viewpoints: James Lavadour* at the Portland Art Museum in 1990. In 1991, co-curators Margareta Archuleta and Dr. Rennard Strickland selected Lavadour's two-panel painting *New Blood* from the holdings of the Heard Museum for the group exhibition *Shared Visions: Native American Painters and Sculptors in the Twentieth Century.* Lavadour received Special Recognition from the Seattle Art Museum's Betty Bowen Awards Committee that same year. Of greatest significance to the expansion of Lavadour's artistic practice was his introduction to lithography in 1990. After Lavadour's first printmaking residency at Rutgers Center for Innovative Print and Paper, he started working across multiple paintings concurrently for the first time. Decades later, Lavadour continues this practice. As explained in-depth in Rebecca Dobkins' essay *The Magnitude of the Gift* (pages 40-51) and in his own words,[12] this experience revolutionized his thinking about multiple aspects of his painting practice: layering, color, and cause-and-effect. His experimentations and collaborations in printmaking were wide-ranging throughout the 1990s, including *Man and Woman* (1994, plate 6), a *ukiyo-e* style woodblock modeled on his painting of the same title (1981, fig. 2) made with visiting master printmaker Tadashi Toda (Japanese, 1936-2000),[13] and intaglio prints published by Seattle's Beta Press (plates 7-8).[14]

Lavadour recalls how he observed several artists from his tribal community leaving over the years for studies at the Institute of American Indian Arts (IAIA) in Santa Fe, New Mexico. Ultimately, each came back, finding employment with the tribe. "The Indian community is super-creative," Lavadour states, referring not only to the visual arts and cultural technologies, but in approaches to politics, economic development, and land use. Yet, a formal arts education, such as the fine training provided at IAIA, did not guarantee that one could make a career as a working artist back home. Lavadour was acutely aware that key elements needed to connect artists with the contemporary art market are usually missing from rural environments. Further spurred by the example of his early mentor Betty Feves and her spirit of community service, Lavadour collaborated with Phillip Cash Cash (Cayuse/Nez Perce) to establish Crow's Shadow Institute of the Arts in 1992. This nonprofit organization promotes creative and educational opportunities for a diverse community of Native and non-Native artists. The economic reach of its print studio is nationally renowned, bringing attention and income to visiting artists through sales of lithographs, monotypes, and monoprints. Its impact in the three decades of operation cannot be overstated, and Lavadour's longtime friend, fellow artist Marie Watt, speaks to its significance personally and professionally in *Jim Lavadour made me cry* (pages 52-55). Lavadour was honored with the Oregon Governor's Arts Award in 1994 in recognition of both his excellence in the visual arts and his role as a community leader. From this point on, his accolades number too many to list. These professional acknowledgements, while deeply meaningful to him, have had less bearing on Lavadour's personal definition of success than his internal standards of excellence do.

As he stretched himself through printmaking, Lavadour also started thinking about how the arrangements of his painted panels could operate philosophically like the parts of a poem.[15] He was moved by the harmony between his multi-directional and multi-sensory experience of the land and poetry that similarly resists linear understanding. For example, a 1997 grid, *Salamander* (fig. 3),[16] now in the collection of the Portland Art Museum, was titled in direct reference to Mexican poet Octavio Paz. Paz's surrealist wordplay in *Salamandra* draws from Indigenous Meso-American stories of salamanders, using their mythological connections with fire and regeneration to explore the human condition. Since the 1990s Lavadour has also looked to the historical example of Chinese literati brush painting and the improvisational spirit of jazz music as traditions in kinship with his own practice.

The body of work Lavadour created during these years melded earth, flame, and atmosphere. Obvious bodily imagery became less prevalent, though he did not completely abandon those visual references yet. *Landscapes,* a major 2001 solo exhibition organized by the Northwest Museum of Arts and Culture in Spokane, Washington, presented twenty of his paintings made between 1987 and 2000, including *Fire and Bones* (1991, plate 4), *Nest of Suns* (1998, Plate 10), and *Flag* (2000, plate 11). Many of these canvases and panels were arranged in the traditional Plateau

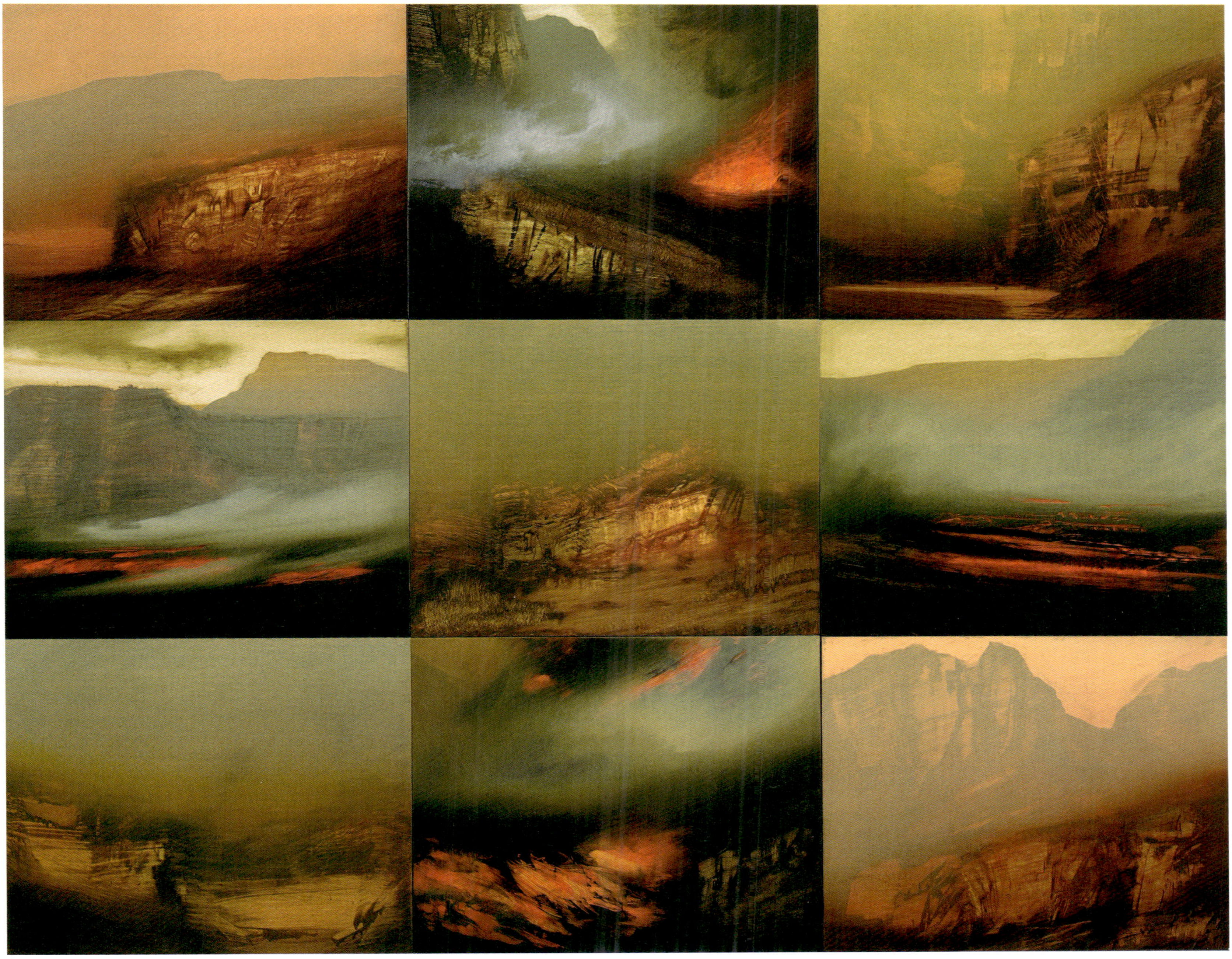

Fig. 3: **Salamander**, 1997. Oil on board, 48 1/16 x 60 1/16 x 2 15/16 inches. Gift from Gary Lewis Moe in memory of Kevin Michael McGee. Portland Art Museum, Portland, Oregon, © James Lavadour, 2015.92.59.

weaving design of a four-pointed star, either on their own or embedded within the grid.[17] Lavadour's long presence on the Umatilla Indian Reservation and immersion in the rich visual culture of his Native community informed these aesthetic sensibilities; while retaining them, he deftly combined such homages with the influences from other forms of expression, maintaining the land as a common thread.

For years Lavadour painted primarily on canvas and linen. By 1994 he had developed such facility with oil paint that he sought a more adequate surface on which to maximize its fluidity. Lavadour switched to gessoed wooden panels, alternating between flat planks and boxes. This deep investment in working with the nature of his materials led to his concept of "interiors," architectural forms that impose structure onto a landscape. Lavadour was fascinated by the effects of turning his work upside down, then back again, to observe the movement of wet paint. He produced a large body of work from these experiments on paper (plate 12). Beginning in 2000, he applied this new physical knowledge to his process of layering paint on panels, reinforcing his conviction that "a painting is an event, not an object." Lavadour's use of these abstracted structural elements appeared throughout his works in this decade, including *Flag* (2000, plate 11), *Bridge* (2001, plate 14), *Point* (2003, plate 15), and an untitled suite of nine lithographs published at the Rutgers Center for Innovative Print and Paper in 2002 (plate 13).[18] A comparison of two of his most significant works from this period, the 16-panel grid *Naming Tanager* (2001, fig. 4), and the 15-panel grid *Blanket* (2005, fig. 5) demonstrates how significantly the interiors impact one's viewing experience.

Looking upon *Naming Tanager,* one is immediately swept into its hazy cliffs and riverbeds, with alternating depths and vantage points.[19] Its palette and *memento mori*-type skulls connect across time: not only within Lavadour's own development and his early use of skeleton imagery in the late 1980s, but also in its implication of the long span of geological time beyond human comprehension. In *Blanket*, Lavadour has upended this sense of time, space, and place further. Vibrant blues, greens, and yellow-oranges suggest not only the appearance of air and water, but their physical sensations. One can track the artist's movement through his turning of panels. Drips of paint defy gravity. Where the earlier work burns, *Blanket* glows. In 2006 Lavadour

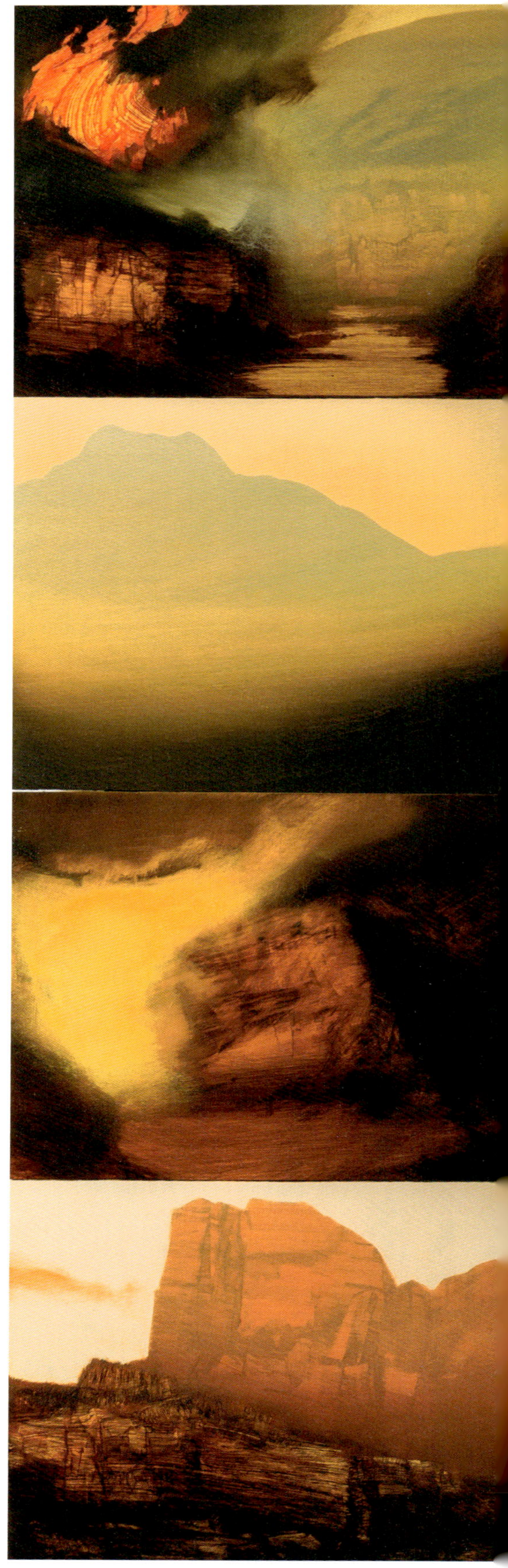

Fig. 4: **Naming Tanager**, 2001. Oil on wood, 72 x 96 inches. overall. Museum Purchase: Eiteljorg Fellowship, acquisition in honor of Bonnie Reilly for her long service to the museum's Collections Council.

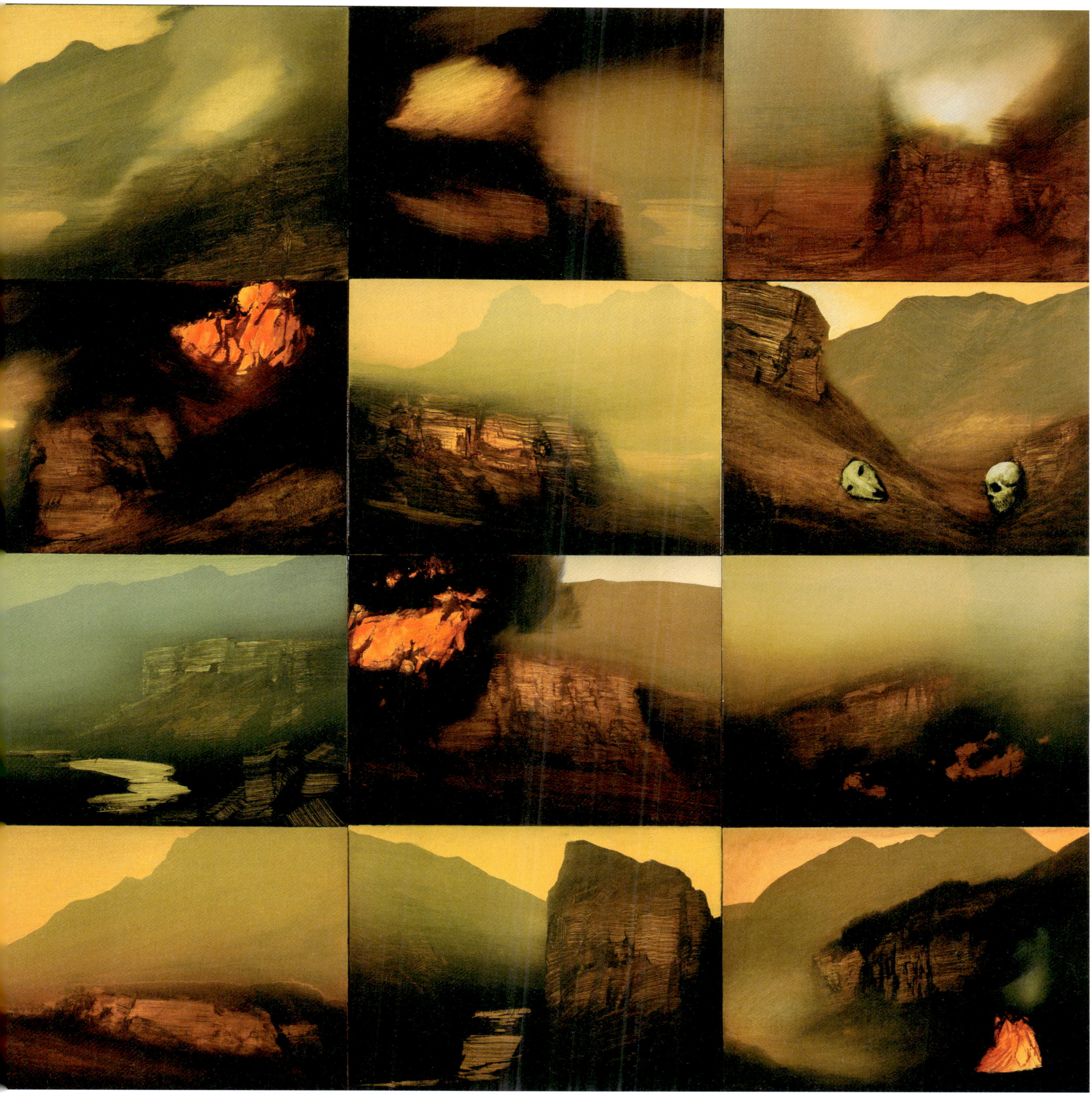

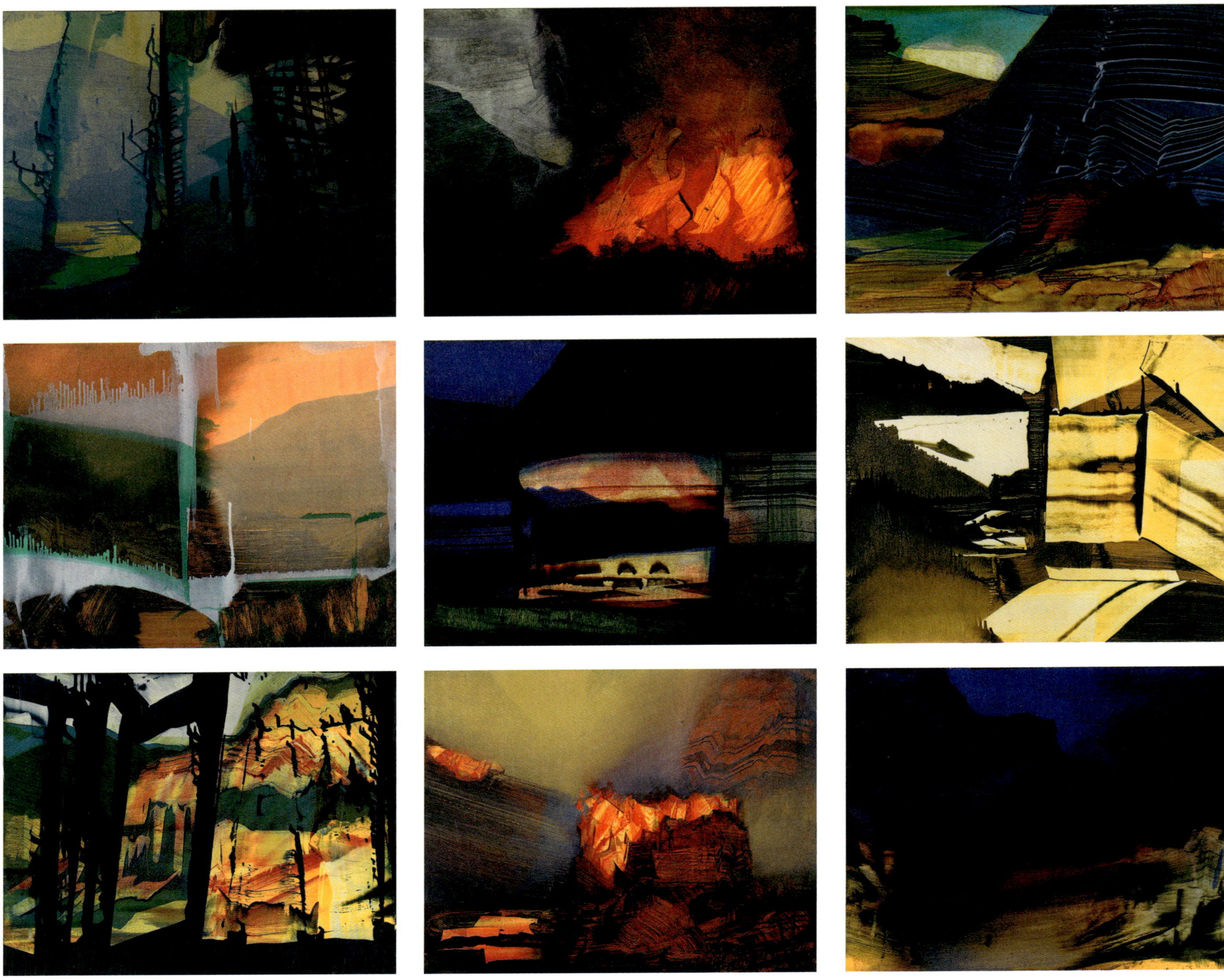

reflected on the evolution of interiors in his work: "After six years both structures have moved from the surface to the background to the surface again in intersecting and rippling layers and patterns. It still adds up to landscape and interiors but the surface of the painting has exploded into time and space. Every painting talks about some ancient thing that is as old as the ground we walk on and connects us all in a shared existence."[20]

During this highly productive decade, Lavadour also engaged his curiosity about the field of physics, particularly the flow of liquids. He had always been attuned to paint's materiality, but the language of physicists better described what he observed in its fluid behaviors. *Ice* (2007, plate 16) showcases Lavadour's innovative method of creating surface effects using a white wash and shiny mica particles. It is also an example of Lavadour's practice of identifying panels that can stand alone. While many of the other paintings made at the same time as *Ice* were ultimately destined for grids, this work achieved the desired visual balance as a single view. In 2008, the Hallie Ford Museum of Art presented *Ice, Blanket,* the luminous *Scaffold* (2000, in the collection of the Tamástslikt Cultural Institute) and nearly twenty other recent works in *The Properties of Paint,* a retrospective of work from 2000-2007. Curator Rebecca Dobkins described this body of work as "jewel-like artifacts of Lavadour's artistic processes and of the physical forces of the natural world."[21]

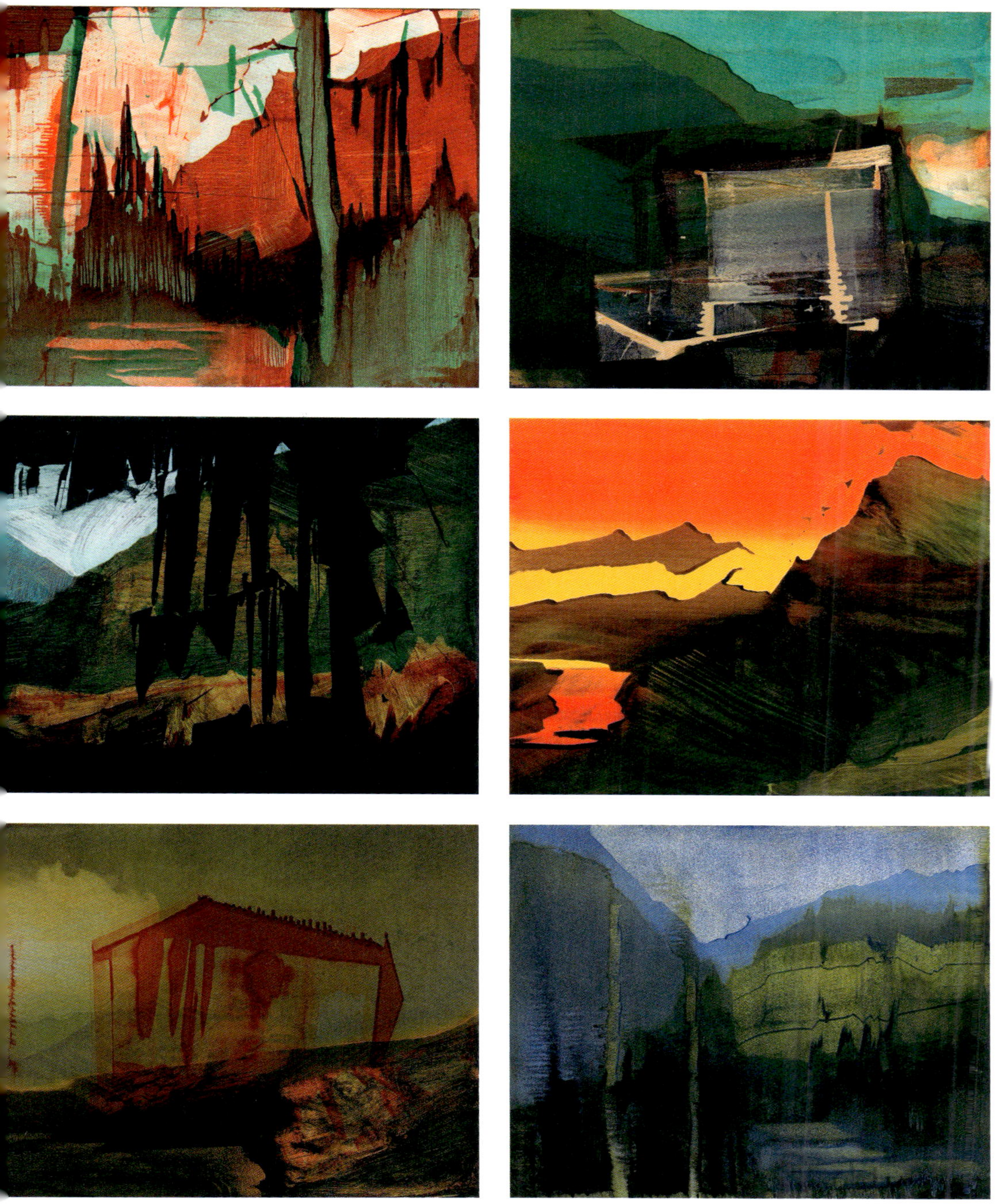

Fig. 5: **Blanket**, 2005. Oil on board, 76 x 156 x 2 inches. National Museum of the American Indian, Smithsonian Institution (26/6079). Photo by NMAI Photo Services.

By the time Lavadour painted *Straight Ahead* (plate 17) in 2010, he had absorbed the lessons of his interiors so fully that he no longer needed to use the box-like visual cues that dominated his work of the preceding period. He has described his use of horizon lines, dividing landscape, middle ground, and foreground, as a way to express moving through the land as one walks it. Whereas painting-as-vortex was fully revealed in his works of the 2000s, as scholar Kate Morris described of Lavadour's painting practice, beginning in 2010 "the vortex form cedes entirely to the matrix [...] allow[ing] him to transcend the two-dimensional limitations of the grid."[22] This calls to mind how Richard Diebenkorn's *Ocean Park* series of the 1970s and 80s examined light on the landscape, rather than the landscape itself. Lavadour drew from his own cache of sensory stimuli for painting *Straight Ahead* and a related work, *Lift,* (2011, plate 18): looking not just at, but out, over, and into.

In 2014, *Out of Range* (plate 20) was selected for the monumental traveling exhibition *State of the Art: Discovering American Art Now,* organized by the Crystal Bridges Museum of American Art in Bentonville, Arkansas. Crystal Bridges's curators identified their mission as bringing together the "most compelling American art being created" from artists not yet fully recognized on a national scale. Meanwhile, Lavadour had achieved a new level of international acclaim. His magnificent grid *Tiicham* ("our land," a meaning that encompasses all living things, fig. 6) appeared in

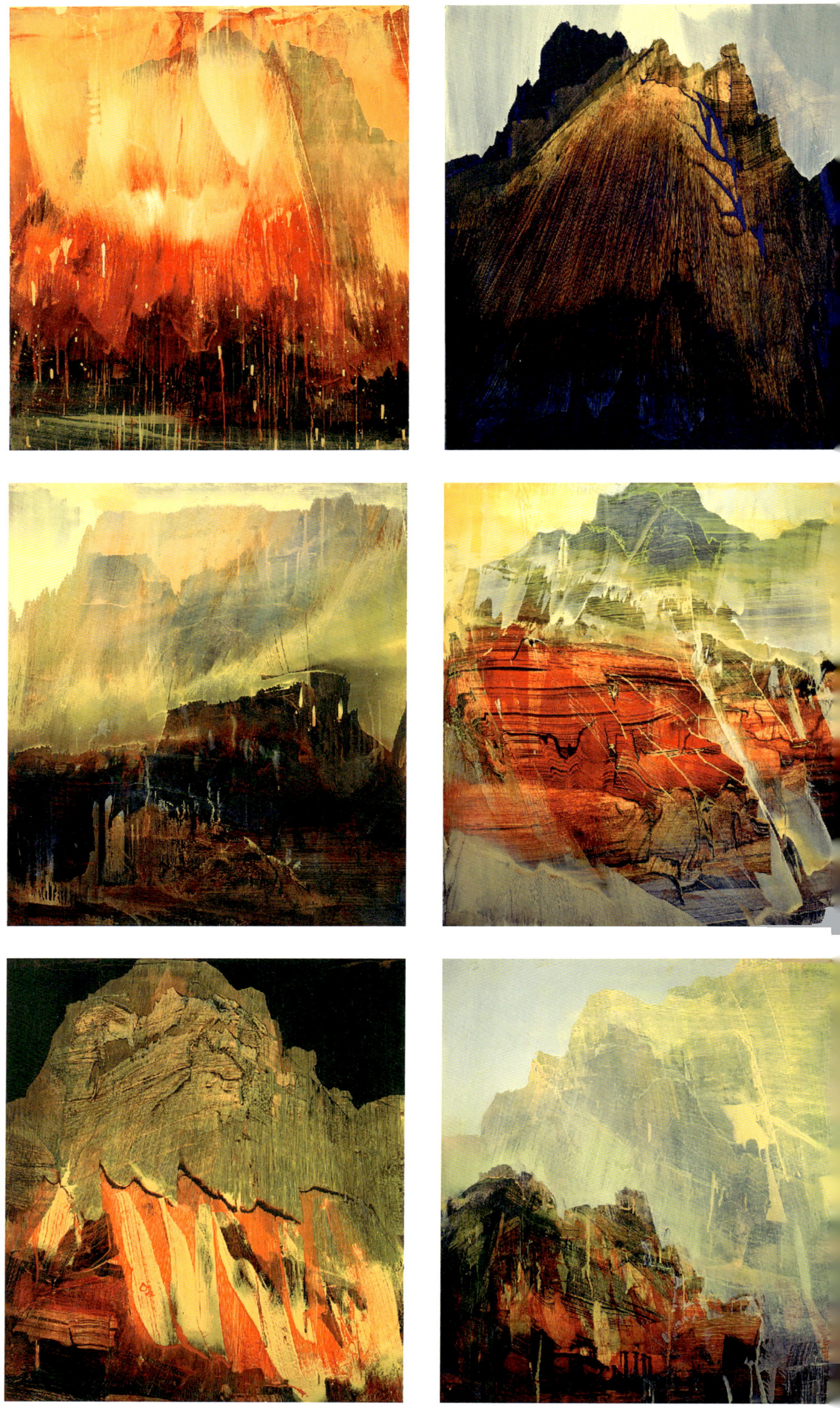

Fig. 6: **Tiicham**, 2013. Oil on Baltic birch panels, 102 x 152 inches. Private Collection.

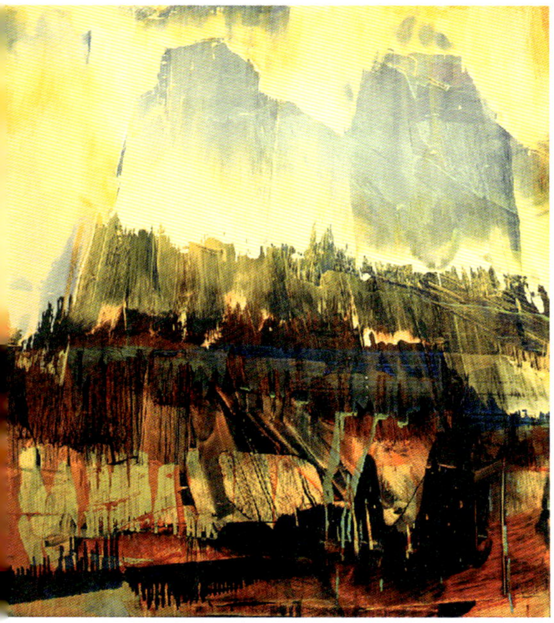
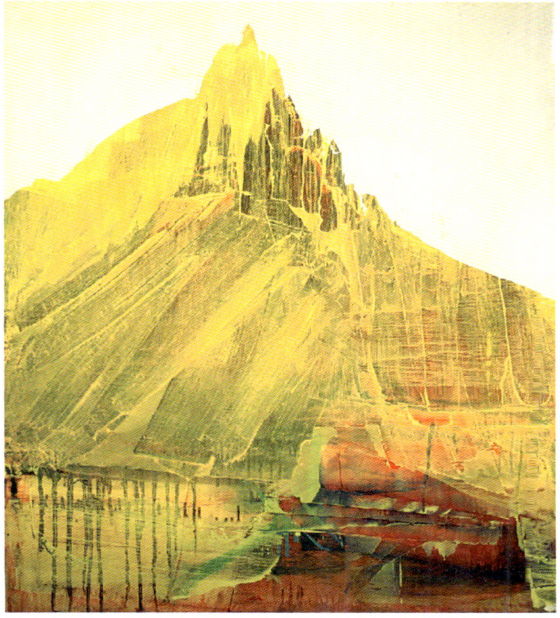
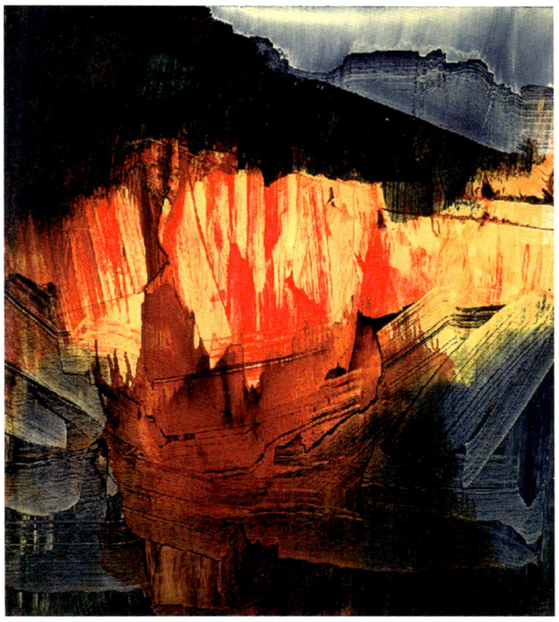
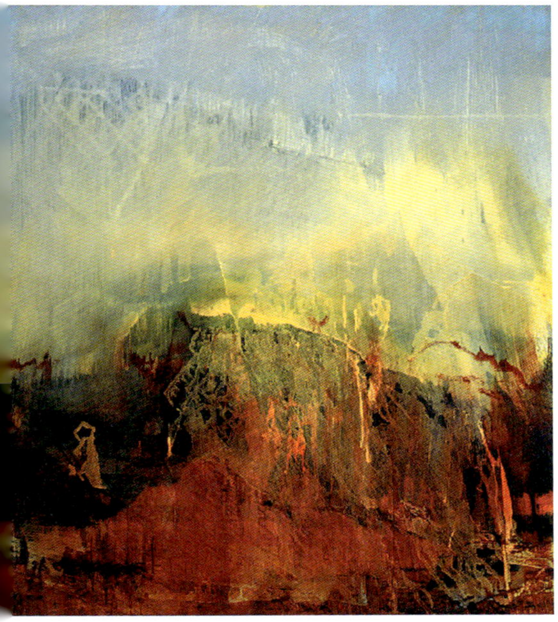
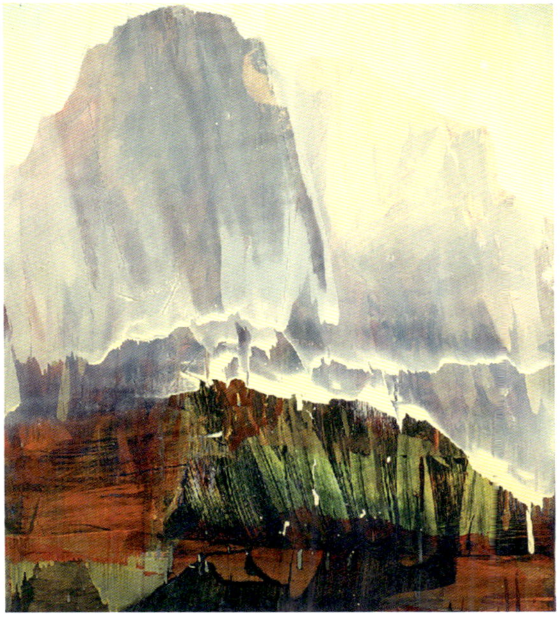
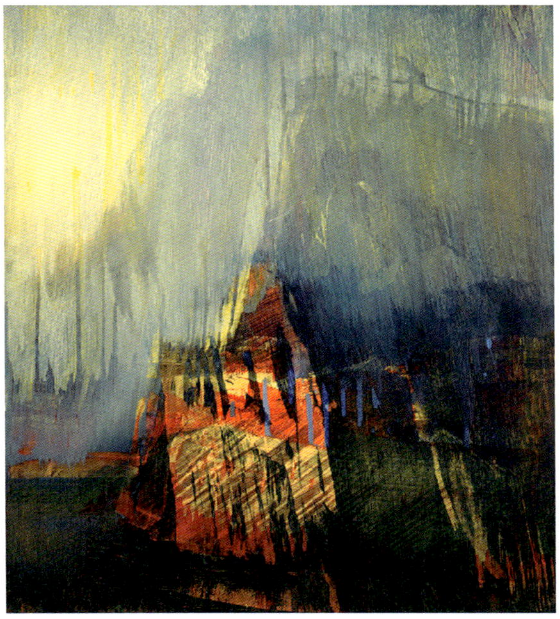
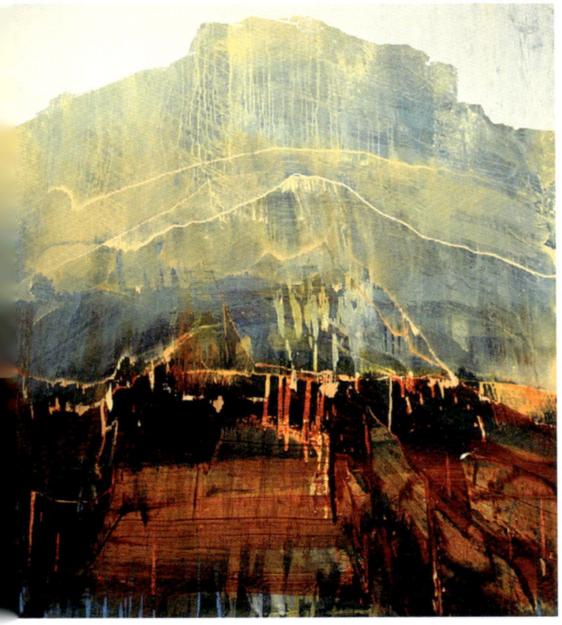
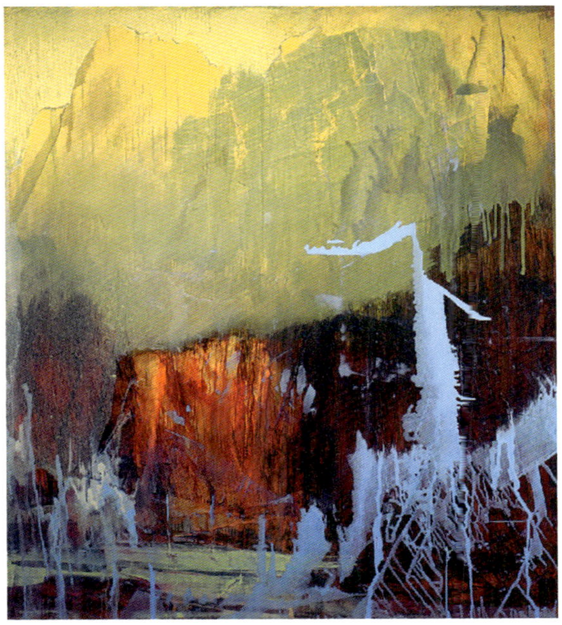
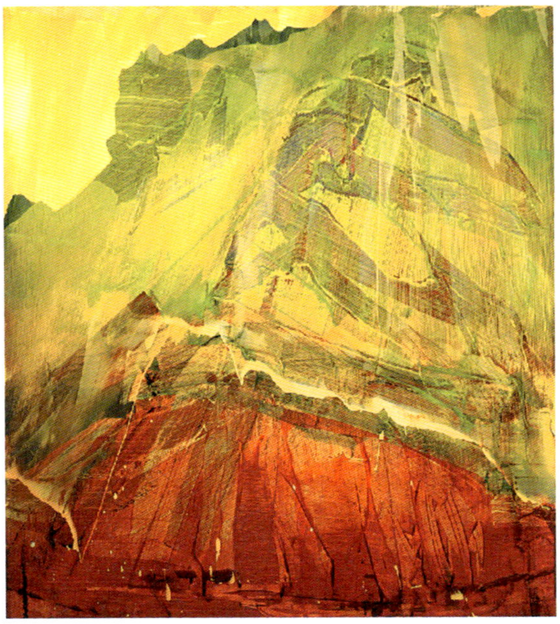

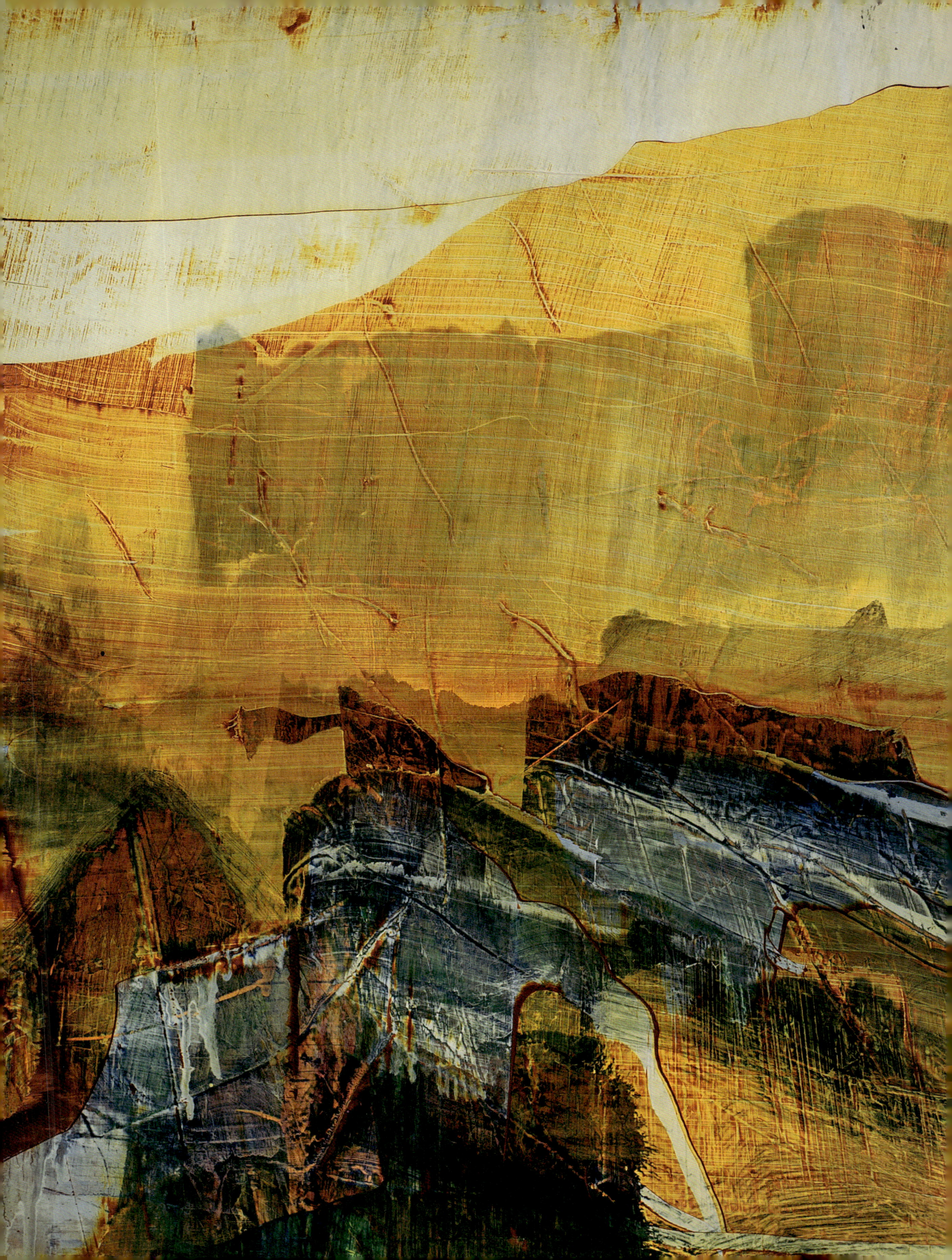

the prestigious 2013 group show *Personal Structures* at the Palazzo Bembo during the 55th Venice Biennale. Gallerist Jane Beebe of PDX CONTEMPORARY ART first recommended Lavadour to project co-curator Carol Rolla. She knew that his approach to painting would resonate with *Personal Structures'* curatorial themes of time, space, and existence, and that Lavadour and his work were ready for this increased level of visibility. Writer and independent curator Meagan Atiyeh, who contributed the monograph on Lavadour for the *Personal Structures* exhibition guide, considers Lavadour's motivations and the emotional trajectory of his work in her essay (pages 56-59).

Lavadour has always shown a great sensitivity to the power of language in shaping perception when naming his works and exhibitions: often drawing from tribal words, song lyrics, Bahá'í spiritual writings, colloquialisms, physics, and his own earlier titles. There is a particularly introspective quality to Lavadour's naming practice. *The New Ghosts of Ceded Boundaries* (2021, plate 29) evoked a tribal history he first pointed to over twenty years earlier. The original green-tinted grayscale suite of *Ghosts of Ceded Boundaries I, II, and III* (1998), directly referenced the treaty in which the Confederated Tribes of the Umatilla Indian Reservation was established and its hunting and fishing rights were negotiated with the U.S. government. The especially bright palette of this later work resists any misunderstanding of Lavadour's "ghosts" as dead and buried. In the 2021 grid, as in *The Ghosts of Many Things* (plate 32) that followed two years later, Lavadour conjures a sense of exuberant spirits in a land teeming with life.

While Lavadour's paintings are not topically political, they still speak from the reality and world of the Confederated Tribes of the Umatilla Indian Reservation homelands since time immemorial, seen from his point of view as a nearly life-long resident and a tribal member. The present retrospective takes its title from two of his works, the six-panel grid *Land of Origin* (2015, plate 21) and its lithographic counterpart (plate 22). Both in their physical presence and the associations embodied in Lavadour's word choice, these variations on making visible one's "Land of Origin" speak to the artist's core understanding of his place in the world and the wellspring from which his painting flows. The doggedness and consistency of this pursuit over the length of his career is evident upon even the most cursory review of his past artist statements, as amply demonstrated in *James Lavadour on Painting,* the edited interview anthology and new interview conducted in 2024 by JSMA executive director John S. Weber for this volume. (pages 60-69).

While Lavadour is widely known for his large grids of painted panels, he takes particular joy in making single-sheet works on paper. He has described these as "easier," since a landscape emerges so readily from his movements across the paper. "It will just happen," Lavadour states, referring to the translation of every brushstroke into evidence of a dynamic event. Unlike the specified relationships between images that Lavadour determines for a finished grid of panels, suites of paintings on paper are meant to be viewed singularly or in any order. He cites his *River Miles* series (2020, plates 24-28) as some of his best paintings on paper to date. Each achieves a balance within itself that encompasses all the life lessons Lavadour has gleaned thus far. Viewed together, they pulsate as interlocking connections across space. During the COVID-19 pandemic, Lavadour found a creative outlet for channeling the uncertainty and isolation of this troubling period. He mined his inventory of works on paper, pulling many that he had started in the mid-1990s, and addressed them as a conceptual group. Lavadour worked back into the original compositions, adding new layers of paint and scumbling. In the resulting *Portfolio: 1994/2021*, these effects mirror the passage of time visually and physically. Lavadour reflected, "paintings hold memories, and to be able to apply what I do now in paint to what I was working on in 1994 has been an astonishing experience. An interesting meditation on how my thinking in paint has evolved over 27 years."[23]

This period of looking back coincided with the timing of Lavadour's interview for the Smithsonian's Archives of American Art Oral History Program by researcher Rebecca Trautmann of the National Museum of the American Indian in spring 2021.[24] It was a crucial time for the growing acknowledgment of his important contributions to contemporary art. In recent years, scholarly and curatorial efforts have recognized Lavadour's status as one of the country's most powerful, original painters while simultaneously acknowledging his influential position within an expanding world stage for Native artists. Lavadour was selected by the late Jaune Quick-to-See Smith (Confederated Salish and Kootenai Nation) for inclusion in two of her last exhibition projects, *The Land Carries Our Ancestors: Contemporary Art by Native Americans* at the National Gallery of Art in Washington, D.C. (2023), and *Indigenous Identities: Here, Now & Always* (2025) at the Zimmerli Art Museum at Rutgers University, New Brunswick, New Jersey.

Smith, the first artist-curator of an exhibition at the National Gallery, chose Lavadour's striking blue and white lithograph *Duotone 2* (2011, fig. 15) to be presented in a checkerboard wall installation within *The Land Carries Our Ancestors*. This strategic arrangement responded to the Dawes Act of 1887 authorizing the United States President to divide tribes' reservations into individual parcels for private Native and non-Native ownership.[25] Alongside works on paper by Andrea Carlson (Ojibwe), Ka'ila Farrell-Smith (Klamath/Modoc), Wendy Red Star (Apsáalooke [Crow]), Diego Romero (Cochiti Pueblo), and several other contemporaries, Lavadour's print was one lens among many through which to consider this legacy and the present-day ties to one's Native homelands. "For us, Native definitions

River Miles V (detail), 2020. Oil on paper, 20 x 28 inches.

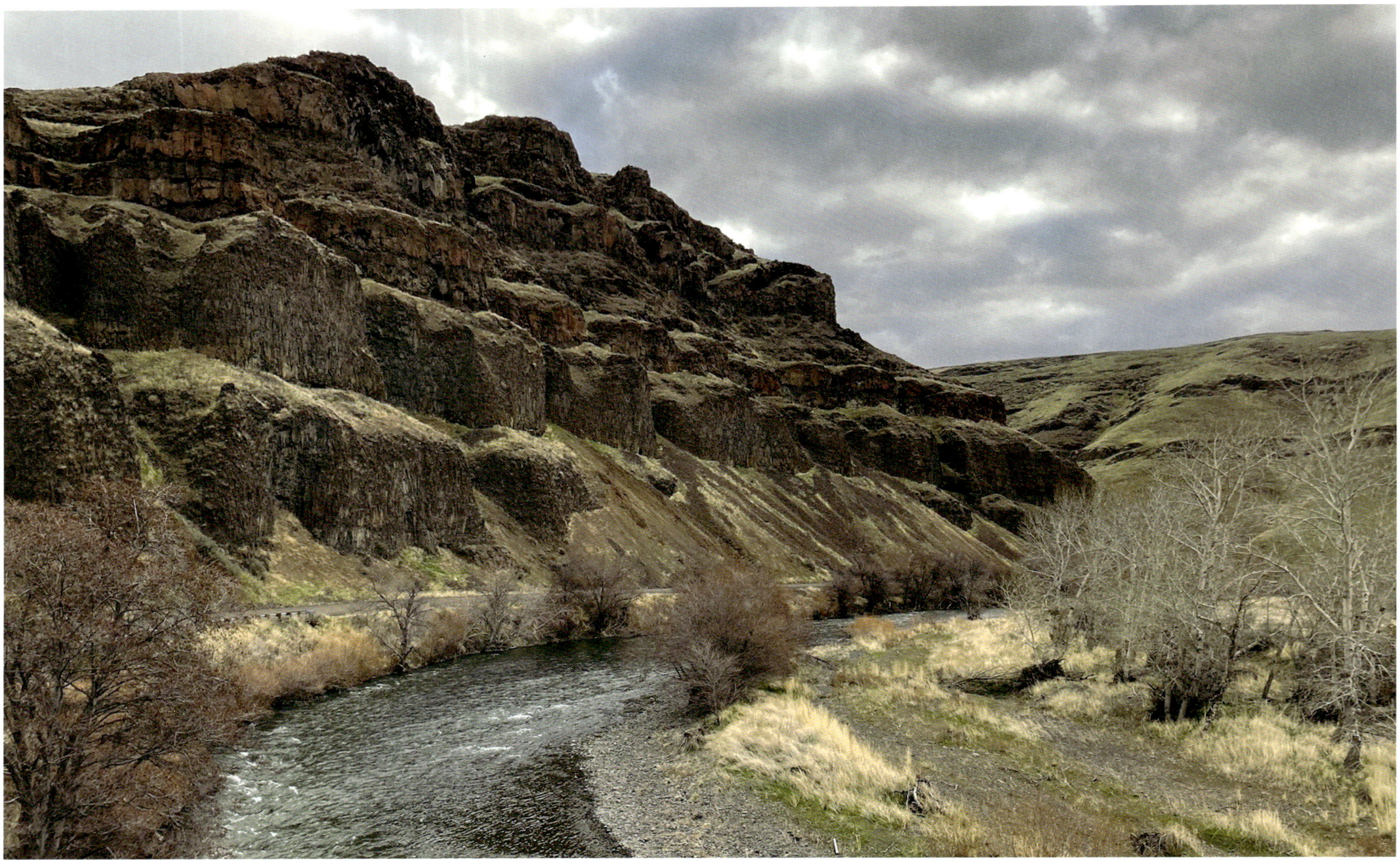

of land/landbase/landscape are always and forever; it is the sacred land of our ancestors. We know that no matter where we go, the dust of the land carries our ancestors," wrote Smith in her exhibition didactics. However, as Morris clarified of Lavadour's mindset, the use of grids central to Lavadour's working method is not shaped by any political statement about land division.

Recent JSMA visitors encountering *Deep Moon* (2004, in the collection of the Jordan Schnitzer Family Foundation), *Torch* (2012, plate 19) and other Lavadour works at the museum often remarked that, from a distance, their initial impression was of sharp, saturated photographs. This is not surprising given the high contrast of Lavadour's illuminated foregrounds and darker backgrounds in those examples. The eye's natural inclination is to grasp onto some recognizable element to give the brain a way to identify and classify what we are seeing. It is this same impulse that leads to the frequent and understandable, yet ultimately inadequate and misguided designation of Lavadour as a "landscape painter." As this essay argues, his works are indeed inspired by the land. But as he insistently notes, his paintings do not depict specific places and are not "pictures." Taken as a whole, the full scope of Lavadour's creative practice clearly extends far beyond traditional landscape painting as art history understands it. For Lavadour, the painting is not even the image one sees on the panel, but the physical process by which an artifact of the event emerges. Accordingly, he has described himself as "an abstract action painter."

James Elkins begins *Pictures & Tears, A History of People Who Have Cried in Front of Paintings* (2001) with an anecdote about then-University of Chicago student Jane Dillenberger, a future trailblazer in the disciplines of modern art theory and religious studies, standing before Mark Rothko and his works in progress in the artist's studio in 1967. These canvases would become the fourteen murals of the Rothko Chapel in Houston, Texas. A year earlier Rothko had written to his patrons, Dominique and John de Menil: "...the magnitude, on every level of experience and meaning, of the task in which you have involved me, exceeds all of my preconceptions. And it is teaching me to extend myself beyond what I thought was possible for me."[26] Dillenberger captured her impressions of this studio visit in a journal entry. Her way of describing the experience nearly sixty years ago resonates with the gravitational pull of Lavadour's contemporary work. "I felt as if my eyes have fingertips," she wrote, "moving across the brushed texture of the canvases." The rest of Elkins' book addresses the profound ability of art to provoke emotional responses, a concept that readily applies to encounters with Lavadour's paintings.

In December 2023, I visited the print studio at Crow's Shadow Institute of the Arts to see Lavadour's most recent lithographs awaiting editioning; these were the result of another of his collaborations with master printermaker Judith Baumann. *Winter* (plate 30) and *Spring* (plate 31) shone like beacons from the table. Lavadour's designs give the appearance, equally, of brushstrokes and palette

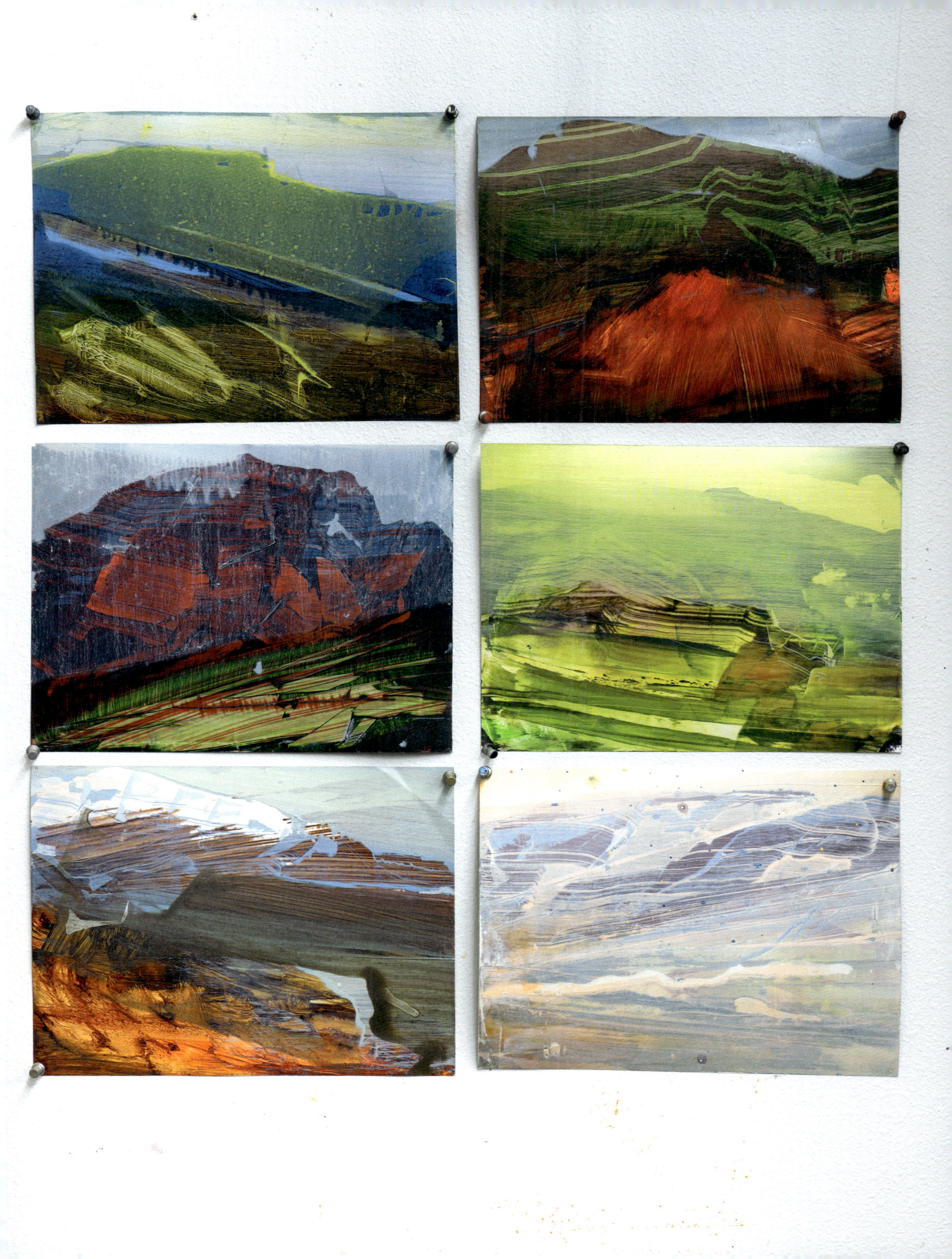

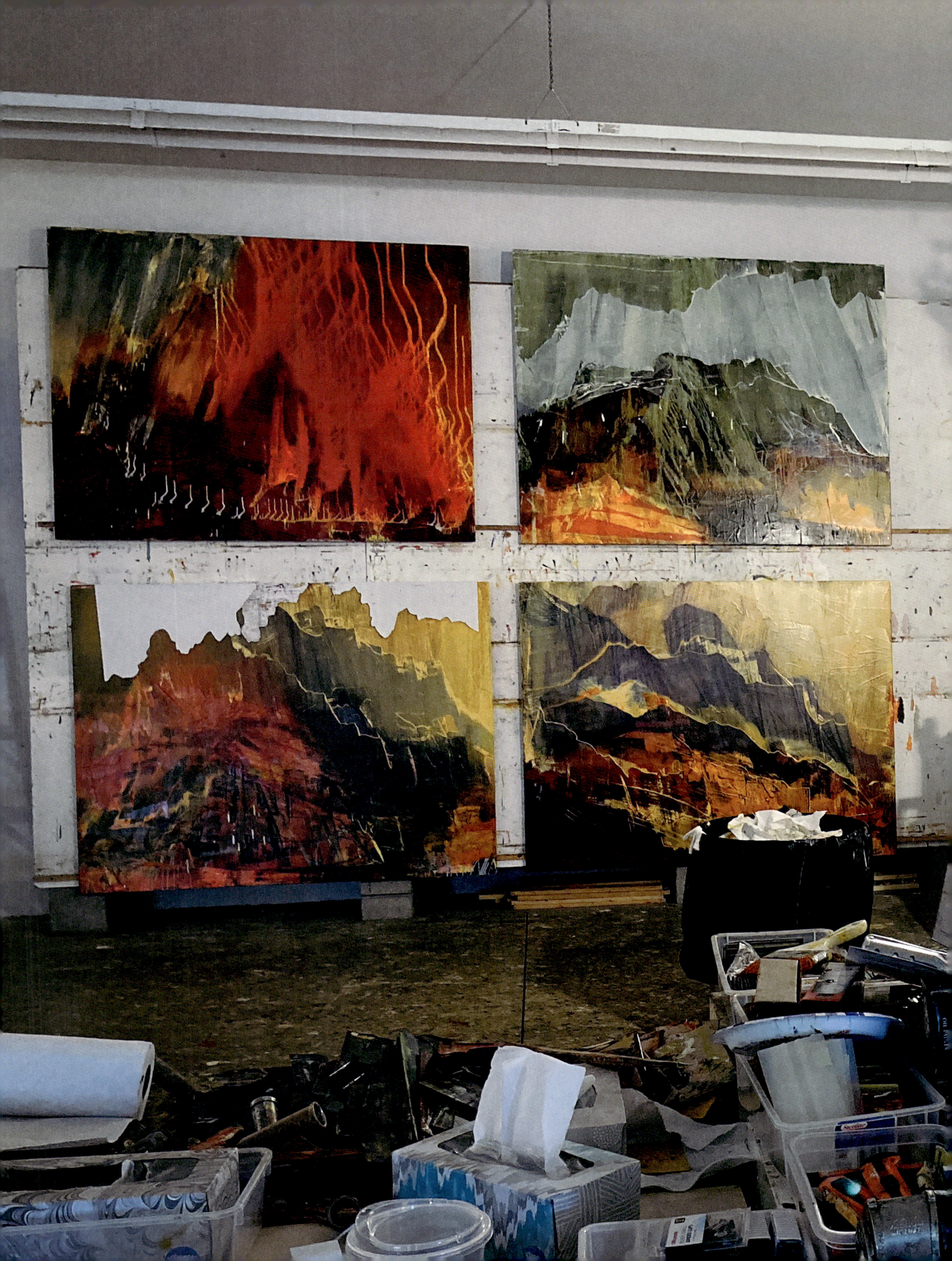

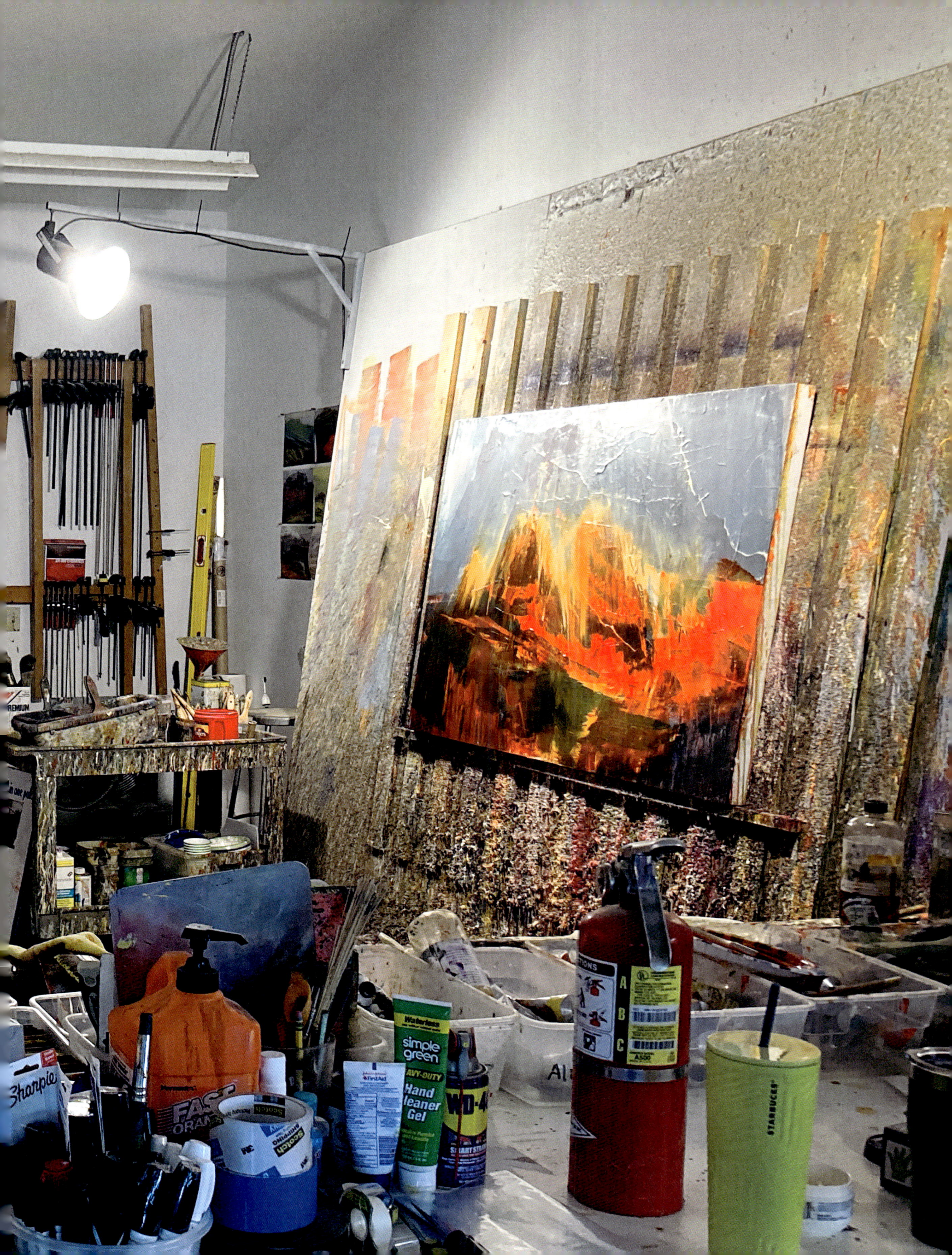
Sharpie
Waterless
simple green
Hand
Gel
WD-40
STARBUCKS

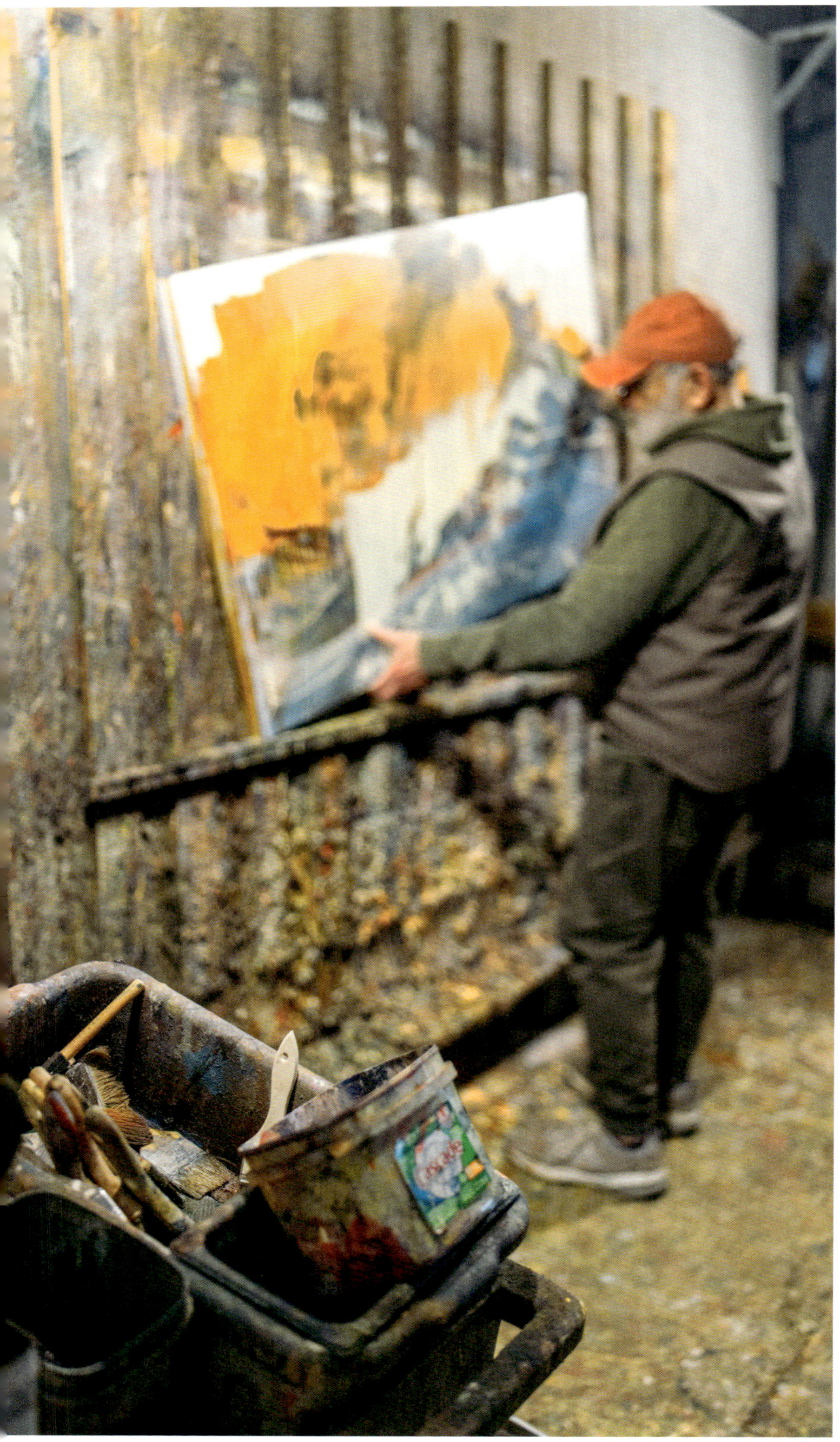

knife scrapes and geological striations or fractures in ice. This goes a step beyond the solid shapes of his earlier two-panel *Summer* (2018-19, plate 23). In *Summer* one sees how the layering of colors plays with both depth—indicating foreground, middle ground, and horizon on the top image—and time—the green stretch of either sunlight or shadow across a wide distance on the bottom. The newer lithographs compel such readings, too, while offering an expression of the artist's movement in painting and the natural rhythms of the earth. Back in his home studio, Lavadour was nearing completion on two spectacular new grids. These became *Bold as Love* (plate 34) and *Lucky Star* (plate 33), each of which represents long-established elements of Lavadour's practice infused with the enthusiasm and foreboding energy of the present historical moment.

Across twelve panels, *Lucky Star* brings together warm, life-giving sunshine and the restorative blues of cool water. *Bold as Love* teeters on the edge of a Caspar David Friedrich-like vision, but is distinctly Lavadour in purpose. Here is where we contemplate nature but here, too, is where we contemplate painting itself. Years earlier Lavadour spoke of wishing he could wrest the term "Romantic Landscape" away from "bloody American history."[27] Unlike the grandiose images of manifest destiny that sought to legitimize outsiders' claims on these lands, in Lavadour's treatment of this subject it is apparent that the power has always been in the land itself. This strength is not one of domination and ownership, but one of connection, reciprocity, and renewal. Lavadour, therefore, offers his paintings as "medicine to the world," proof of his active participation and his commitment to welcoming untold possibilities.

"Does the painting lift the spirit?," Lavadour asked his audience—but really, himself—in a recent conversation at PDX CONTEMPORARY ART.[28] He was surrounded by his newest body of work, comprised of grids, stacked diptychs and triptychs, and paintings on paper that seem to have taken the unbridled energy of *Bold as Love* and *Lucky Star* as their springboards. The forward momentum of Lavadour's practice over five decades as a working artist is just one story told within *James Lavadour: Land of Origin.* Despite being the most comprehensive survey of his work thus far, this retrospective cannot claim to tell the full breadth of such a remarkable artist's career and legacy. Yet we offer the exhibition, like each of Lavadour's paintings and prints, as an invitation through which greater understanding and appreciation may be found.

Endnotes

1 Marli Miller. "The Blue Mountains," The Oregon Encyclopedia. https://www.oregonencyclopedia.org/articles/blue_mountains/, April 17, 2023. Accessed October 14, 2024.

2 As quoted in Jaclyn Moyer, "The Many Legacies of Leticia Carson," *High Country News*, published June 1, 2023. https://www.hcn.org/issues/55-6/history-the-many-legacies-of-letitia-carson/. Accessed March 18, 2025. Lavadour's ties to Oregon history span beyond the reservation, notably in regard to Leticia Carson, his great-great-great-grandmother who was born into slavery and became one of the first known Black women to settle in Oregon. Carson's daughter Martha married a Walla Walla and Métis man, Narcisse Lavadour, in 1868, making James Lavadour a direct descendant of this union. The artist gifted a five-panel painting to the Leticia Carson Elementary School in Corvallis, Oregon, in his relative's honor in 2022. Lavadour's brother, celebrated basket weaver Joey Lavadour (b. 1954), is among the group of collaborators currently working to preserve the photographic history of generations of Métis (descendants of mixed French Canadian and Indigenous ancestry) in collaboration with Whitman College through the Métis Family Photo Archive project. See "Research Project Leads to Groundbreaking Photo Archives," *Whitman Magazine*, Winter 2024, https://www.whitman.edu/whitman-stories/whitman-magazine/winter-2024/research-project-leads-to-groundbreaking-photo-archives. Accessed July 21, 2025.

3 Vicki Halper. *James Lavadour: Landscapes*. Northwest Museum of Arts & Culture and University of Washington Press, 2001, p. 12. Halper's essay provides a thorough biography of Lavadour and a chronology of the artist's career through 2001.

4 Unless otherwise noted, all quotations from James Lavadour are taken from the author's interviews with him, by phone or at the artist's studio in Pendleton, Oregon, between March 2023 and February 2025, or from Lavadour's comments during a program at PDX CONTEMPORARY ART on May 31, 2025.

5 Halper, p. 14.

6 W. Jackson Rushing, "What the Ground Says: The Art of James Lavadour," *Into the Fray, Eiteljorg Museum of American Indians and Western Art* and University of Washington Press. 2005, p. 71.

7 Sheila Farr. "Desolation, Transformation: James Lavadour's landscapes of the mind," *Seattle Times*, Sept. 16, 2005. https://archive.seattletimes.com/archive/20050916/lavadour16/desolation-transformation-james-lavadours-landscapes-of-the-mind. Accessed May 12, 2025.

8 *James Lavadour on Painting*, John S. Weber, ed., interview anthology in this catalogue. Pp. 60-69.

9 *Sunset at the Lariat* and *Now My Cowboy's Gone* (both 1984), now in the collection of the Smithsonian National Museum of the American Indian, were initially purchased by the Indian Arts and Crafts Board, Department of the Interior in 1984; *Reservation Voodoo* (1985), in the collection of Seattle Art Museum, appeared in two group exhibitions at that museum in 1987 and 1989.

10 Artist statement. JSMA record of the exhibition.

11 Prior to this, Lavadour typically used blue underpainting.

12 *James Lavadour on Painting*.

13 Master printmaker Tadashi Toda of Kyoto, Japan, and James Lavadour presented an intensive workshop for Whitman College art students at Keiko Hara's Mokuhanga Project Space in Walla Walla, Washington, from April 4-7, 1994. Toda used 20 carved blocks and 36 colors to create this edition. Lavadour advised on the selection of inks to match his 1981 image of two figures. The result (printed to exact scale with the original painting) captured the mood and palette of Lavadour's early work. Mokuhanga Project Space Workshops. https://www.mokuhangaprojectspace.com/workshops. Accessed July 18, 2025.

14 Lavadour made multiple variations in his proofs while working with Beta Press and explained that entire collection of images is considered *Dreaming of Whirlwinds*. Email from James Lavadour to Danielle Knapp, February 20, 2025.

15 Kate Morris expands on this revelation in her discussion of Lavadour's work. *Shifting Grounds: Landscape in Contemporary Native American Art*, University of Washington Press, 2019, p. 12.

16 *Salamander* was among the images Lavadour submitted with his successful grant application to the Joan Mitchell Foundation in 1998, receiving a prestigious Painting Fellowship.

17 Both Vicki Halper and Rebecca J. Dobkins address this topic in their catalog essays for *James Lavadour: Landscapes* and *The Properties of Paint*, respectively.

18 Another work from this period, *Flag 2* (2001), was the first acquisition to the State of Oregon underwritten by The Ford Family Foundation's Art Acquisition Program in 2011.

19 Scholar Joyce Szabo situated Lavadour's work within the lineage of Native artists documenting historical events to those forging new understanding of the present and future: "His multiple-panel *Naming Tanager*, 2001, not only offers indications of how the artist felt in the place of places that inspired him, but also, through its very size and power, pulls viewers into that landscape." Joyce Szabo. "From Vibrant Colors to Somber Tones: Painting at the Juncture of Two Centuries," p. 41. The Eiteljorg Museum's Native Art Now! programming included a traveling retrospective exhibition featuring 39 works made by participants in the Eiteljorg Contemporary Art Fellowship program and acquired for the museum's permanent collection. *Native Art Now!: Developments in Contemporary Native American Art since 1992*, Veronica Passalacqua, et al. eds. Eiteljorg Museum, 2017.

20 James Lavadour, artist statement, July 2006.

21 Rebecca Dobkins and James Lavadour. "James Lavadour: The Properties of Paint," Hallie Ford Museum of Art, 2008, p. 7.

22 Kate Morris. *Shifting Grounds: Landscape in Contemporary Native American Art*. p. 73.

23 James Lavadour, artist statement, 2021.

24 Oral history interview with James Lavadour, April 29 and May 13, 2021. Archives of American Art, Smithsonian Institution. https://www.aaa.si.edu/collections/interviews/oral-history-interview-james-lavadour-22037. Accessed April 14, 2025.

25 This legislation upended communal land stewardship and further coerced Indigenous landholders to assimilate into a capitalist society.

26 https://rothkochapel.org/learn/about/. Accessed August 23, 2024.

27 James Lavadour, artist statement, November 15, 2003.

28 Lavadour engaged an audience of members of the Portland Art Museum's Native American Arts Council and Contemporary Art Council on May 31, 2025.

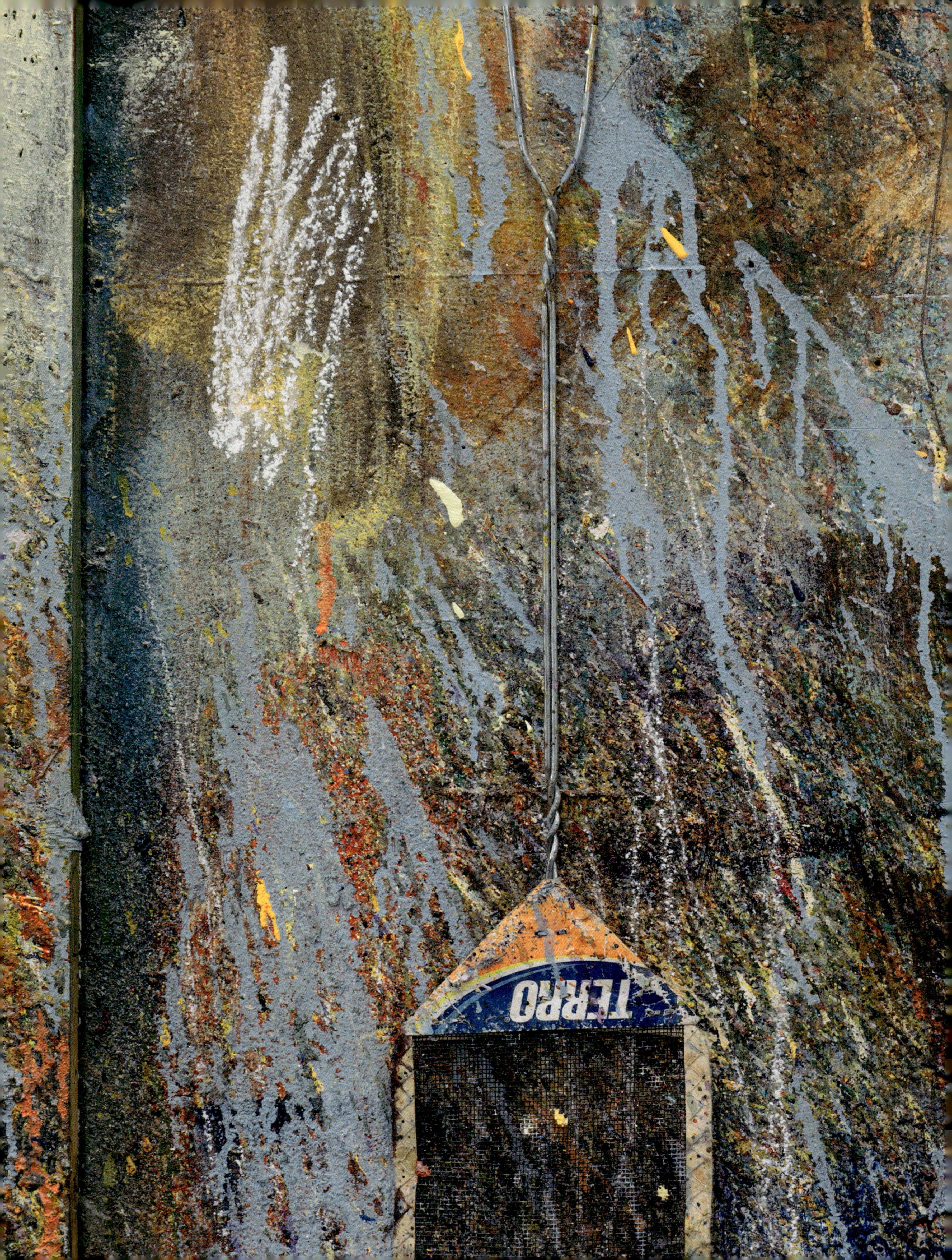

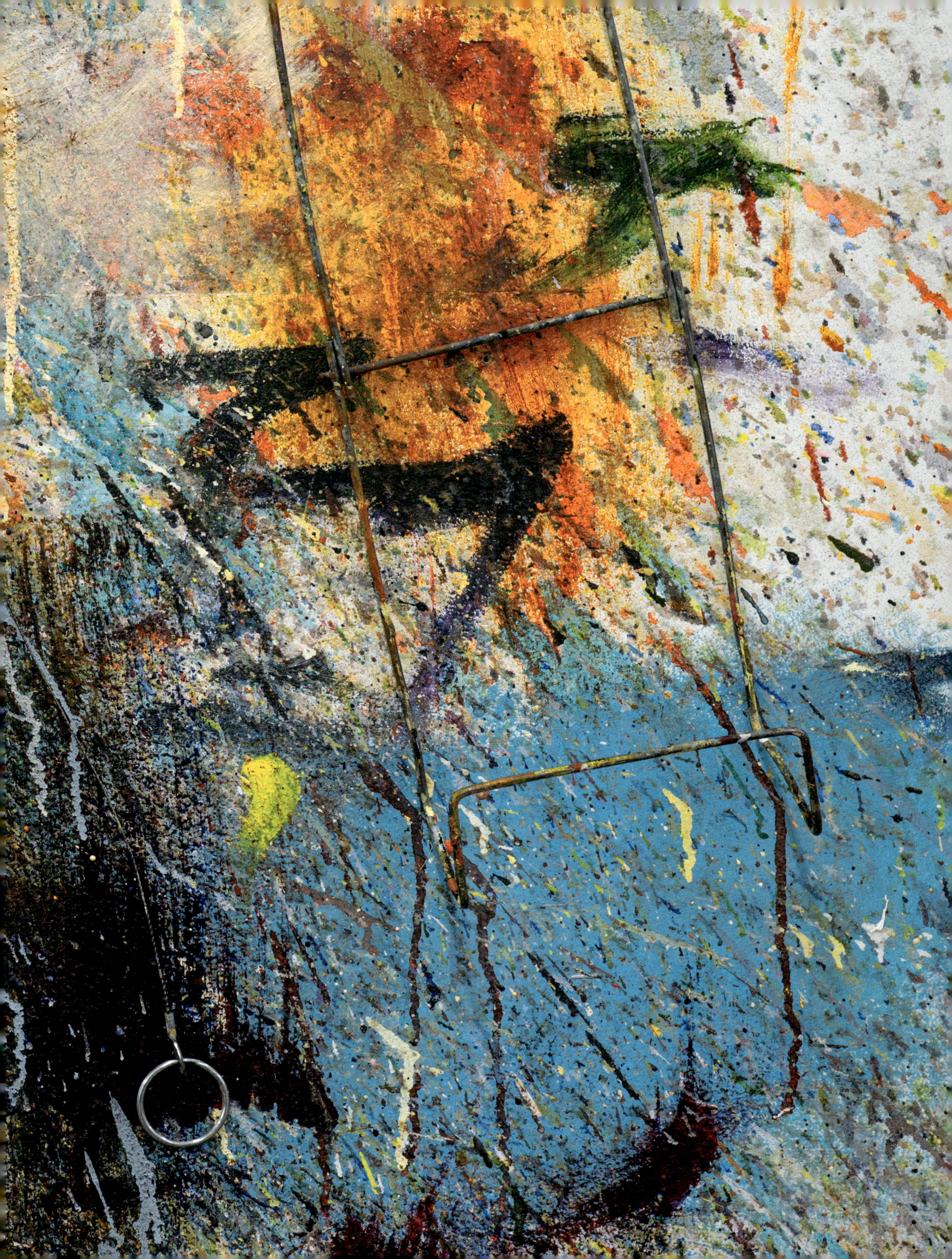

THE MAGNITUDE OF THE GIFT: James Lavadour and Crow's Shadow Institute of the Arts

Rebecca J. Dobkins

James Lavadour began dreaming of creating an arts center on his homelands of the Confederated Tribes of the Umatilla Indian Reservation (CTUIR) well before the actual founding of Crow's Shadow Institute of the Arts in 1992. In the 1970s and 1980s, Lavadour worked for the CTUIR in various capacities, and at the same time struggled to develop a career as an artist, painting in relative isolation and without access to fine arts education or the infrastructure of the mainstream art world of galleries, dealers, and museums. He recognized that dimensions of this struggle were shared by the many creative people in his community, whether they were working in fine or traditional arts. Lavadour wanted to find a way to bring resources to the Umatilla Indian Reservation, and in turn, bring his community's creativity to the world.[1]

What Lavadour could not have foreseen was the degree to which his vision came to fruition. From its scrappy beginnings in 1992 as a cobbled-together print studio in the then-unrenovated St. Andrew's Mission school building, Crow's Shadow now holds a place in the firmament of the contemporary art world, with its prints finding their way into prestigious venues and collections such as the Museum of Fine Arts, Boston, the National Gallery of Art, the National Museum of the American Indian, and the Whitney Museum of American Art, among many others. Prominent Seneca artist Marie Watt, who has long called herself "the poster child of Crow's Shadow," speaks of the "magnitude of Jim's gift" in creating this lodestar, not only for her, but for all Indigenous artists.[2] This essay reflects upon the magnitude of the gift of Crow's Shadow and how it both fed and drew from the wellspring of Lavadour's artistic career.

A LEAP BECAUSE OF FAITH

Lavadour spent his early childhood on the Umatilla reservation, but in 1959 he moved with his family to Walla Walla, Washington, where he graduated from high school in 1969. In this small college town, he had some exposure to art education, as well as to the bohemian ideas of the era. Lavadour also had his first introduction to the Bahá'í faith, with its emphasis upon the oneness of humanity, the centrality of service to community, and art as a legitimate life pursuit that uplifts the human condition. In 1975, Lavadour and his young family returned to the reservation to live, a move influenced by this belief in service and desire to serve his community, even though at the time he had no clear idea of what he might do for a living or what form this service would take.

Lavadour's move took place in what can now be understood as an historical moment of Indigenous nation-building. It was a time of return from diaspora by other tribal citizens, particularly those of his generation and a generation earlier who had been subject to federal urban relocation policies, as well as many who had served in the military, especially during the Vietnam war. In 1974, the CTUIR had adopted an Overall Economic Development Plan, with land and water resources at its center and with a vision of creating a robust tribal infrastructure.[3] To Lavadour's surprise, the first job he found with the tribe was as an artist in curriculum development. Through that and later positions, he regularly came into contact with many of the most culturally knowledgeable people on the reservation, elders such as Sam Cash Cash, Philip Geyer, Elizabeth Jones, Ike Patrick, and Carrie Sampson. He got to know talented leaders in tribal government including Antone Minthorn, a visionary elected official and advocate for sovereignty, and Mike Farrow, a tribal administrator who modeled the importance of recruiting exceptional personnel and creating effective organizational structures in the service of achieving tribal goals. Lavadour refers to the education he received at the elbows of these and other elders and leaders as his "college."

A seminal moment in these early years back on the reservation was when Lavadour and other extended family members went before the CTUIR General Council to be enrolled, something initially encouraged by Antone Minthorn, but really insisted on by his aunt Hazel Lavadour Jackson. At the meeting, one of the key questions put to the petitioners was, "Why do you want to be a tribal member?" Lavadour recalls saying, "If I'm enrolled, I promise to serve the tribe to my best abilities for the rest of my life." He immediately had the feeling, "Oh my God, what have I done?" Yet he took that promise seriously and has lived out this pledge, both through his own art making and ultimately through the vehicle of Crow's Shadow. Lavadour thinks of this promise as one that has bound him to the reservation; however, Crow's Shadow, in serving the tribal community, has brought the world to the reservation and the reservation to the world.

INTERTWINED TRAJECTORIES

From its conception, Crow's Shadow intersected Lavadour's art world career, both on and off the reservation. The space that Crow's Shadow first and still occupies, the St. Andrew's School, physically embodies this inseparability. Lavadour was familiar with the old school building, then and now owned by the region's Catholic diocese, in part because it had been used for tribal education programs when he worked for that department. When the two-story building was vacated in the 1980s, both Phillip Cash Cash (Cayuse/Nez Perce) and Lavadour rented classrooms to use as studio space, even as this was a very novel concept on the reservation. Cash Cash, who became one of the founders of Crow's Shadow, graduated from the Institute of American Indian Arts high school program in 1979 and later attended Pacific Northwest College of Art in Portland. He returned

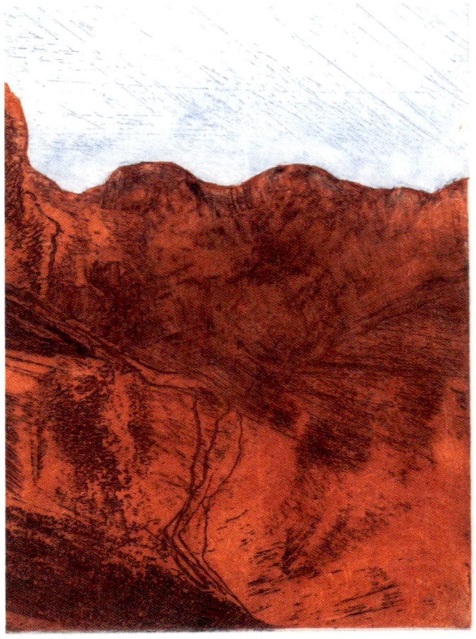
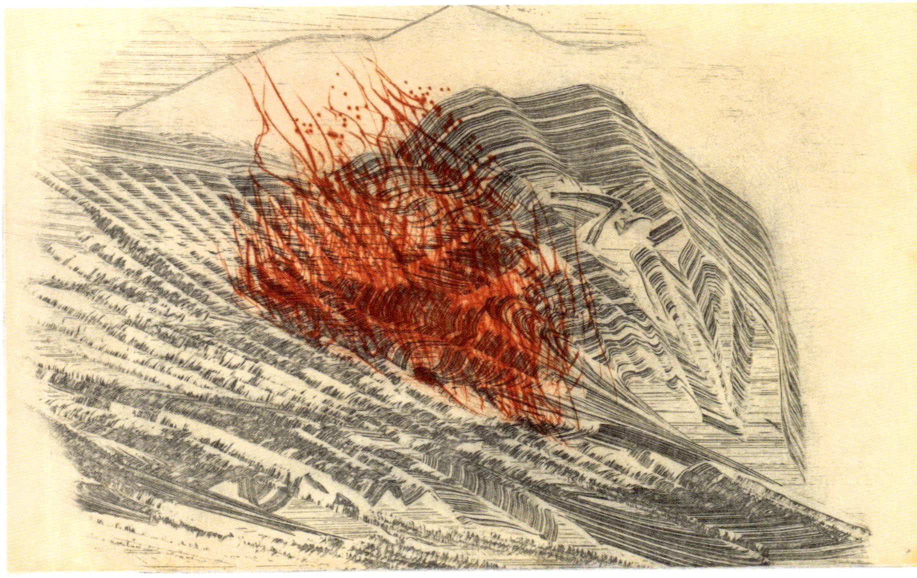
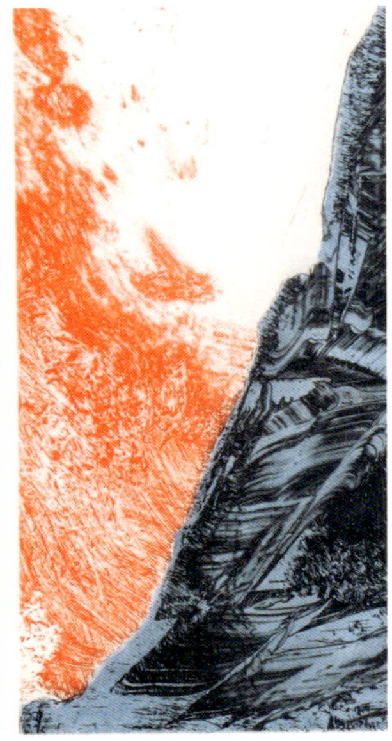
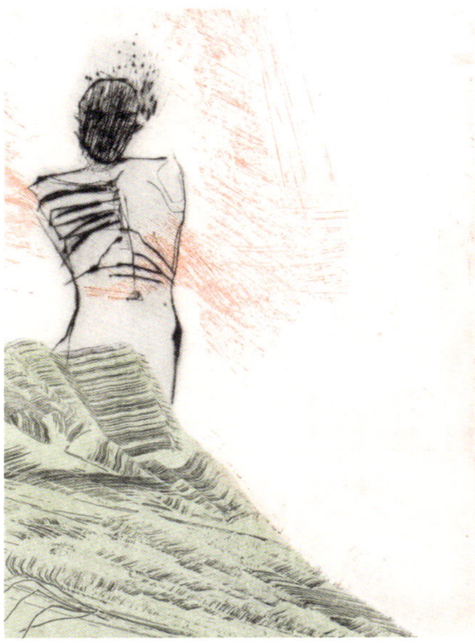
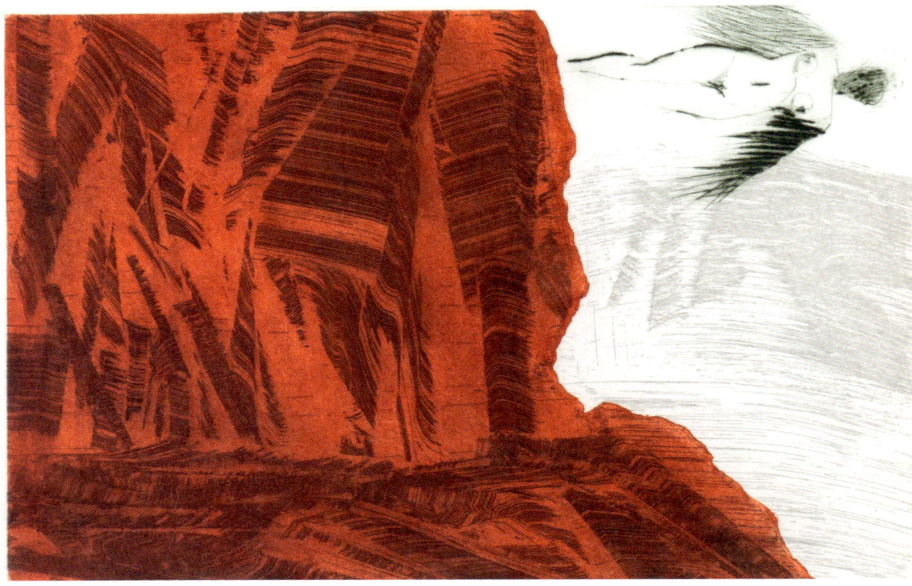
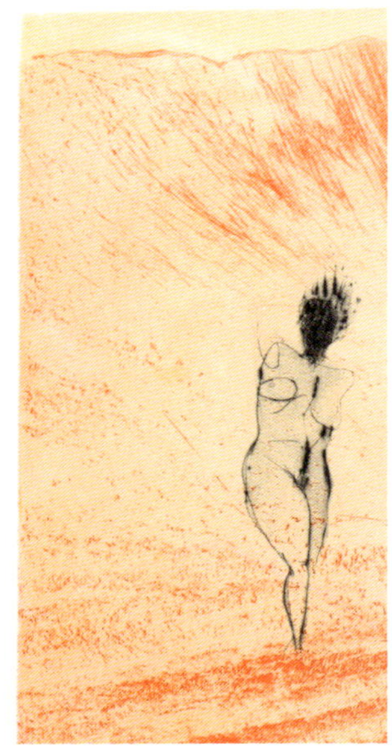

to the CTUIR in 1983, where he pursued his art practice and held positions with the CTUIR and federal agencies. Lavadour not only had studio space at St. Andrew's, but lived there as well, from the 1990s through the early 2000s.

After showing in exhibitions like the 1983 Oregon Biennial at the Portland Art Museum and being selected for public art projects by the Washington State and Seattle Arts Commissions in the early and mid-1980s, Lavadour had moved closer to working full time as an artist. He had received early critical support from the Pendleton-based ceramic artist, Betty Feves (1918-1985), whose encouragement, guidance, and material support were vital.[4] Feves, who grew up in eastern Washington but had studied art and art education and lived in New York City, was a creative, insistent advocate for the arts and played a major role in creating the arts programs at Blue Mountain Community College. Through what she called the Pendleton Artist Advocate Project, Feves raised funds from local art patrons so that Lavadour could work solely on his art for a year in 1985. Her example as a community activist who made space for the arts and artists to thrive in Pendleton inspired Lavadour as he envisioned a reservation-based arts organization.

Lavadour's painting was also shifting. His earlier figurative work was giving way to expressive, abstract landscapes. In 1990, Lavadour applied and was selected for a residency at what was then called the Rutgers Center for Innovative Print and Paper (now known as the Brodsky Center, housed at the Pennsylvania Academy of the Fine Arts in Philadelphia as of 2018).[5] This proved transformative, both for Lavadour's painting and as a catalyst for what became Crow's Shadow. Lavadour worked there with master printer Eileen Foti, and he equates this first encounter with printmaking as a sort of conversion experience. As a self-taught artist, without art school training, Lavadour was new to printmaking techniques and the collaboration experience at the heart of the process. Foti's wealth of knowledge and technical know-how, along with her generosity in sharing it, was inspirational. As Jim remembers, "I'm an isolated artist, and printmaking is sort of like being a member of the band. You've got a part, you write the song or you're the lead, but you're not the entire thing, you're not the one that makes it successful. I just really enjoyed that very much."[6]

Lavadour credits Foti with teaching him how to use red effectively by layering it on top of yellow, and after 1990, fiery reds appeared as never before in Lavadour's paintings. From the Rutgers residency, Lavadour "took away, more

Dreaming of Whirlwinds (detail), A/P 3, 1994. Color aquatint, soap ground etching, and drypoint, 35 x 46 inches. Published by Beta Press, Seattle. Collaborating Master Printer: Marcia Bartholme. Private collection.

than anything else, that feeling of really learning something fundamental and vital to my whole process. I use that in everything I do today, in terms of layering."[7] Lavadour recounts how, prior to this experience, he had worked from beginning to end on each individual painting; after the residency, he began to work on multiple paintings at once, in layers of color in a fashion parallel to printmaking, becoming much more productive as a result.

In addition to this sea change in artistic process, Lavadour returned home convinced that a print studio could be the model for the art center he had imagined on the reservation. Foti, like many printmakers before her, believed in the potential of printmaking to create social transformation, as it facilitated the democratization of art making and access to broader venues. She was also experienced with employing printmaking to facilitate exchange and communication across geographic and cultural borders.[8]

In 1991, Cash Cash also had a printmaking residency, in his case at the Tamarind Institute at the University of New Mexico, the premier center for lithography in the United States. Cash Cash's experience reinforced that of Lavadour, and the stage was set for the creation of an art center with printmaking at its heart. Lavadour's wife at the time, JoAnn, was also deeply committed to the concept, and suggested the name Crow's Shadow, the title of a 1988 painting in one of the artist's first sold-out shows, a watershed moment in his career. Cash Cash wrote a grant proposal that resulted in the first significant funding for Crow's Shadow, and in 1992, Crow's Shadow Institute of the Arts (CSIA) was incorporated. Lavadour gives great credit to the original board members, especially tribal members Patrice Hall Walters (Umatilla), Raphael Hoffman (Nez Perce), Jo Motanic Lewis (Umatilla), and Antone Minthorn (Cayuse), and the first executive director, Marie Hall, all of whom gave countless hours of their "blood, sweat, and tears" to launch the organization. Another key contributor was Tom Hampson, who had worked for the CTUIR for years and who served as a consultant for CSIA in the early days, fundamentally shaping its future.[9]

For Lavadour, Cash Cash, and the other founders, the essence of Crow's Shadow was and is to provide opportunities and the means for artists to thrive. From the beginning, the mission included traditional artists, and Lavadour "understood how important it was," even though that was not the path he had taken in his own art practice.[10] In the 1990s, especially, there were few organized classes on the CTUIR to teach beading or weaving or drum-making or other arts. Crow's Shadow developed a model for supporting traditional arts that was, according to Lavadour, fairly simple: "Organize people, give them a telephone, provide them with a place, the whole mechanics.... The person doing the workshop [had] the responsibility for who they wanted to teach and how they wanted to teach."[11] In this way, those with cultural knowledge shared it in the ways they wished and those seeking knowledge had a place to learn; Crow's Shadow gave people a place to go, offering camaraderie and acceptance. Creating space for traditional arts to thrive developed alongside the creation of the print studio program.

THE 1990s: A GENERATIVE ERA IN CONTEMPORARY NATIVE ARTS

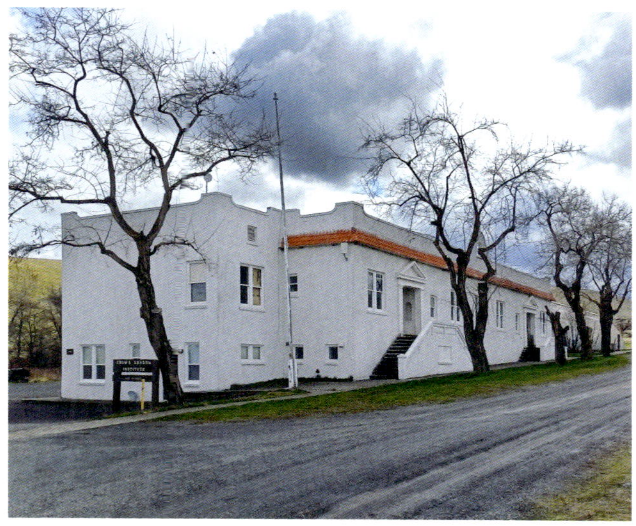

Crow's Shadow Institute of the Arts. Photograph by Danielle Knapp.

The birth of Crow's Shadow in the 1990s coincided with the growing visibility of Native American arts as a result of the longtime advocacy of Native artists, curators, and activists. The Columbian quincentenary in 1992 was initially presented by U.S. federal government channels as something to be celebrated, but artist-curators such as Jaune Quick-to-See Smith (Salish and Kootenai, 1940-2025) were adamant that Native American voices and visions be heard and seen. Smith organized important exhibitions in this period, among them *The Submuloc Show–Columbus Wohs* in 1992-94 that explicitly responded to the Columbian invasions.[12] Over the course of her career, Smith consistently turned to printmaking as one way of advocating for Native American contemporary art and disseminating it broadly.[13] One of the most significant exhibitions Smith curated in the last years of her life, *The Land Carries Our Ancestors: Contemporary Art by Native Americans,* at the National Gallery of Art in 2023, prominently featured prints, including eight produced at CSIA.[14]

Lavadour was included in another watershed exhibition, *Shared Visions: Native American Painters and Sculptors of the Twentieth Century*, organized by the Heard Museum in 1991 and co-curated by Margaret Archuleta (Tewa/Hispanic) and

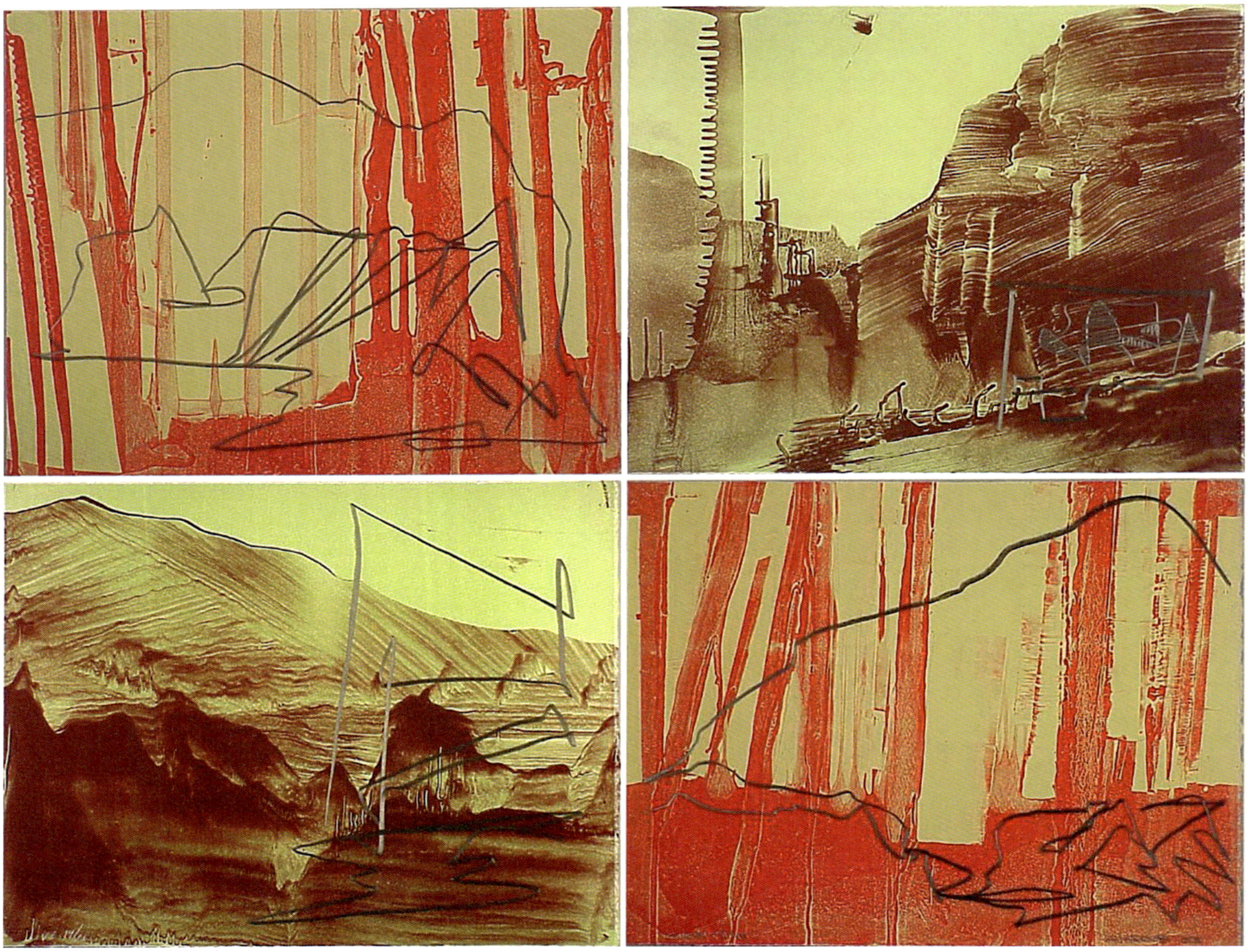

Fig. 7: **Ghost Camp**, from an edition of 16, 2002. Four-color lithograph with hand drawing in graphite pen, 17 x 21 ¾ inches.
Crow's Shadow Institute of the Arts Archive, Hallie Ford Museum of Art, Willamette University (CSP 02-114 (a, b. c. d).

Rennard Strickland (Cherokee and Osage).[15] This seminal traveling exhibition included over seventy artists and revealed how Native American artists incorporated Western modernist movements such as abstract expressionism and went beyond narrow definitions of "traditional" Native art. Lavadour expanded his community of artists through events associated with this project, including a major symposium in Phoenix. His travels there allowed him to experience the southwestern landscape for the first time, including the Grand Canyon.

As Lavadour was curated into more and more group exhibitions of Native American art in both the U.S. and Canada, he became acutely aware of the ways contemporary Native American artists were marginalized from the mainstream contemporary art world, despite an apparent acceleration of institutional interest in Native art.[16] It became part of the CSIA mission to span this divide, a commitment codified into the CSIA logo: its two parallel lines are transected by a diagonal conduit crossing the barrier between these art worlds, going in both directions.

CSIA AS A CONDUIT FOR NATIVE ART AND ARTISTS

For CSIA's first decade, Lavadour was deeply involved in the organization on nearly a daily basis. He was living and working, taking care of his family, and serving on the board of CSIA, all literally in the same place—the St. Andrew's Mission school building. Lavadour recalls that there were times when he couldn't distinguish between his advocacy for Crow's Shadow and his job as an artist, such as when he made pitches for the organization at events where he was exhibiting his work. His time was divided between developing this new arts center and making his own art. He kept circling back to his life commitment to contribute to the tribe; Crow's Shadow manifested that commitment.

Reflecting on those early years, Lavadour believes that the most important thing he did was to attract the right people to work with and at CSIA, whether on the board or as staff. To Lavadour, Crow's Shadow existed to discover and nourish the potential of the CTUIR community and the broader community of Indigenous artists. One of the key supporters was the Rutgers printmaker Eileen Foti, who helped set up the initial print studio and press at Crow's Shadow. Trained as a master printer at Tamarind Institute, Foti established the studio in accord with Tamarind's exacting protocols for lithography and its documentation. When it came time to hire a full-time master printer, the CSIA board chose Tamarind-trained printer Frank Janzen in 2001, who brought those protocols to shape what became Crow's Shadow Press in 2002.

In September 2001, Lavadour, along with CSIA board members and supporters such as Foti, organized a groundbreaking, three-day symposium, Conduit to the Mainstream, to which key Indigenous artists, academics, and printmakers were invited.[17] The object was to discuss the status of contemporary Native arts and envision how Crow's Shadow could help artists break into the mainstream. The attendees ranged from luminaries of the Native art world, such as Kay WalkingStick (Cherokee) and James Luna (Luiseño), to curators such as Archuleta and Strickland, all of whom Lavadour had cultivated relationships with in his own art career. Marie Watt, the youngest artist in attendance, attests to the extraordinary impact of being introduced to these stellar Indigenous artists and other arts professionals, who in turn began to include her work in various projects. She recalls that 2001 was a time before social media existed in any meaningful way, and information about Indigenous arts had to be scavenged in exhibit brochures, catalogs, and the occasional book. The face-to-face dimension of the Conduit gathering generated relationships and new energy and commitment to her studio practice.[18] While not a direct outcome of the Conduit gathering, it seems hardly a coincidence that in 2005, just a few years later, both Watt and Lavadour were chosen for the then still-relatively new Eiteljorg Contemporary Art Fellowship, considered by many to be the most prestigious in the field.[19]

Janzen attended the Conduit to the Mainstream symposium in his new role as CSIA master printer. Immediately afterwards, his tenure (2001-2017) began with the residency of Edgar Heap-of-Birds, who produced an eighteen-color lithograph as the first print editioned by the newly established Crow's Shadow Press. As Lavadour began his own collaborations with Janzen, he chose to donate the sales of every edition to Crow's Shadow, helping create a stronger financial foundation and a regular income stream for the Institute. In addition, collectors of Lavadour's work became interested in the work coming out of Crow's Shadow, becoming regular supporters, whether through purchasing prints or making other kinds of donations.

The first lithographic suite that Lavadour and Janzen collaborated on was **Ghost Camp** (2002, fig. 7), a grid of four four-color images that reveal cross-fertilization between Lavadour's painting practice, with its drips and scrapes, and the layering inherent to printmaking. The next major effort between Lavadour and Janzen was the **Early Spring in February** series in 2004 (fig. 8), eight two-color images that collectively explore a wide palette in rendering the

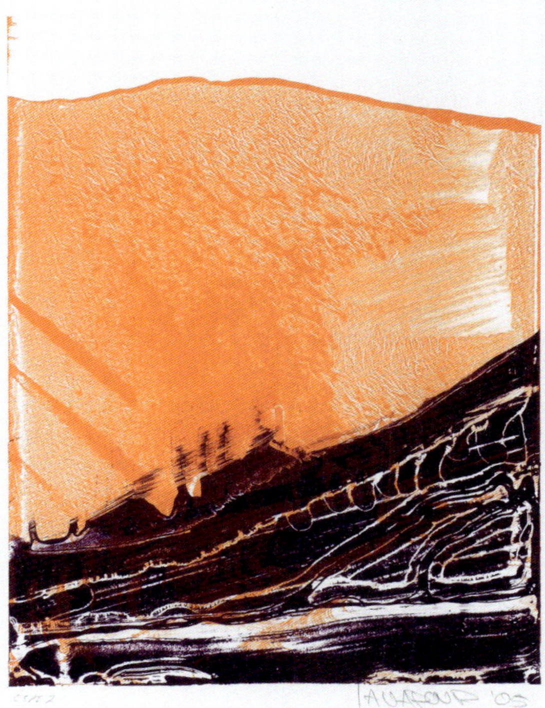

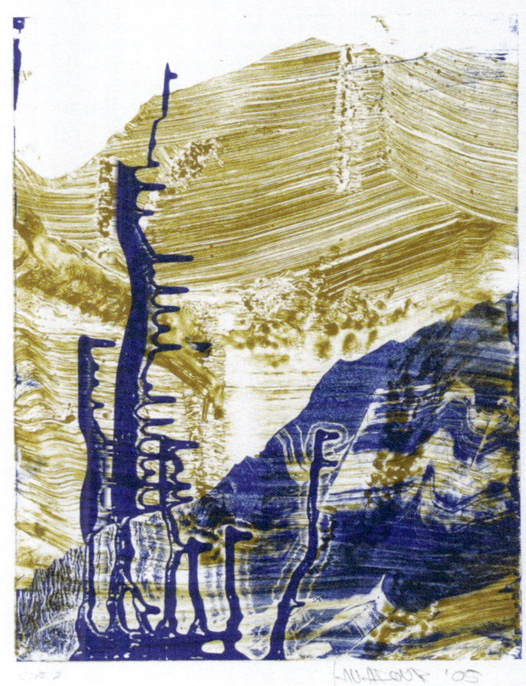

Figs. 8-9: Two prints from the **Early Spring in February 2005 Suite**, ed. 46/50, 2005. Two-color lithographs, 11 x 8½ inches. (each). Crow's Shadow Institute of the Arts Archive, Hallie Ford Museum of Art, Willamette University (2006.044.004 and 2006.044.002).

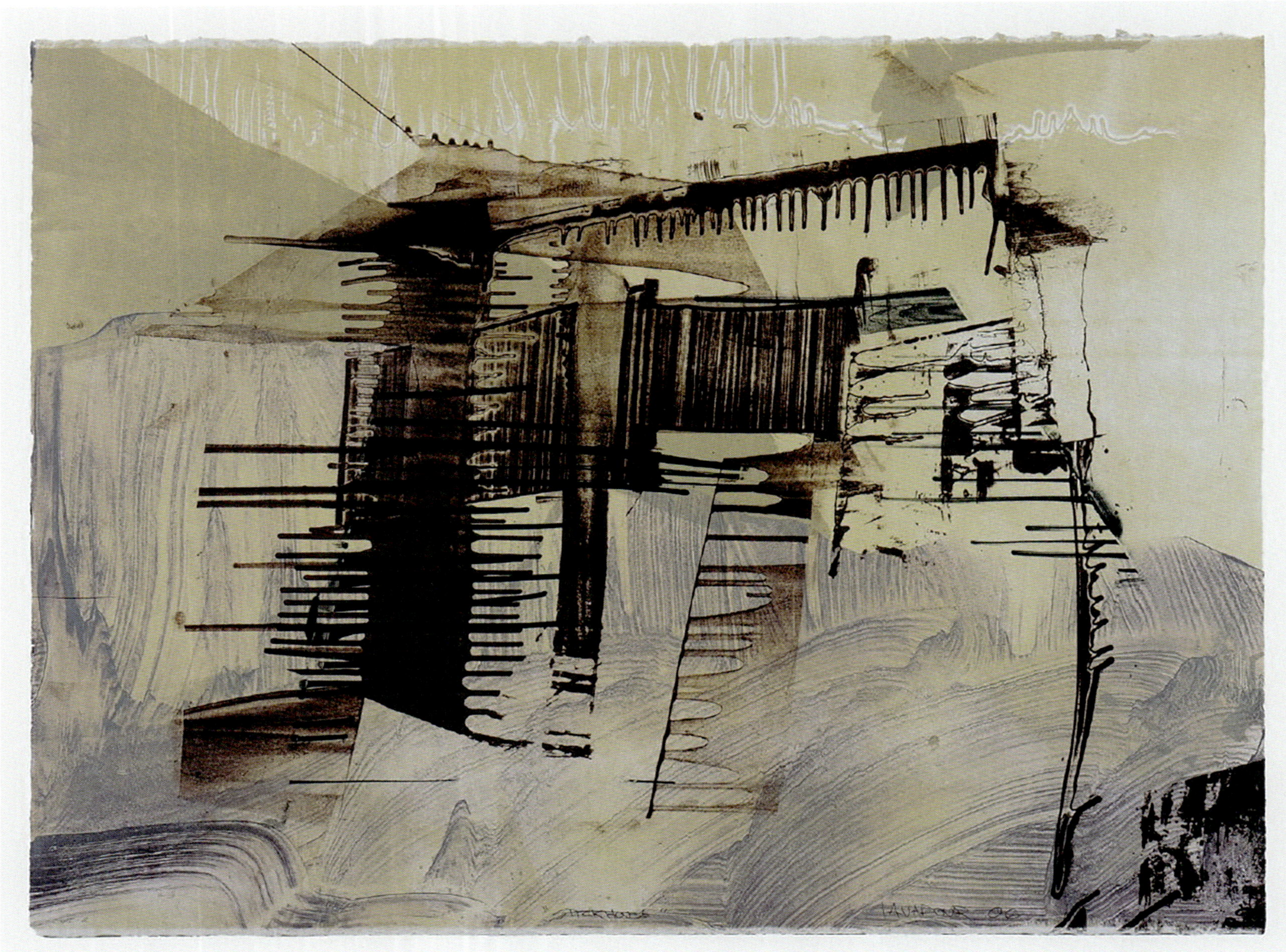

Fig. 10: **Stick House**, from an edition of 30, 2006. Six-color lithograph, 22 ½ × 30 inches. Crow's Shadow Institute of the Arts Archive, Hallie Ford Museum of Art, Willamette University (CSP 06-101).

mood and transition from winter to spring on the Columbia River Plateau. In 2006, Lavadour worked with Janzen to edition a complex image, **Stick House** (fig. 10), that, like **Ghost Camp**, evokes the enduring relationship between Indigenous peoples and their homelands through abstract reference to shelters built not only upon, but in kinship with the land.

Lavadour continued making prints at Crow's Shadow through Janzen's tenure, including a series of twenty-one monotypes initiated in 2008, completed in 2010, although most were not published until 2019. In 2011, Lavadour completed the **Duotone** series of four lithographs, each with intensely saturated layers of two shades of the same color (green, blue, or red/pink), a departure from his prior prints and their generally contrasting palettes. In 2015, Lavadour and Janzen collaborated to create a grid of four three-color lithographs, **Land of Origin** (fig. 11), that in its complexity and scale is a powerful culmination of the decade and a half working relationship between artist and printmaker.

THE WORLD COMES TO CROW'S SHADOW

CSIA was deemed a "Golden Spot" program by The Ford Family Foundation of Oregon in 2010, marking a significant turning point in the Institute's history. The designation, given to just a few residency centers in Oregon that the Foundation considers to be distinctive environments for artistic creativity, came with financial support for both Crow's Shadow and the individual artists awarded residencies. To be eligible for Golden Spot awards, artists had to live in Oregon, be at mid-career, and have a promising exhibition history.[20]

The Golden Spot program not only provided regular external funding for artist residencies, but linked Crow's Shadow to a broader Oregon arts ecosystem as well as to the art worlds of the resident artists themselves: the galleries that represented them, the venues where they displayed work, and the networks in which they operated. Several

Indigenous artists who live in Oregon were awarded Golden Spot residencies, including Brenda Mallory (Cherokee), Wendy Red Star (Crow), and Sara Siestreem (Hanis Coos), but Crow's Shadow also attracted a wide range of non-Indigenous artists, such as Arnold Kemp, Storm Tharp, and Samantha Yun Wall.[21]

For Lavadour, the rationale for including non-Indigenous artists was straightforward: all artists who came to work at Crow's Shadow became bridges to the outside world. At the same time, by offering artists a welcoming space for creativity, Crow's Shadow became a gift back to the world. As visiting artists came to Crow's Shadow, they shared information and techniques that became part of its cumulative history, and when they left as CSIA alumni they could validate its worth and importance, effectively raising its profile. Throughout this period, Lavadour recalls that the board consistently filtered every decision it made through the sieve of the CSIA mission: "to provide educational, social and economic opportunities for Native Americans through artistic development."[22] As the board understood, bringing non-Indigenous artists who enriched CSIA and the CTUIR community, strengthening both, ultimately promoted opportunities for Native American artists.

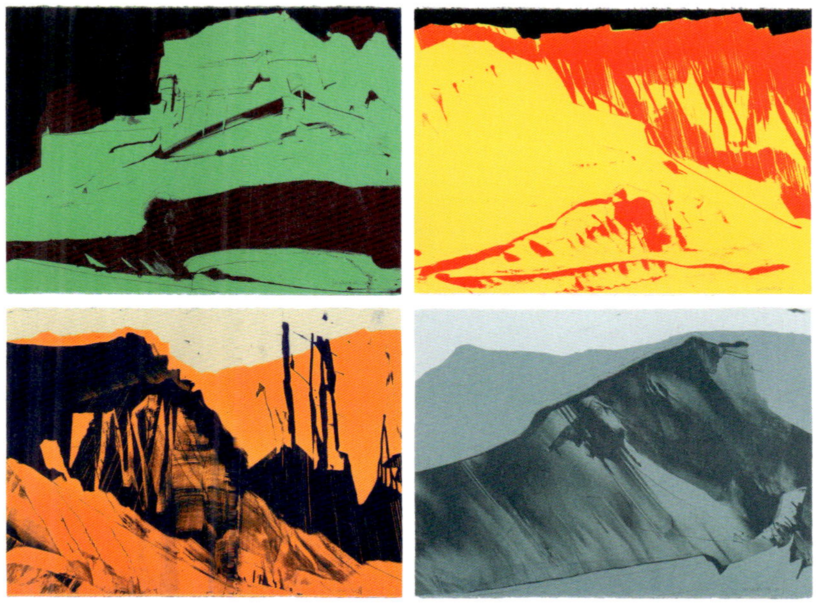

Fig. 11: **Land of Origin**, ed. 2/18, 2015. Three-color lithographs, 22 ½ x 30 ¼ inches. (each). Crow's Shadow Institute of the Arts Archive, Hallie Ford Museum of Art, Willamette University (CSP 15-101).

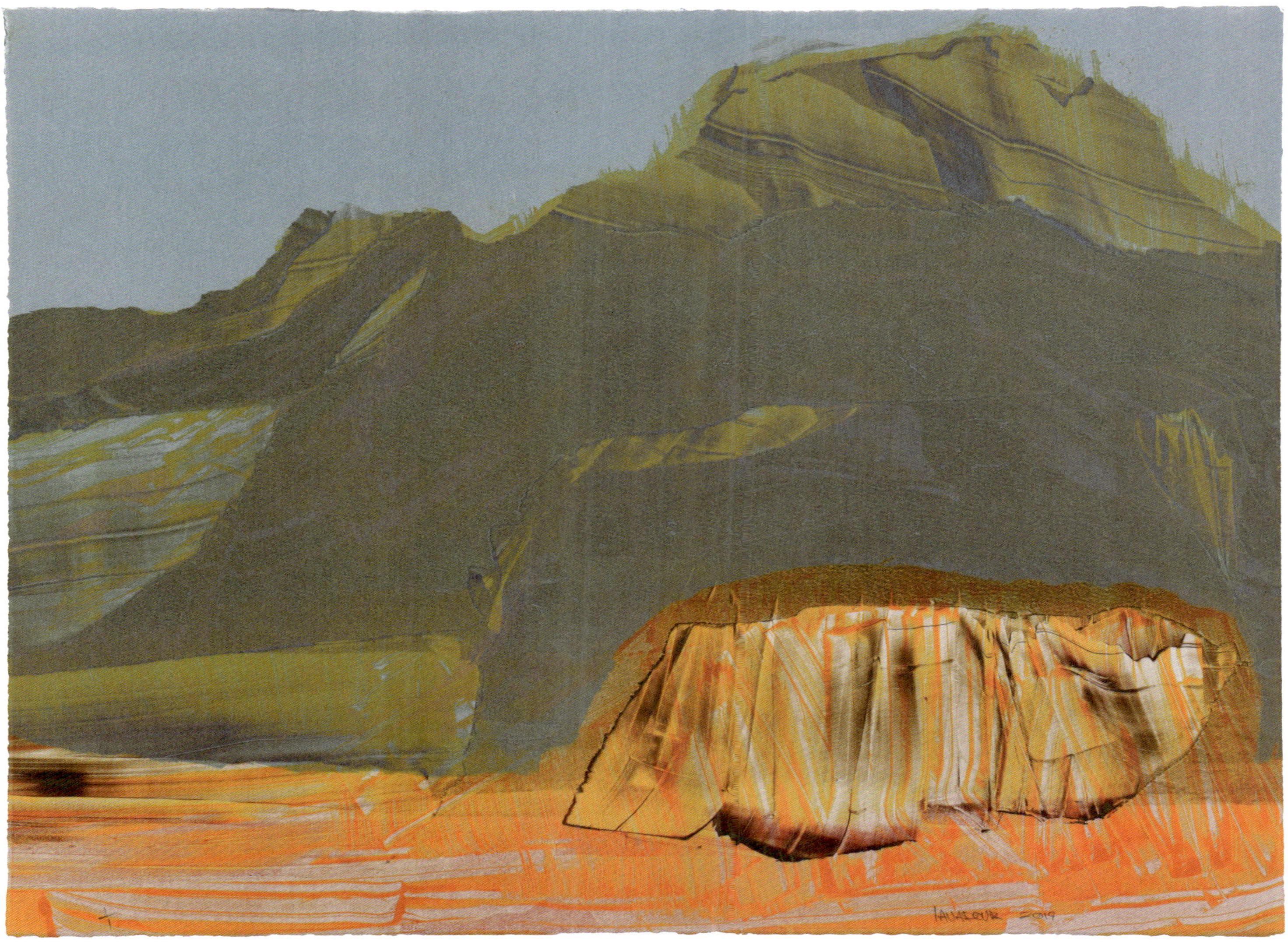

Fig. 12: One print from the **Crow's Shadow Suite**, 2010. Monotype, 22 ½ x 30 inches. Hallie Ford Museum of Art, Willamette University (2019.014). Photograph by Dale Peterson.

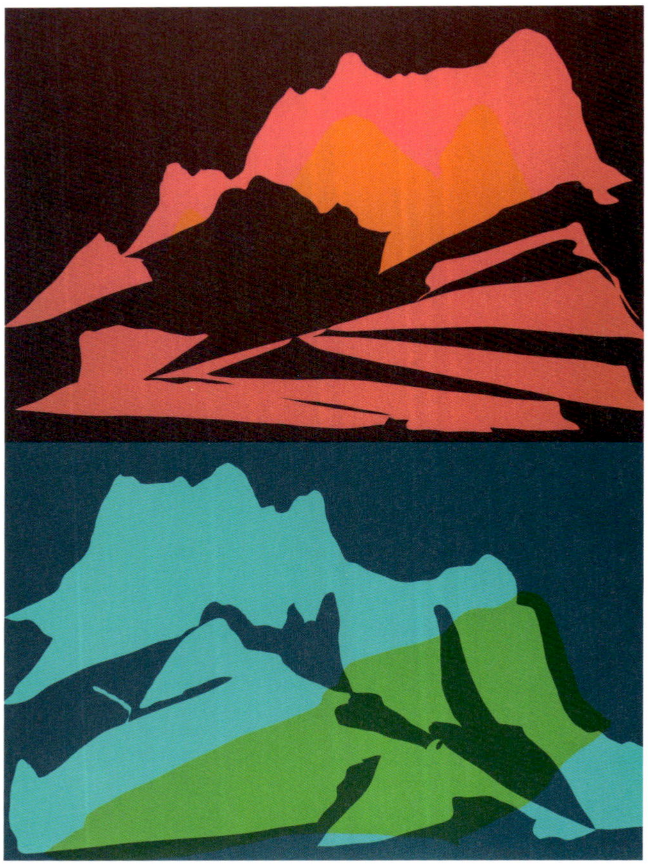

Fig. 13: **Summer**, ed. 8/30, 2018-19. Six-color lithograph, 30 x 22 inches. Jordan Schnitzer Museum of Art, University of Oregon.

Crow's Shadow's improved financial stability during the 2010s allowed Lavadour to step back somewhat from day-to-day involvement. In 2014, Karl Davis, with degrees in art history and a background in gallery administration, became CSIA executive director, a position he held until 2023. Davis increased the Crow's Shadow budget, revenue, and staffing and, building on its track record of artist residencies and the reputation Lavadour had earned for his own work, secured support from nationally prominent arts organizations, notably the National Endowment for the Arts in 2018.

During this period, CSIA prints, including those made by Lavadour, made it into significant museum collections and circulated in exhibitions. Among those were a 2014 exhibition of CSIA prints at the National Museum of the American Indian, *Making Marks*, and a 2017 *CSIA at 25* exhibition organized by the Hallie Ford Museum of Art that traveled to other selected venues. That same year CSIA won the Oregon Governor's Art Award, a recognition of its impact upon the state's arts ecosystem. In 2019, the *New York Times* prominently featured an article on CSIA in its arts section, "Increasing Exposure for Native Artists," lauding the impact Crow's Shadow had achieved to date.[23] By the early 2020s, Crow's Shadow prints were in the collections of the Library of Congress, the Museum of Fine Arts, Boston, the Whitney Museum of American Art, and the Eiteljorg Museum in Indianapolis, among many others.

In 2017, Frank Janzen retired and handed the reins to another Tamarind-trained printer, Judith Baumann, who remained at CSIA until 2024. According to Lavadour, Baumann, who had a background teaching drawing and printmaking at the university level, helped elevate printmaking at CSIA and specifically helped him to experiment with color and form. Collaborating with Baumann as well as with earlier printers often led to breakthroughs in his painting practice: "Every time I made prints, I experienced a very productive period right afterwards." Part of that productivity came from the sense of accomplishment from having a successful collaboration with a creative partner, a process at the heart of printmaking. With Baumann, he felt he was beginning to figure out some things about printmaking that, in his words, had been "plaguing him" since the beginning, given that printmaking requires rendering images in their opposites.[24]

Lavadour and Baumann collaborated on three lithographs during her tenure: **Summer** (2019, fig. 13), a six-color lithograph with two images stacked upon each other, similar to the form of **This Good Land** (2017, fig. 14), but distinctive with its colors of pink, red, orange, green and blue. **Spring** (2023, plate 31) and **Winter** (2023, plate 30) are independent yet related works, with intense colors signaling each season's essential energy. As with the prints editioned with Janzen, Lavadour employed his painterly process of scraping and layering, yet these later works reflect the artist's ongoing refinement of contrast between movement and stillness.

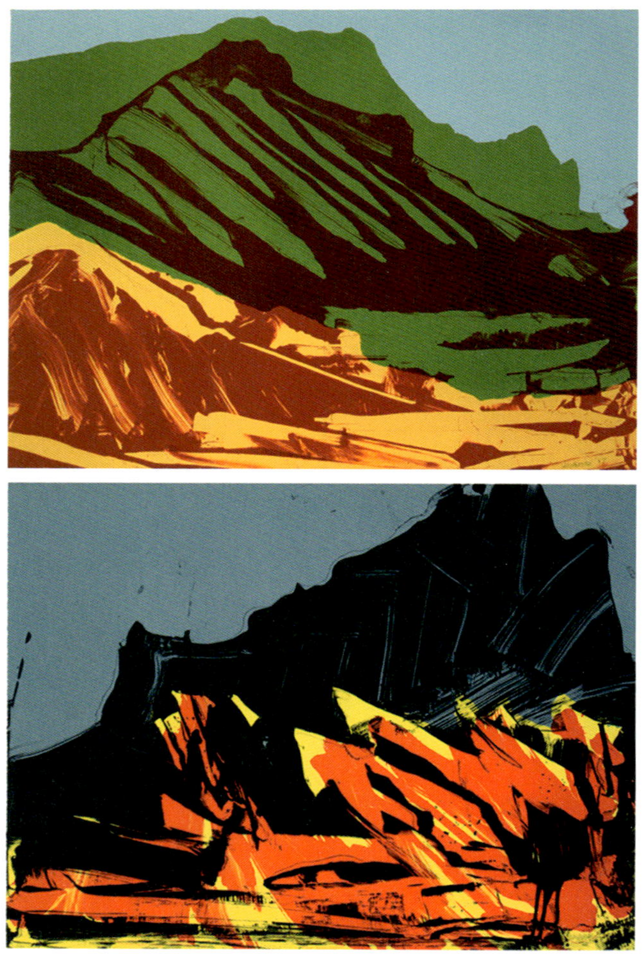

Fig. 14: **This Good Land**, 2017. Four-color lithograph, 60 x 39 ½ inches. Crow's Shadow Institute of the Arts Archive, Hallie Ford Museum of Art, Willamette University (CSP 17-101 (a,b).

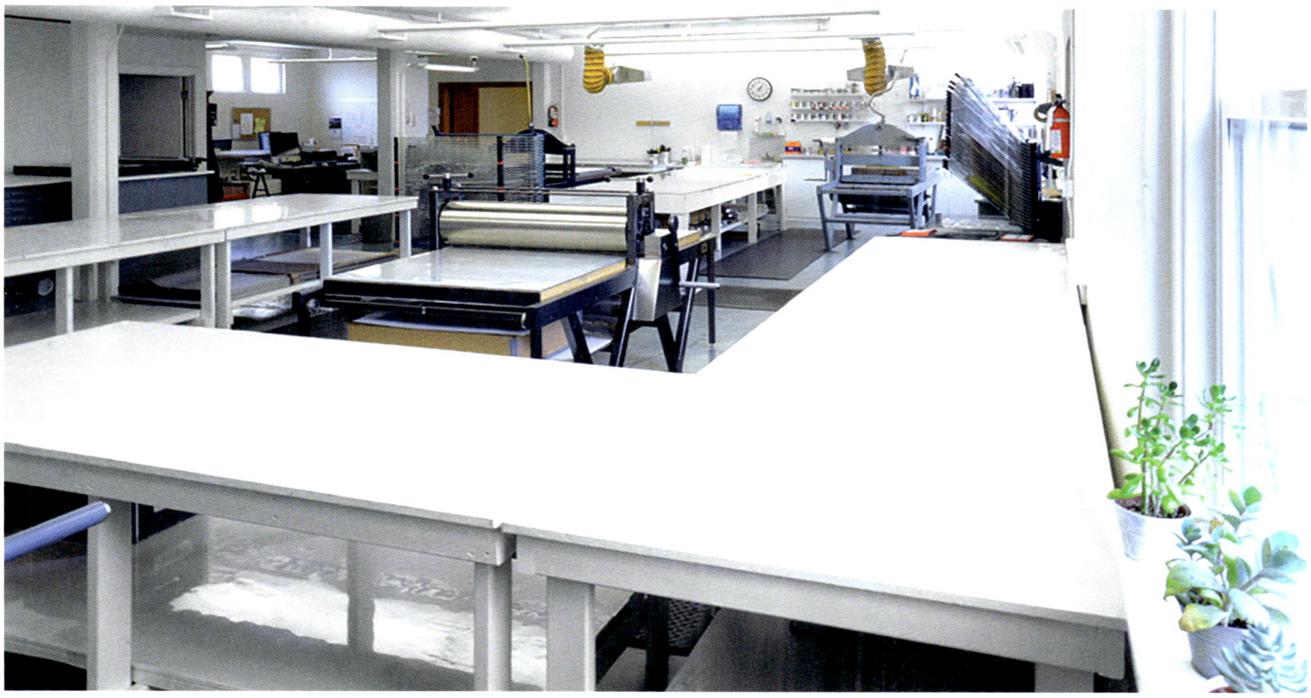

THE ENDURING GIFT OF CROW'S SHADOW

For the milestone exhibition at the National Gallery of Art in 2023, *The Land Carries Our Ancestors: Contemporary Art by Native Americans,* curator Jaune Quick-to-See Smith faced the daunting challenge of how to represent the diversity of Indigenous artists across mediums, regions, generations, and genders.[25] The National Gallery had not had an exhibition of Native American fine art since the 1950s and had no paintings by Native artists in its collection until 2020, when it acquired **Target** (1992) by Smith, a mixed-media work from the earlier era of Columbian quincentenary critique. Smith ultimately selected nearly fifty artists, a striking sixteen of whom had done residencies at Crow's Shadow. Of the over fifty works in the exhibition, eight were prints produced by Crow's Shadow Press. These are but two measures of the impact Crow's Shadow has made in its more than three decades of existence.

Smith wrote in the accompanying exhibition catalog for *The Land Carries our Ancestors* that the works she chose were "so much more than beautiful objects on display in a museum. While they might not fit into the mainstream of Euro-American perceptions of landscape, they do represent our enduring connection to land."[26] On one wall of the exhibition, framed prints and other works on paper were arranged in a two-level pattern with corners touching to invoke a checkerboard. This was a direct reference to the fragmenting of Indigenous lands by the 1887 Dawes Act that divided collectively-held tribal homelands into individual allotments, with many lands ending up in non-Native possession. The CTUIR is one such 'checkerboard' reservation; in the twenty-first century, however, it and many other tribal nations are acquiring parcels of land back. Smith intended for the works within the arrangement to signal the ongoing persistence of Indigenous connections to land across generations and regions, working against the devastation of U.S. government policies.

Displayed on that wall were several of the Crow's Shadow prints Smith selected for the exhibition, including Lavadour's lithograph **Duotone 2** (2011, fig. 15). For Lavadour, the lush blue drips and lines in this image "are identical to the snaking and braiding of river channels," as they have shaped the land and people's lives upon it for millennia.[27] His work brought the presence of place, of the Umatilla, Walla Walla, and Cayuse homelands, into the nation's temple of world art, a temple that has so belatedly opened its doors to Native American visions. This and all the works created at and by artists associated with CSIA served as testimony to the success of the Crow's Shadow mission that Lavadour has so long advocated: to provide opportunities for Indigenous artists and to serve as a conduit to the broader, mainstream art world—and for that world to be enriched by Indigenous creativity.

When asked to sum up the significance of the creation of Crow's Shadow, Lavadour identifies the community of the Confederated Tribes of the Umatilla Indian Reservation—not himself—as the fundamental wellspring of its contributions: "I'm...very idealistic about human potential and creativity....[Crow's Shadow is] serving humanity. It wasn't just for us, it wasn't just for our community. That's the kind of potential our community has. To give something big to the world. That's what the world needs.... That's the kind of people we are."[28] The magnitude of the gift of Crow's Shadow is immeasurable and ongoing. James Lavadour is to be honored for nurturing it from the wellspring of his own and his people's creativity.

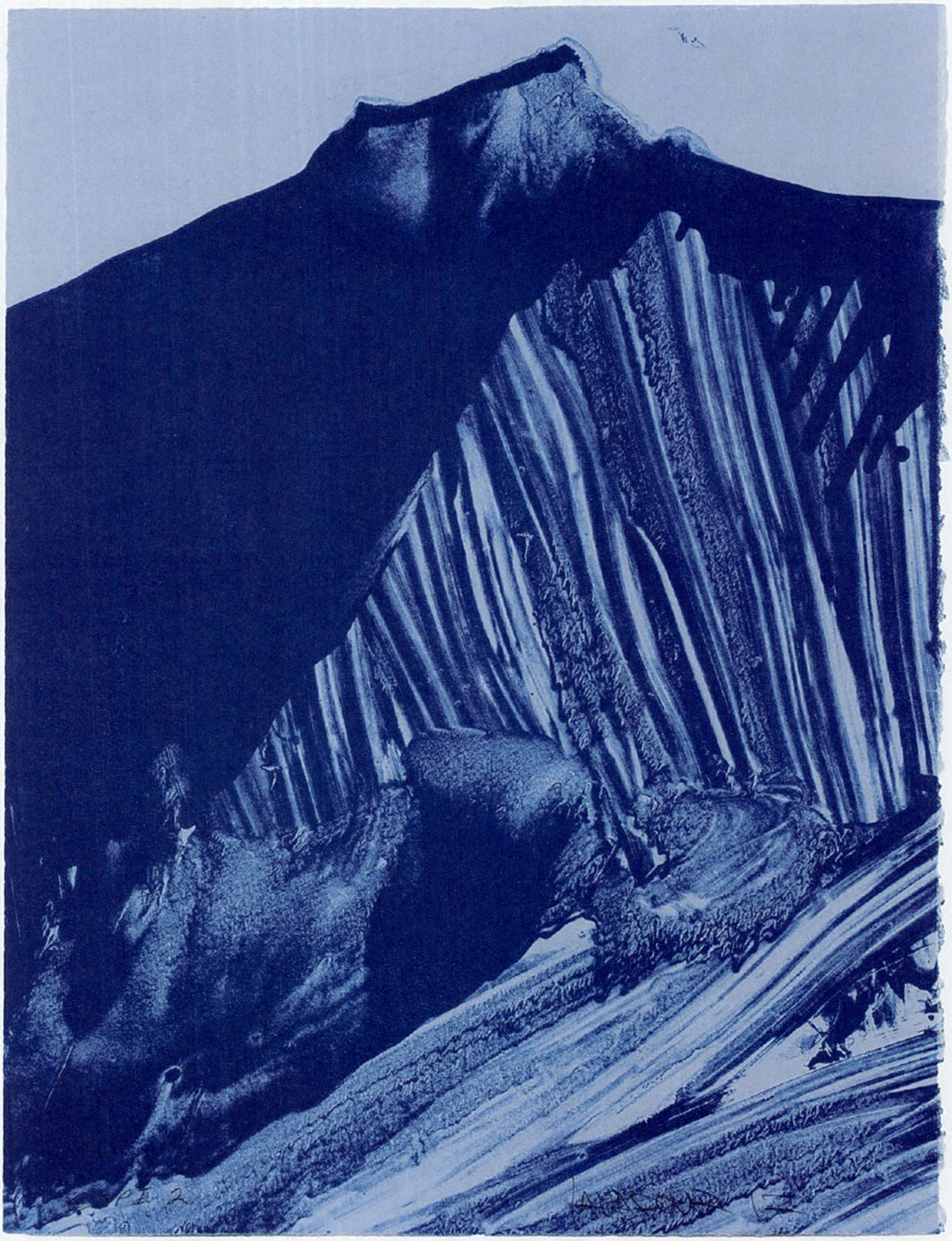

Scholar and curator Rebecca J. Dobkins, PhD, is Professor Emeritus of Anthropology and American Ethnic Studies at Willamette University and has organized major exhibitions of work by James Lavadour (Walla Walla), Marie Watt (Turtle Clan of the Seneca Nation of Indians), and Rick Bartow (Mad River Wiyot), among many others, as Curator of Native American Art at the Hallie Ford Museum of Art in Salem, OR.

Endnotes

1 This essay draws from recorded conversations between the author and James Lavadour on January 13-14, 2025, as well as many prior discussions. In addition, I rely extensively on Prudence F. Roberts' essay, "Crow's Shadow Institute of the Arts at 25: A History," in *Crow's Shadow Institute of the Arts at 25*, heather ahtone (sic), Rebecca J. Dobkins and Prudence F. Roberts (authors). Hallie Ford Museum of Art, 2017, pp. 11-29.

2 Conversations between author and Marie Watt on January 23-24, 2025. Also see Rebecca J. Dobkins, *Marie Watt: Lodge*. Salem, OR: Hallie Ford Museum of Art, 2012, pp. 32, 43, 46.

3 See Roberts, "Crow's Shadow Institute of the Arts at 25," p. 13.

4 Betty Feves moved to Pendleton in 1945, accompanying her husband Dr. Louis Feves, who worked for the Indian Health Service and became the physician for the Lavadour family; he delivered James Lavadour into the world in 1951.

5 See the Brodsky Center at Pennsylvania Academy of the Fine Arts, https://brodskycenter.com/. Accessed March 4, 2025.

6 Conversation with the author, January 13, 2025.

7 Ibid.

8 Roberts, "Crow's Shadow Institute of the Arts at 25,"pp. 12-16. Lavadour also printed with master printer Marcia Bartholme at Beta Press in Seattle in 1994-95. Those prints, along with the rest of the Beta Press collection, are now in the collection of the Tacoma Art Museum. See https://tacoma.emuseum.com/collections/19384/beta-press-collection. Accessed March 4, 2025.

9 Correspondence with the author, April 2, 2025. For more detail about the history of CSIA's founding and early years, see Roberts, "Crow's Shadow Institute of the Arts at 25," pp. 12-17.

10 Conversation with the author, January 13, 2025.

11 Ibid.

12 Jaune Quick-to-See Smith, *Submuloc Show/Columbus Wohs: A Visual Commentary on the Columbus Quincentennial from the Perspective of America's First People*. Atlatl, 1992. Lavadour's work was not included in this exhibition.

13 See Josie M. Lopez, "Printmaking as Resistance and Survival," in *Jaune Quick-to-See Smith: Memory Map*, by Laura Phipps et al. Whitney Museum of American Art, 2023, pp. 44-48.

14 Smith, *The Land Carries Our Ancestors*. National Gallery of Art in association with Princeton University Press, 2023.

15 Margaret Archuleta, Rennard Strickland, Joy L Gritton, and W. Jackson Rushing, *Shared Visions: Native American Painters and Sculptors in the Twentieth Century*. Heard Museum, 1991.

16 One of the most historically significant exhibitions Lavadour participated in during this period was *Land, Spirit, Power: First Nations at the National Gallery of Canada* show in 1992. See Diana Nemiroff, Robert Houle, and Charlotte Townsend-Gault, *Land, Spirit, Power: First Nations at the National Gallery of Canada*. National Gallery of Canada, 1992. In contrast, it took the National Gallery of Art in the U.S. until 2023 to mount a similar group exhibition (*The Land Carries Our Ancestors,* curated by Jaune Quick-to-See Smith).

17 For more about Conduit to the Mainstream, including a list of attendees, see Roberts, "Crow's Shadow Institute of the Arts at 25," pp. 17-18.

18 Conversation with the author, January 23, 2025.

19 James H Nottage, *Into the Fray: The Eiteljorg Fellowship for Native American Fine Art, 2005*. Eiteljorg Museum of American Indians and Western Art in association with University of Washington Press, 2005..

20 D.K. Row, "Ford Family Foundation announces 'golden spots' grants to three nonprofits," *The Oregonian*, October 15, 2010.

21 For a list of artists who had residencies at CSIA from 2001-2016, see ahtone, Dobkins and Roberts, *Crow's Shadow Institute of the Arts*. Hallie Ford Museum of Art 2017, pp. 150-154.

22 See Crow's Shadow Print Archive webpage, Hallie Ford Museum of Art, Willamette University, https://hfma.willamette.edu/collections/crows-shadow/index.html, accessed March 25, 2025.

23 Alex V. Cipole, "Increasing Exposure for Native Artists," *The New York Times*, March 15, 2019. Also see: https://www.nytimes.com/2019/03/12/arts/crows-shadow-institute-native-american-art.html, accessed January 20, 2025.

24 Conversation with the author, January 13, 2025.

25 See Shana Bushyhead Condill, "The Dust on Our Feet," in Smith, *The Land Carries Our Ancestors*, pp. 29-37.

26 Jaune Quick-to-See Smith, "Land/Landbase/Landscape," in Smith, *The Land Carries Our Ancestors*, p. 26.

27 James Lavadour, artist statement, in Smith, *The Land Carries Our Ancestors*, p. 92.

28 Conversation with the author, January 13, 2025.

Fig. 15: **Duotone II**, 2011. Lithograph, 15 x 11 ⅛ inches. Crow's Shadow Institute of the Arts Archive, Hallie Ford Museum of Art, Willamette University (CSP 11-116).

Jim Lavadour made me cry

Marie Watt

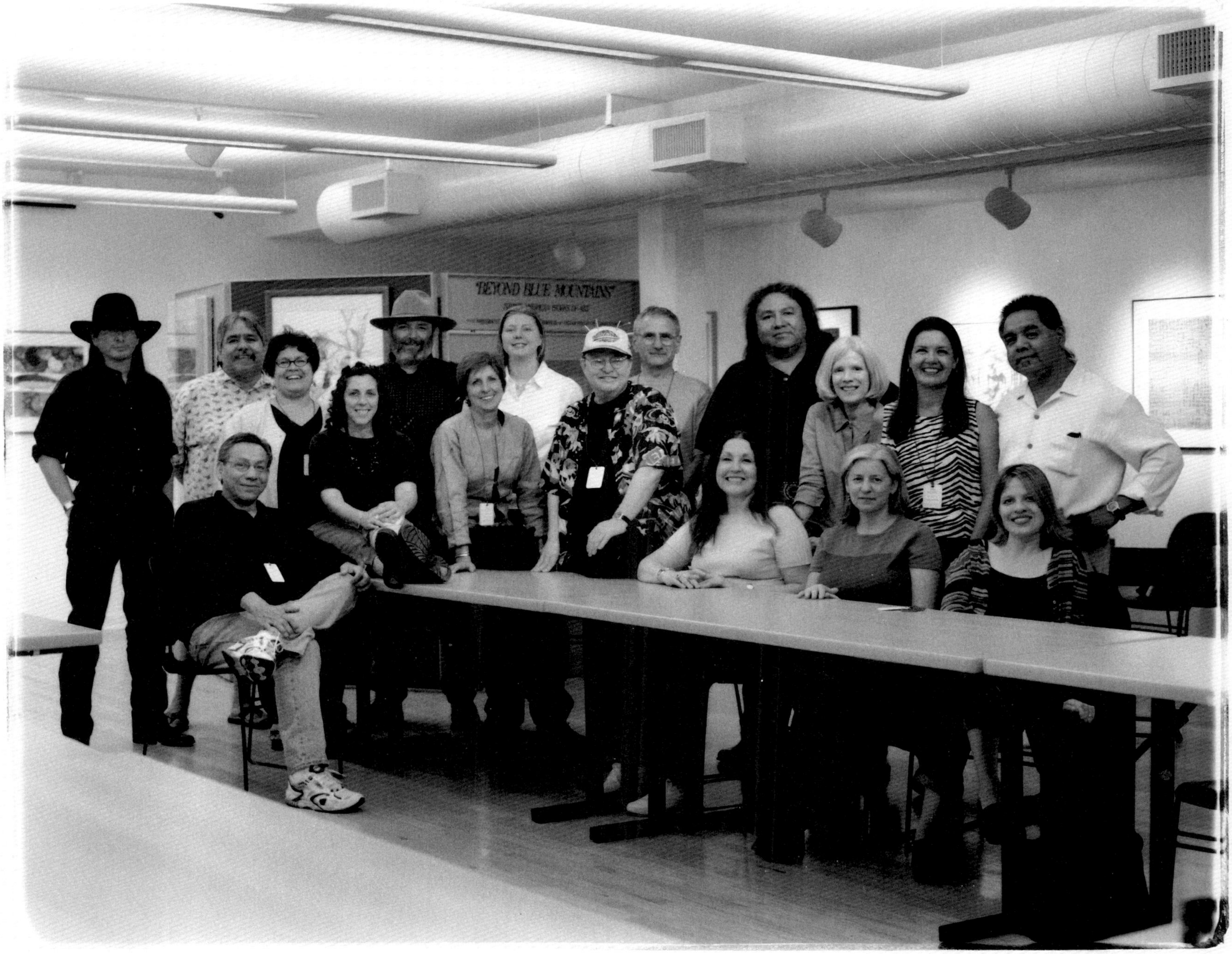

Conduit to the Mainstream participants, including James Lavadour (back row, fourth from left) and Marie Watt (front row, far right). Photography by Pat Walters.

For a long time, I have jokingly referred to myself as Crow's Shadow Institute of the Arts' poster child. The organization was founded in 1992 by James Lavadour (or as I know him, Jim) as a print studio and gallery located on the lands of the Confederated Tribes of the Umatilla Indian Reservation, in the old Catholic mission school on St. Andrew's Road. I call myself Crow's Shadow's poster child not simply because of the sheer number of times I've printed there (five). Neither is it because of the deep friendships I have developed over the course of these visits, nor the transformational experience of making the drive from Portland, where I live, through the chute-like Columbia River Gorge, finally arriving at the foothills of the Blue Mountains. The reason I acknowledge myself in this way is because I can trace every single opportunity and success in my career as an artist over the past twenty-plus years back to Crow's Shadow: the place, the land, and the community it and Jim have nurtured, are an extension of home.

My husband wants me to start this with a story in which Jim Lavadour made me cry. This is embarrassing for both Jim and me—especially since, within our small circle of mutual friends and colleagues, Jim was chided for this. But before I get to that, I need to give context to my relationship to Crow's Shadow, and Jim Lavadour, as an artist and my friend.

I wish I could recount the exact moment when I first learned about James Lavadour, the artist, because after all these years I can't remember not knowing about him. In the late eighties and early nineties it was nearly impossible to see work by contemporary Indigenous artists in academic art history curricula, catalogs, monographs, or exhibitions unless they had been curated by a peer (think of the dual hats worn by artist-curators like Jaune Quick-to-See-Smith, Truman Lowe, Harry Fonseca, George Morrison, Peter Jemison, and many others). It might have been the

1992 catalog *Land, Spirit, Power*, published through the National Gallery of Canada, Ottawa, that finally gave me a touchstone that aggregated the work of dozens of contemporary Indigenous artists—Rebecca Belmore, James Lavadour, Kay Walking Stick, Carl Beam, Alanis Obomsawin, and others. As a fellow artist with roots in the Pacific Northwest, Jim's paintings spoke to me. He had his own visual vocabulary and yet his investigations—the project and process that comes with the work of being an artist—felt radical and new, yet also familiar. Art historically, I saw a connection to painters like Gerhard Richter, Mark Rothko, and Helen Frankenthaler, as well as the Northwest Mystics like Mark Tobey, Morris Graves, and Hilda Morris.

In 1997, after completing my MFA in painting and printmaking at Yale, I moved to Portland, Oregon, a few hours west of the Confederated Tribes of the Umatilla, Walla Walla, and Cayuse. I first met Jim when I was teaching at Portland Community College (PCC). It was the spring of 1997, and he had been invited to participate in the annual *Art Beat* arts and culture event, which drew in creatives locally and nationally to lecture and perform at the college. Each invited participant had an assigned committee member contact, and I was Jim's. I was thrilled to meet him, and brimming with nervous excitement. Here was an established, nationally acclaimed artist whose work I had not only followed scrupulously but also deeply admired. Little did I know that this first introduction—one in which I was completely star-struck and tongue-tied—would lay the groundwork for my relationship with Crow's Shadow.

In 2001, I was invited to the *Conduit to the Mainstream* symposium at Crow's Shadow Institute of the Arts. In this moment, the organization was a youngling. It had just hired its first Master Printer, Frank Janzen, and had not yet embarked on printing with its first invited artist, Edgar Hock E Aye Vi Heap-of-Birds. In many ways, the symposium was an informal opening ceremony, christening, and community gathering. The intention was to discuss how Crow's Shadow would serve a vital role within the Confederated Tribes community, and simultaneously how the professional printing program would support a confluence of local and national Indigenous artists, and their adjacent communities. The institute was articulated as an engine, propelling economic sovereignty while sustaining the integrity of making for so many Indigenous artists navigating the contemporary art world.

The symposium was held in the former St. Andrew's School house, which had been converted into an art institute, print studio, and cultural program space. While the land wasn't given back to the tribe, the transformation of the mission school into a space of Native art and Native ingenuity was certainly an act of reclamation, and something to be celebrated. At the symposium, I was surrounded by giants in their respective fields, including artists Kay Walkingstick, James Luna, Rick Bartow, Joe Feddersen, and Truman Lowe; as well as curators Joanna Osborne Bigfeather, Margaret Archuleta, Prudence Roberts, and Rennard Strickland. Heavy hitters in the print world were also present, including Mari Andrews from Crown Point Press, Marjorie Devon from Tamarind Press, and Eileen Foti from Rutgers Center for Innovative Print & Paper. With Crow's Shadow Institute of the Arts, and Jim Lavadour as a (reluctant) leader, a trail was about to be blazed in which community, and specifically a multidimensional Native community, was front and center.

In part, it was front and center because of its rootedness in place. This was a novel, revolutionary idea where, instead of being relegated to antiquity and fetish, the reservation was setting the terms for engagement between Native art and the art world. The discourses and decorums were established by the land and the place, and the people of it: in short, bringing the world to the reservation, as opposed to bringing segmented fantasies of the reservation to the world. This gathering further reinforced notions of community that extended beyond the academic and philosophical, reaching to the familial and the relational, connected by place and carried into the world by its participants. Crow's Shadow centered deeply ingrained Indigenous notions of relationality before there was a word for it. I departed the *Conduit to the Mainstream* symposium buoyed by Crow's Shadow's vision, new friendships, and a belief, deep in my gut, that this organization represented something uniquely beautiful, powerful, and necessary.

The next year, in 2002, I was invited to print at Crow's Shadow with the esteemed Tamarind-trained printer Frank Janzen. It was the first time I worked with a Master Printer or the medium of lithography. Printmaking was my entry point to being an artist, which is to say I had some experience in a print studio, but the opportunity to work with an expert like Frank opened up a universe of creative possibilities. By nature of their work and training, a Master Printer comes equipped with an extensive knowledge of materials, techniques, and color theory, as well as the chemistry of printing, to the point where it can appear to be alchemy. To be a good collaborative printer, it takes a certain touch of personability and incredible artistic agility. It's not uncommon for individual printers to have areas of focused expertise reinforced by a broad skillset, from which they pull to meet the needs of individual artists they work with. At Crow's Shadow, Frank Janzen came to the organization with deep knowledge of lithography, but also worked with me on making multi-colored woodblock relief prints. Later, Judith Baumann similarly worked in lithography, but her areas of expertise extended to relief techniques, screenprinting, digital applications in print, and letterpress.

For me, there was a particularly generative opportunity in these repeated collaborations: the ability to develop a printing muscle memory. Trials and proofs, failures and successes, growing into an intuitive collaboration. Hitting the ground running each time became a little bit easier, and the running itself got faster, taking me further each time. It is most common to visit Crow's Shadow for a two-week period. In the first week, tests and discussions yield image plates and ideas. In the second week, color trial proofs are the name of the game; that is, unless you are good at running out the clock (like myself) and find yourself color trial proofing and making plates in tandem. After this, the prints are editioned at the studio: this takes time and is a laborious process that changes depending on the number of color plates and the size of the edition. At some point, the prints are signed and numbered by the artist and stamped with the printer's and studio's chops.

When I was at Crow's Shadow making my first edition of lithographs, Jim and his then-wife, Roberta Lavadour, lived in the old mission school on the floor above the studio. Over the course of the residency, I was occasionally invited up for a visit. This is how I became friends with Jim and Roberta. During one of these visits, I decided to share one of my samplers, a stitched non-print work, in progress. Somehow, our conversation evolved (or, perhaps devolved) into Jim bluntly telling me I needed to work harder. Maybe my memory of this moment is imperfect. Maybe what he was truly telling me was that I needed to keep working, to produce many, perhaps dozens, more of these samplers. But at that moment, when Jim's words punctuated the air, I started to tear up. This feedback hit me in the gut. I was at the time balancing my full-time teaching load at Portland Community College with my art practice, carving out time from my weekends to produce lithographic editions at Crow's Shadow. Truth be told, I felt like I had been working very hard. Now, in all fairness to Jim, what he was saying was a reflection of the stratospherically high expectations he holds for himself and that he respected me enough to hold me to them as well. His painting and creative process are rigorous, to say the least.

As long as I have known Jim, he rises before the sun, tinkers on studio correspondence, and then sets out to watch the light rise over the horizon of the Blue Mountains. At times he is accompanied by a herd of pronghorn or other animal relations. He then goes to the studio and paints. Jim has dozens if not hundreds of panels gestating at any point in his studio. Nestled in this moment—in Jim's words—in this memory, was a seed that rooted in me. I have found now that he was hinting at the fact that the more artworks an artist makes, the more they know (or even at times, realize they don't know), and that an abstracted, individual piece of the puzzle is not enough, and shouldn't feel like enough. The example Jim set, and the stories that he told about his own beginnings, flipped a switch in me. I began to see that with discipline and hard work, it might be possible to one day work as an artist full time. I cannot help but sit here for a moment and reflect on how this conversation imprinted on me and affected my path, creating so many possibilities in my career, and a momentum forward.

After the *Conduit to the Mainstream* symposium, and having the opportunity to print at Crow's Shadow, a steady stream of opportunities began to flow my way, and each one grew out of a relationship I had formed there. I was invited by the artist-curator Truman Lowe to participate in the *Continuum* exhibition, a solo exhibition opportunity at the Smithsonian National Museum of the American Indian's George Gustave Heye location in New York. I received a sabbatical from PCC to work on this project. Projects with Marge Devon at Tamarind Press (the *Migrations* print project) and Margaret Archuleta at the Institute of American Indian Arts Museum (now the Museum of Contemporary Native Art) followed (*Blanket Stories: Ladder*). Through Jim and Crow's Shadow, I met Mark and Patty Anderson and the Walla Walla Foundry family, who introduced me to bronze casting and CNC technology applied to carving reclaimed wood. I believe all of these opportunities, while he could not have predicted them, were and continue to be part of Jim's vision and legacy: that is, Crow's Shadow would be a conduit to an ecosystem of opportunities for artists who were also caught in a ripple emanating from Crow's Shadow's mission, vision, and altruistic community of reciprocity.

And the story of connectivity doesn't end. Flash forward to early 2025 when I was invited to print at Tandem Press at University of Wisconsin Madison, where Truman Lowe served as the Chair of the Art Department in the 1990s. I cannot help but ask myself if I would have been invited to UW if it weren't for my connection with Truman. We can also see Jim's legacy, and the legacy of what he created at Crow's Shadow, in newer organizations, like Forge Project or Native Arts + Culture Foundation, which have different missions but share the core values of recognizing the land, crafting networks of support, and amplifying Indigenous voices. New opportunities and connections arise each day, for so many people, all thanks to a wave created at Crow's Shadow. Every day I feel so fortunate to be a ripple in this wave, and that one day, many years ago, Jim Lavadour made me cry.

Artist Marie Watt is a member of the Turtle Clan of the Seneca Nation of Indians whose work draws on images and ideas from Haudenosaunee (Iroquois) protofeminism and Indigenous teachings. Her practice is interdisciplinary, incorporating printmaking, painting, textiles, and sculpture. Watt conducts both solo and collaborative projects, but in all of them she explores how history, community, and storytelling intersect.

For the Next World

Meagan Atiyeh

> "I've been thinking a lot about the role of intuition. It's a sensual kind of experience of the world, and of time and place. It's almost a place where your body digests time. That's a place I try to access and have always."
>
> –Julie Mehretu

There is almost no sound at the edge of the open wheat fields where James Lavadour paints. In this lack of shifting traffic, planes, voices passing, and urban buzz, the Blue Mountains that backstop the fields hold a muted, consistent sway. This quiet, paired with the domestic quiet he has carefully nurtured over the decades painting in retreat on the Umatilla Indian Reservation, is a receptive ground for a worldview shaped by Bahá'í teachings, Ravi Shankar, jazz improvisation, and the Indigenous heritage of his community.

I've had the good fortune to know Jim for some time. To have talked with him about his paintings for hundreds of hours. Jim has a psycho-emotional facility critical to artists, underappreciated and unreachable by most of us. He is compelled to untie a particular conceptual knot. He is bothered by not working, and chases the experience of painting, daily. He engages in a precise, but untethered attention that is otherwise described by the Zen concept of Mushin, literally "no-mind," or spontaneous action, or Samadhi, from the *Bhagavad Gita*. Mihaly Csikszentmihalyi described a Flow state of complete immersion that Lavadour found immediately resonant and has referenced to explain both formal and conceptual completeness in his practice for many years.

In his studio, a new body of work begins in the emotional shadow of the last to leave. A mix of anxieties push and pull as the new panels arrive, perhaps a shifted scale or aspect ratio from the last grouping, requiring a squinting of the mind to reset and a movement of the body to adjust to the new edges. There may be thirty panels anew. Two, three... nine might be up on the studio wall at a time, waiting for the first marks.

The immediate understanding of Lavadour's painting is as landscape. Over the trajectory of his mature career, this has shifted from ink mistakable as photograph, to abstract interiors without horizon, and then stepped back again into a tension between these two poles. In the making of his paintings, abstraction is a precursor to the horizon lines. The period of layering washes, scrapes and drips is a free dive. He approaches the panels, trudging around the edges of a lava flow, entering to push a new layer across, maybe working on some or all on the studio wall, with a similar arc, color, or gesture applied to each. Panels turn and reorient in an all-over approach. "When I make paintings, sometimes I feel like I'm right at the edge of perception, of what can be seen," he has described. "There are comets and neutrinos whizzing by. I feel like I'm in motion when I'm there."[1]

As the panels progress, horizon lines and mountain edges tether and define the emergent compositions. Although figurative, the horizons and basalt formations, plateaus and gorges Lavadour renders are not depictions. They are intuitional gestures, pulling from his inherent knowledge of the land and from a refined daily practice that filled notebooks with hundreds of gestural pencil marks.[2] Panels

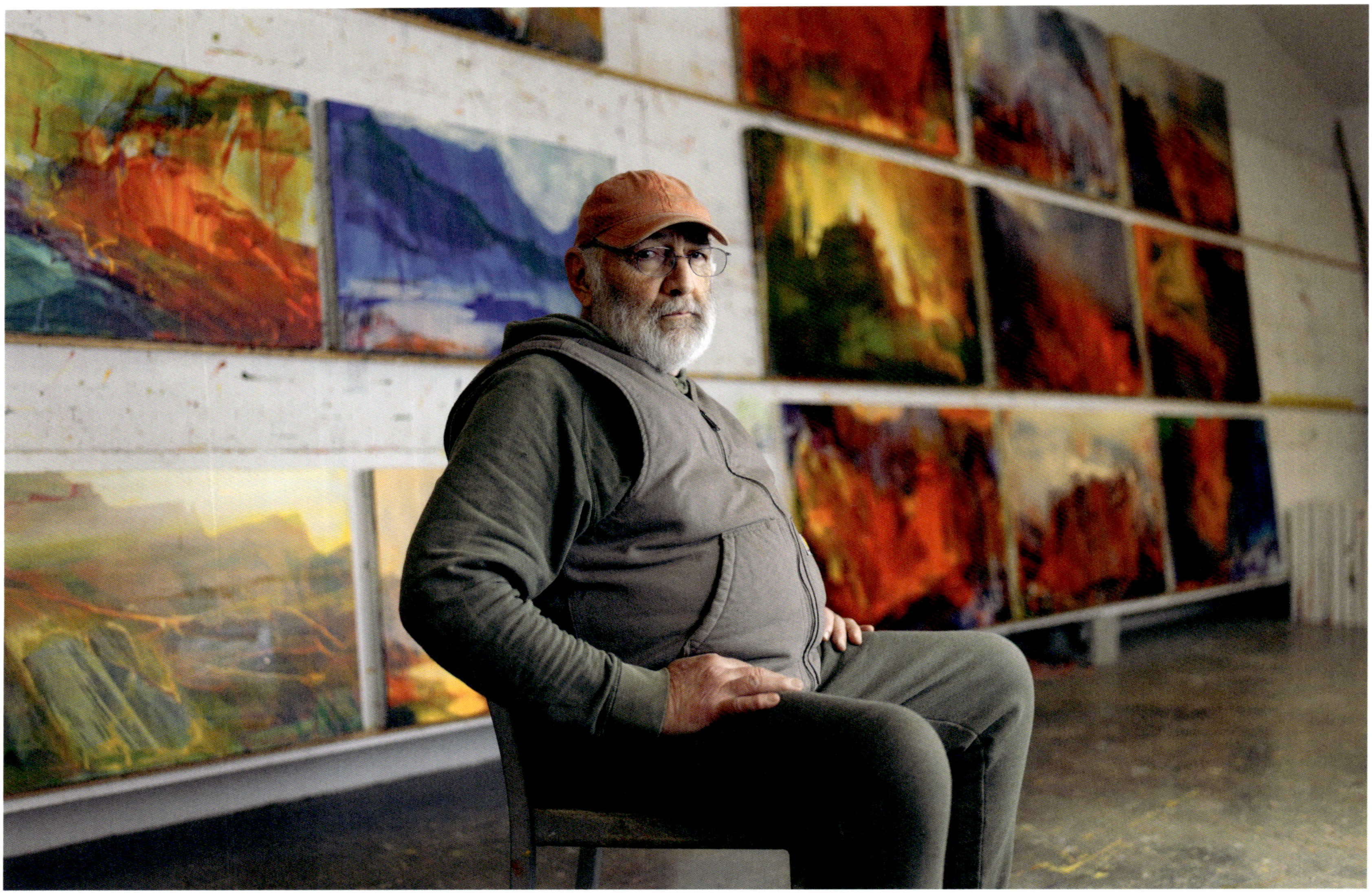

are reorganized or set aside as they give him trouble or spark connections. And many might fly through, if a color and a mark is travelling well and popping to his eye. Red days.

When his mother was living, and in his care, he would drive her through the hills and along the river, as a break from the day's paintings, listening to Bob Dylan and talking like old friends. On the fumes of the painting but slowly settling back into the wheat fields. His drives, like his walks, are filled with buoyancy. On visits to Portland, I drove Jim through the looping helix of the urban highway system, arching high across the Marquam Bridge, down to the Willamette River then lifting back across the Fremont with views of the widening river and cargo ships, train yards below, and again. His exhilaration with the ride was the same he gave to his drives in Umatilla, slowing to point to a basalt wall that had made our friend the rock-hound and photographer Terry Toedtemeier squeal, a small house along the river that he'd watched for his entire life, the smell, the haze of the season...

In a new afternoon quiet, a return visit to the studio to look again before the layer is set, to decide what of the session will stay. His study of the developing compositions is intensely felt. A new kind of attention, he considers the panels now with sobriety, doubt, revelry, concern. It is a tenuous time for the looker and the paintings. And in this way, the group of works advance with a shared DNA of minerals, fractal properties and emotion. It is not a direct line, and many days' marks are erased. The paintings' sweet spots and movements become more nuanced and thus harder to consider together. This middle ground–the point where he is grappling with a number of paintings that have come along together and may succeed or fail together on any given day–it is a point of struggle.

Jim's life in the studio is paramount, daily, with few breaks and less travel. Over the years, he has given some of this time to partners and families, children, grandchildren, Crow's Shadow Press. The paintings are the one full record of his life, however. One where he sees each struggle, spark, relation, birth and death, even as we cannot.

I think of Jim globally in concert with the booming cannon of abstract expressionists or gestural abstraction, both mid-century American, later European or contemporary Diasporic artists. His appreciation for other painters is guttural and full of warm envy. He has reached great successes, including the Venice Biennale, important museums and patrons, including Alice Walton. In a regional context I think he is unmatched, but significantly influential. I've seen Jim's marks attempted again and again by young painters searching for their place.

In terms of an Oregon art historical context, I see sympathies with Louis Bunce, although Bunce was much more a chameleon of styles, employing cubism, abstract expressionism, and surrealism. But Bunce as well worked on a global level while being very much a Pacific Northwest painter who proclaimed:

"My visual world is the West, in particular the largeness and dramatic variety of the Oregon country, from the greybound, hushed harmonies of the Pacific coast to the upheaval of black and white in the high plateaus. Nature, the material of my vision, suggests the style in which the painting is cast and the subject cannot be detached from those elements which suggest it.... I seek an order which will reveal the inner life, the substance and pulse of space and light, which nature, in a surprising procession of form, color and rhythm, parades before my eye mind."[3]

I especially see Bunce in Lavadour's grids: These last formal rhythms Jim assembles as he reorders panels to experience the energy they create bouncing through or pushing away from one another. When a grouping meets his eye in a certain moment, it can become final, as one multi-panel piece, and not likely to be split by future hopeful collectors. The largest of these so far is the 36-panel *Conduit* that Lavadour arranged for Converge 45, with Kristy Edmunds as Artistic Director and me as organizer for her "You in Mind" exhibition at Disjecta Contemporary Art Center (now Oregon Contemporary). Following rejected offers for purchase by a collector who wished to parse and separate the grouping of panels, this work has now been placed permanently on a most fitting wall at the Portland International Airport.

Here, *Conduit* is an important bookend to a masterwork, large-scale 1958 painting by Louis Bunce.[4] Bunce's cubist painting, commissioned for the airport, stirred up a good deal of Oregonian concern in its day. It has been written that "people wanted a picture of an airplane and instead Bunce gave them the feeling of a lift-off."[5] Lavadour echoes: "My painting went from trying to mean something to being a process of revealing an aspect of reality that's not visible in the paradigm in which we exist." In other words, he says: "It doesn't *mean* anything. It *is* something."[6]

When I send Jim Julie Mehretu's sentiment on intuition and the body that reminds me of him, he responds:

"I think of it as the ecstatic experience where I can see and feel without limitations if only for an instant. When I was younger, I could luxuriate in the experience. I thought it would expand with age, but no. Like a broken mirror fractured in a thousand pieces. I get glimpses of light as I sift and rummage through the infinite flow. But it is so sweet and precious I will take whatever I can find. I can't stop searching I'm beginning to think that as it dims in this world, it is what makes the heart yearn for the next world."[7]

Writer, independent curator, and arts consultant Meagan Atiyeh is Senior Advisor to The Ford Family Foundation's Visual Arts Program, a major initiative to benefit Oregon artists through direct grants and support to organizations that nurture their careers. Prior to her current role, Atiyeh oversaw the State of Oregon's Art in Public Places Program and managed visual arts programs for the Oregon Arts Commission for over two decades. She has written extensively on Oregon artists, including James Lavadour, with whom she has worked closely on several past projects.

Endnotes

1 Sheila Farr, "Desolation, Transformation: James Lavadour's Landscapes of the Mind," *The Seattle Times*, 2005, https://www.seattletimes.com/entertainment/desolation-transformation-james-lavadours-landscapes-of-the-mind/, September 16, 2005.

2 These were shown along with painting at the Maryhill Museum's 2002 exhibition "James Lavadour: Intersections."

3 Louis Bunce, quoted in Thomas C. Colt, Jr., ed., *Louis Bunce: A Retrospective Exhibition*. (The Portland Art Museum, 1955), pp. 8-9.

4 Louis Bunce. *Portland International Airport Mural*, 1958, Oil on canvas, 70 x 228 inches Collection of the Port of Portland.

5 "Louis Bunce: Art Collection at PCC," Portland Community College, https://www.pcc.edu/art-collection/artist/louis-bunce/, accessed April 21, 2025.

6 Sheila Farr, "Desolation, Transformation: James Lavadour's Landscapes of the Mind," *The Seattle Times*, https://www.seattletimes.com/entertainment/desolation-transformation-jameslavadours-landscapes-of-the-mind/, September 16, 2005.

7 Conversation between the author and the artist, 2025. Also, see: Hilarie Sheets, "'It's a Sensual Kind of Experience of the World': Julie Mehretu on Why She's Letting Intuition Guide Her Art Practice Now More Than Ever," *Artnet*, https://news.artnet.com/art-world/julie-mehretu-creativity-1946621, March 22, 2021.

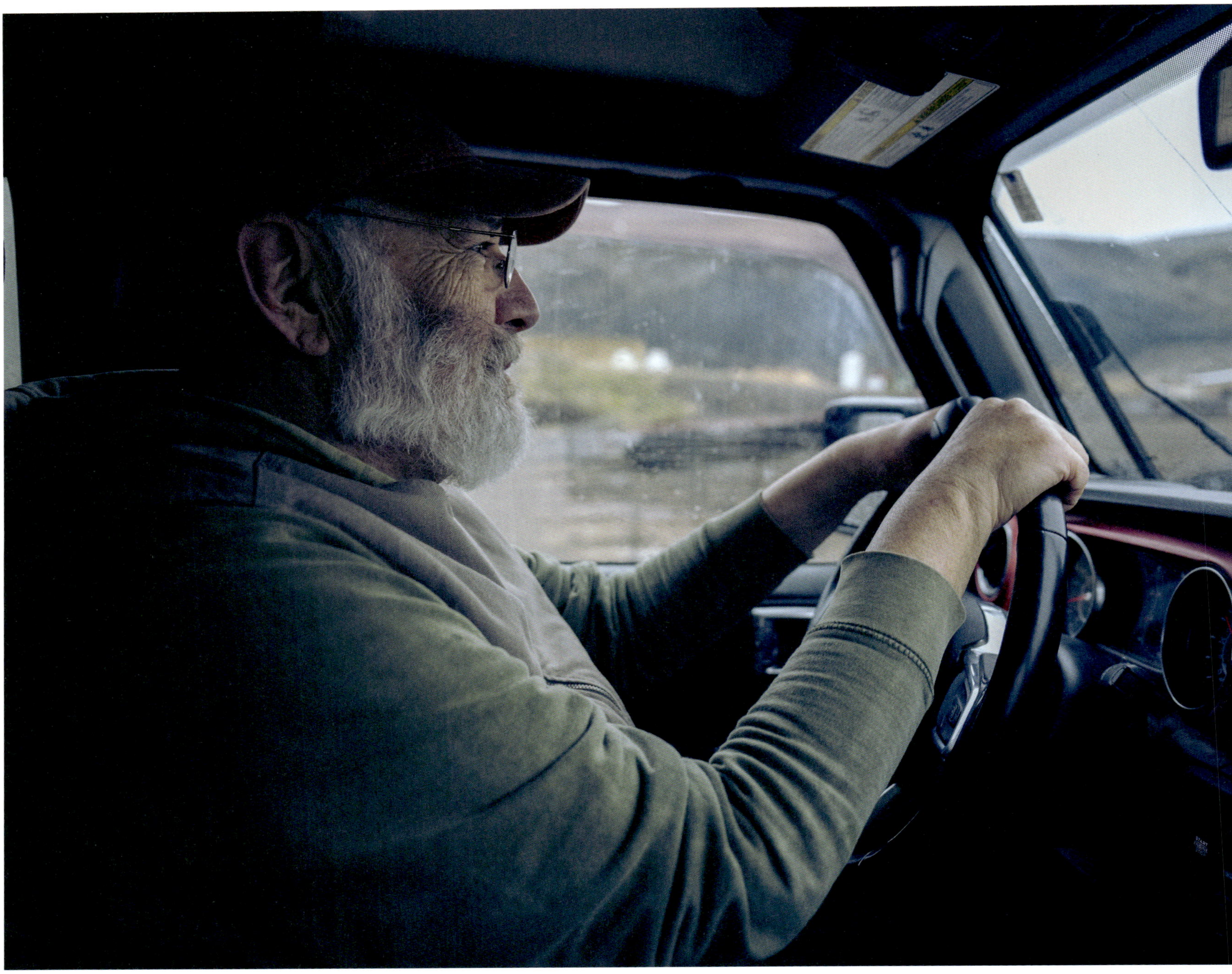

James Lavadour on Painting

Edited by John S. Weber

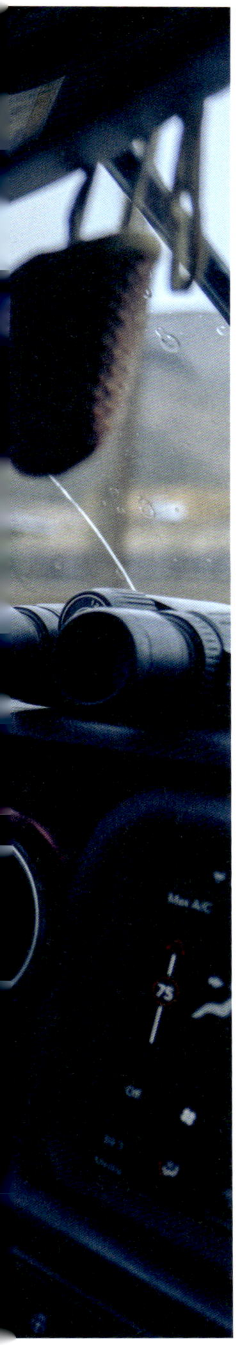

Since his work began attracting the serious attention of galleries and museum in the 1980s and 1990s, James Lavadour has spoken regularly with journalists, curators, and art critics about his ideas, his working process as a painter, and how his life experience informs his painting. This anthology compiles quotations from five of those conversations over a period of nineteen years, integrated with a new interview. The quotes are organized thematically rather than chronologically, demonstrating a remarkable consistency in Lavadour's thinking over time and an acute self-awareness of how he approaches his practice.

Background Thoughts

Where I come from there is the earth and the heavens, and we are made of the same stuff. The creator put the fish, the berries, the meat, and the water here to take care of us, but what of me is also part of nature? I approach nature as a way of learning about who I am and what I am. I began to collect my information about making paintings from the physical act of engaging with nature by walking or sticking my hand in a stream to understand what it is. Instead of looking at it, I felt it. You lay down on the earth and take a nap on the hillside or you drink good water after exerting yourself on that hillside. All of those things become a part of your body memory, your muscle memory. –2008

I was an avid hiker and early on I realized the connection between the kinetic experience of hiking and the physical experience of painting. I became aware of this microcosm-macrocosm thing, that the events happening on the land–sedimentation, hydrology, erosion–were the same as the stuff happening with paint on the canvas. –2012

The landscape is a structure and very simple. It's an undulating mass that is in constant flow. You know, flow in the movement of our own body and the way we move through the world. It's not something which is contained in a picture like a snapshot. It's got a horizon. A middle ground and a foreground, period. After a while, landscape becomes a part of just the way you move. The land has informed my body. Walking on the land over years and years will inform your muscles and your bones and the way you breathe and the way you think. It informs your dreams. It becomes the matrix for this experience of your life. –2005 (Lake)

I did the skeletal figures for a long time. I'd drive by these cliffs and see the basalt, the way it fractures. There's every figurative possibility that you can imagine in those fractures–eyes, figures, eyes looking back at a mask. I always looked at a rock sticking out of a hillside as a head. And I'd see a big hillside and all these heads are old, they speak of the universe, the origin of the planet, and they go way back. So I always thought of those formations as being figurative, and in a sense, sentient. I'd see those faces looking back at me.

I realized that everything that's out there is in here. And so it became a big question of what of me is out there. I began to approach nature and hiking as a way to understand who I am, and what I am, and how I am, and where I am. Exposure and sensual perception and the daily accumulation of bits and pieces of knowledge that sticks with you is what I made the paintings out of. –2024

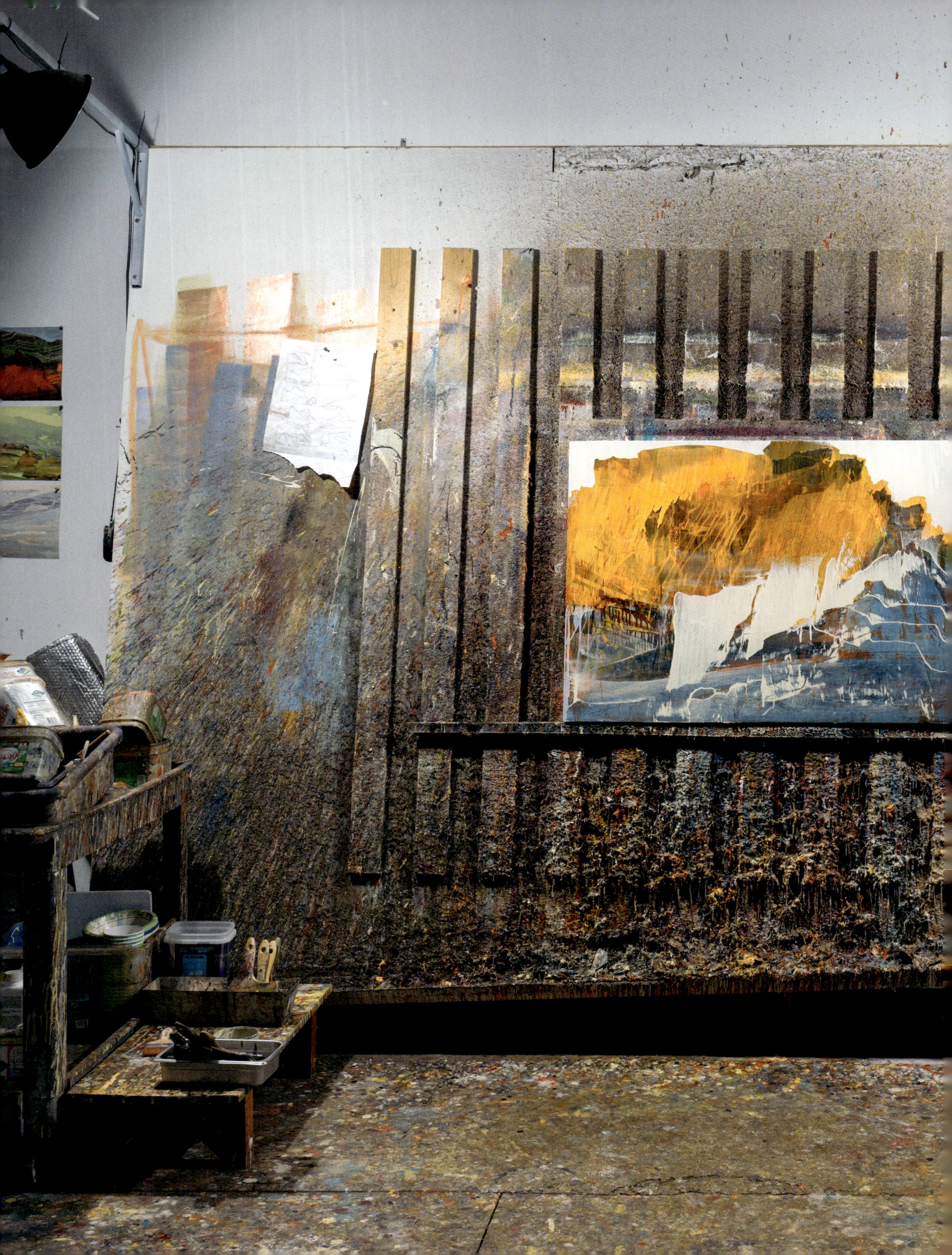

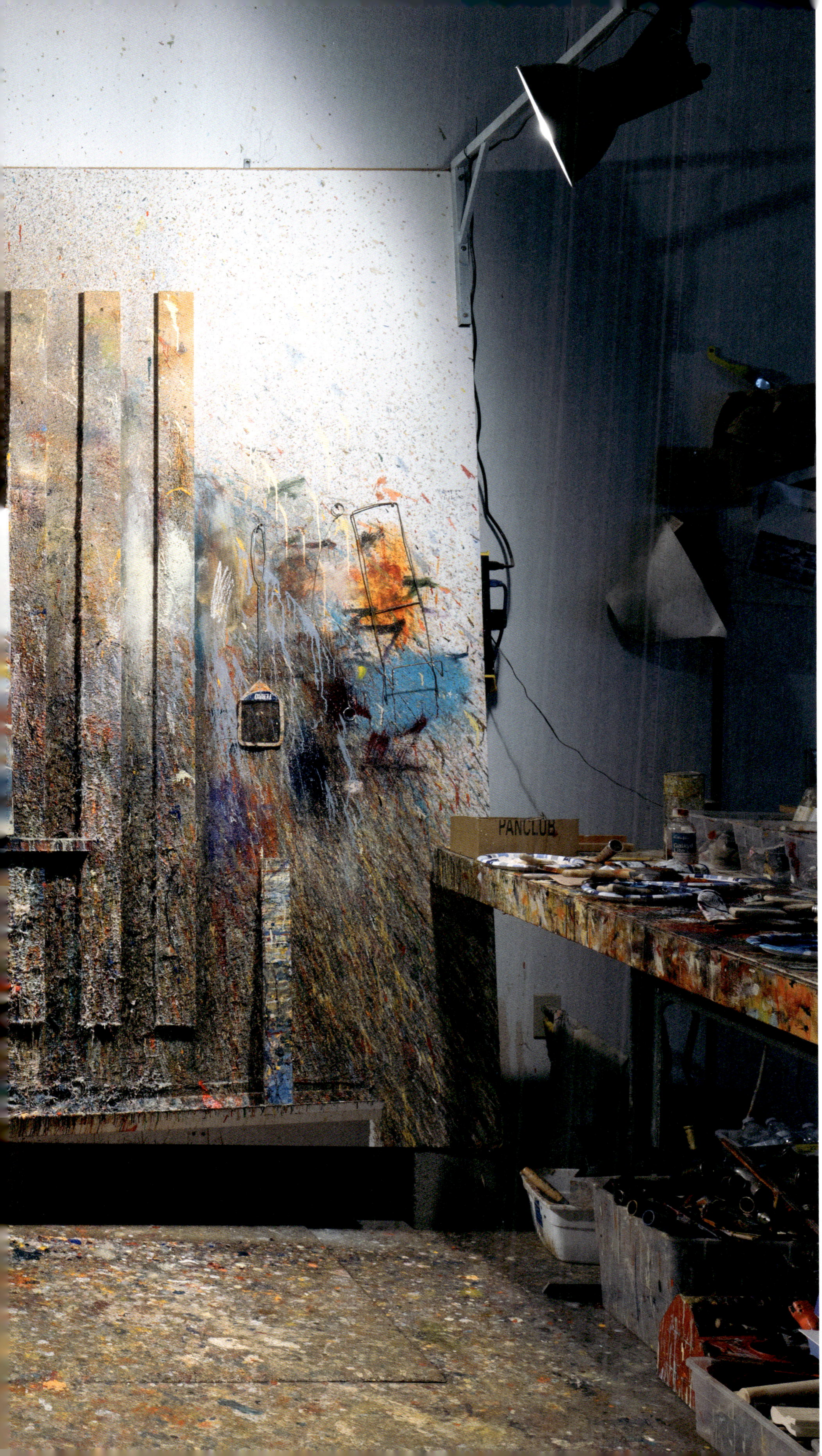
PANCLUB

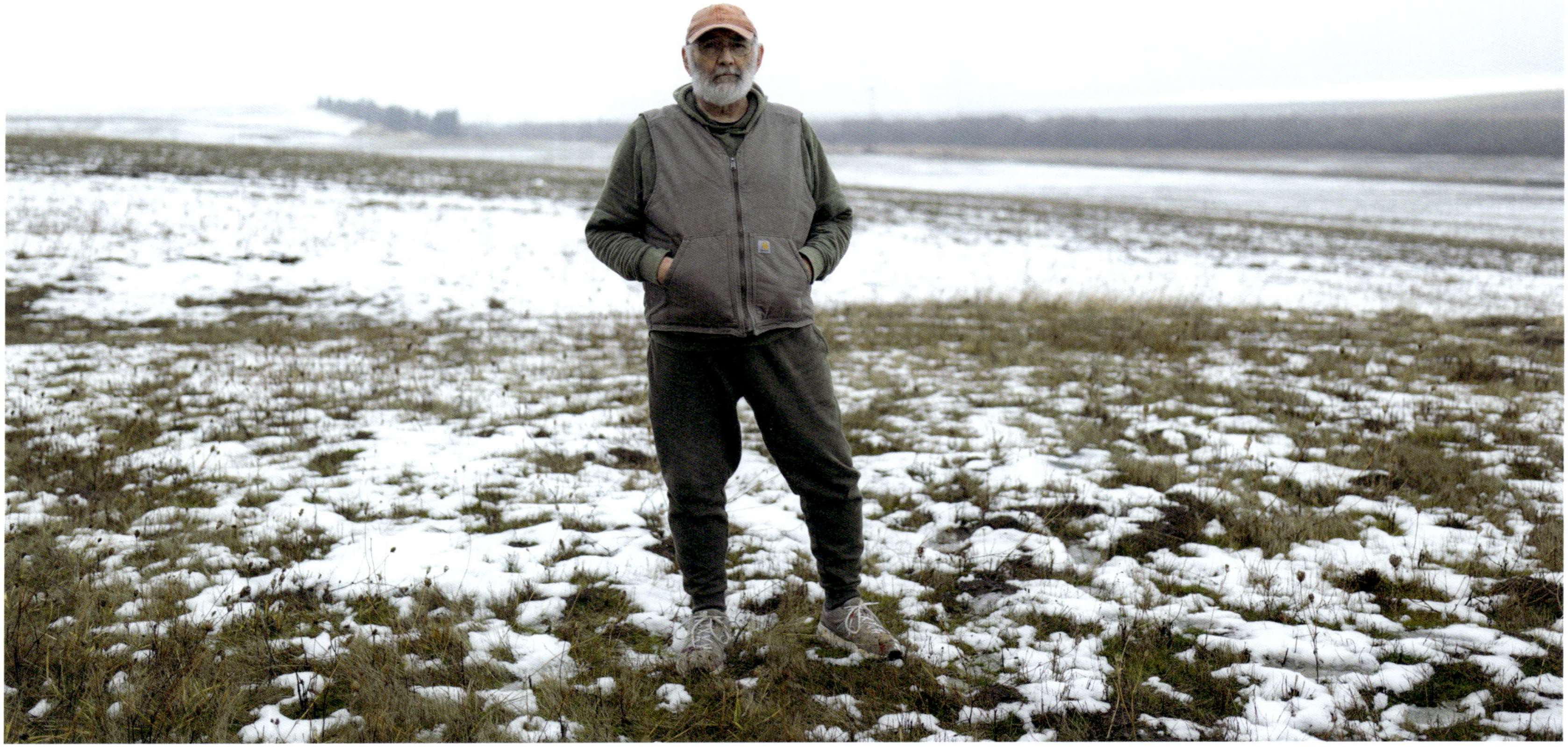

Insights

My main interest has always been about the properties of paint, what paint does. One of the things that paint does is that it is organic and does the same sort of things that dirt does, that anything in the natural world does. It has the same processes: erosion, sedimentation, flow. –2008

My first love is watercolor. The organic event of pigment in water on a surface makes all these patterns that are identical to the landscape. They're there, it's hydrology, you know, all the things that happen down in these micro spaces are exactly what's happening out in the environment. Here, the water is puddling in various places, puddling and flowing and eroding, and sedimentation, and the whole hydrological process of the forming the land is the same exactly as what happens in paint. –2024

I saw the same processes in watercolor settling in on a piece of paper as rivers and mountains. That was the first principle that struck me early on and I realized that ever since I was a child I was fascinated by those particular processes. –2008

My painting went from trying to mean something to being a process of revealing an aspect of reality that's not visible in the paradigm in which we exist.... It doesn't mean anything. It is something. –2005 (Farr)

I don't consider myself depicting or representing anything. I am nature. A painting is an event of nature, it's not a depiction of nature. It is nature. So when I work, I layer one layer of paint on top of another, on top of another, and the circumstances that add up are these things that we recognize. Our brains recognize them as part of the world we live in, but they're not pictures of the world, they're events of the world. –2012

Process and Making

All I had in my mind when I started painting was maybe a horizon line up there, and down here is where all the action is. I developed this whole way of drawing. It's kind of loopy and looks sort of like a contour drawing. I did thousands of them in notebooks. 50-second, 20-second drawings on each page. And I began to realize that the mark I was making was my mark. I wasn't looking at something and making its likeness. It was like when you write your name, you know, that's your mark.

So I had to figure out what to do with my mark, because I can't get away from it. And the more I begin to explore it, the more I realized that it related to all of this {he points to the land}, this land, this line that we're following on the road, and that horizon, and the way the erosion has created all of that, and those hills and drainage. I realized that what's what I am, I'm that same exact thing. —2024

To paint is a multifaceted activity. It is not just one thing or working at one level. You are using your muscles, your mind, your heart and your ears that each have their own strata. It is not just one thing. It is in motion and I began to see my body of work not as one painting at a time but that I am working with the energy of an entire body of work. —2008

My paintings are always discovered later. Sometimes they appear to me as I'm doing them, but they are events, and I'm not really aware of all the implications of the event. They can be perceived in many different ways.

I reveal paintings, I don't really create paintings. They come out of the process, they don't come out of my imagination. —2024

I had to figure how to control that process by developing certain structures that came out of walking and just moving your body. The whole physiological aspect of moving on a piece of land and how that influences your physical motions and how those motions bring your body into the landscape. When you move your arm in a certain way, it causes all of these events to happen. That is how I started my whole landscape theory. It is a fairly simple process, putting paint on a piece of canvas and scraping it, stretching it, layering it and all of those things. It is not rocket science. —2008

I got this fellowship to go to the Rutgers Center for Innovative Print and Paper where I was working on a litho press. I'd never worked in litho before and never done printmaking. It was a totally alien experience. Printmaking is one layer at a time, one color at a time, and you're working backwards, and you're working in black and white. My brain doesn't work that way, and it's just very difficult to think that way. But printmakers are collaborative artists, you know, and I had a great printmaker working with me, Eileen Foti, and she just walked me through it and showed me how to do these layers.

After that, all of a sudden, it just clicked what I was doing in painting. And I went home, and I started working frantically, one layer at a time. I'd start hundreds of paintings. And then I'd come back around and do the next layer, the next layer, the next layer of all these different piles. And eventually, they started appearing, a new thing started appearing, and it was extremely exciting. I was more excited about painting than I've ever been in my entire life. I felt like I had just discovered something really, really fantastic. And I just had so much energy, and I made a lot of paintings. This is around 2000 to 2010. It was an extremely fertile, prolific period, because all of a sudden I realized that I knew everything I needed to know, and I was able to isolate the different stages. Before, I just made a painting, I didn't really know how I did it, I just intuitively did it. But with printmaking, I could go in these stages, and I could do anything I wanted. —2024

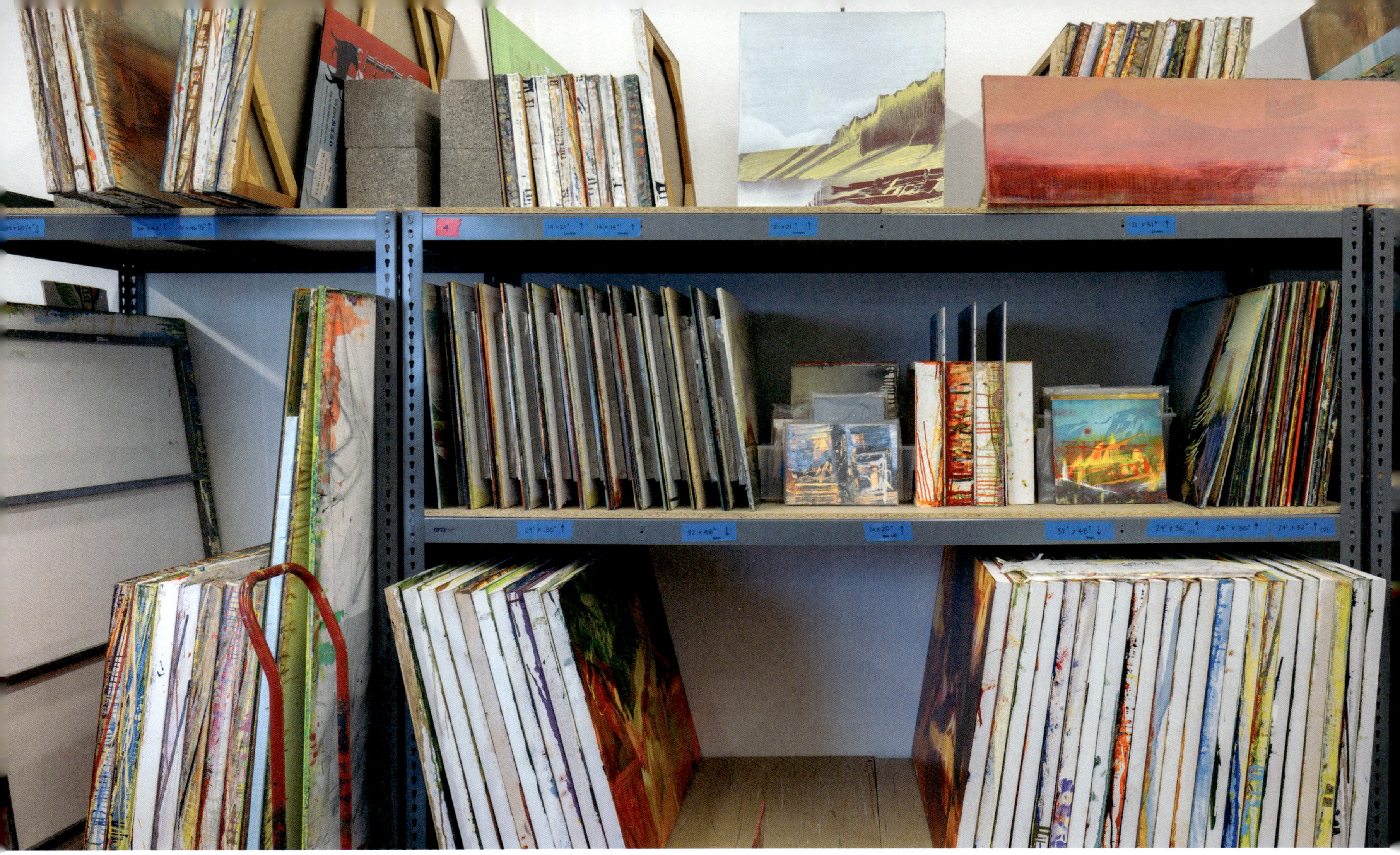

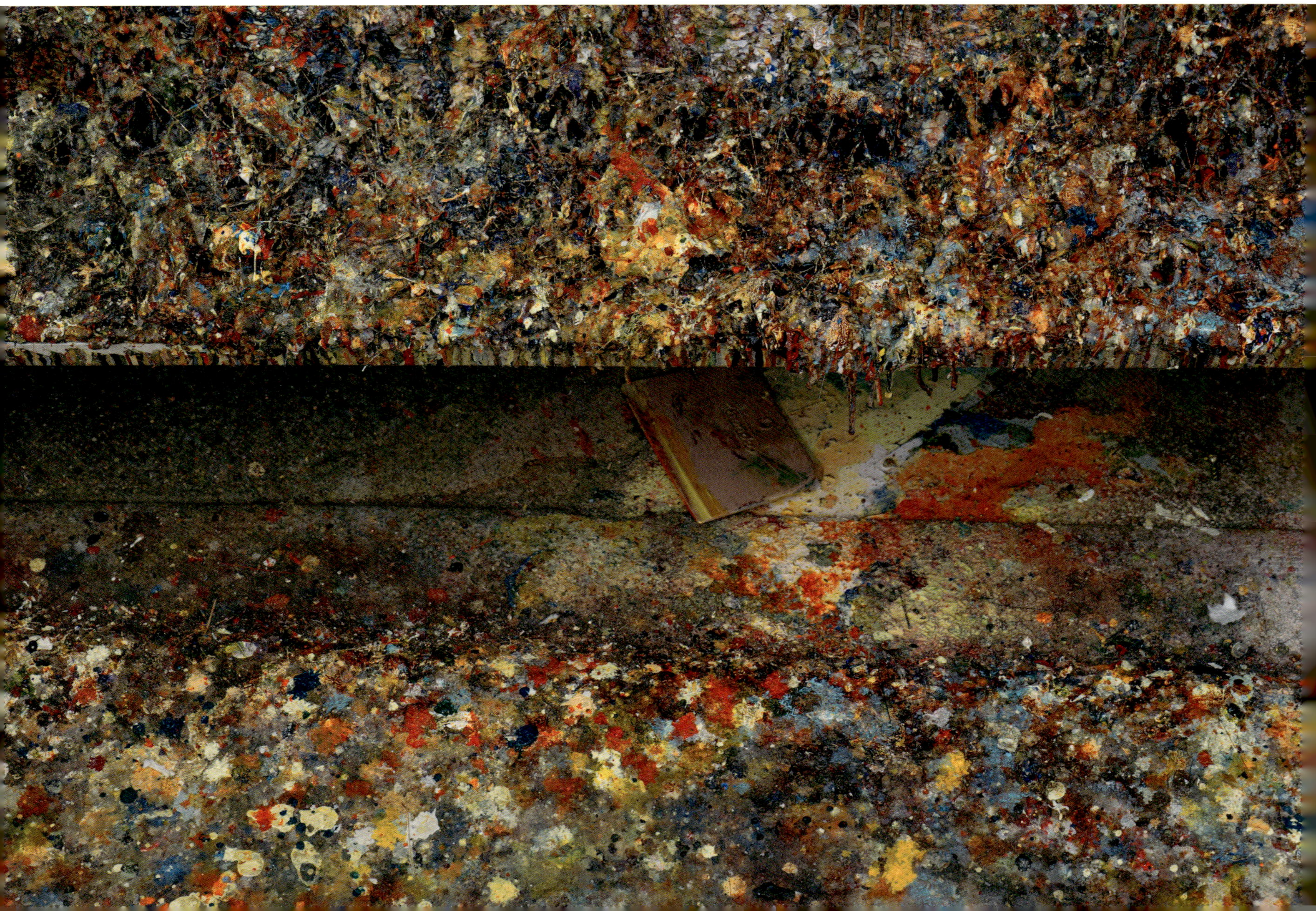

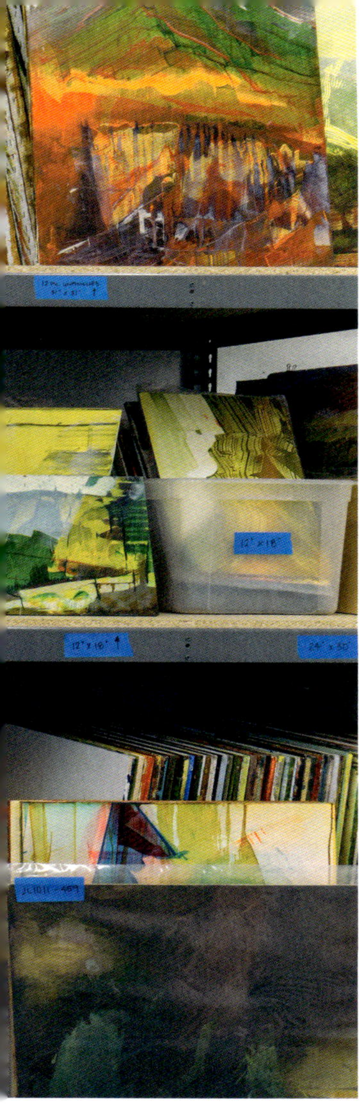

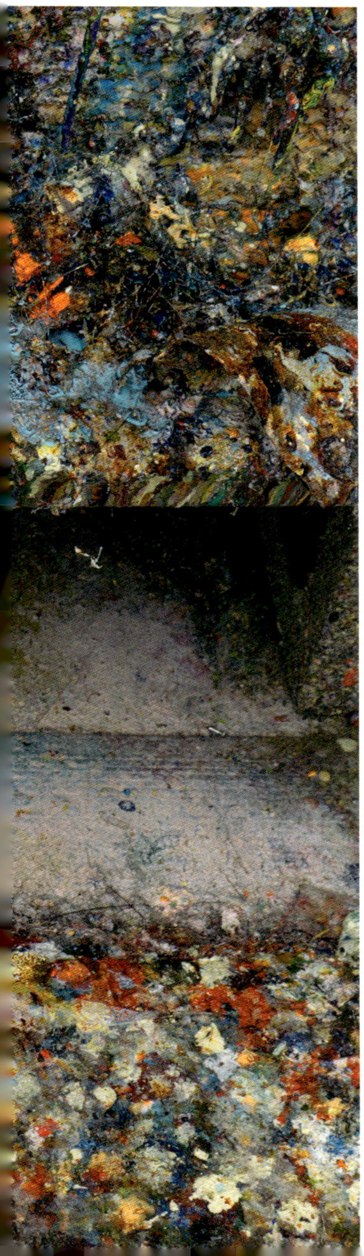

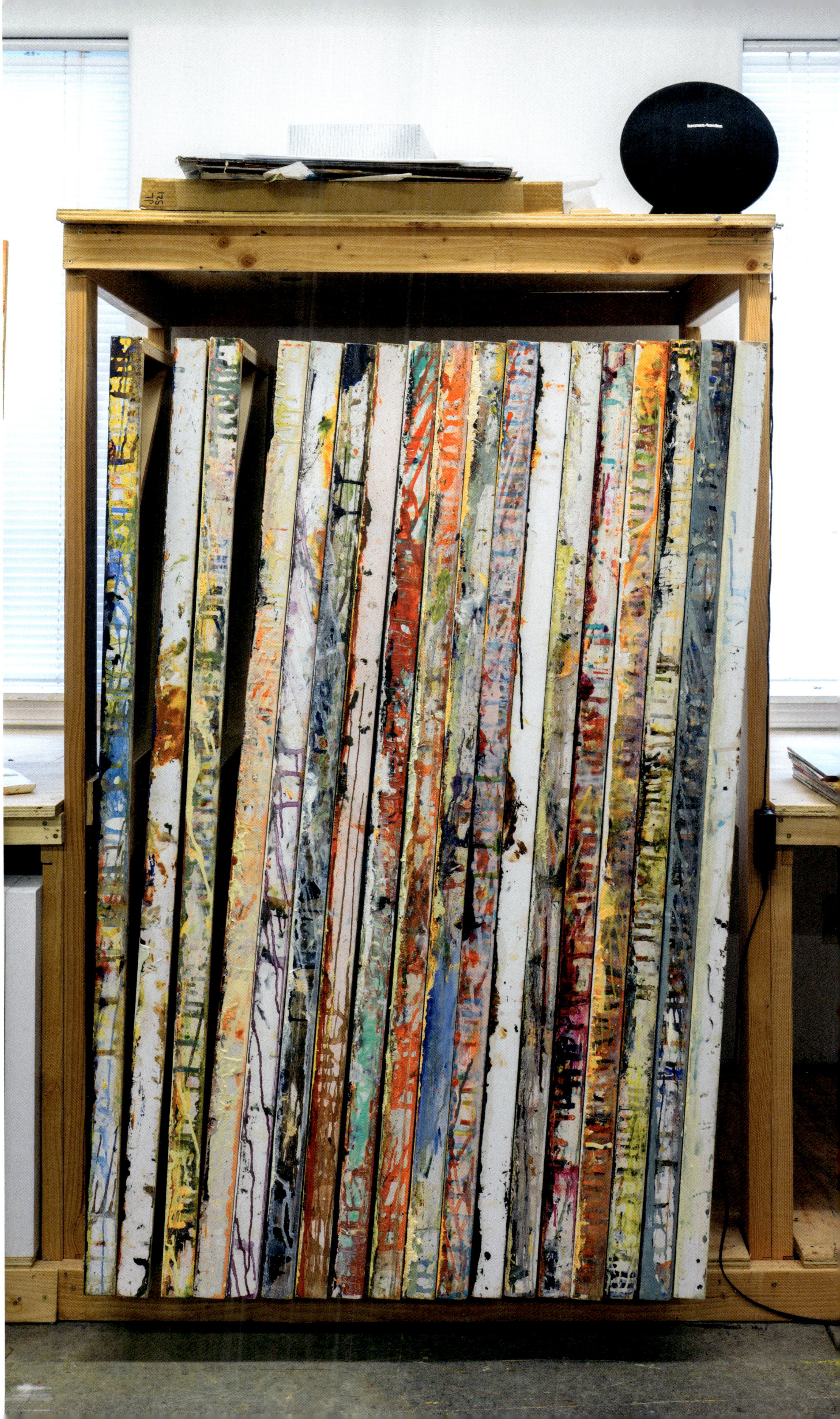

I realized that I had two basic things that I work with in my paintings: the first is organic flow which is the landscape. The second was an architectural grid or abstraction which is based on the human perception or response to the natural world. Those two ideas have always been my right hand and my left hand. They were polar opposites of one another. I used to do either abstracts or landscapes. At this point, they intersected in this collision.... The abstracts became more like landscapes and the landscape became more like architectural structures with a cellular structure that had spaces within spaces within spaces. –2008

Process and Making

I started listening to jazz, and the improvisational process. The way that a group of musicians from all over the place get together in one spot and make music. If you listen to Ornette Coleman, John Coltrane or any of those people they are all strong individual musicians. They are all doing a particular thing and they are moving in and out of one another, countering one another or wrapping around and opening an opportunity for another musician. I began to think that was the perfect way of thinking about making an image, especially in printmaking. Printmaking is totally painful for me and it was excruciating to have to slow the process down. Once I began to understand the language and the process of it, that knowledge really opened my productivity. I could take what I was doing and separate it into stages over a period of time instead of having my whole emotional investment at this one moment where if it does not work out, I am crushed. –2008

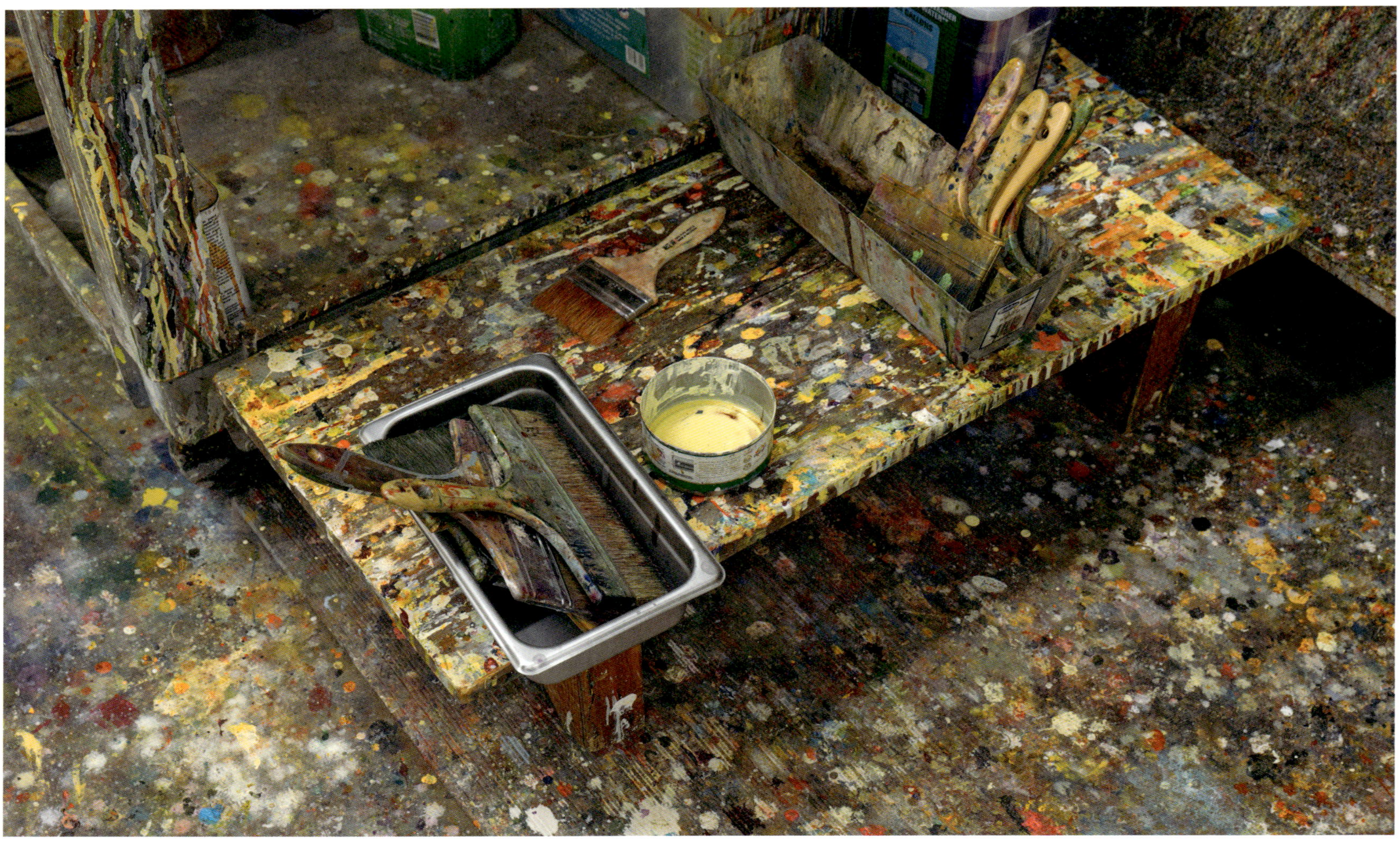

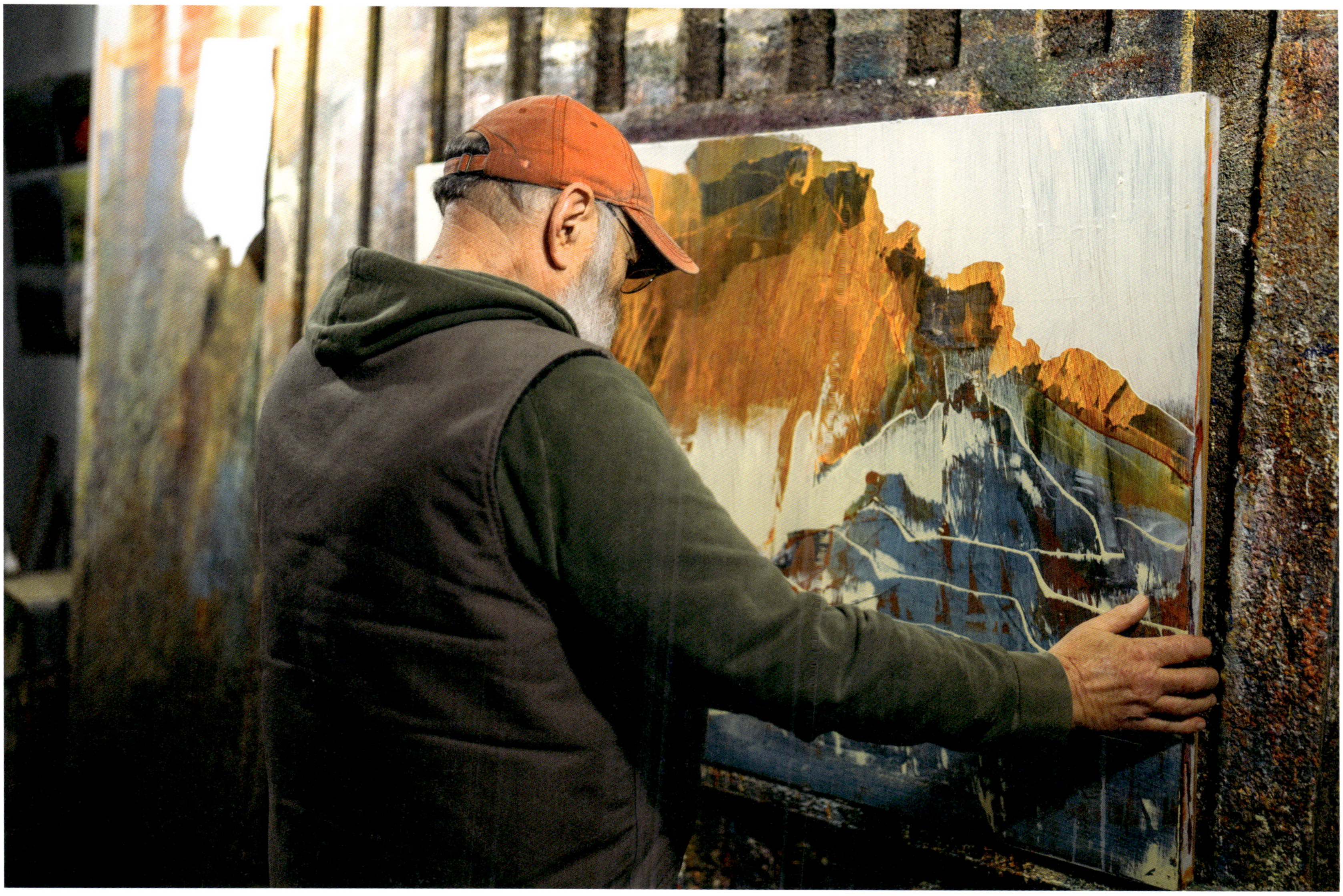

Starting Points

I always think of starting a painting like rolling a rock downhill. It just keeps going and going and going until it hits its angle of repose. But on that journey down I come up with new techniques every day, and it just takes time. I can't visualize it to begin with. I can't say, oh, this needs some red, or this needs something else. I have a method of working I think of as binary. You know, if it zigs, then the next move is a zag; if it's cool, the next one's warm. If it's opaque, the next one is transparent. –2024

Usually, I start with a color.... When it is all still wet I might start scraping into it and then letting it dry. It does not have any form to it yet, it just has a dimensional mass. I might do dozens of panels all at once with a few variations. I just let the palette evolve until it starts shifting. You get bored of one thing and so you pull in something else. That whole process takes time to build up hundreds of those panels. Every once in a while, one of those might be close to a finished piece.

Then the painting becomes dimensional. The first layer is about physiological expression, but after that you begin to deal with time and structure. It is about the geology, the architecture of painting. You become more cognizant and aware of your experience. You are always trying to get the most out of the least effort rather than blasting it each time. Paint is beautiful and it has its charms no matter what stage it is at, so you want whatever it is producing at the time to be visible through successive layers of time.

It is more like being a jazz musician because you are responding to all of the previous layers. After the physiological scrape where you are not thinking about what you are doing, at the next step you are looking at what you are doing and how to interact with the previous actions. How to counter or balance what is already there? What color approach are you going to use this time? –2008

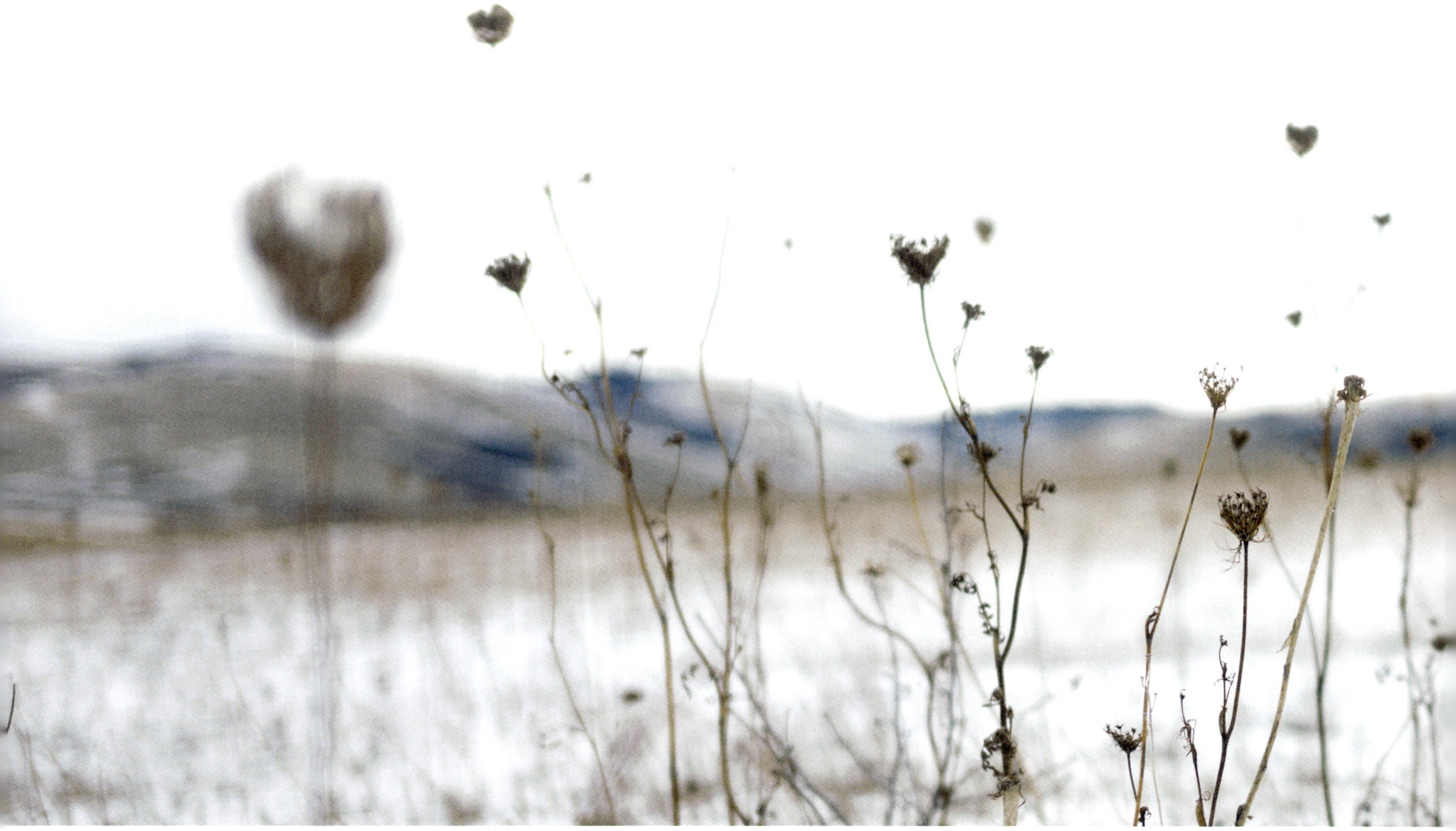

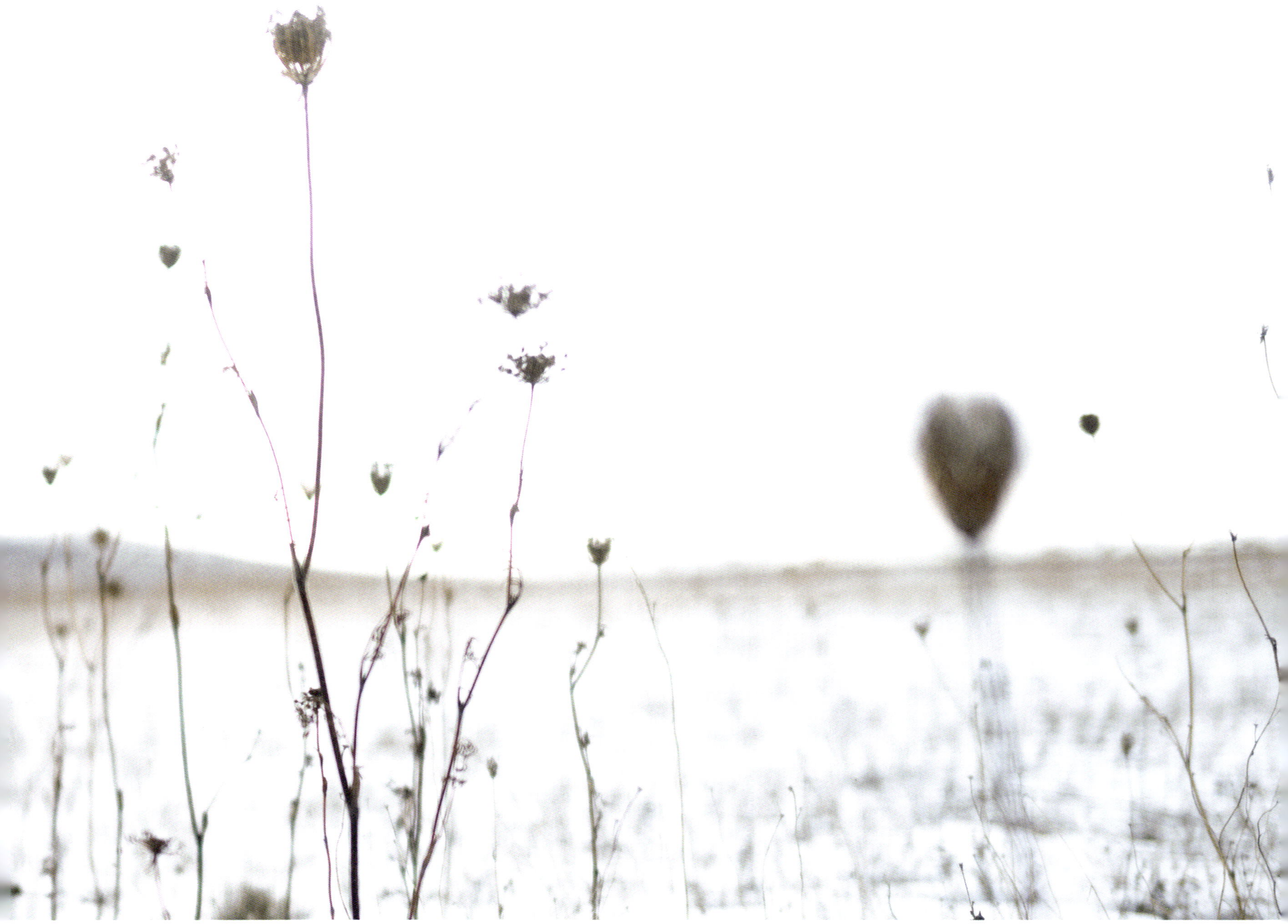

Art and Life

I'm trying to be optimistic about life. I feel I'm working for world peace. That's my job, and that's why I make art–to lift the human heart, to elevate it. That's all I can do.

I think of painting as my life, and whatever's going on in life, I've got to figure out time for painting, how I'm going to be in the studio. Because painting is a type of knowledge that you have to renew every day. It's not something you can read about and relax on. It requires active participation in the world.

So my painting is living in the world, it's alive, and it's not fantasy, it's something right in your face, the energy of it. I don't know how to describe it.... It's like I've got my nose in the groove of the world, like a phonograph needle, and the world is just spinning around, and this is what comes out.

To me, these paintings are medicine to the world. —2024

Interview sources:
John S. Weber, 2024, for *James Lavadour: Land of Origin* exhibition catalogue
Joe Nickell, 2012, for *The Missoulian*
Arcy Douglass, 2008, for portlandart.net
Eva Lake, 2005, for PDX Contemporary Art
Sheila Farr, 2005, for *The Seattle Times*
Gerry Stroph O'Scannlain, for *Open Spaces*, 2004

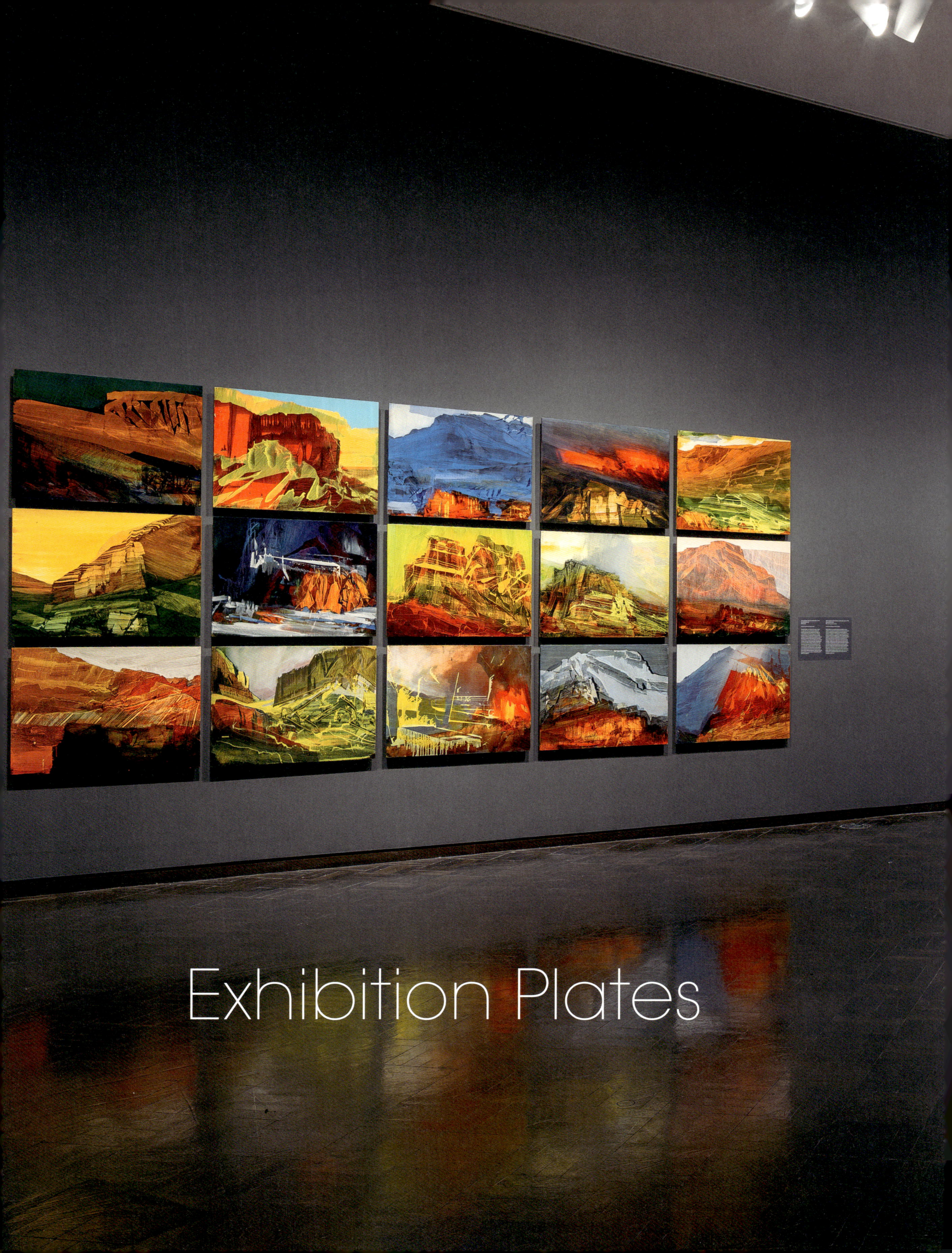

Exhibition Plates

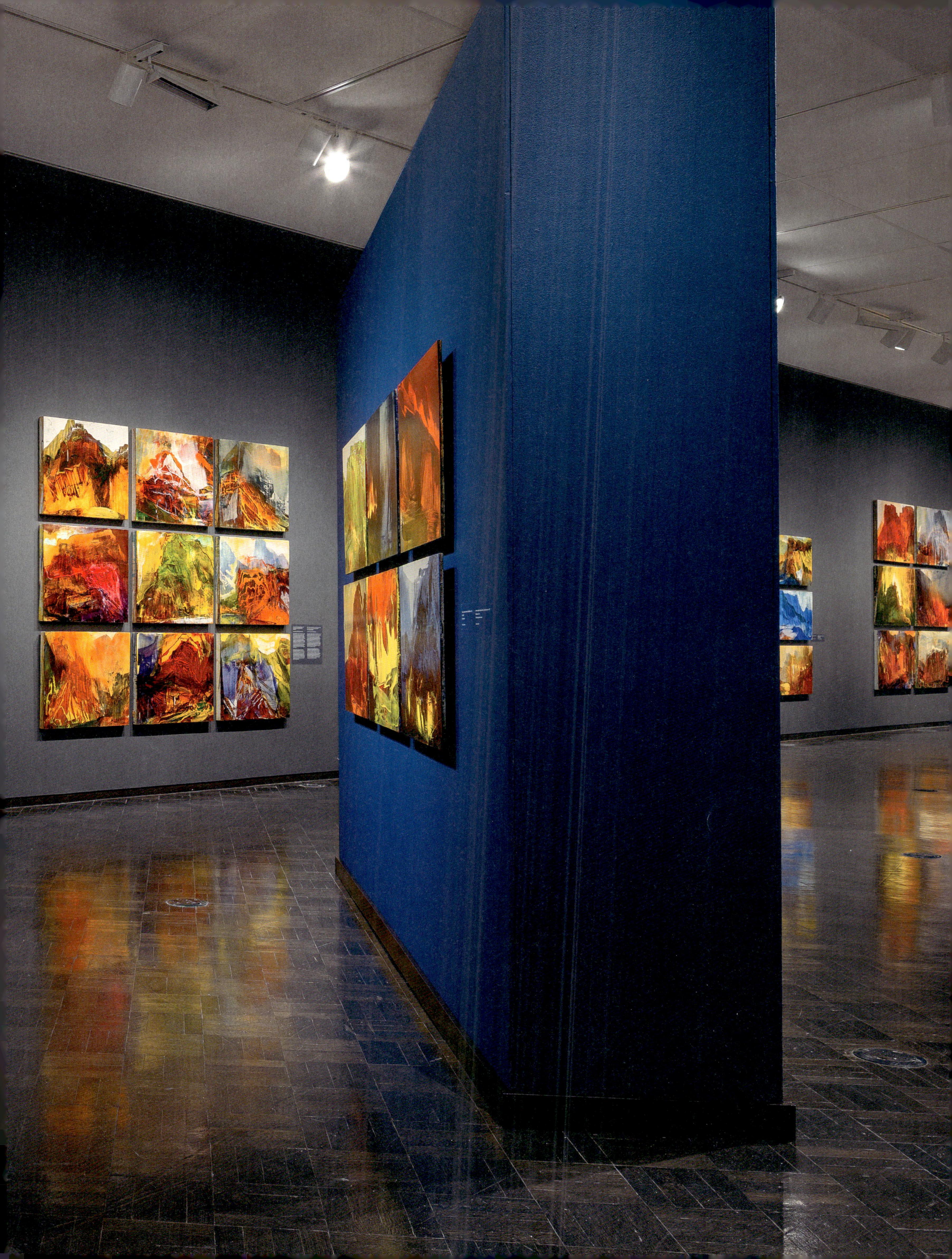

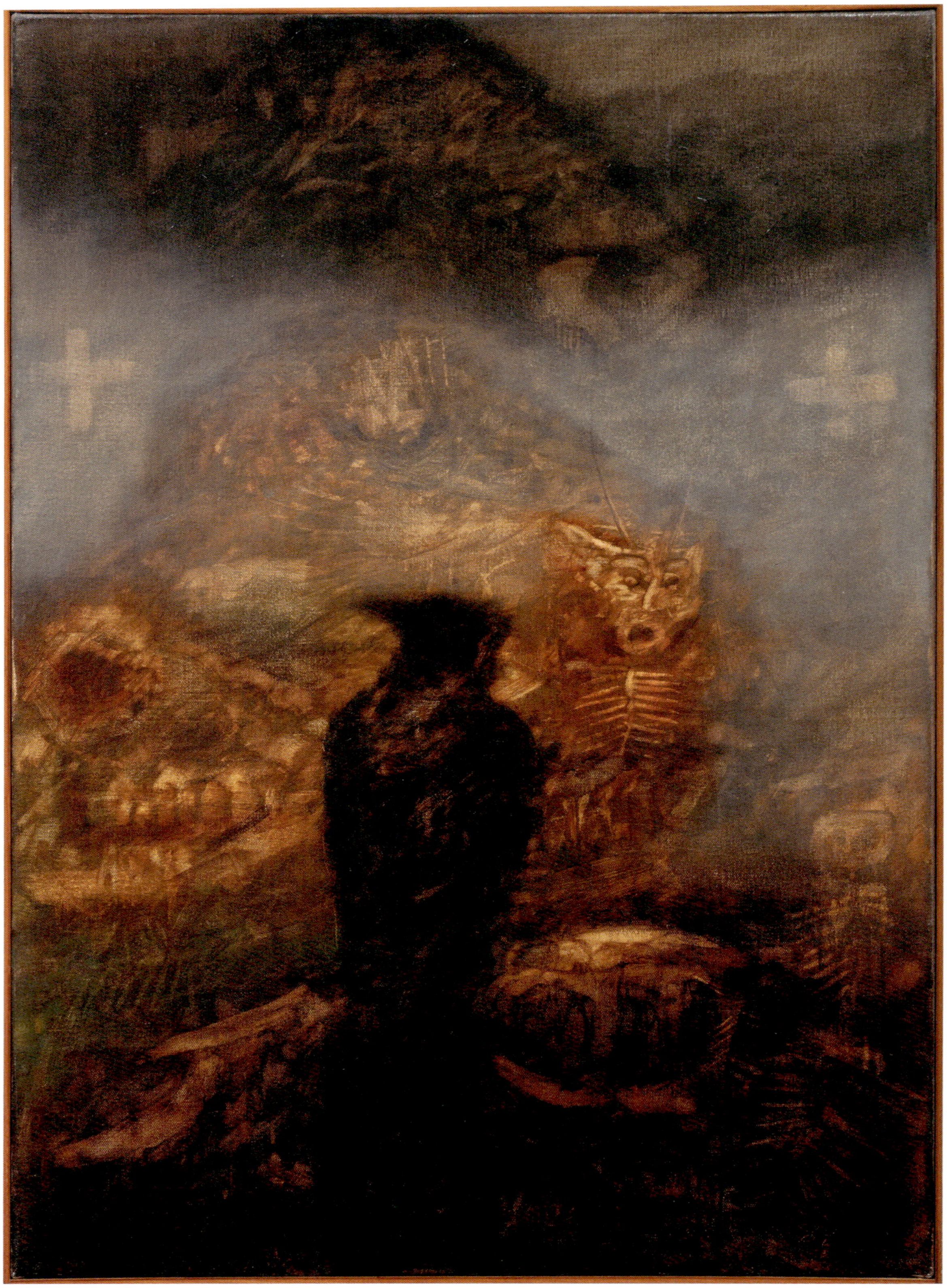

Plate 1: **Crow's Shadow**, 1987. Oil on canvas, 48 ¾ x 34 ¾ inches. Lazar-Stock Collection.

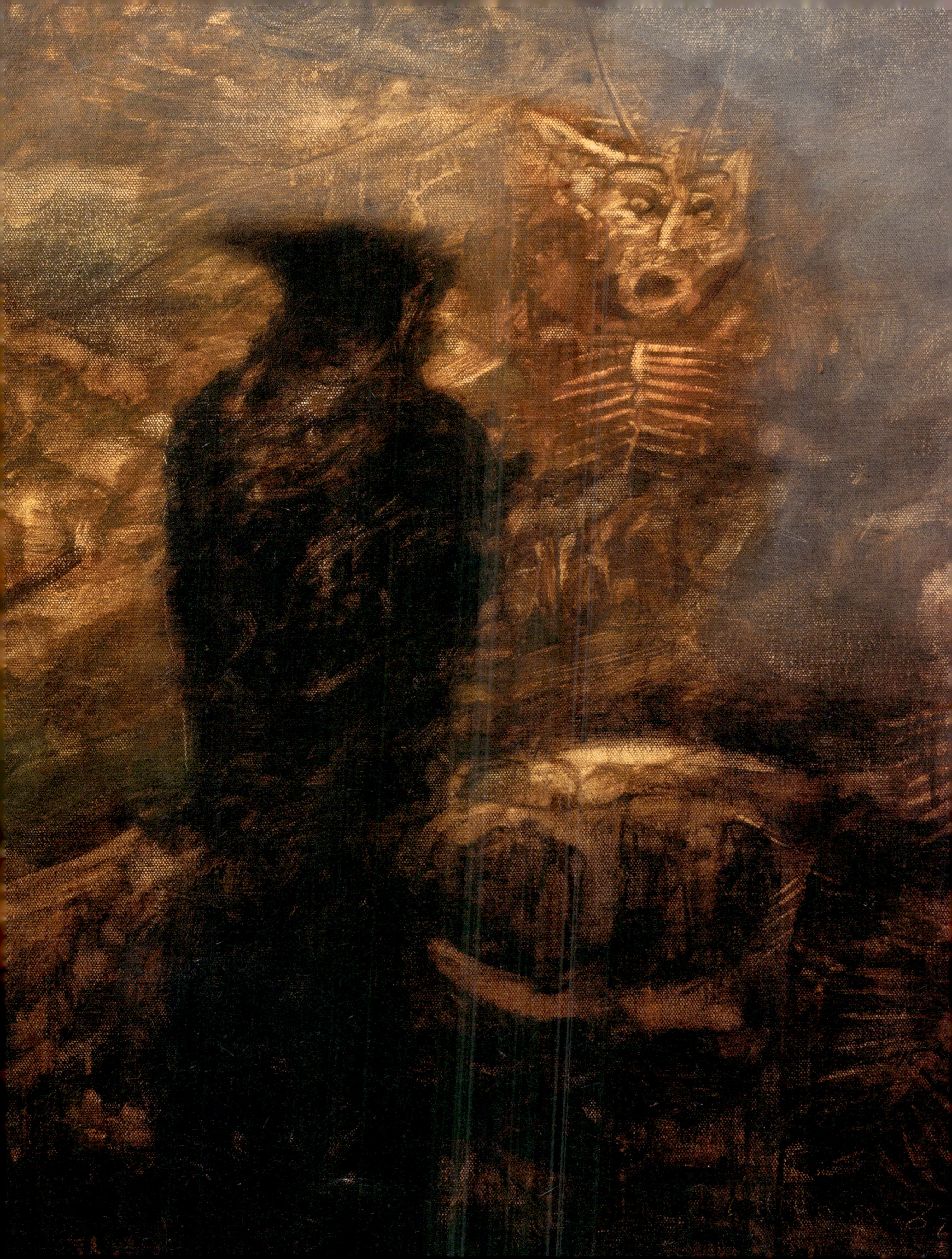

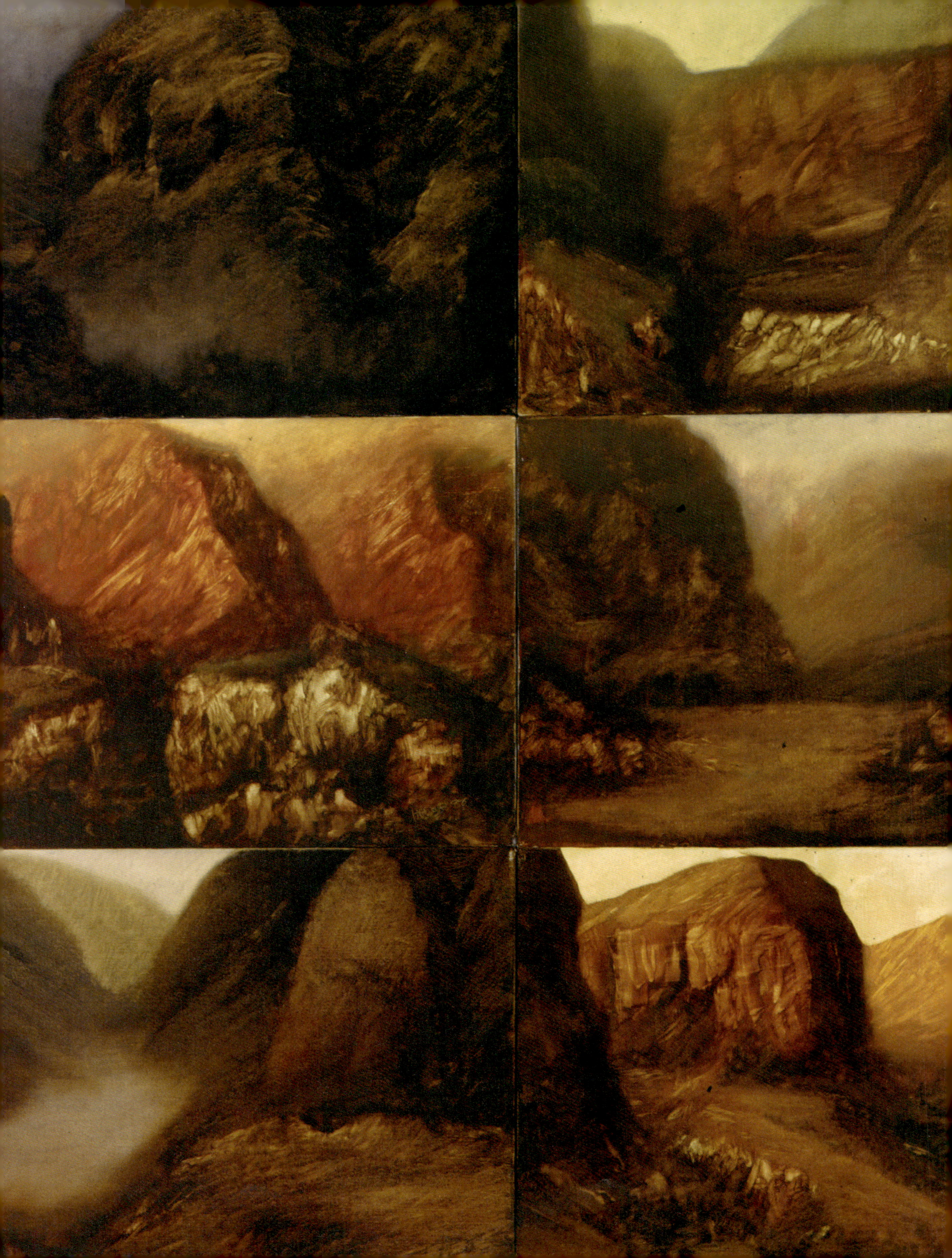

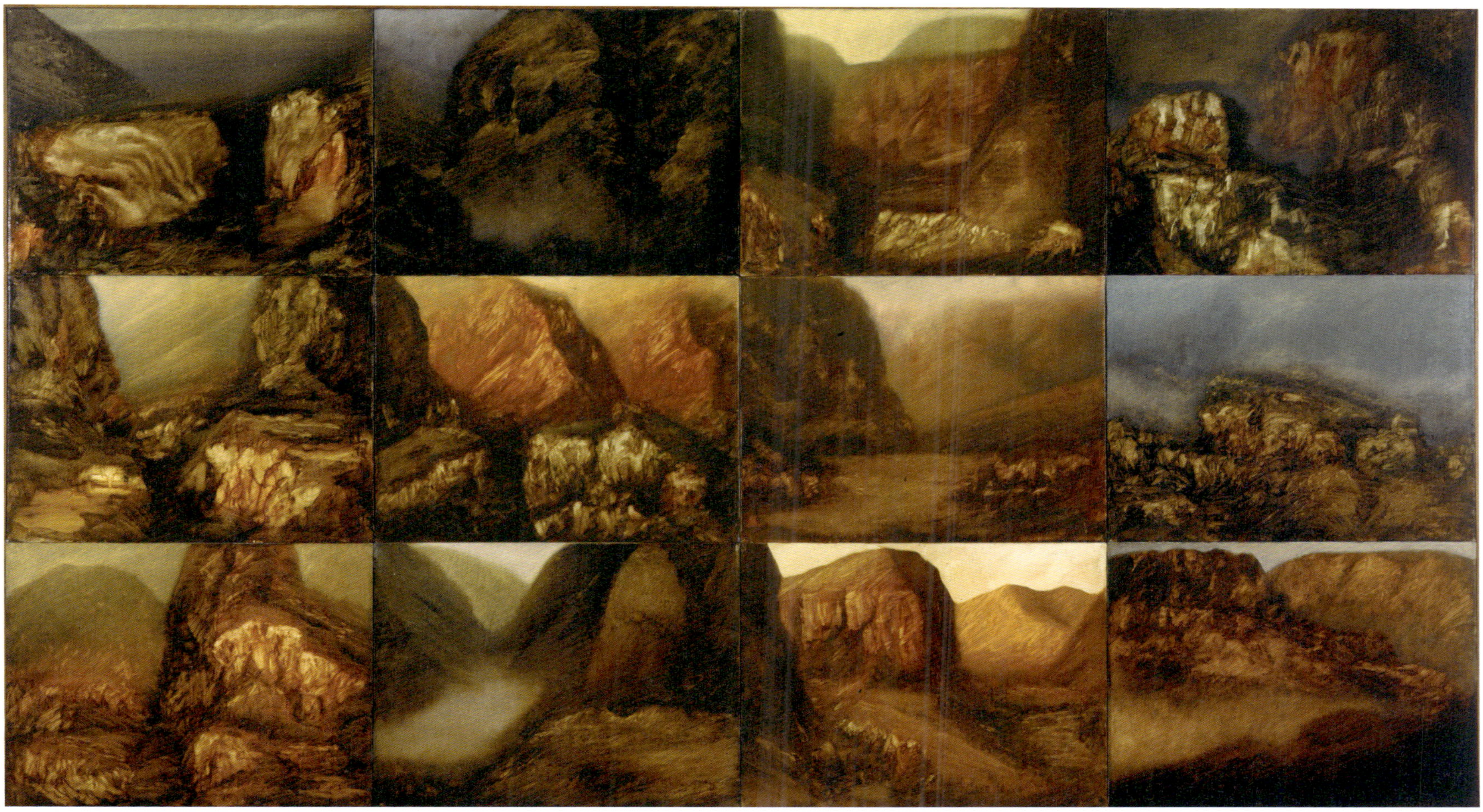

Plate 2: **The Seven Valleys and The Five Valleys**, 1988. Oil on canvas, 55 x 96 inches. Whitney Museum of American Art, New York; Gift of Ida Cole.

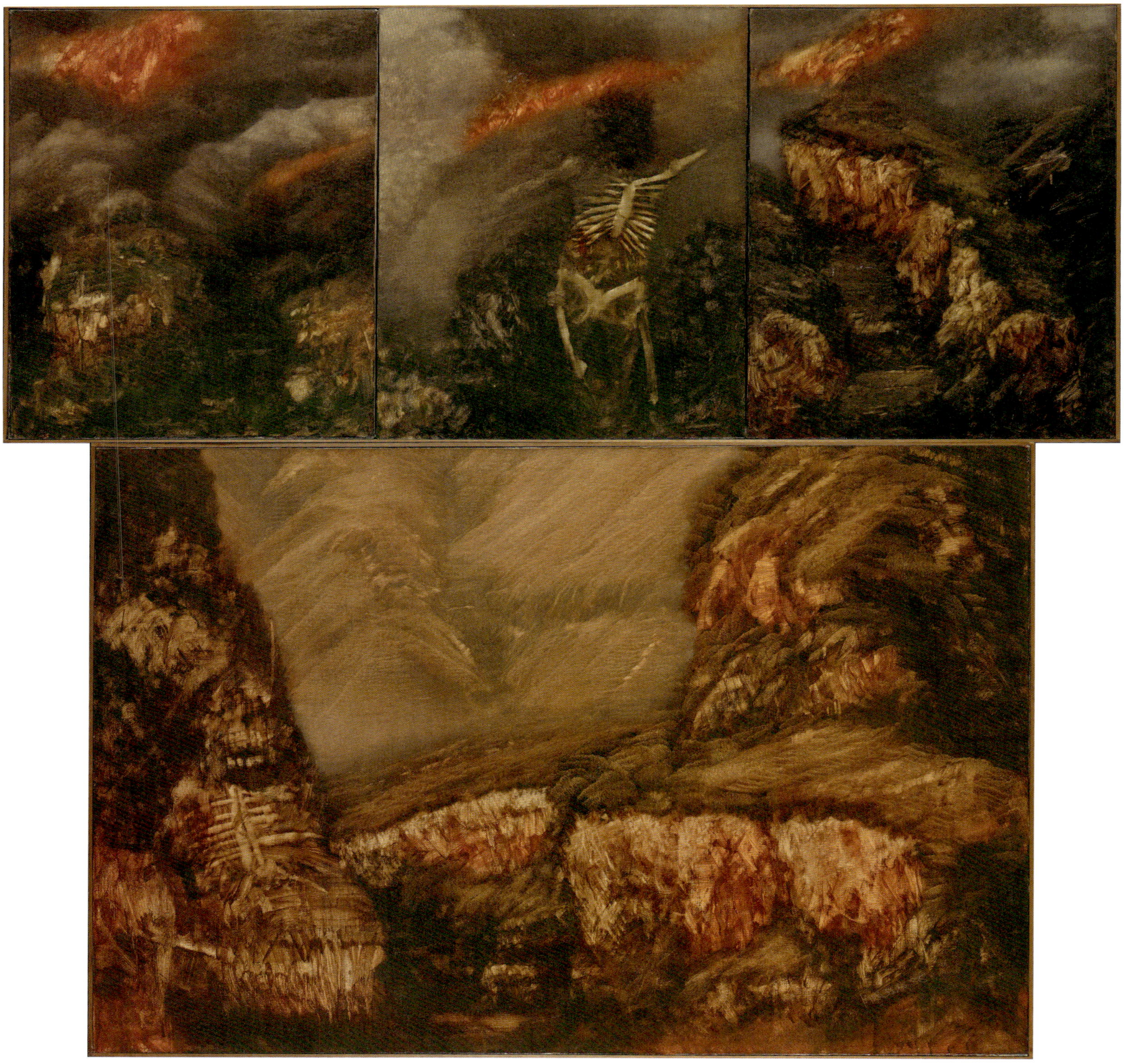

Plate 3: **Boom!**, 1988. Oil on canvas, 74 x 72 inches. Denver Art Museum: Native Arts acquisition funds, 2015.538A-B. © James Lavadour.

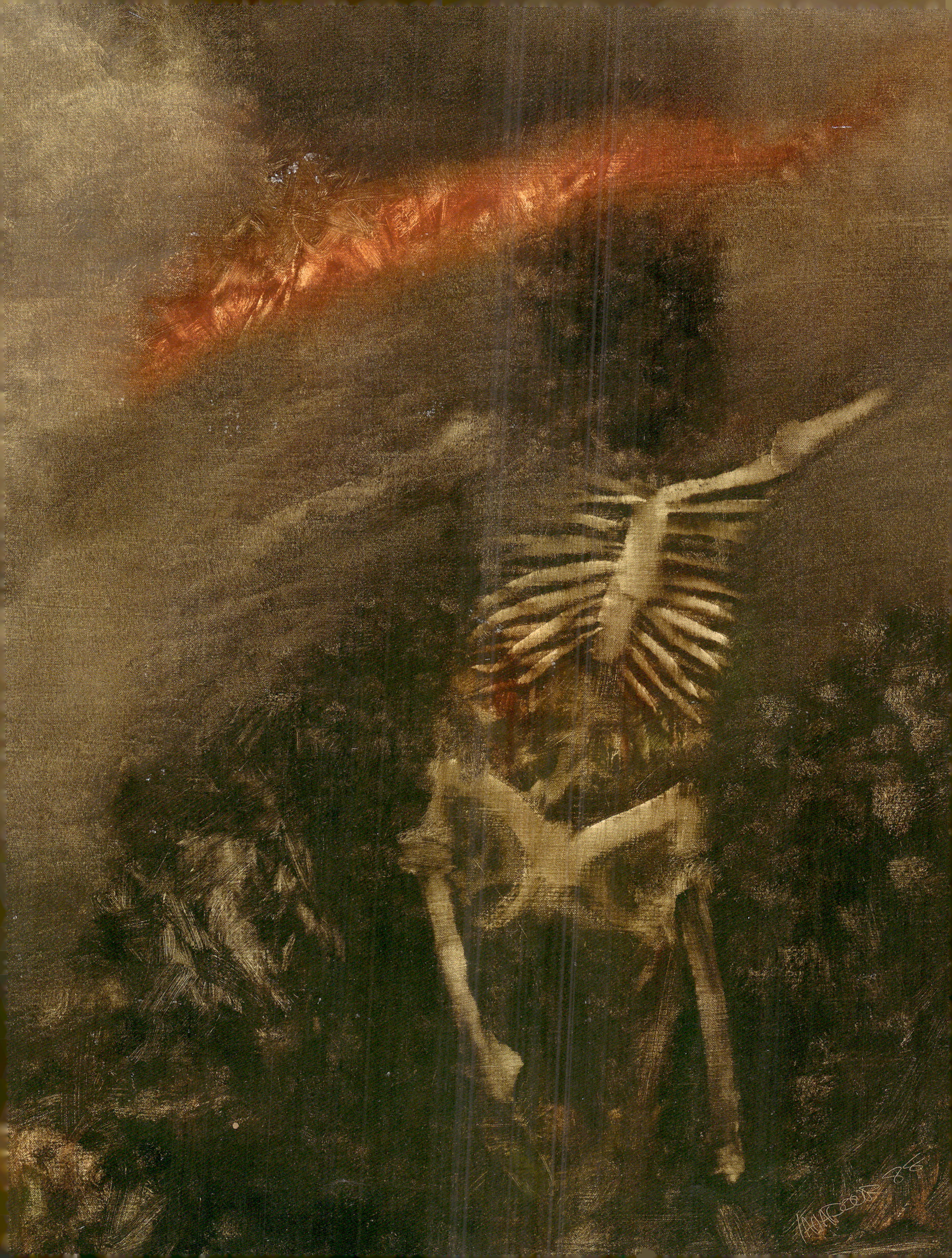

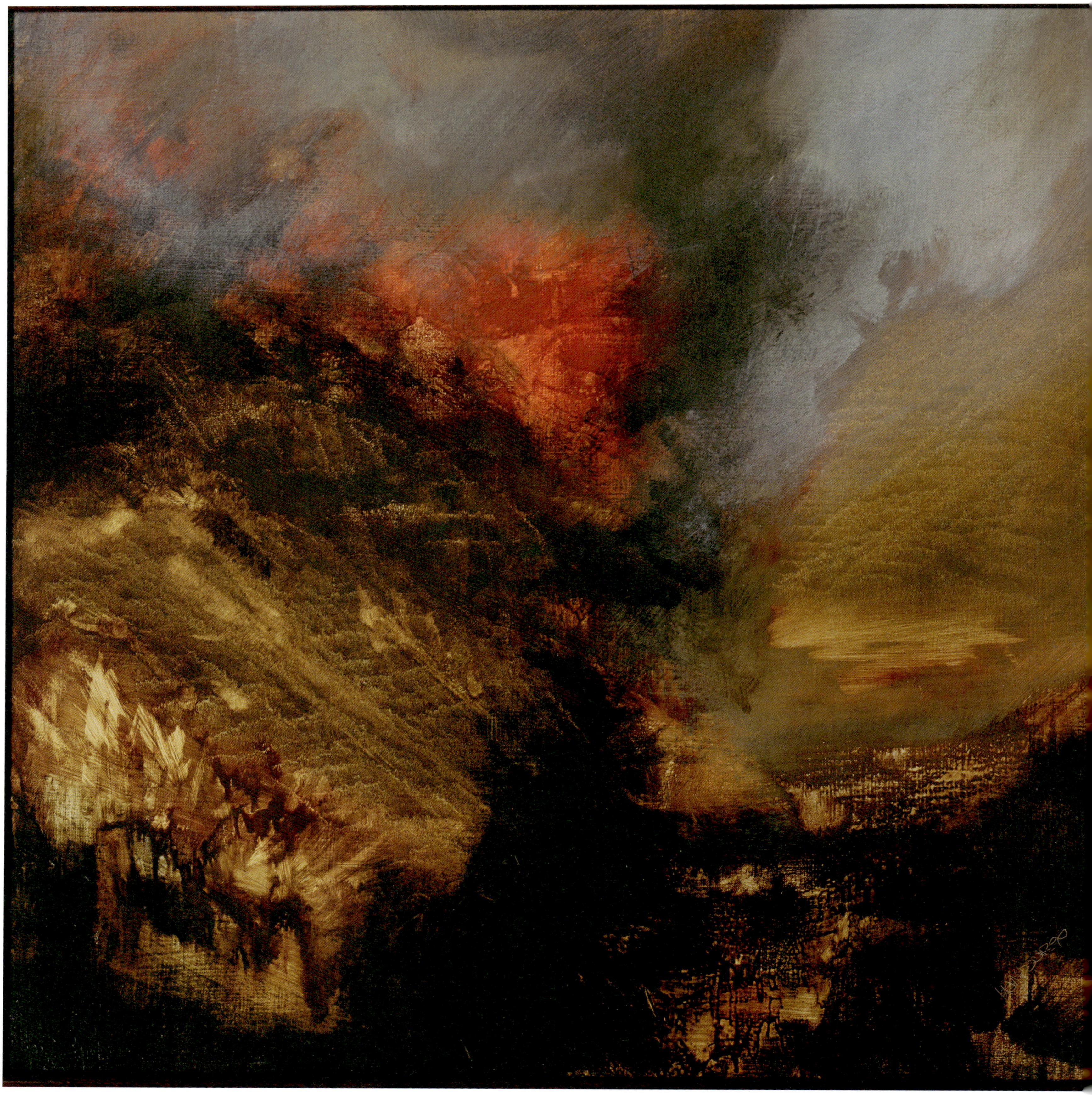

Plate 4: **Fire and Bones**, 1990-91. Oil on linen, 31 x 62 inches. Boise Art Museum Permanent Collection.

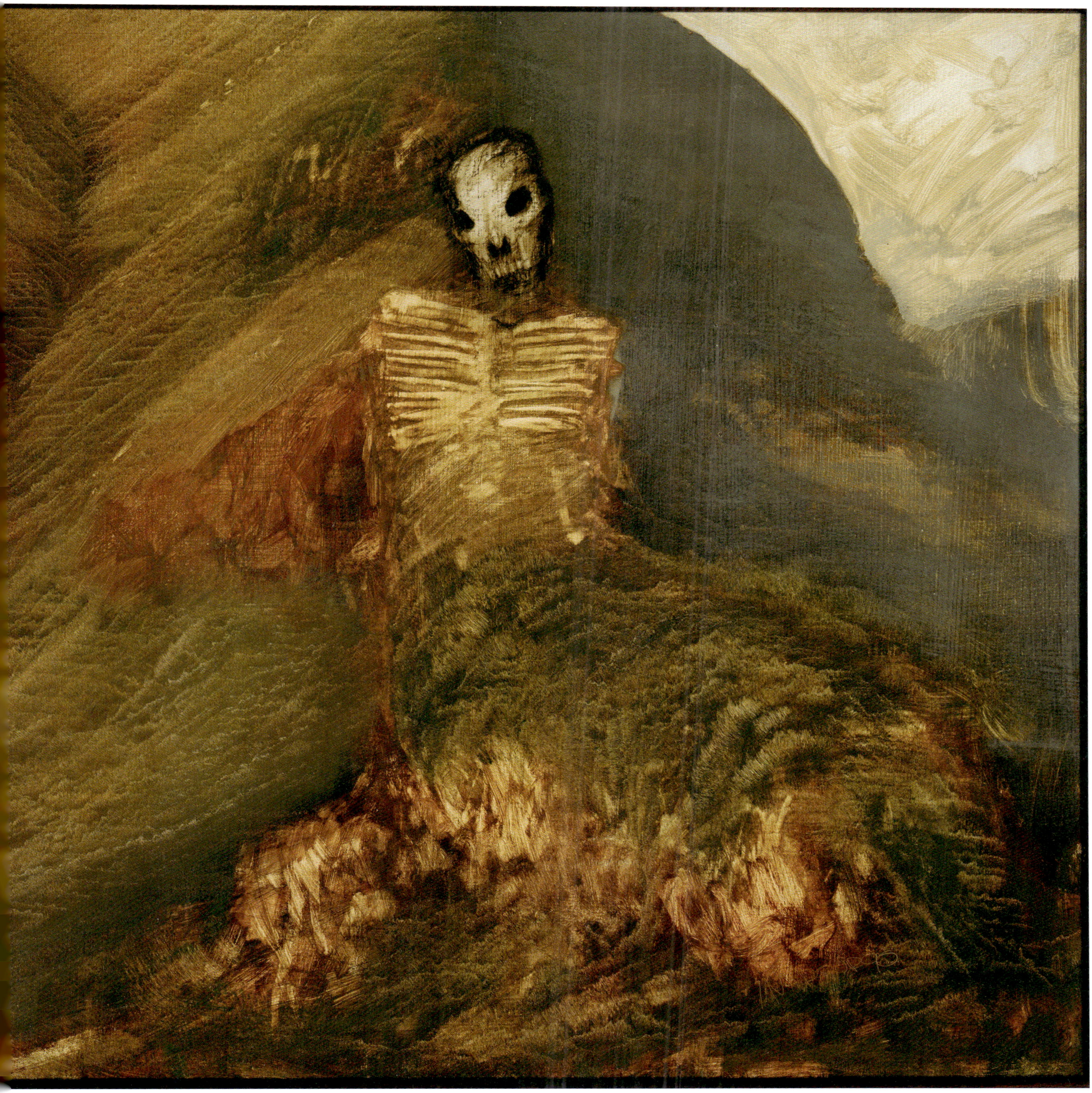

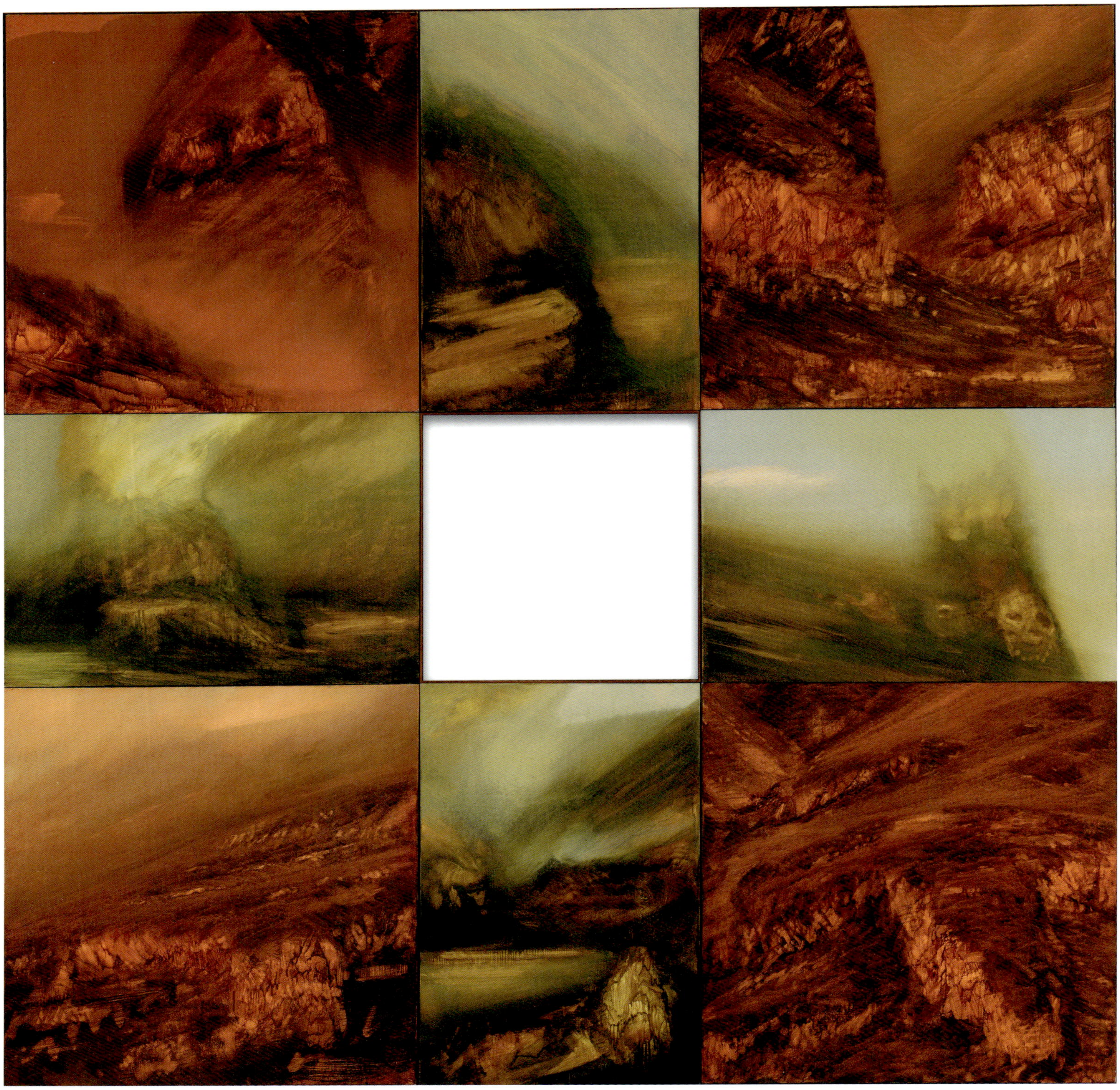

Plate 5: **Release the Sun**, 1990-91. Oil on linen, 83 x 83 inches. Tacoma Art Museum, Gift of Rebecca and Alexander C. Stewart.

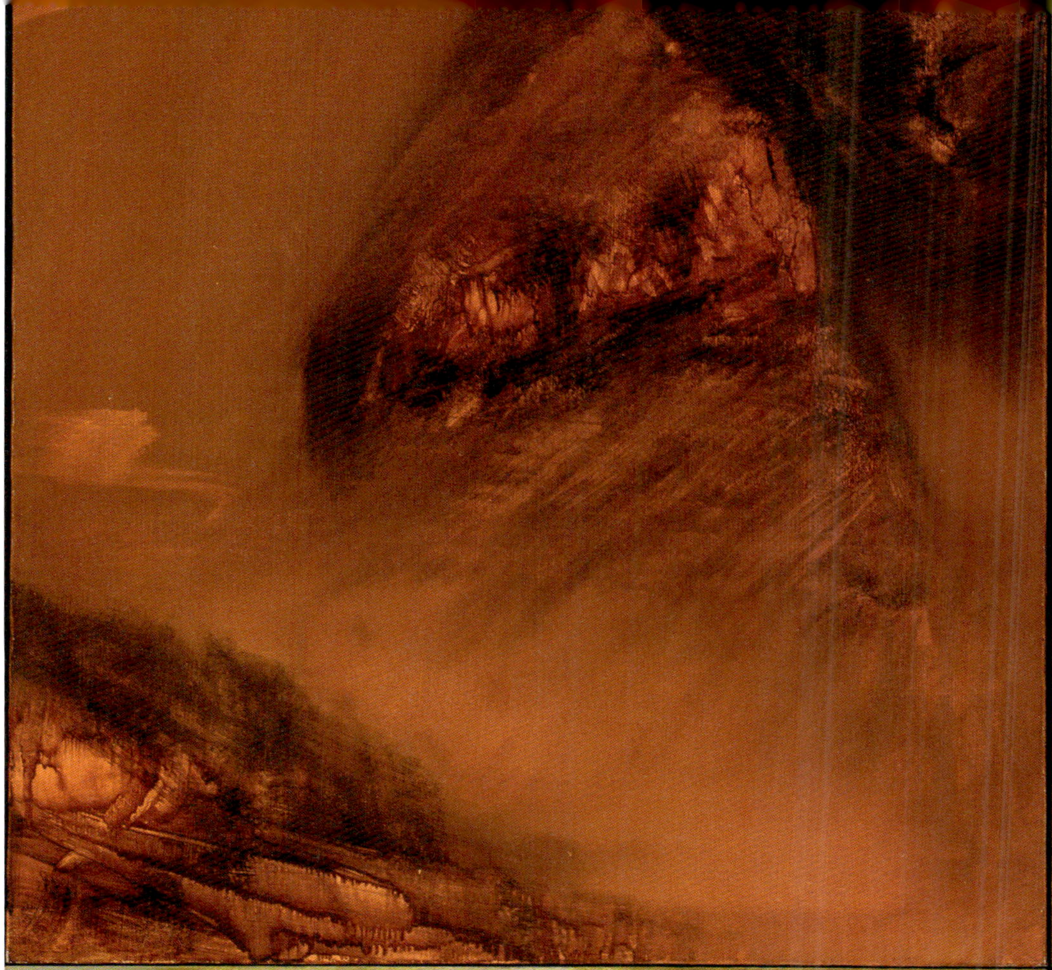
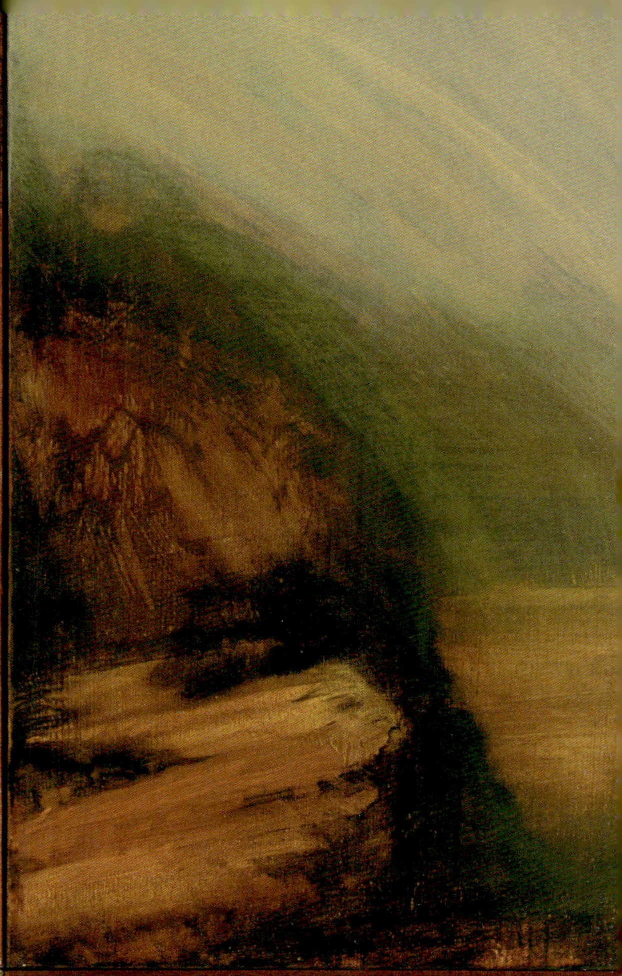
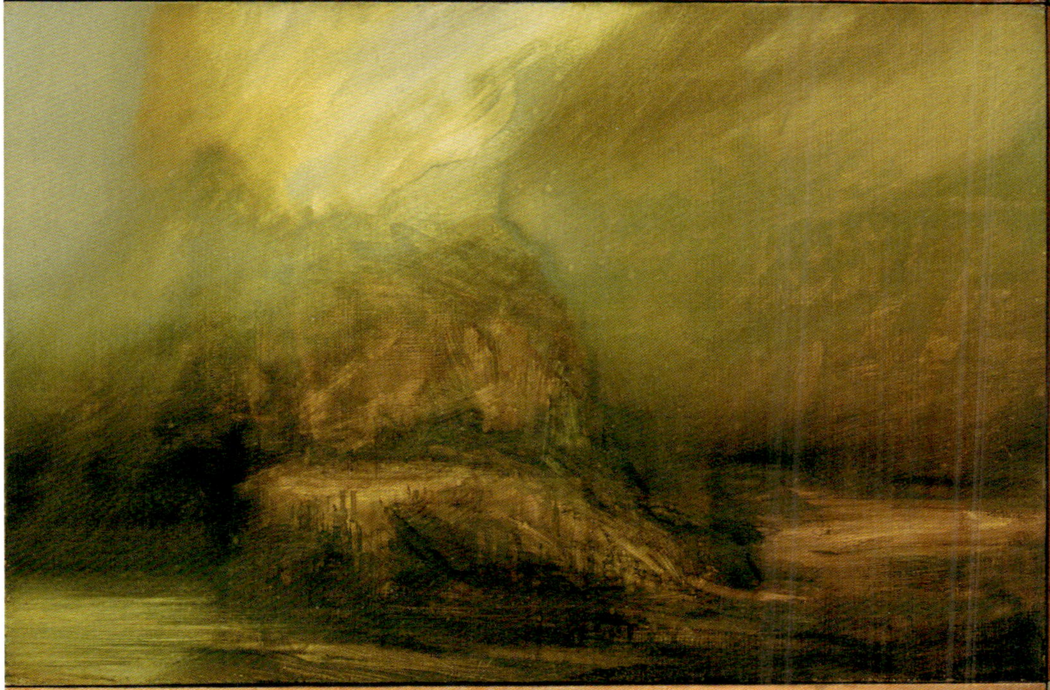
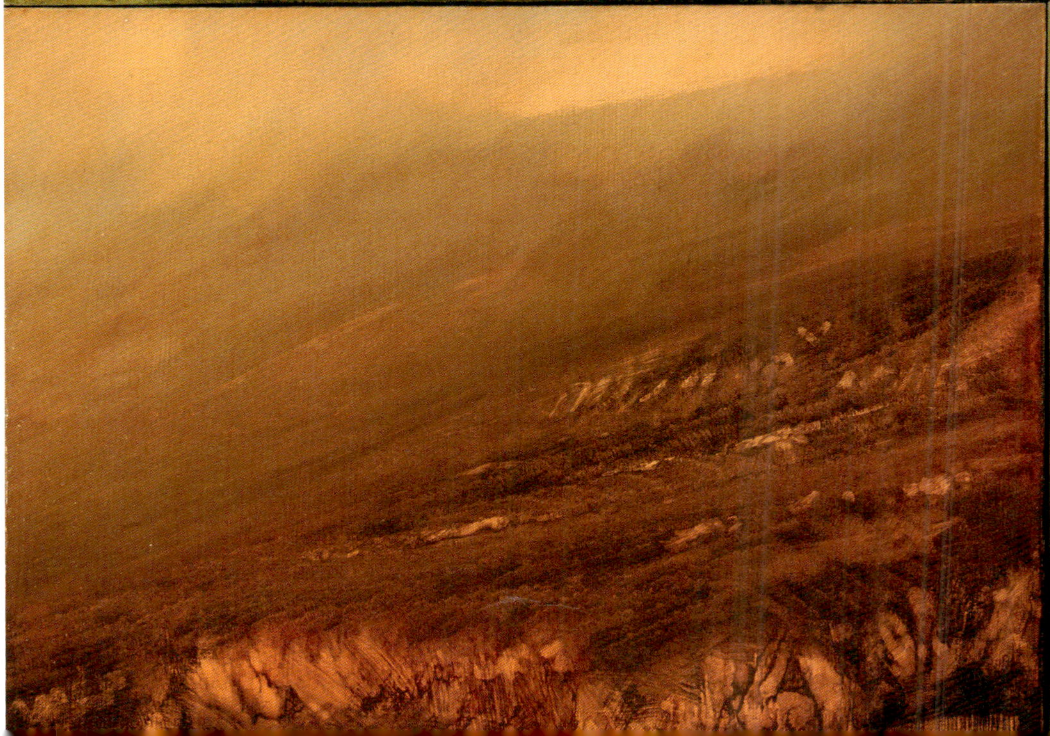
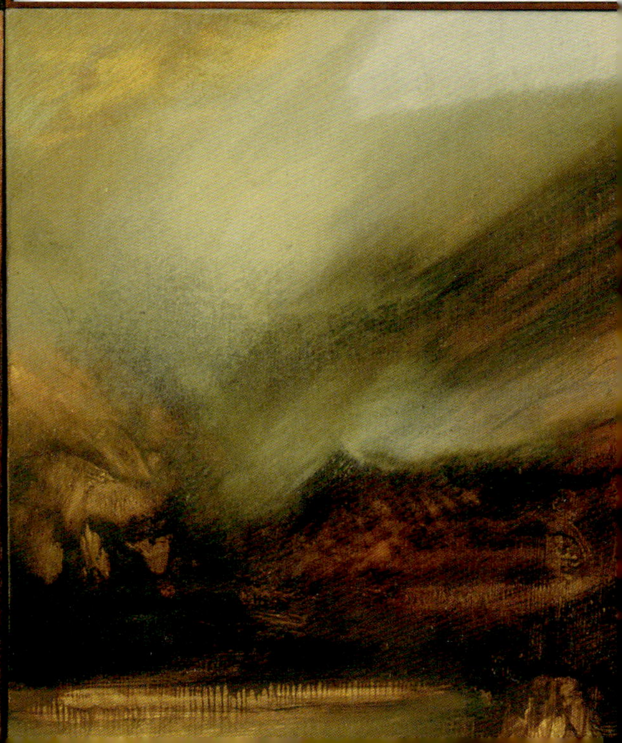

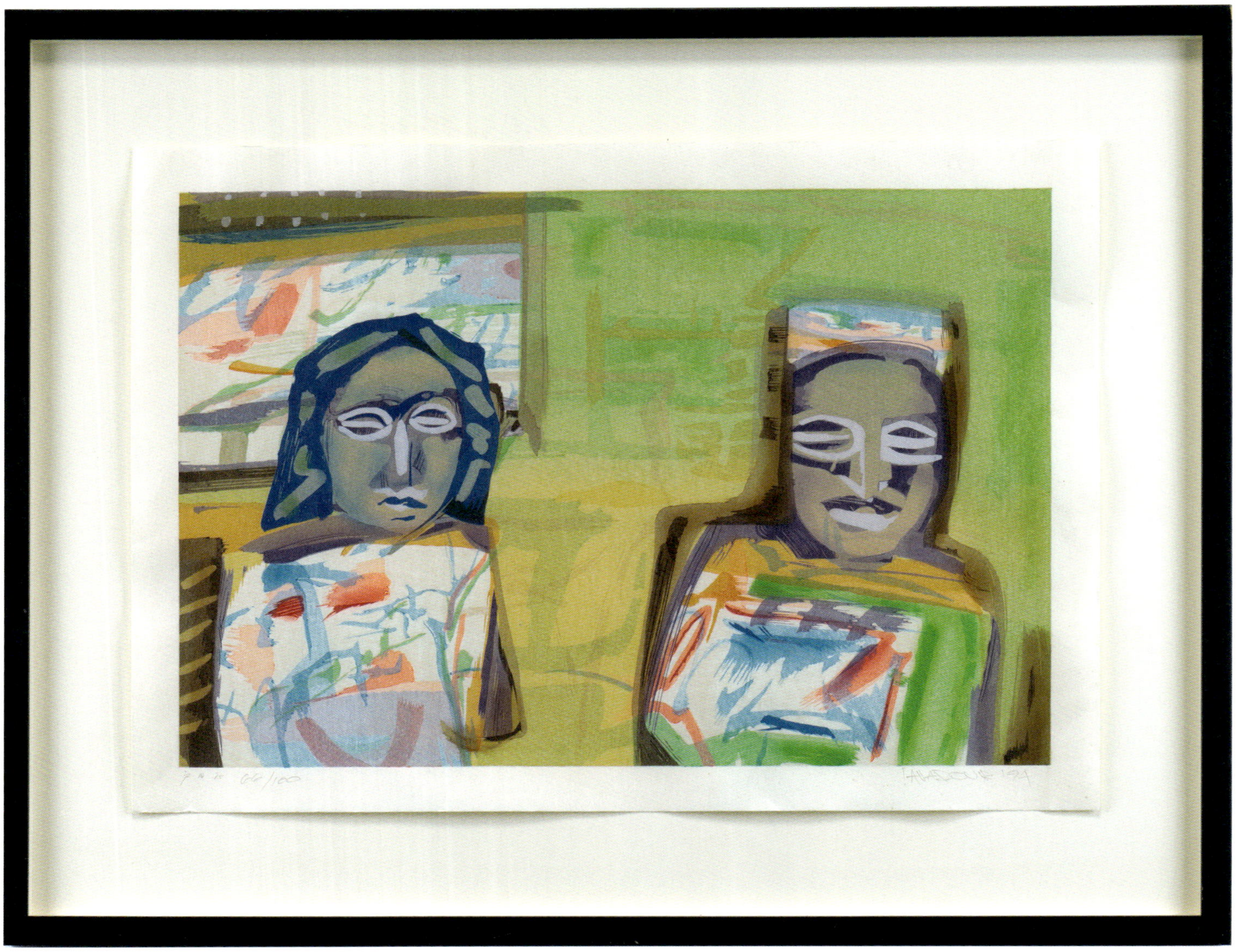

Plate 6: **Man and Woman**, ed. 66/100, 1994. Woodblock print, 24 ¼ x 31 inches. Courtesy of the artist.
Opposite page, bottom: **Man and Woman** (detail), 1981. Oil on paper, 24 ¼ x 31 inches. Courtesy of the artist.

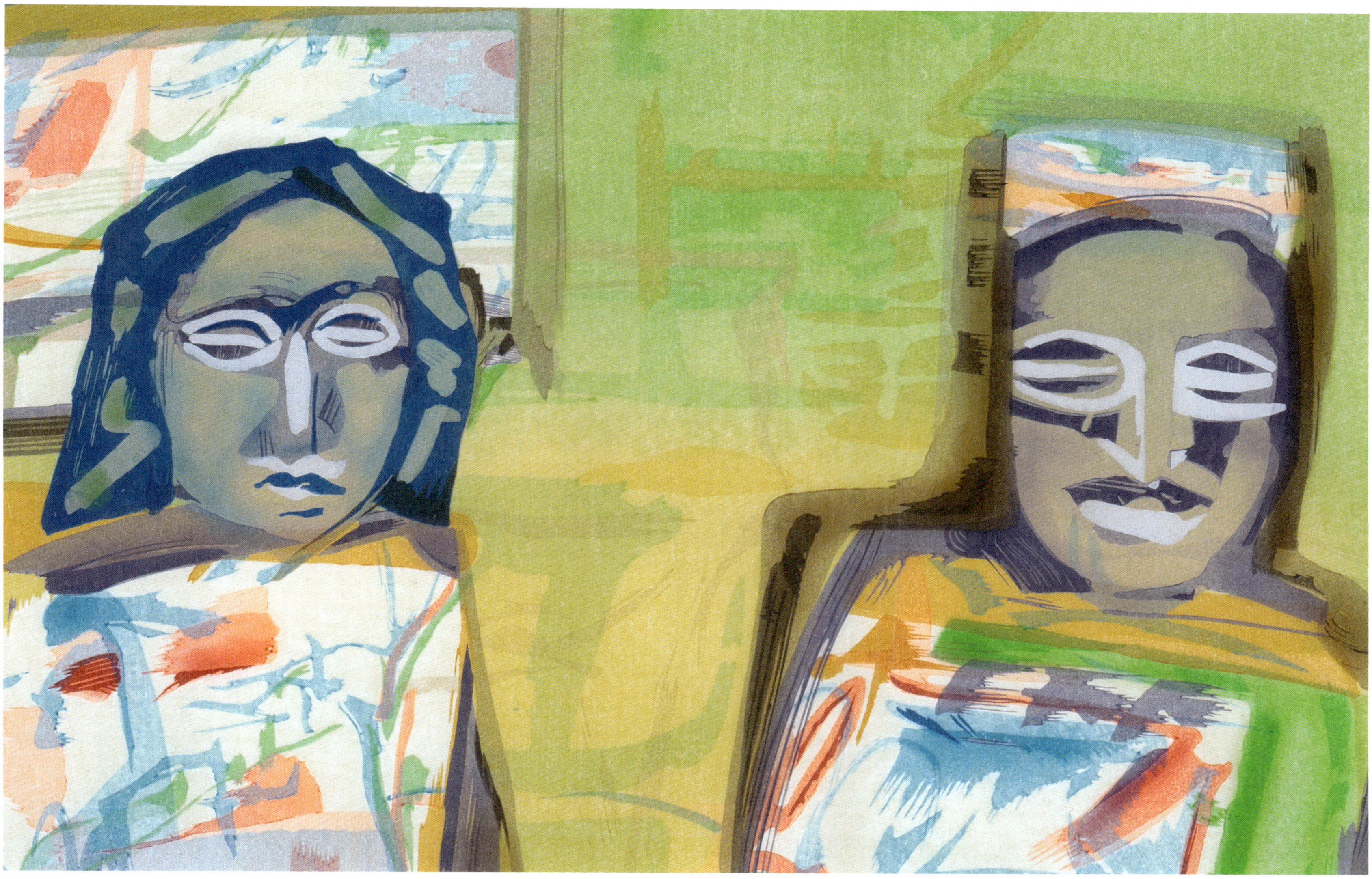

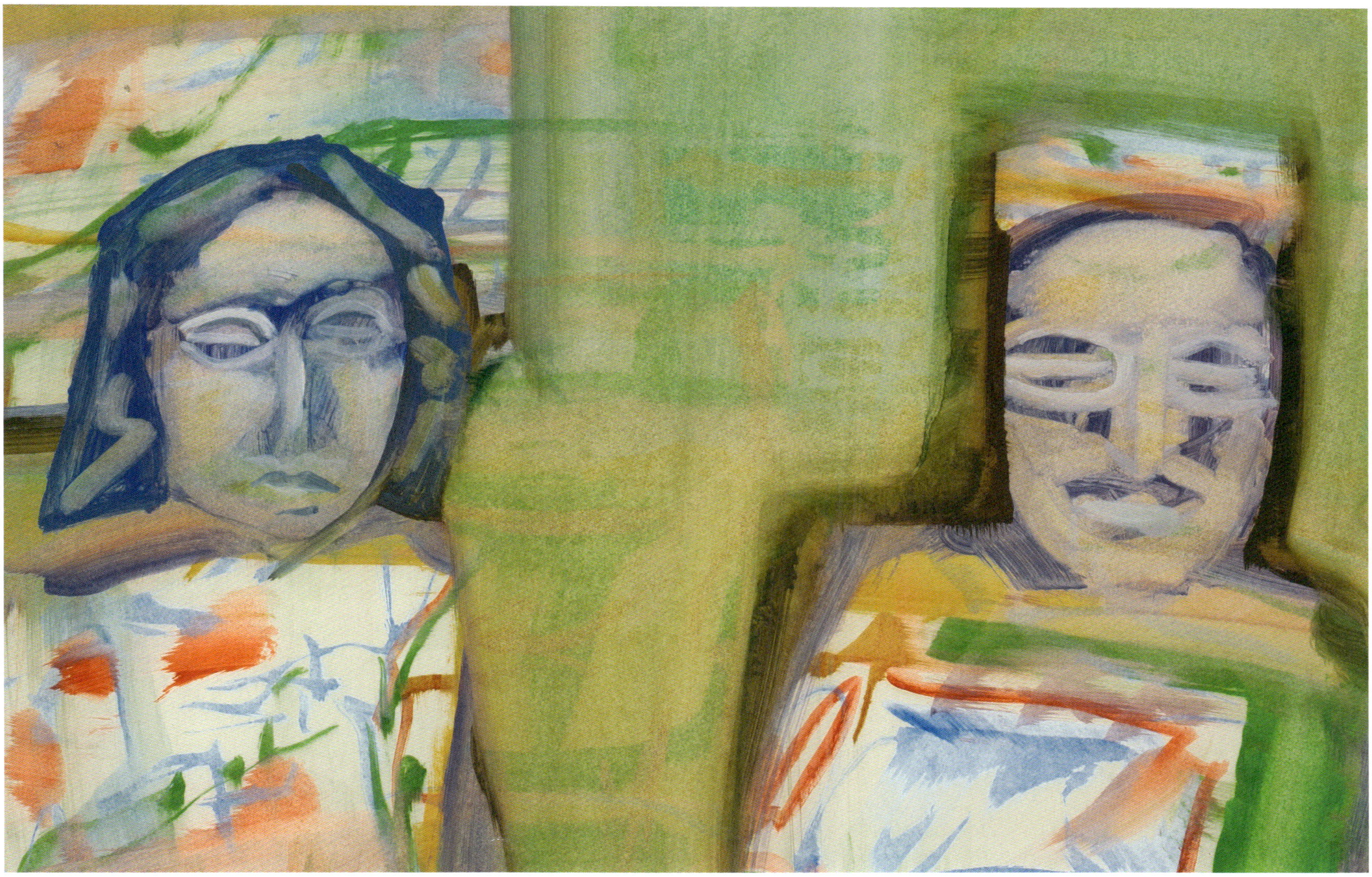

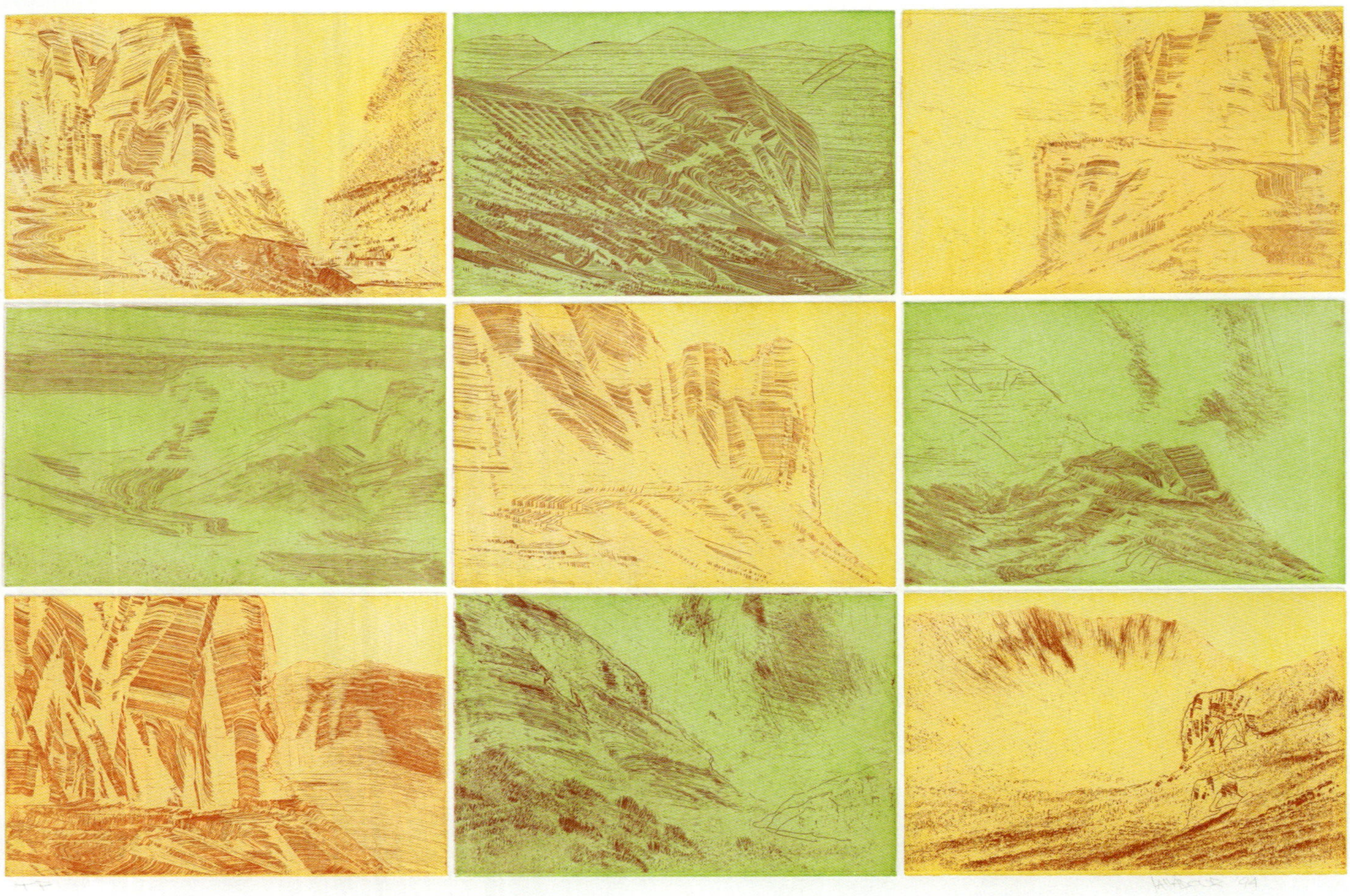

Plate 7: **Dreaming of Whirlwinds**, T/P, 1994. Color aquatint, soap ground etching, and drypoint, 35 x 46 inches. Courtesy of the artist.

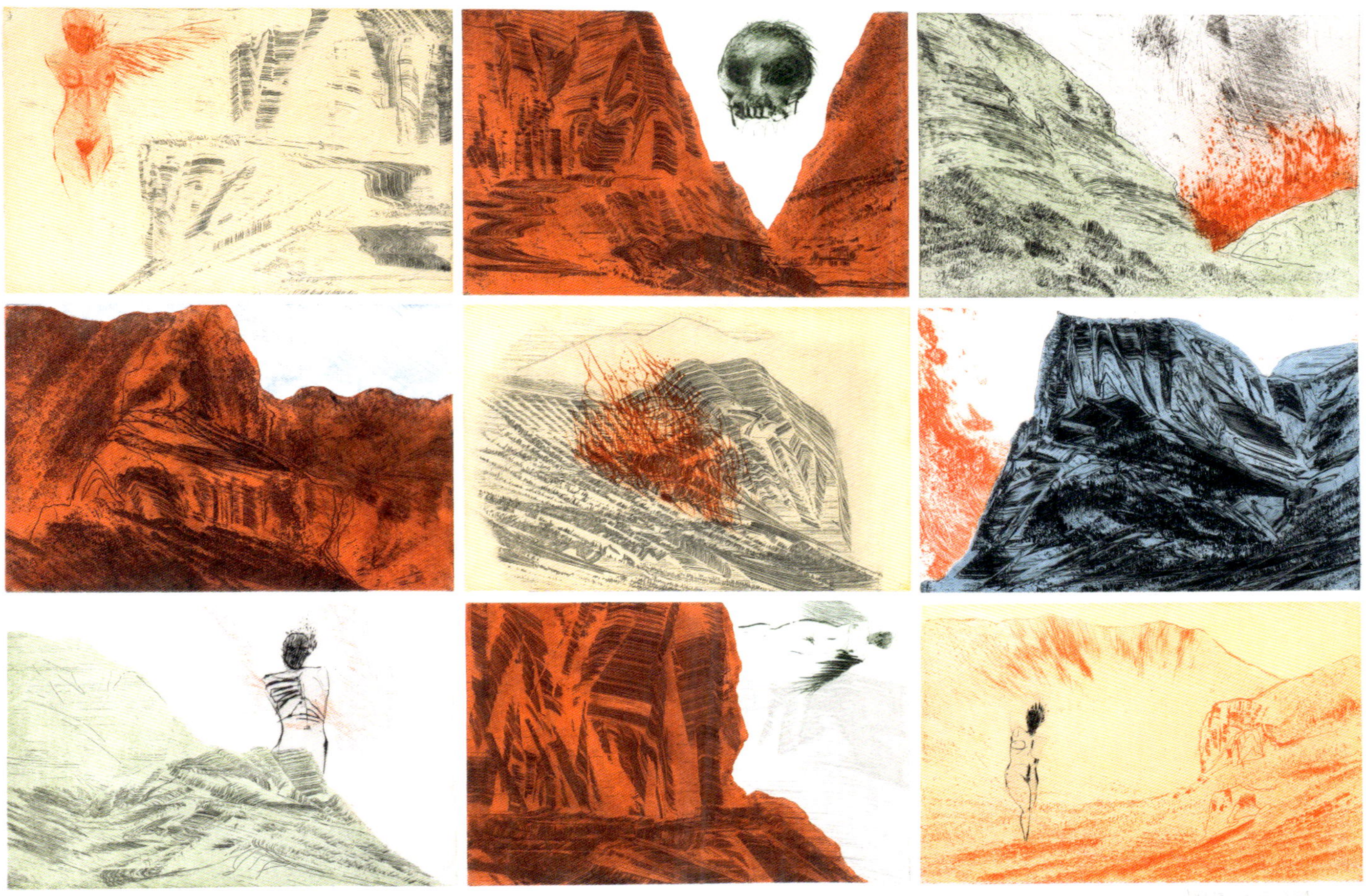

Plate 8: **Dreaming of Whirlwinds**, A/P 3, 1994. Color aquatint, soap ground etching, and drypoint, 35 x 46 inches. Private collection.

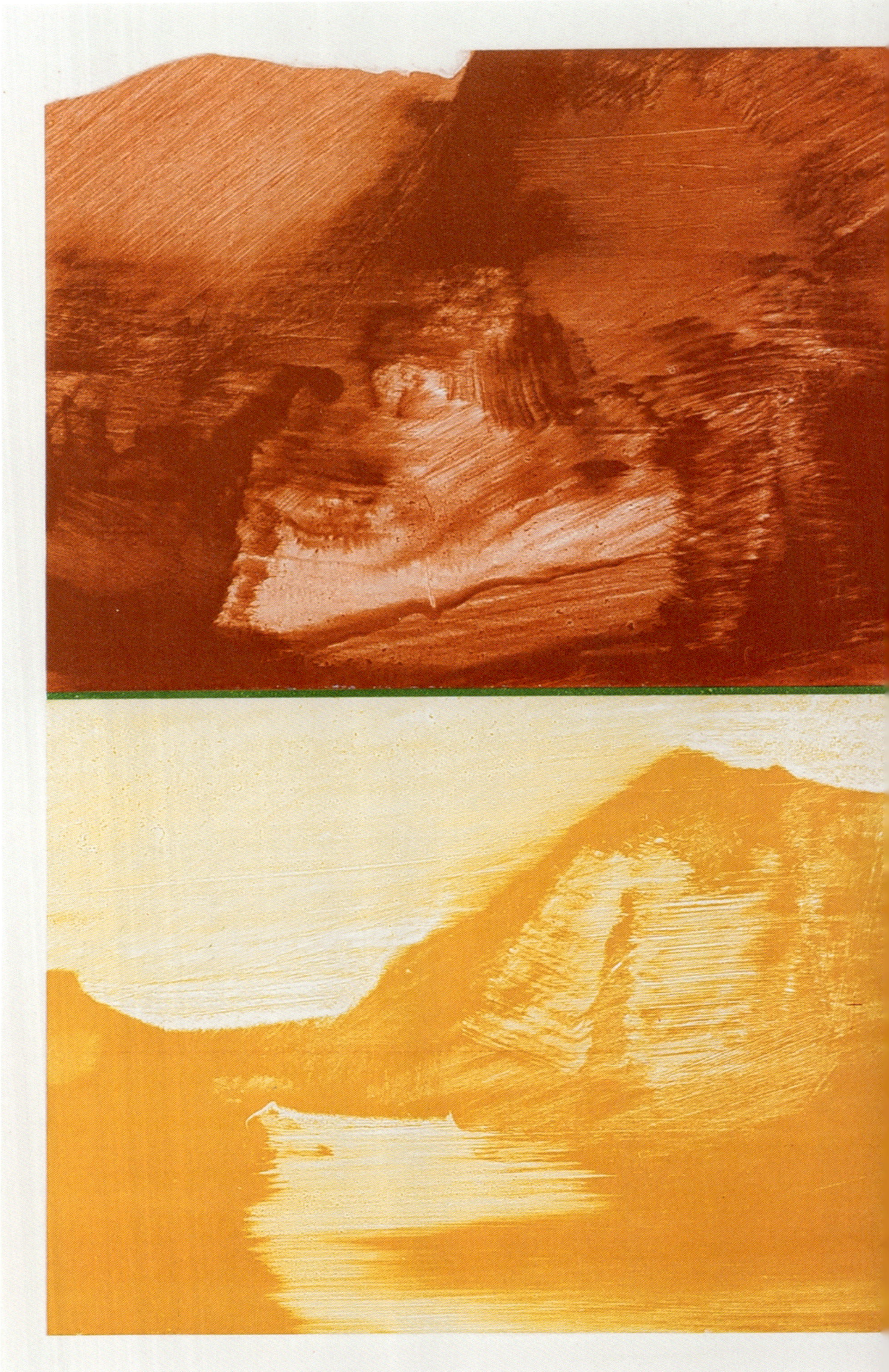

Plate 9: **Untitled**, T/P, 1997. Waterless lithograph, 18 x 21 inches. Published by 21 Steps Studio. Collaborating Master Printer: Jeff Ryan. Courtesy of the artist.

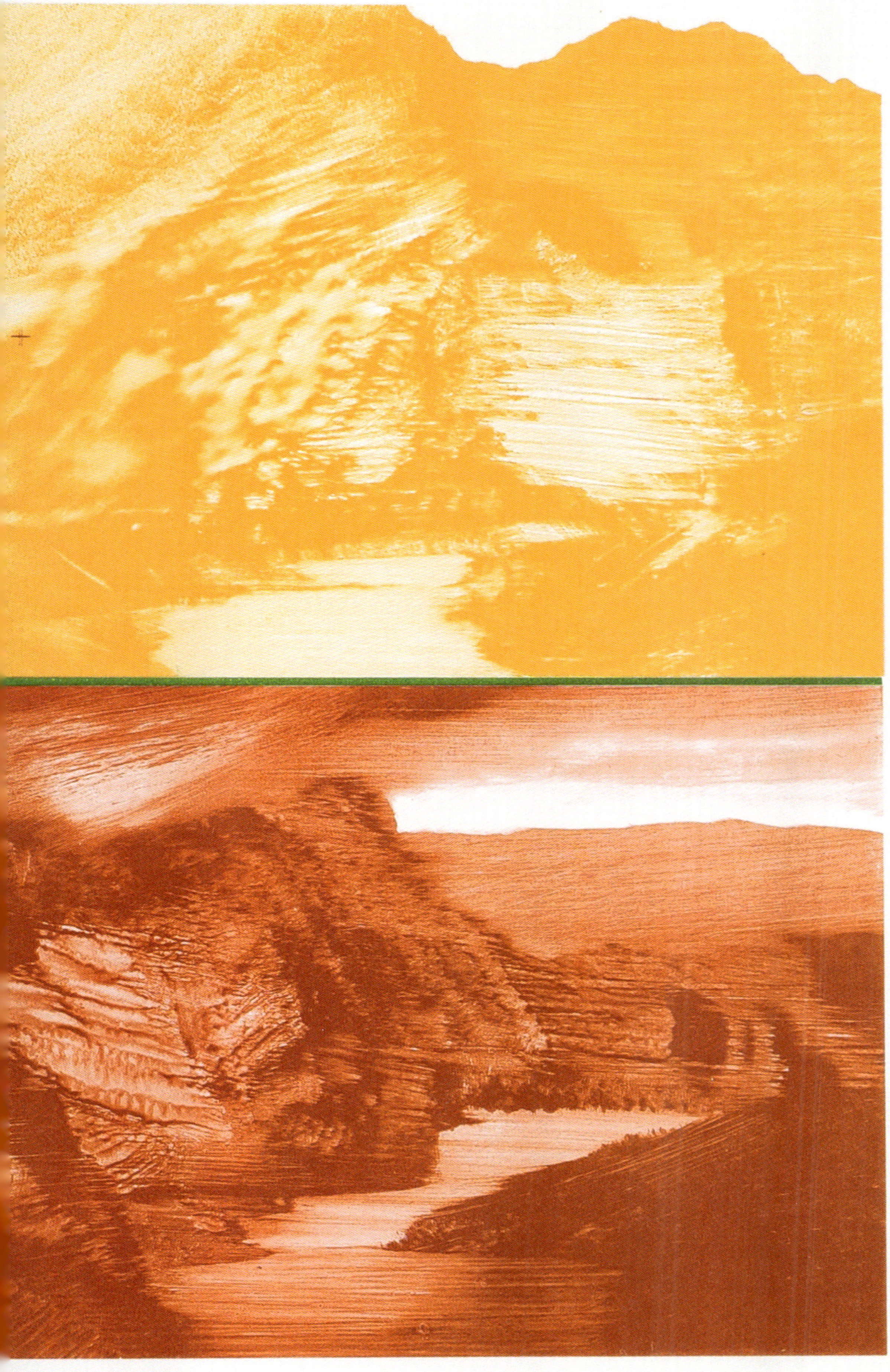

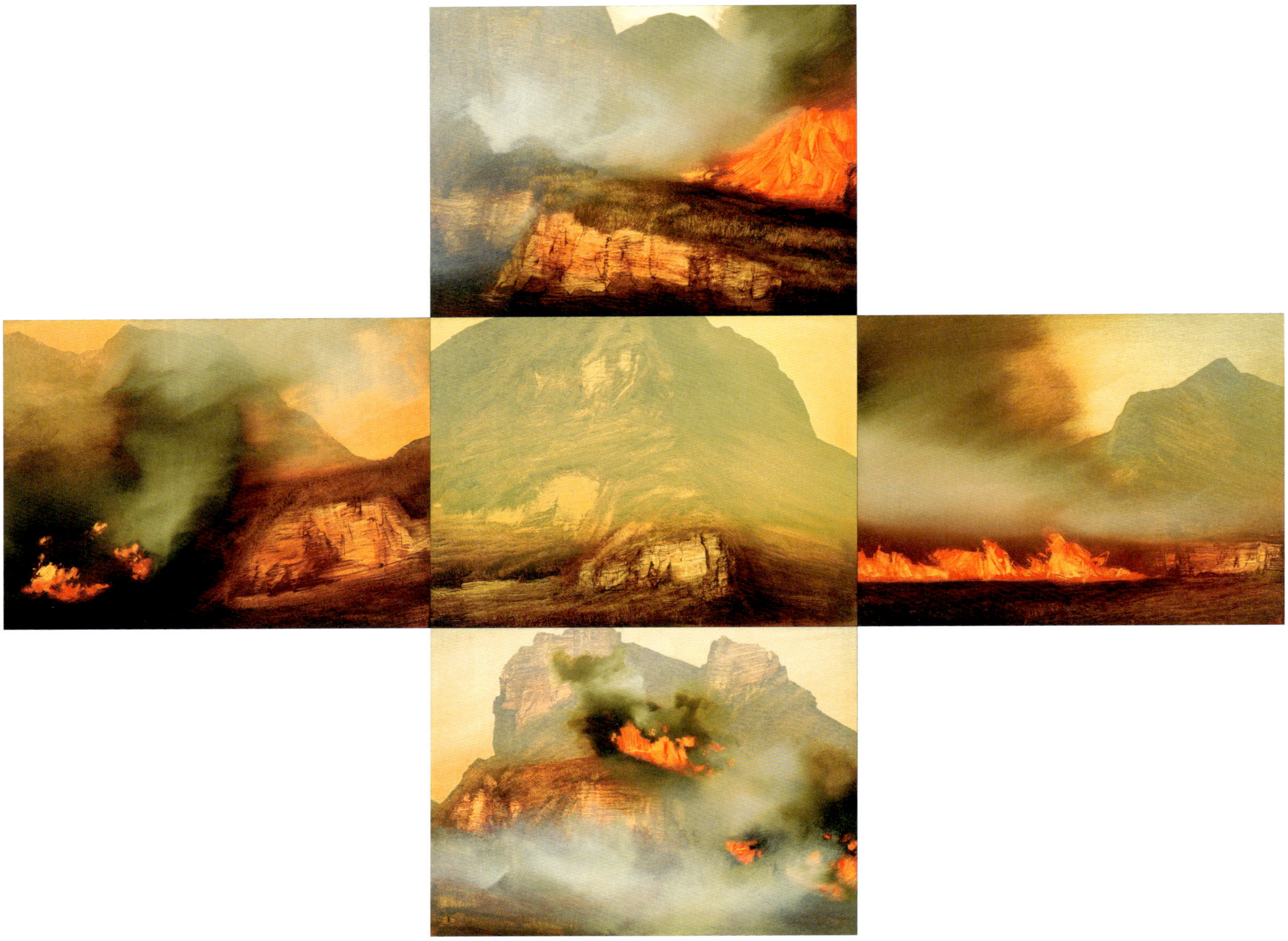

Plate 10: **Nest of Suns**, 1998. Oil on panel, 72 x 96 inches. Courtesy of the Northwest Museum of Arts and Culture, Museum purchase, 2003 (4041.1).

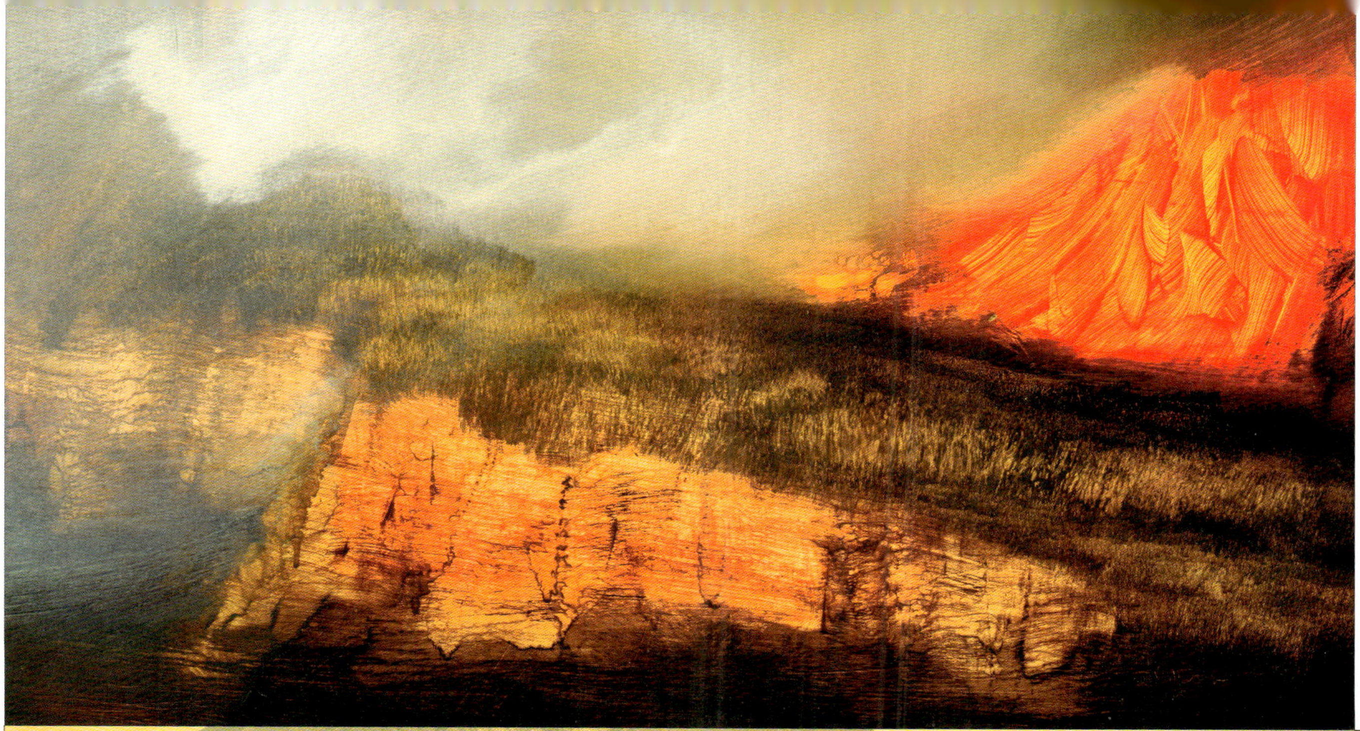

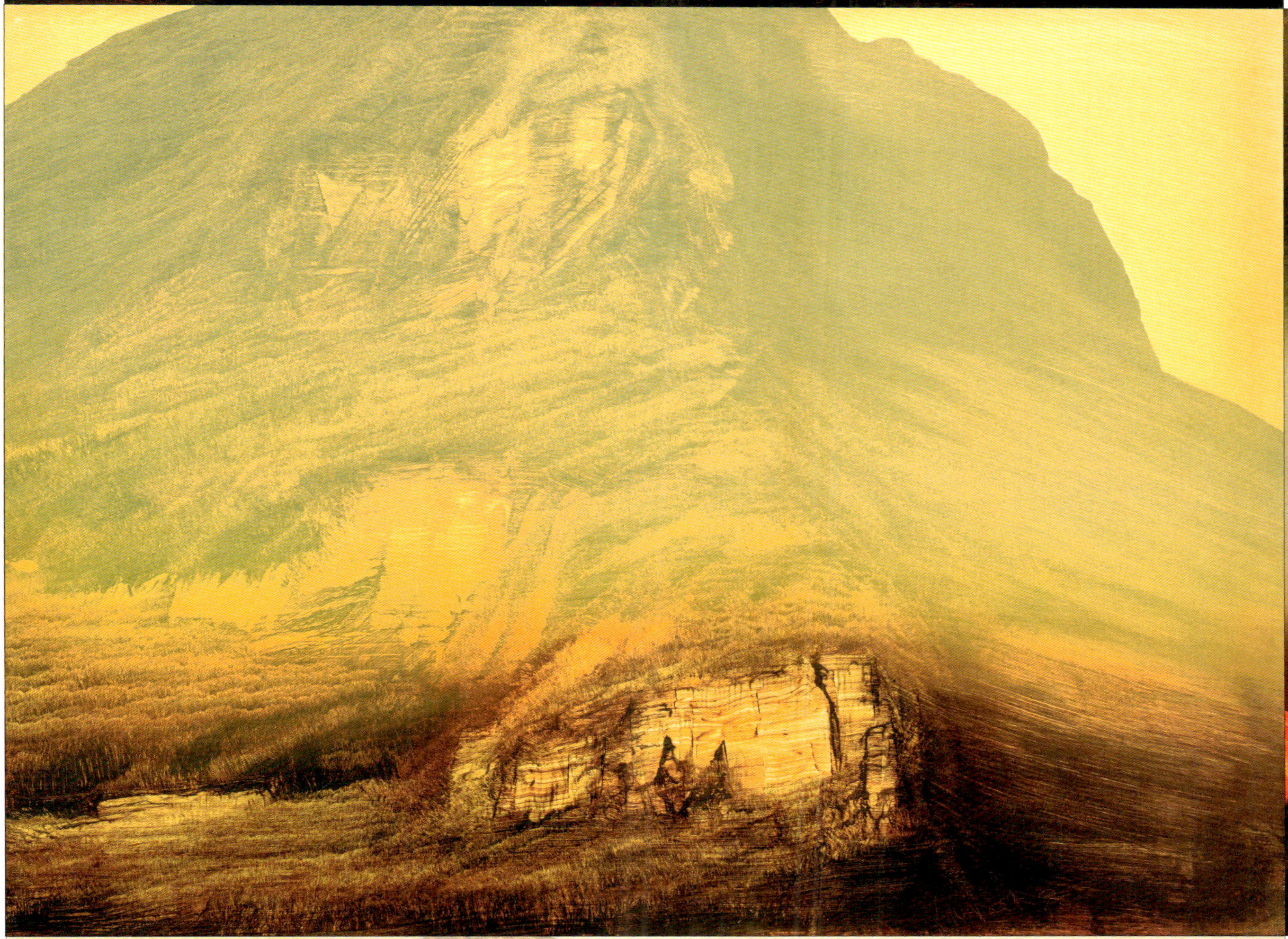

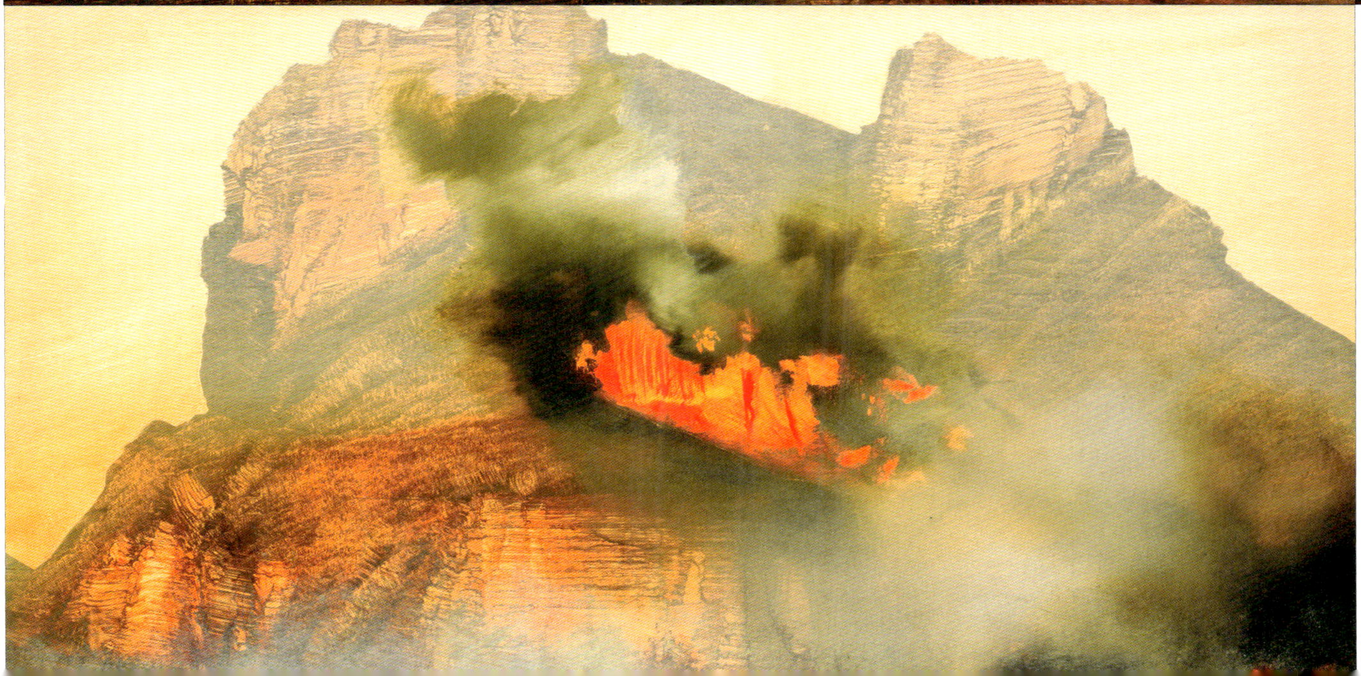

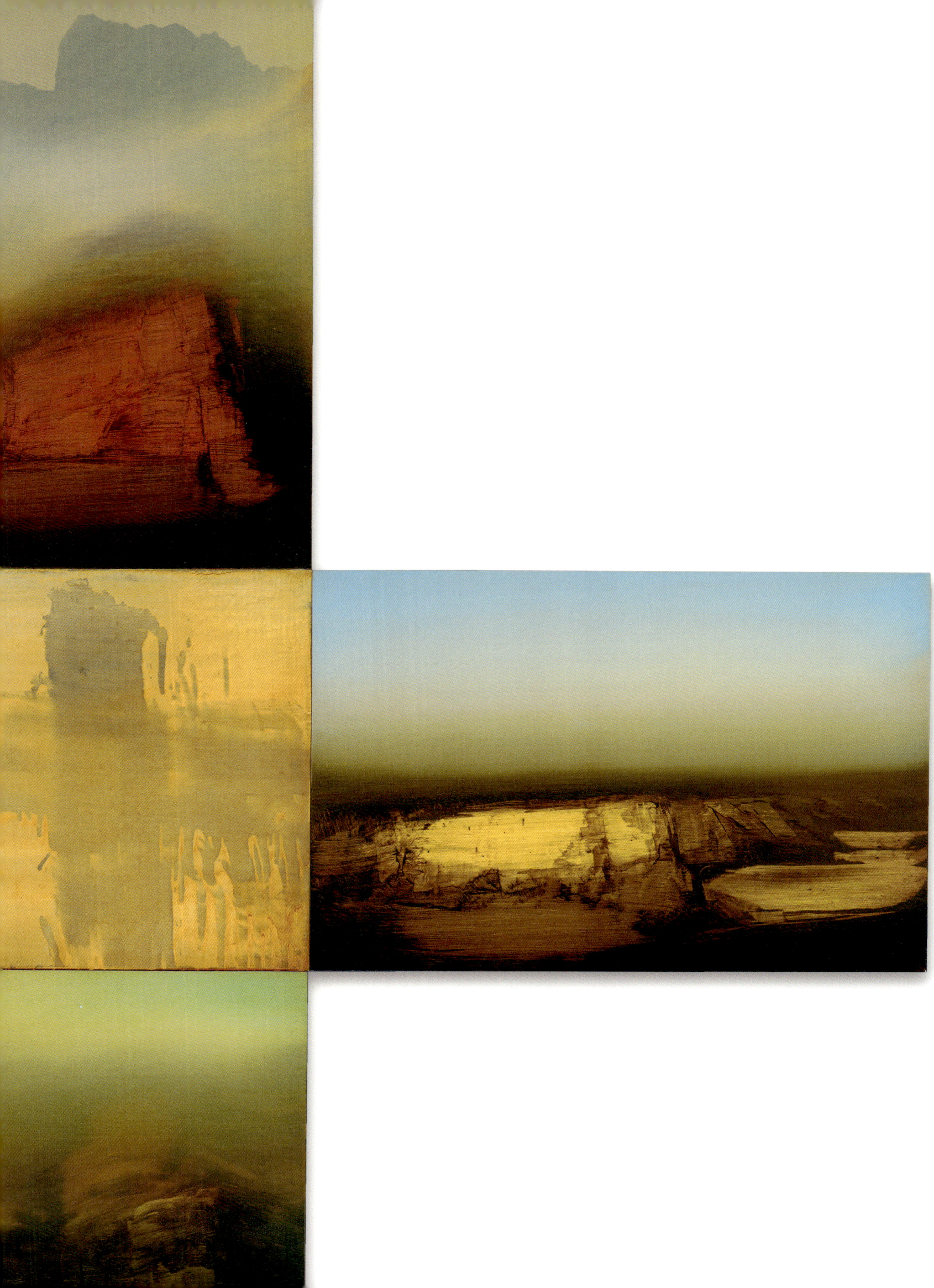

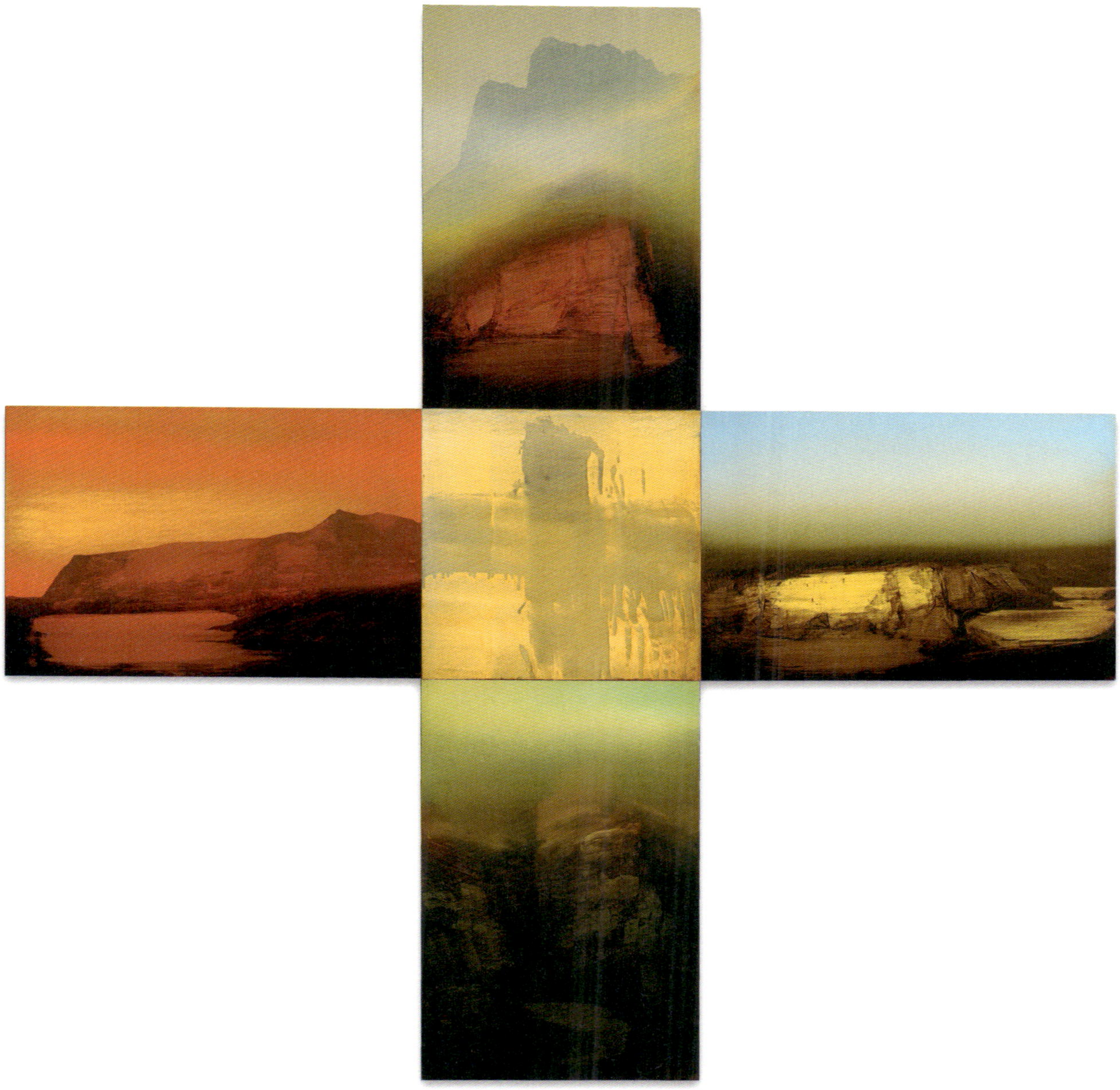

Plate 11: **Flag**, 2000. Oil on panel, 80 x 80 inches. Tacoma Art Museum, Anonymous gift, 2022.1.

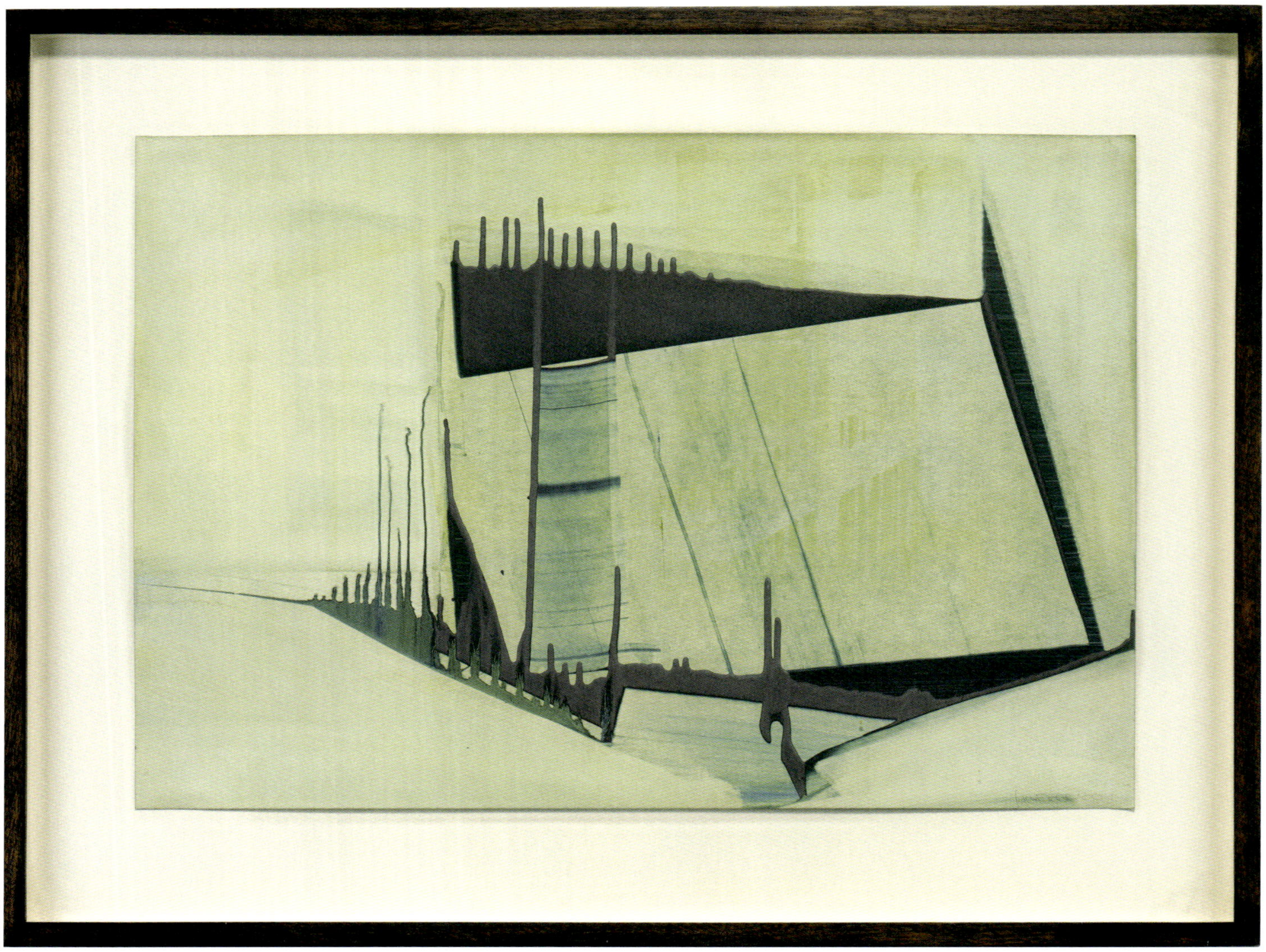

Plate 12: **Untitled**, 2000. Oil on paper, 27 x 35 inches. Courtesy of the artist.

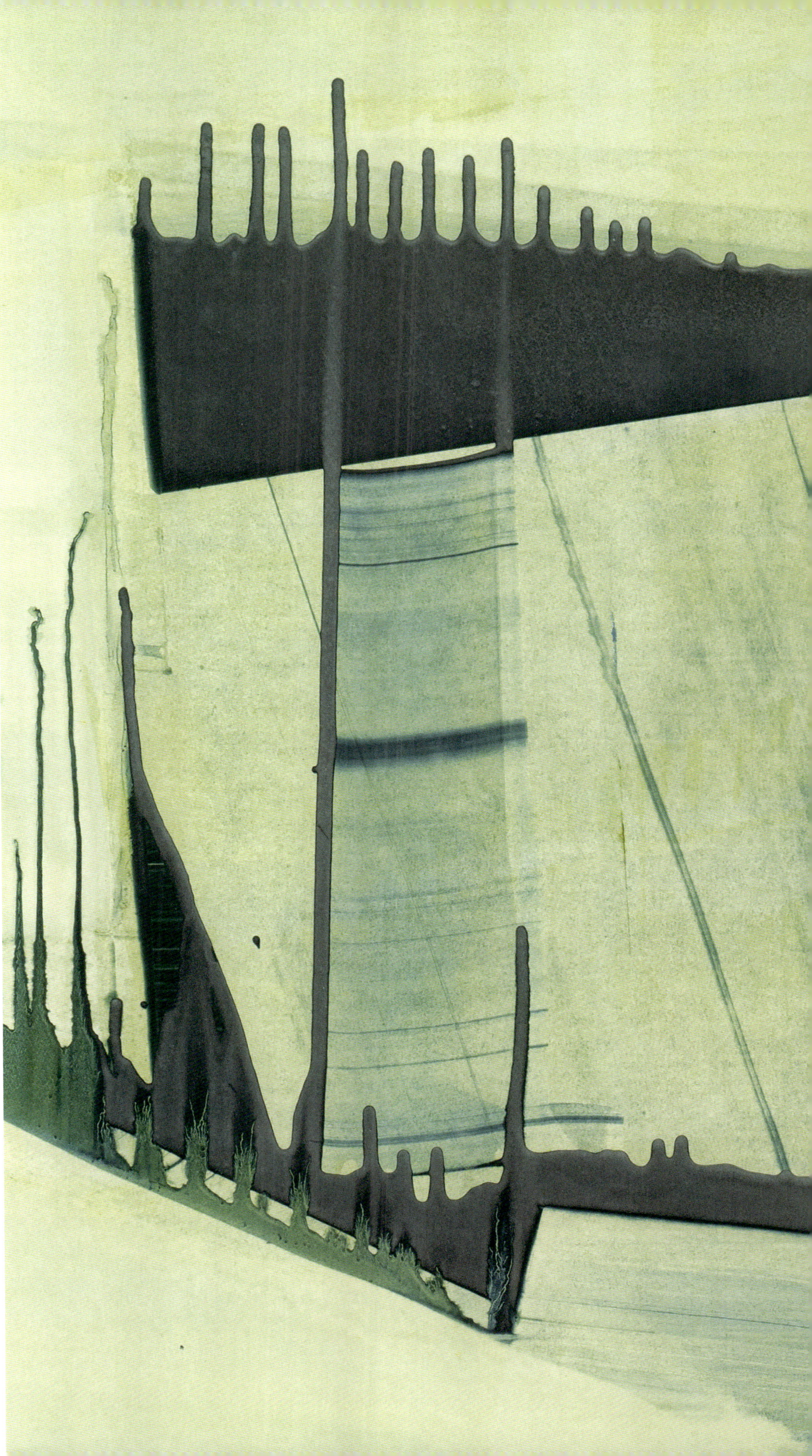

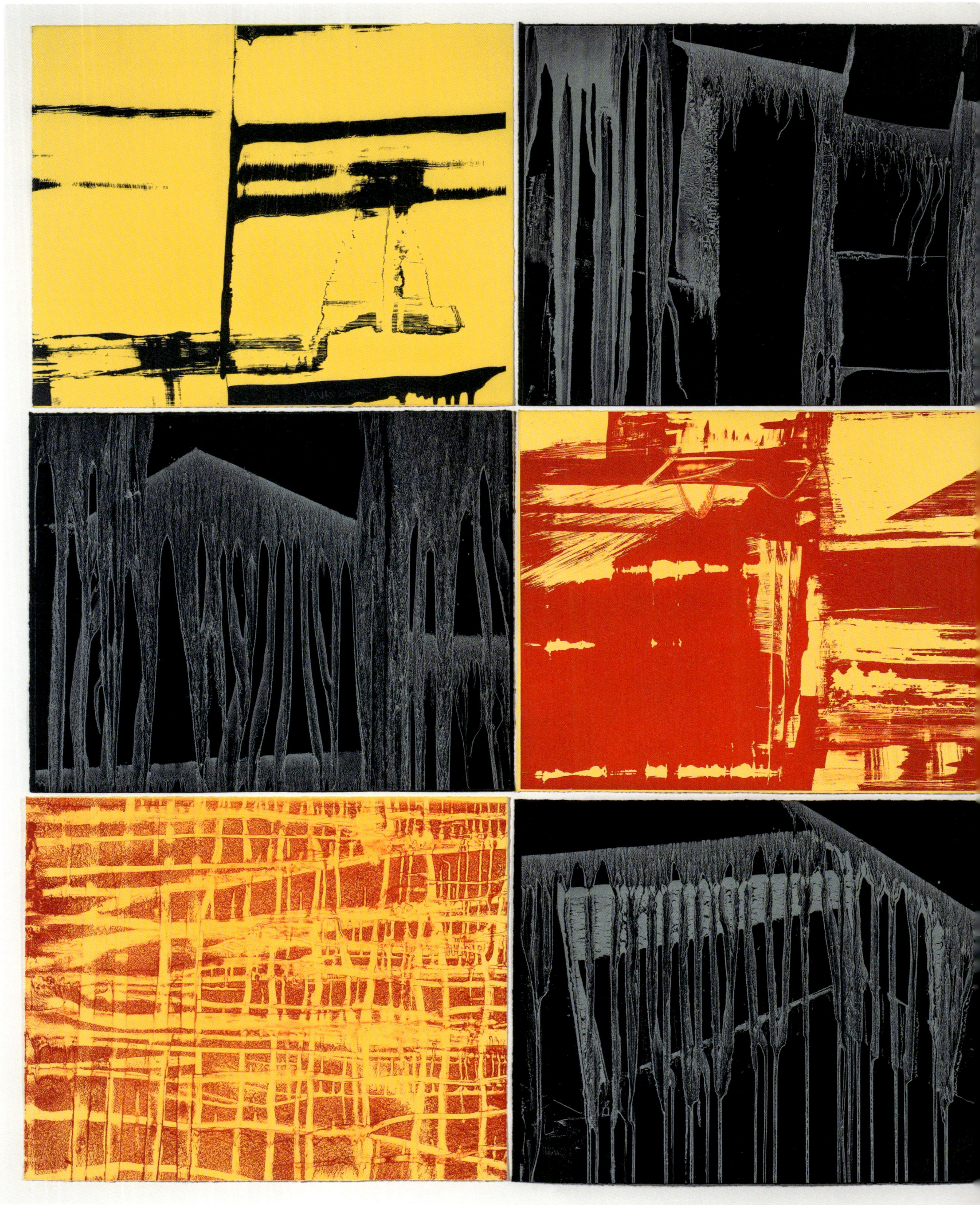

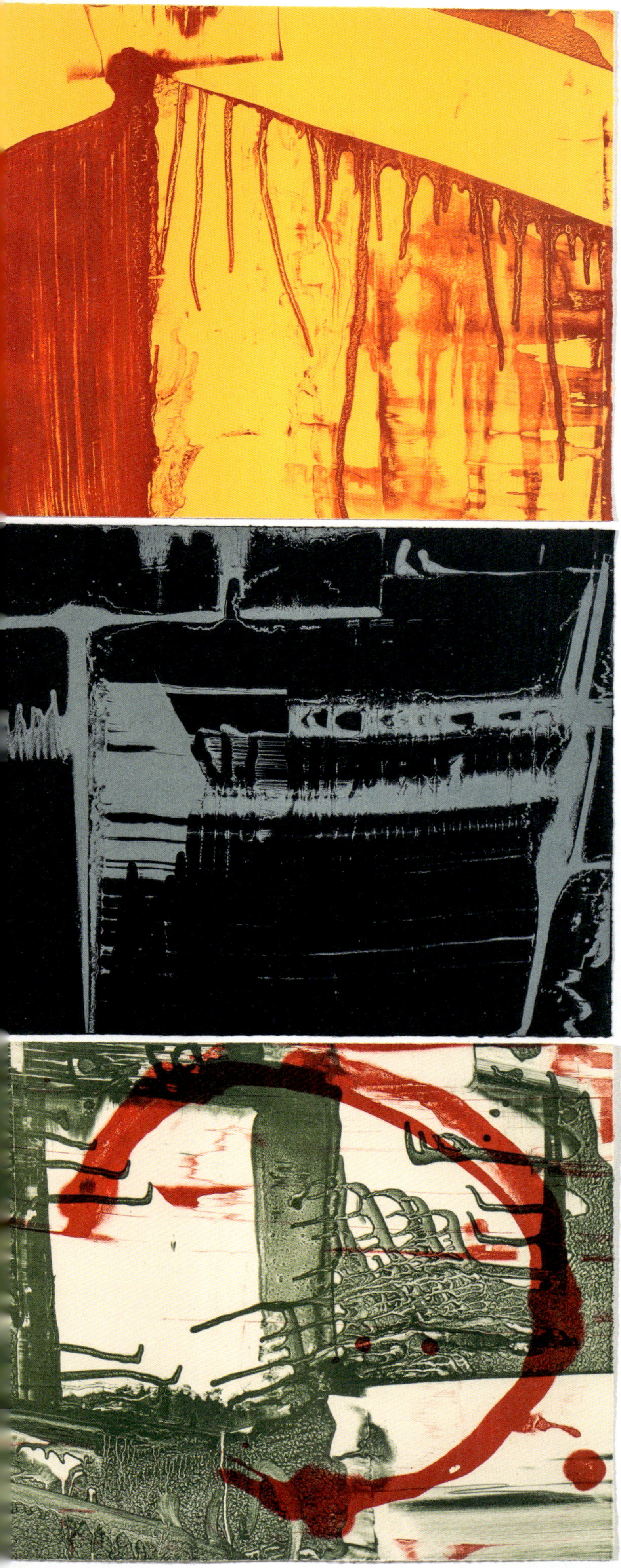

Plate 13: **Untitled**, ed. 18/18, 2002. Lithograph, 42 x 51 inches. Published by the Brodsky Center at PAFA. Collaborating Master Printer: Eileen M. Foti. Courtesy of the artist.

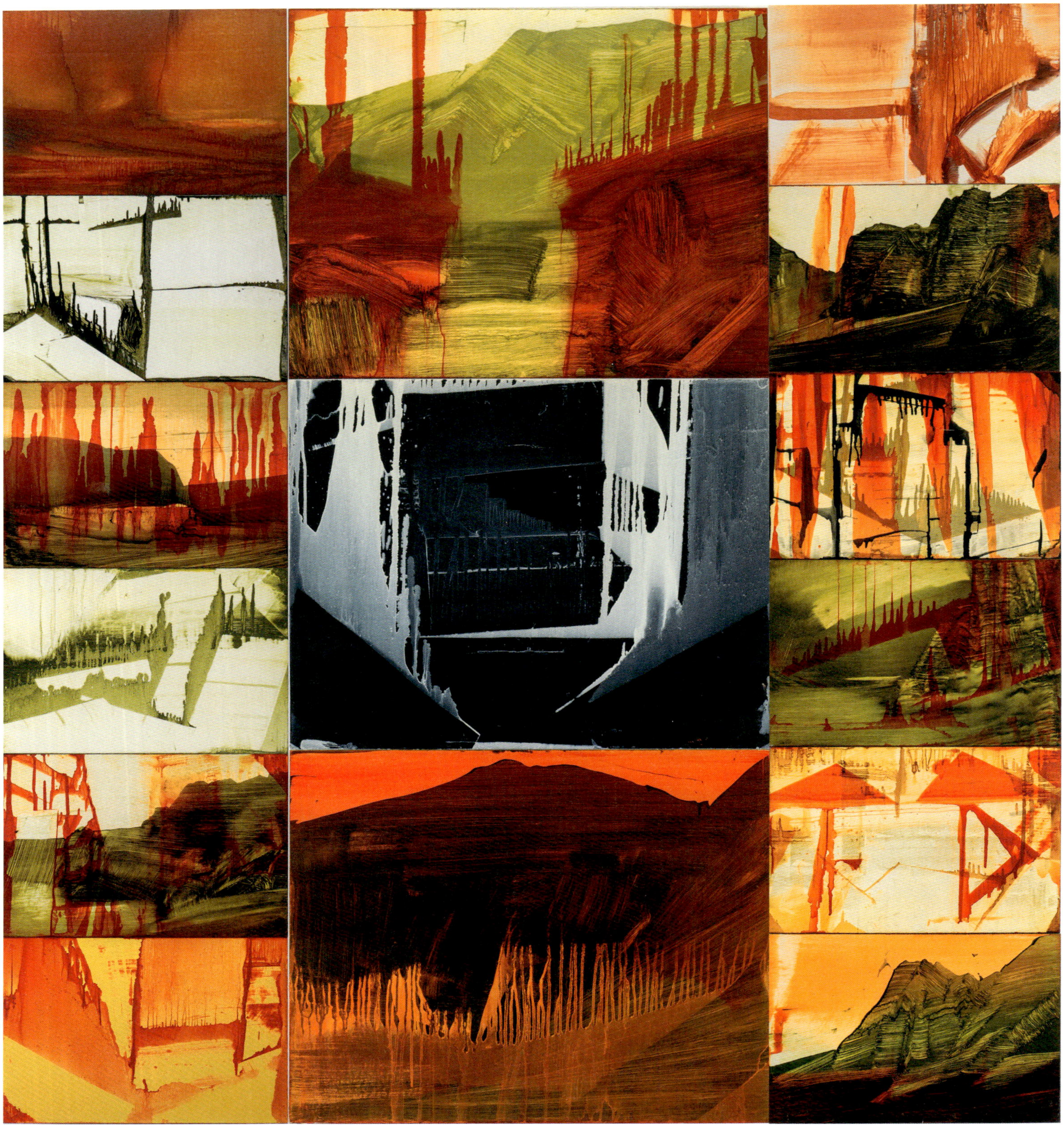

Plate 14: **Bridge**, 2001. Oil on panel, 54 x 72 inches. Courtesy of the artist.

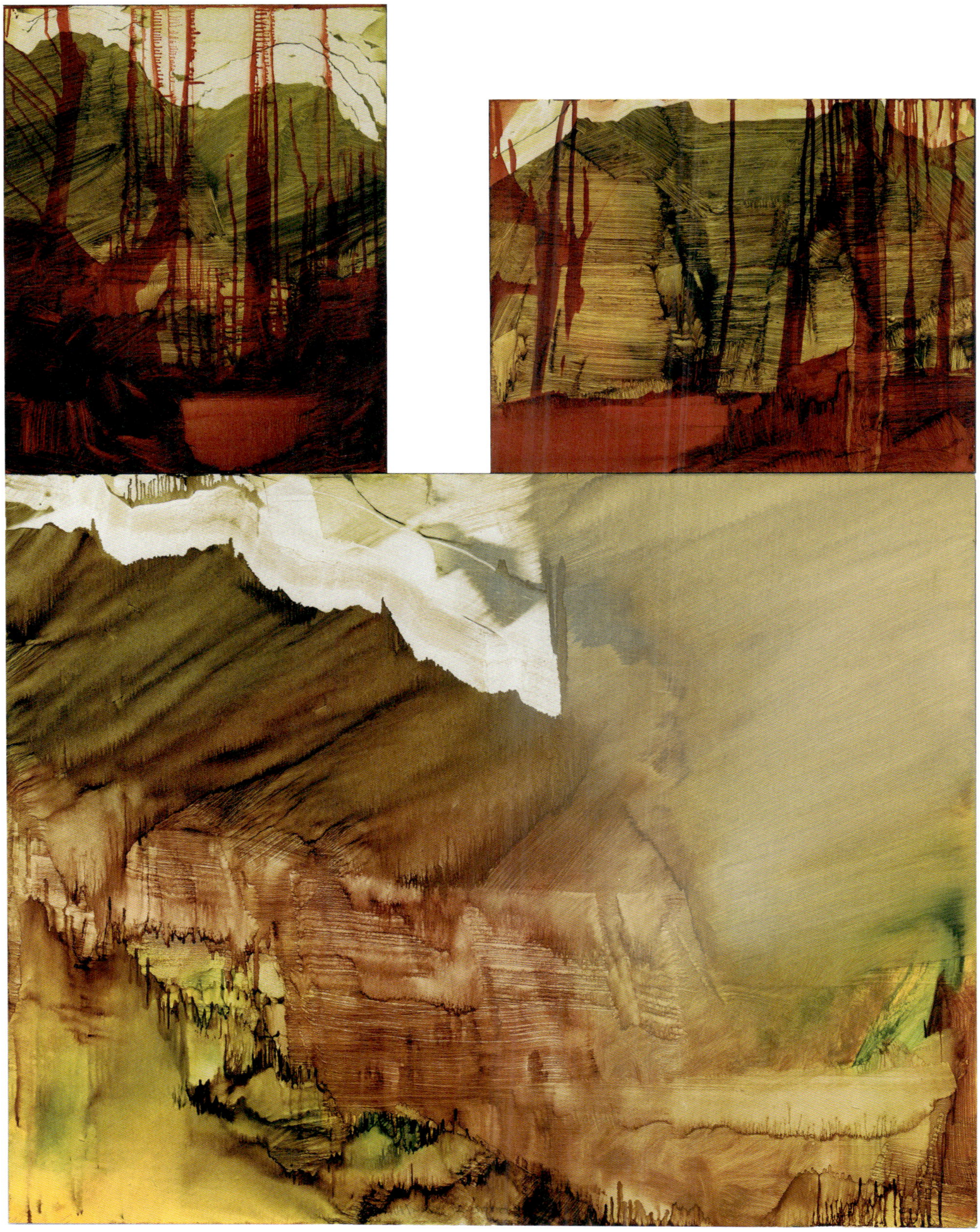

Plate 15: **Point**, 2003. Oil on plywood, 78 x 60 inches. Boise Art Museum Permanent Collection; Gift of Driek and Michael Zirinsky.

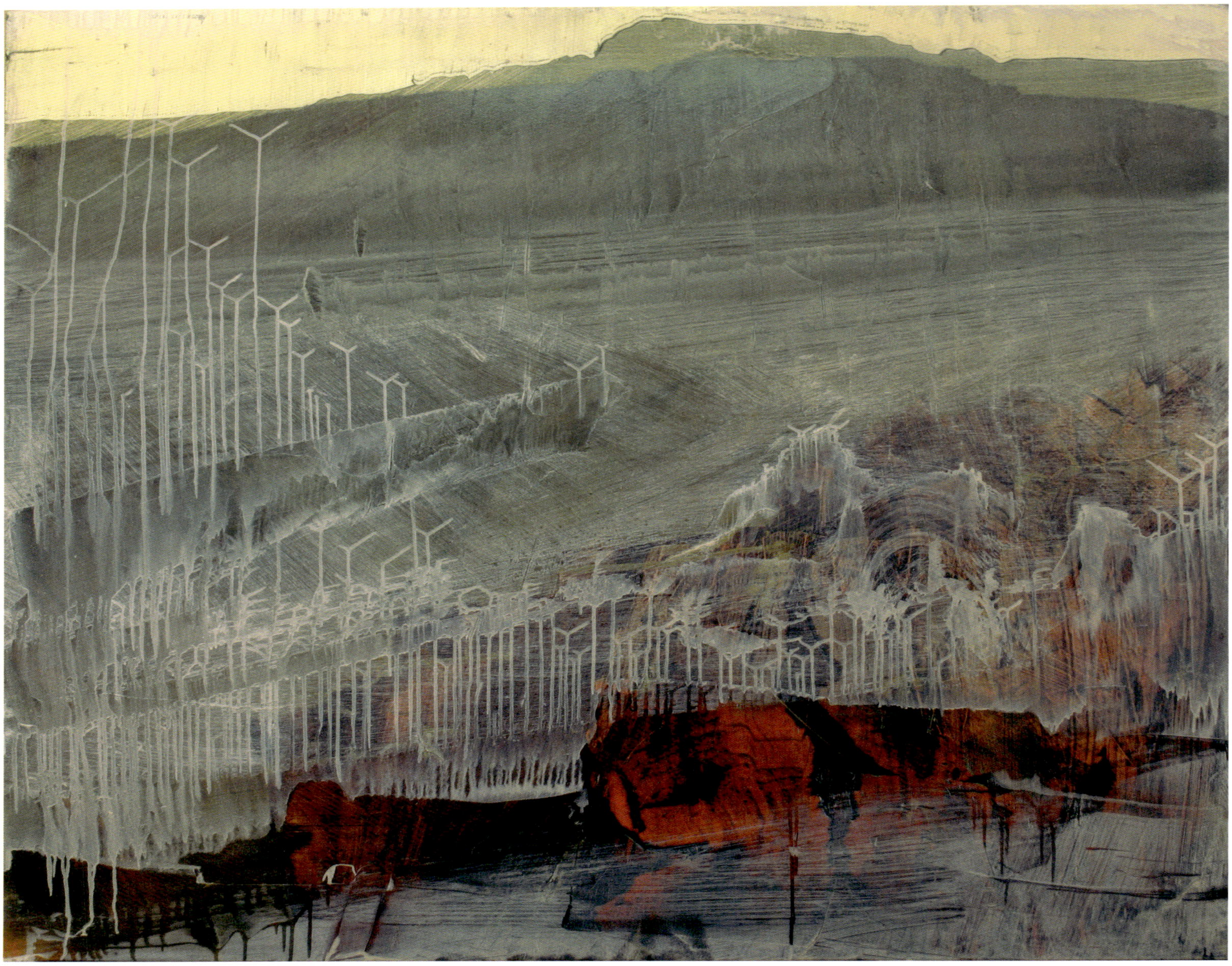

Plate 16: **Ice**, 2007. Oil on panel, 48 x 60 inches. Collection of the Hallie Ford Museum of Art, Willamette University, purchased with funds from an endowment gift from the Confederated Tribes of Grand Ronde, through their Spirit Mountain Community Fund.

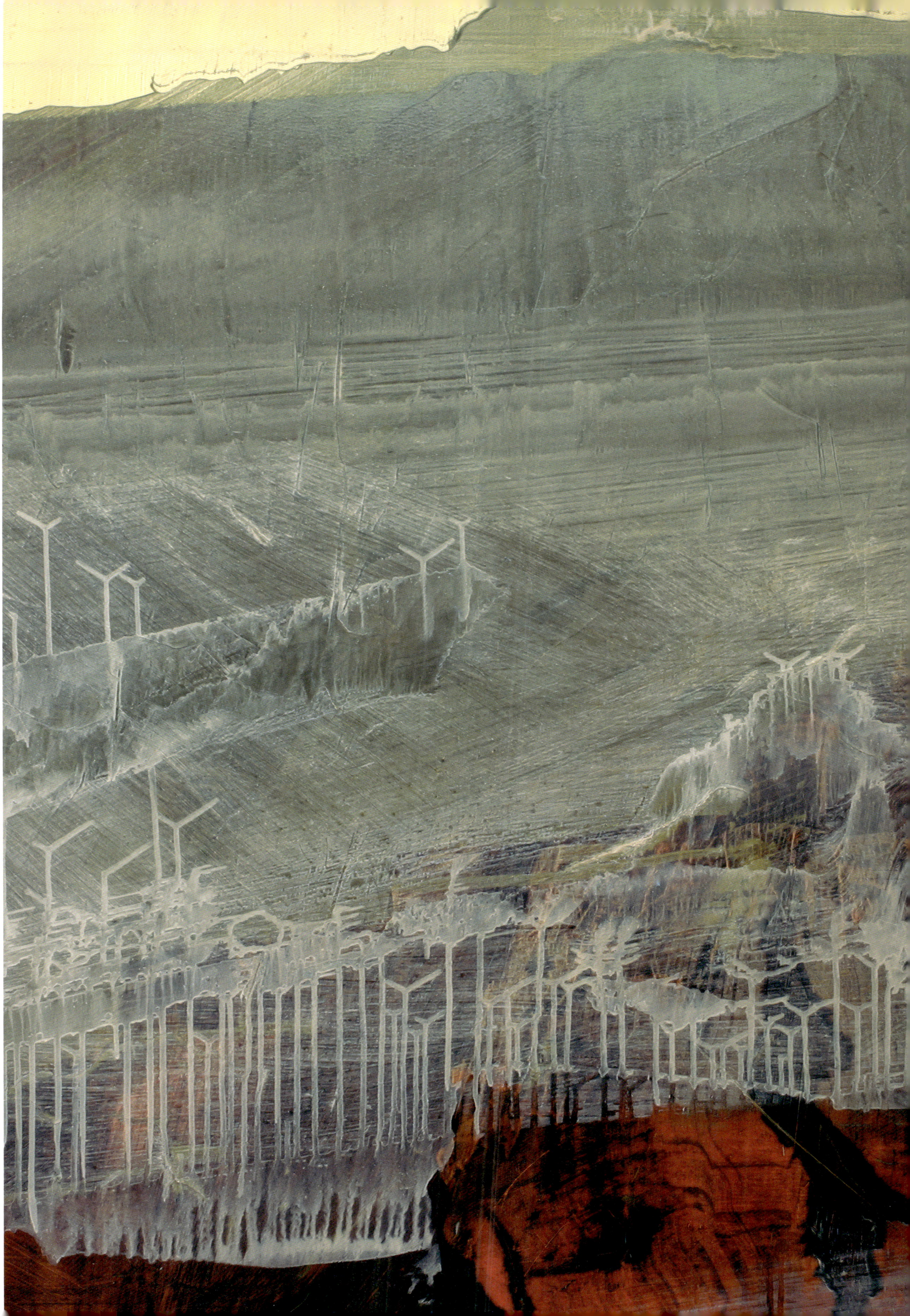

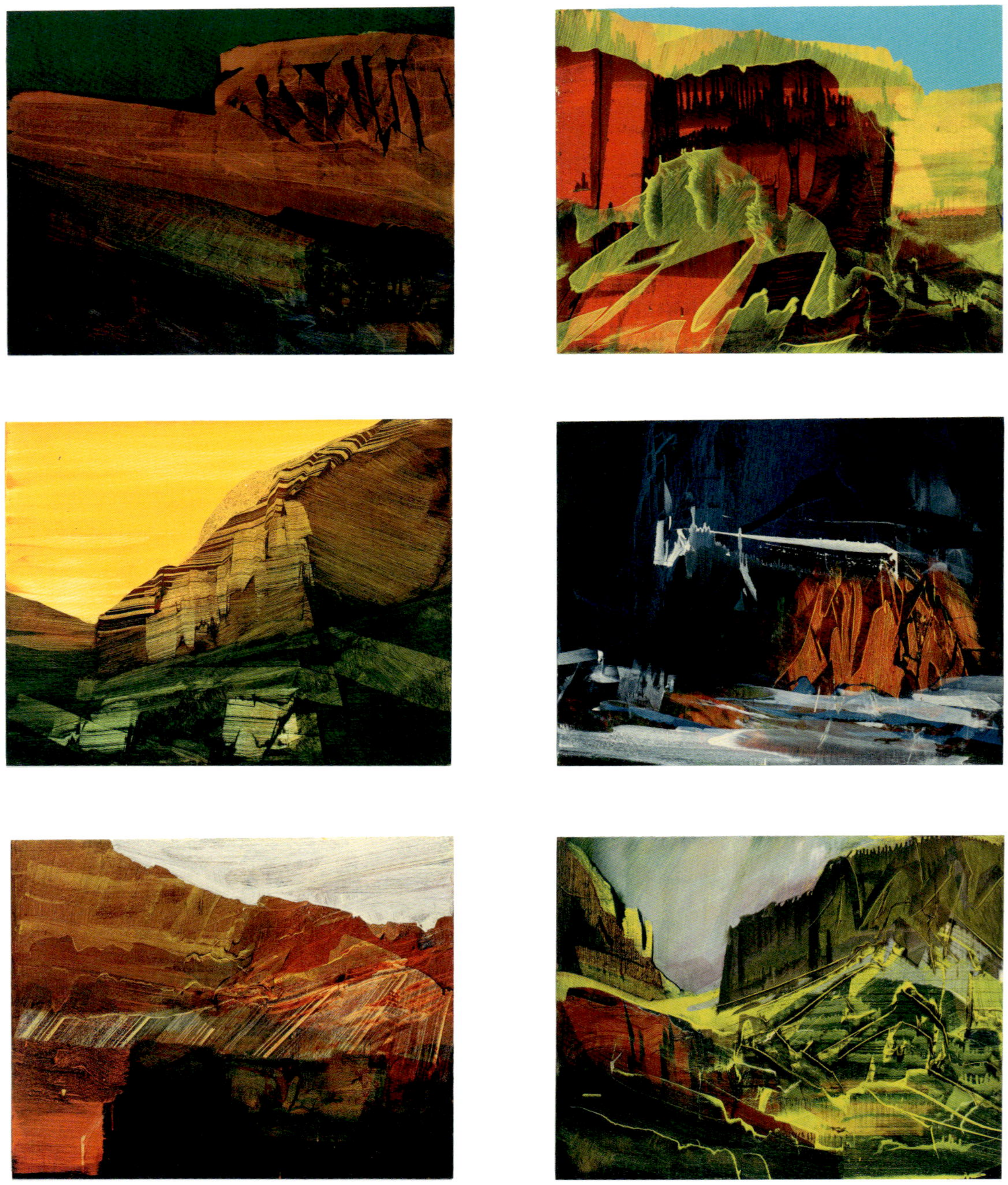

Plate 17: **Straight Ahead**, 2010. Oil on panel, 76 x 158 inches. Collection of Overmeyer-Dougher Family.

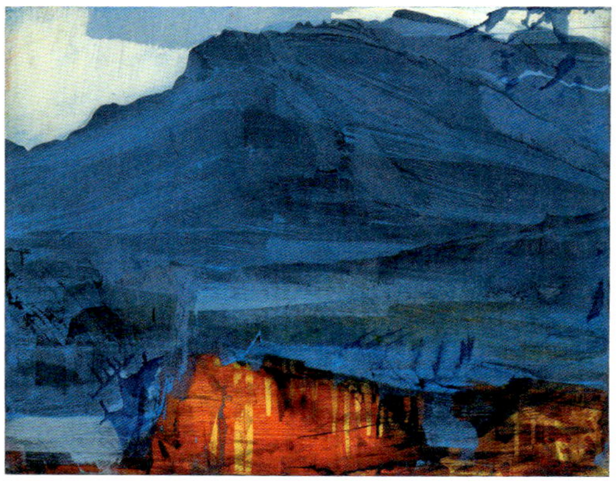
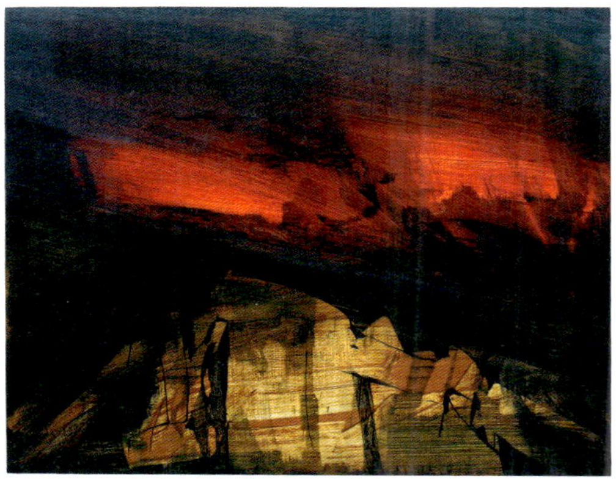
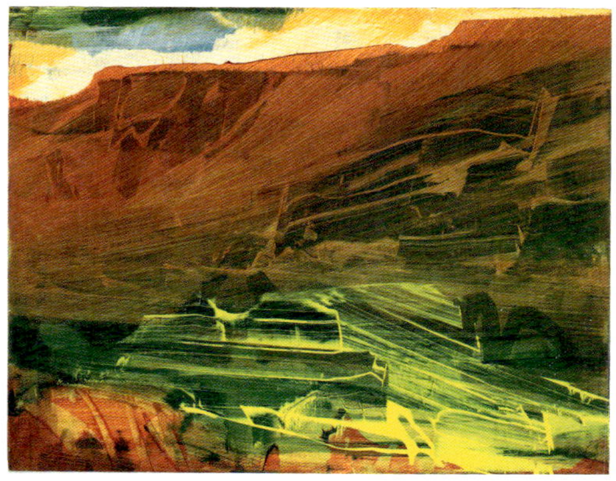
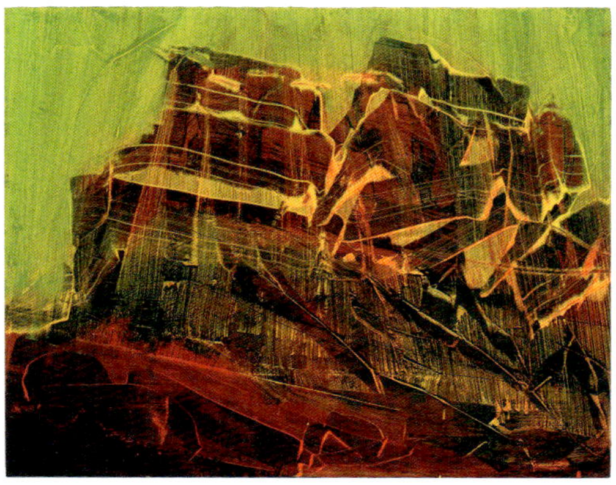
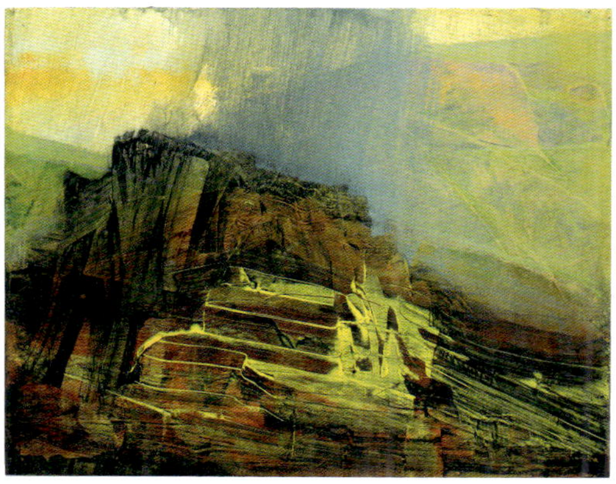
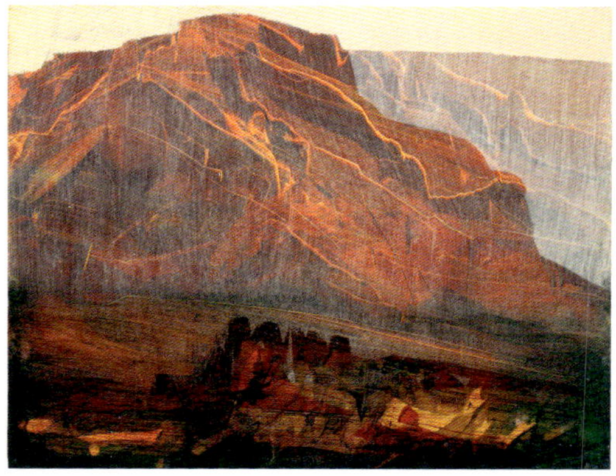
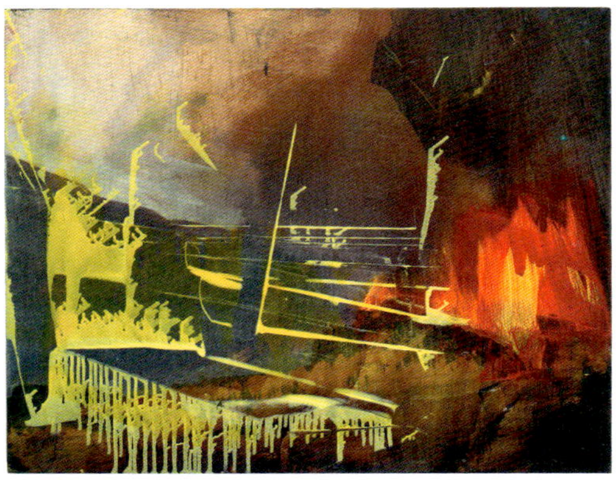
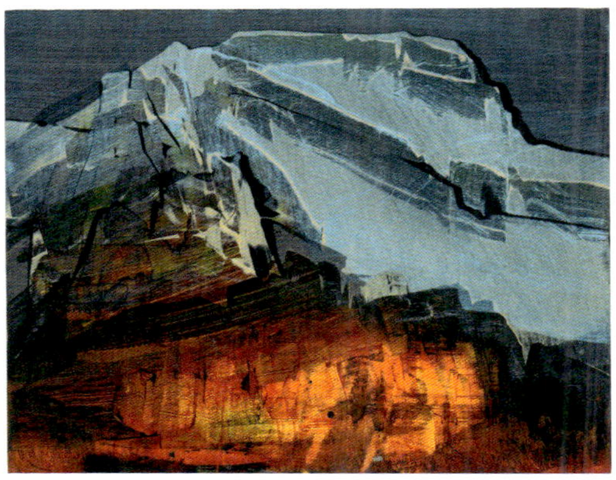
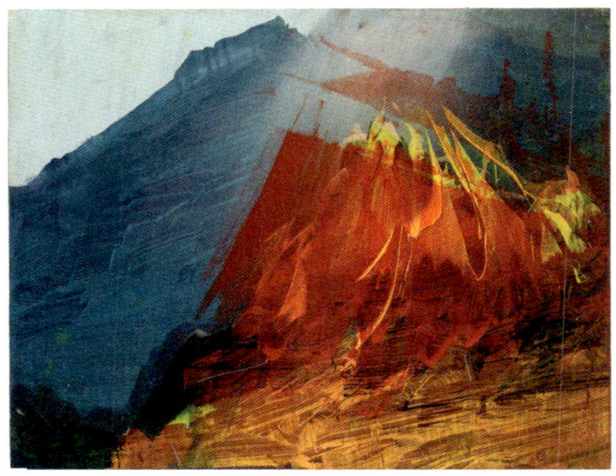

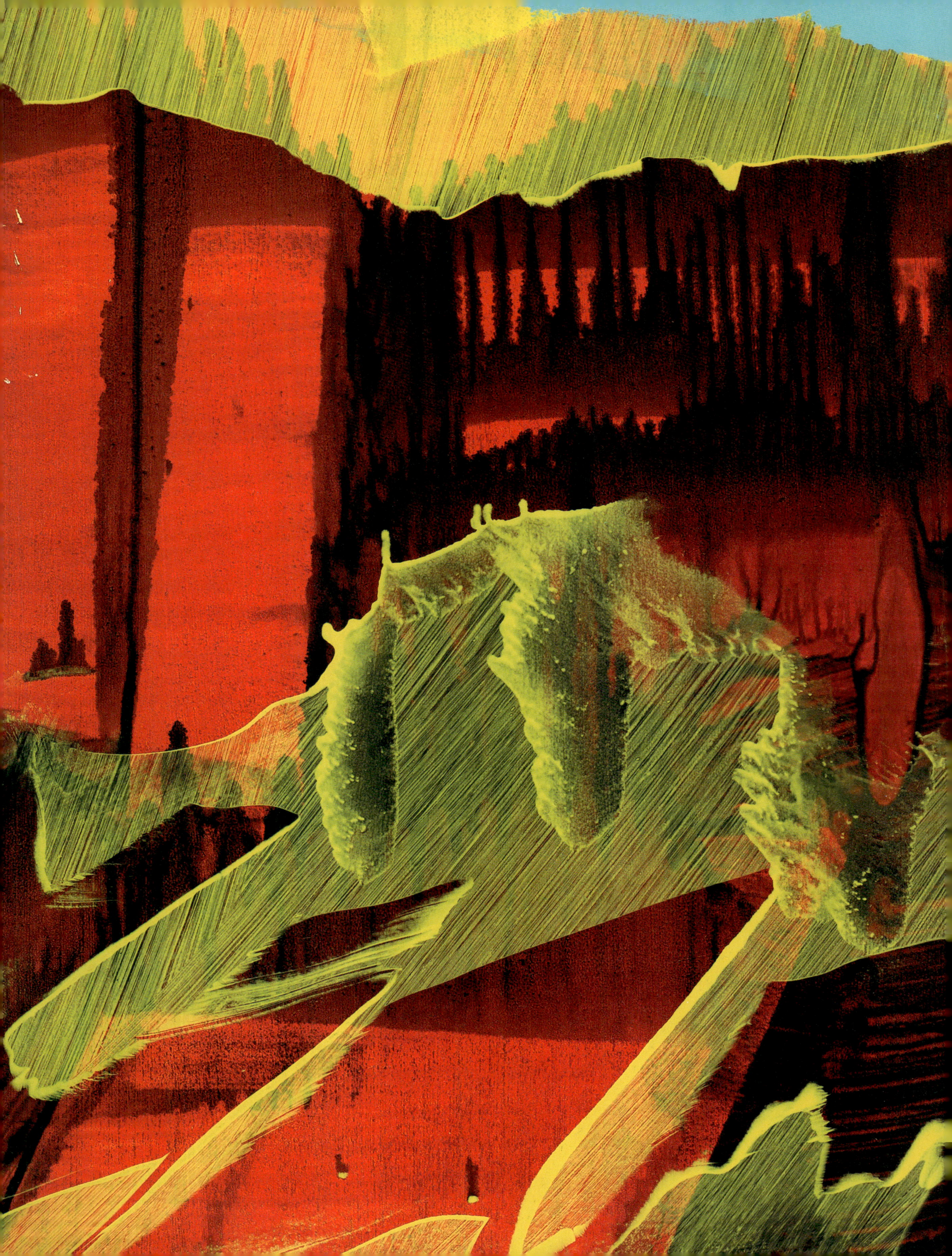

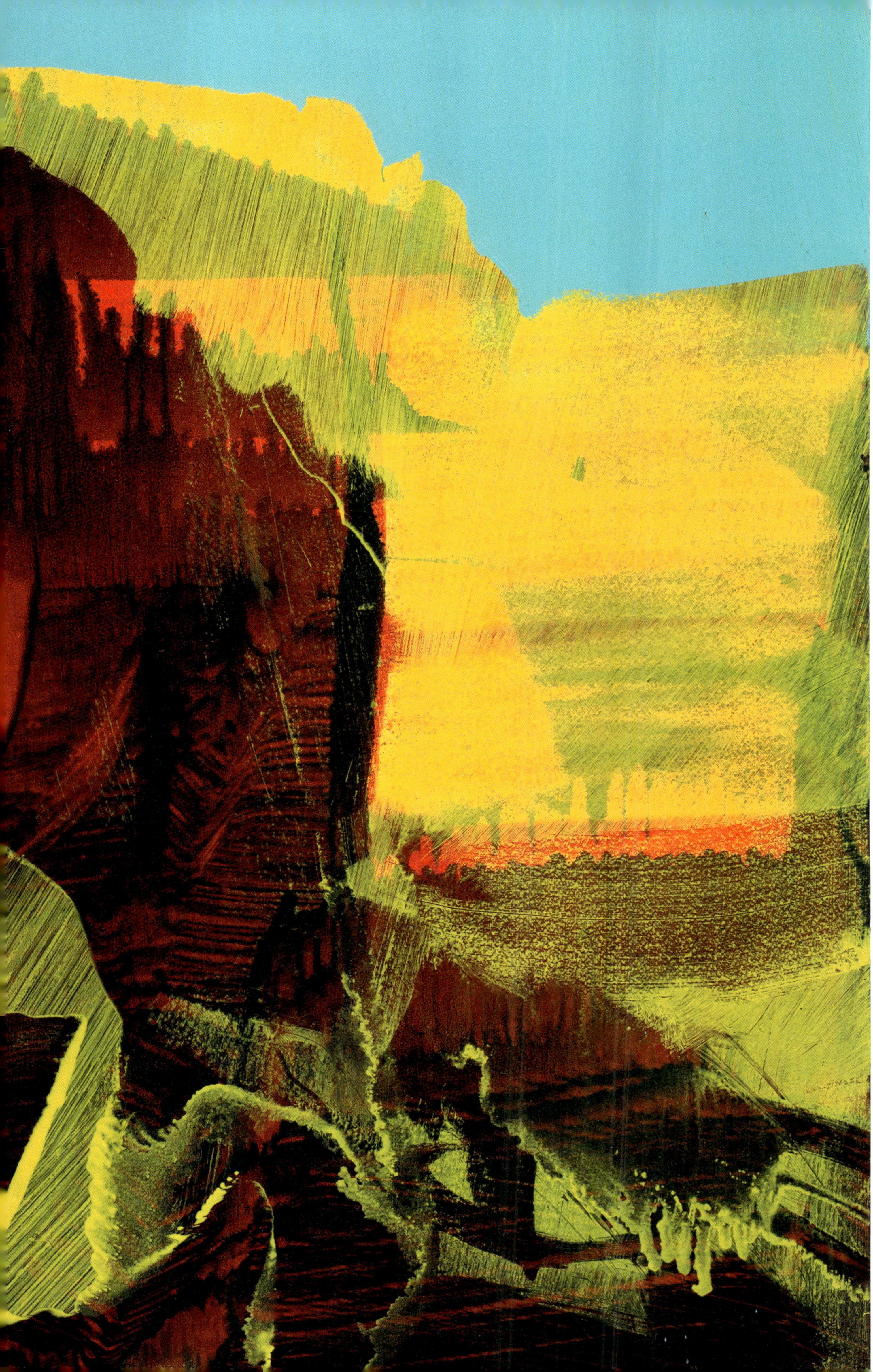

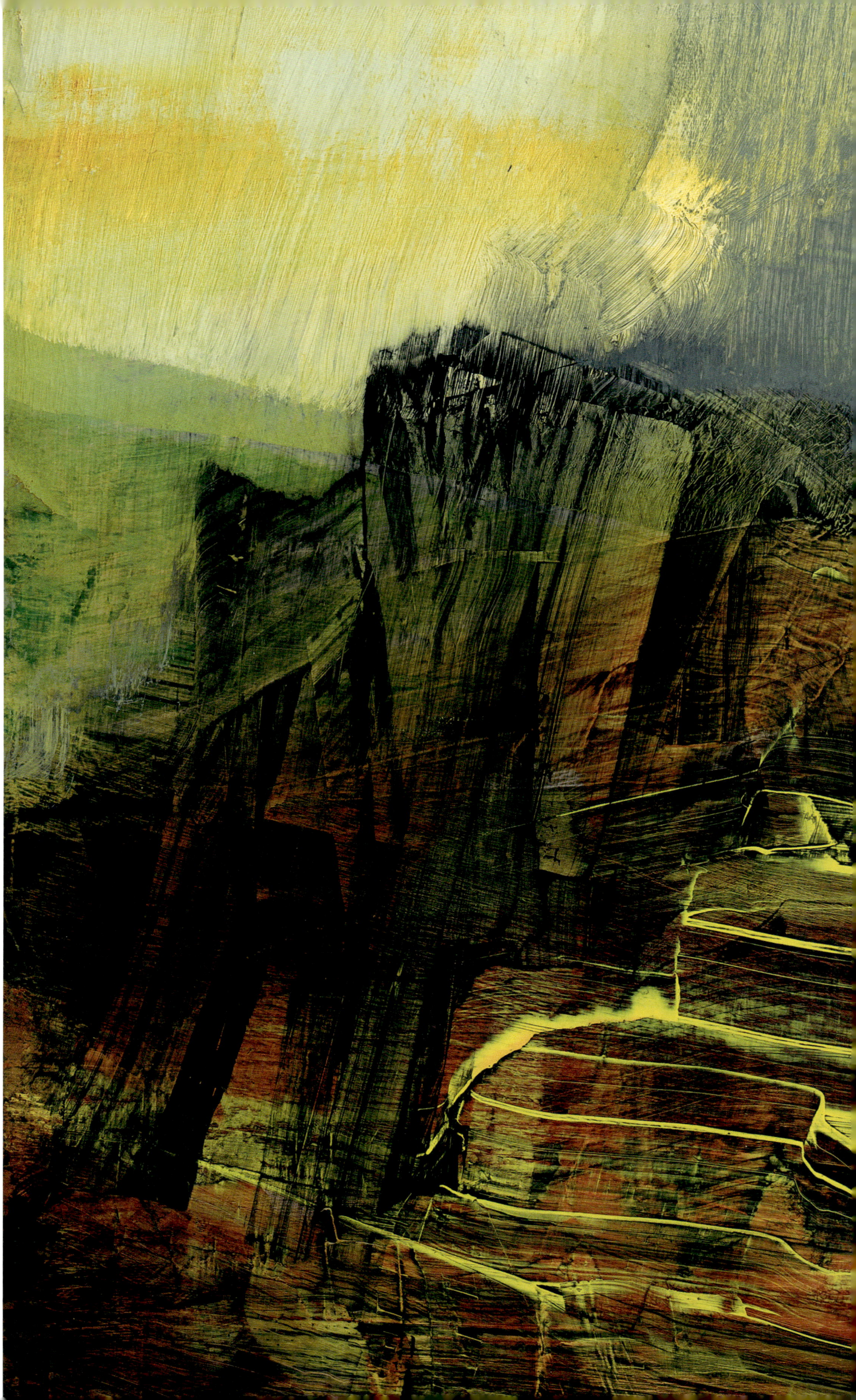

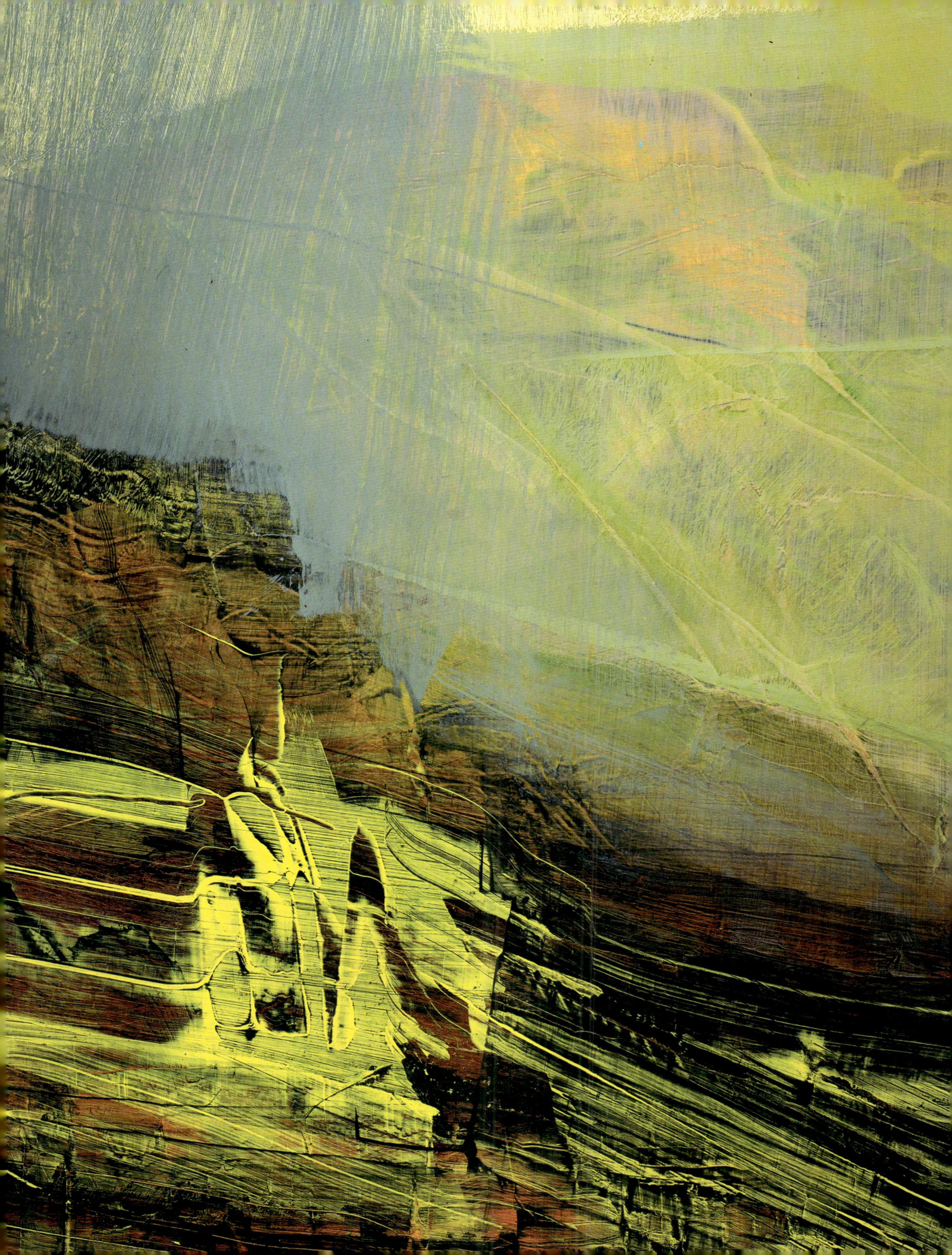

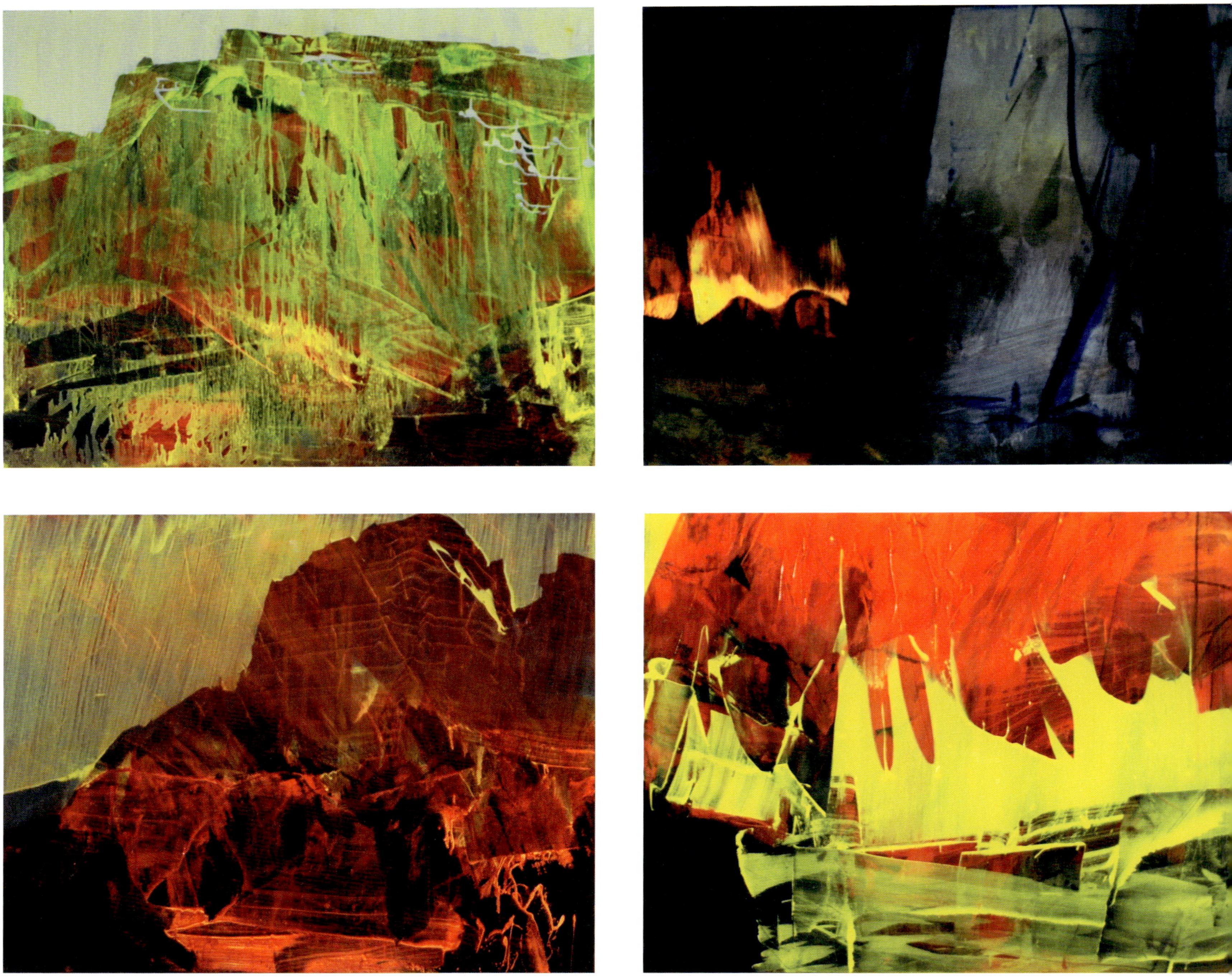

Plate 18: **Lift**, 2011. Oil on panel, 50 x 94 inches. Private Collection.

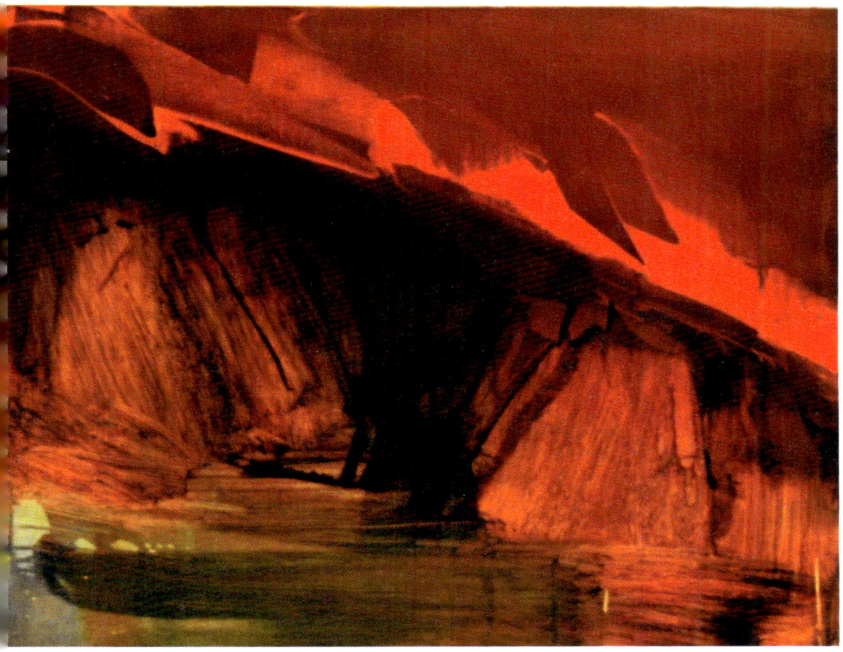

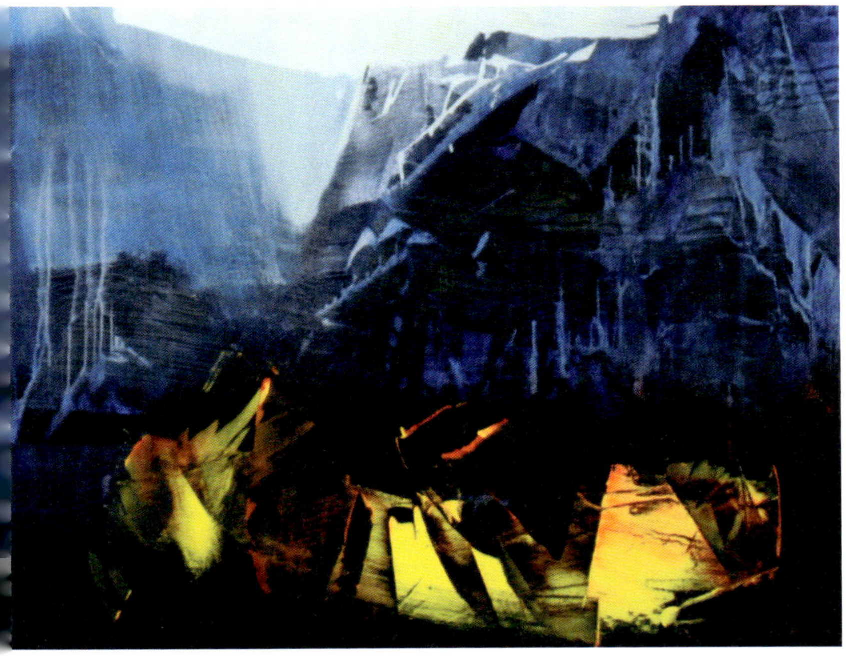

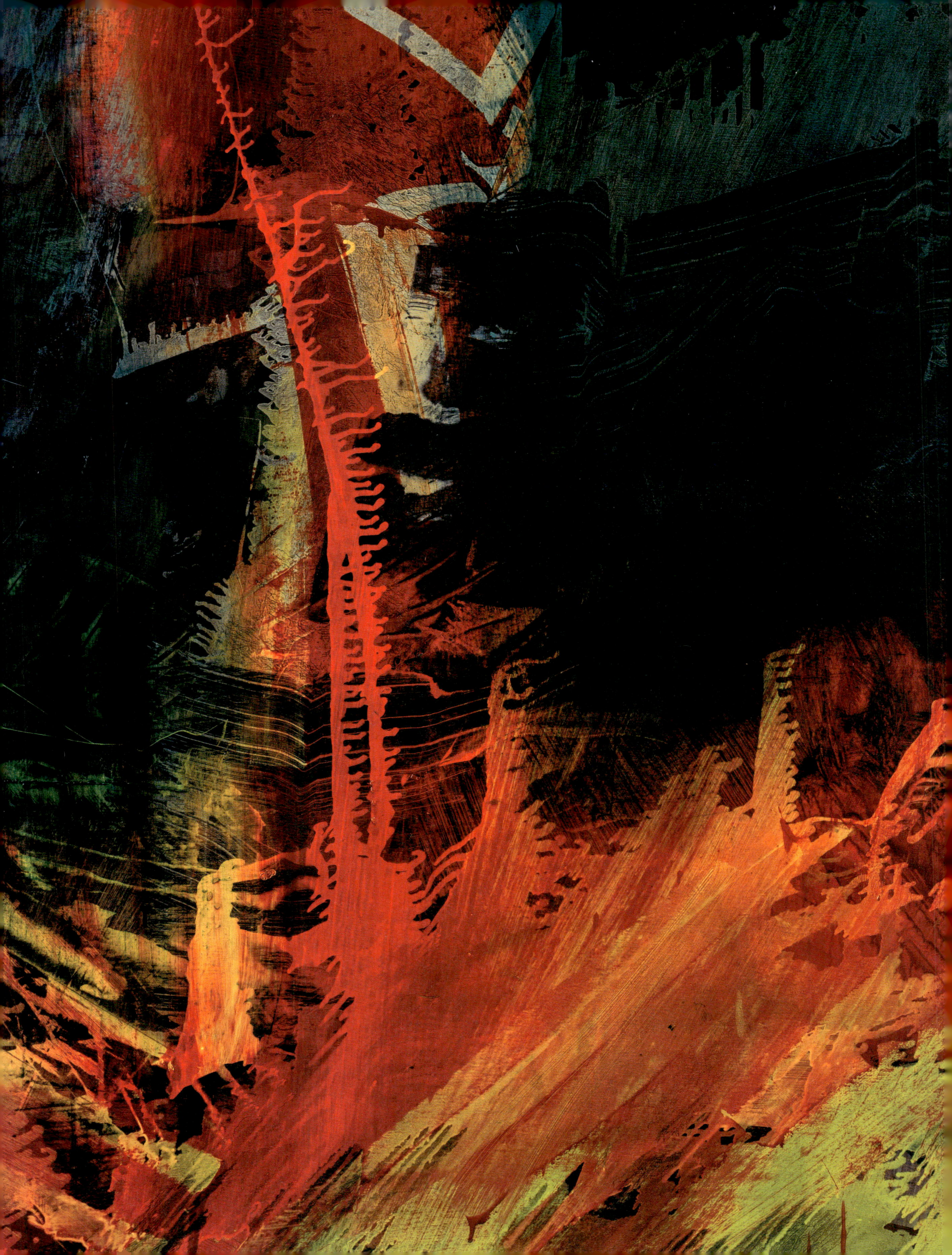

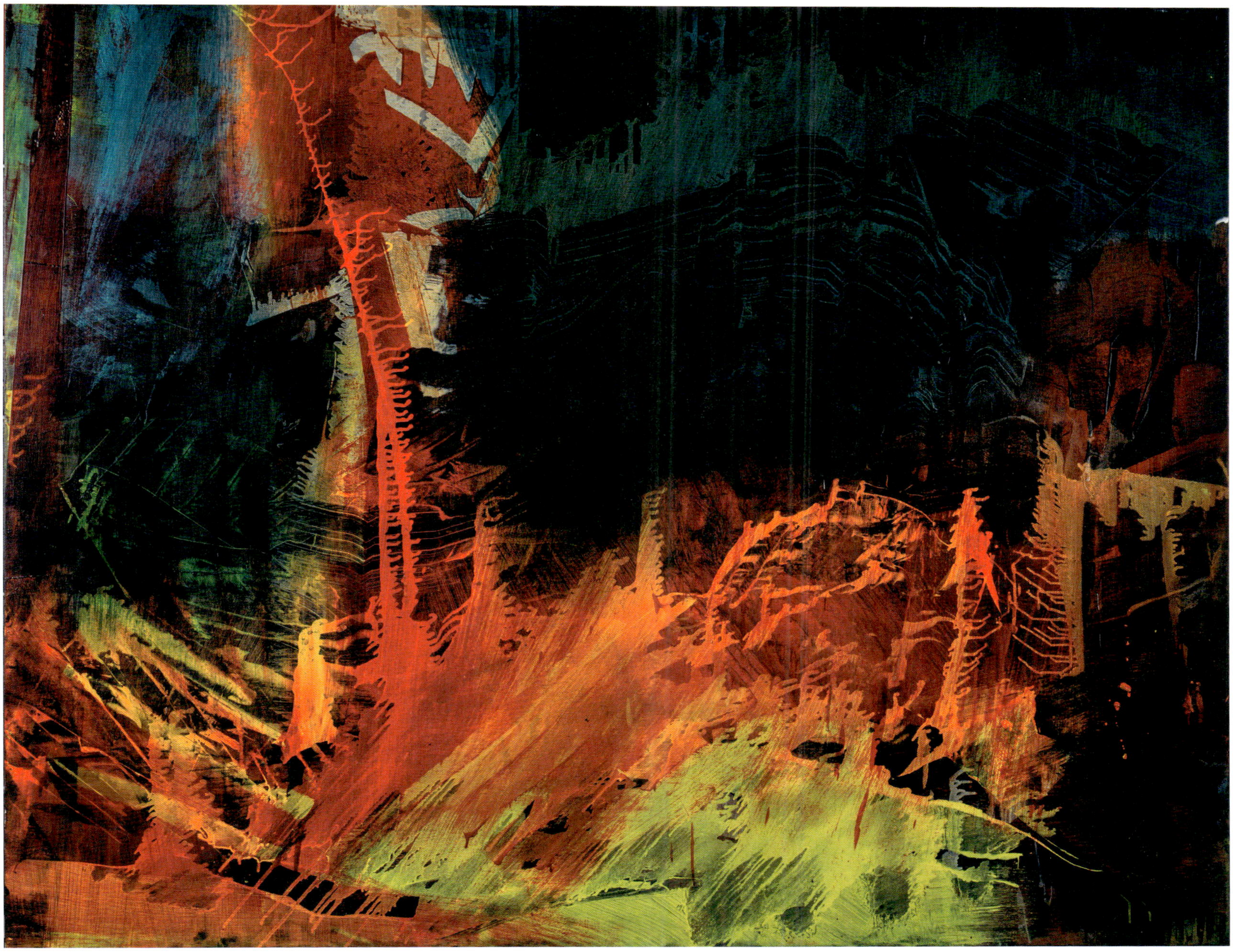

Plate 19: **Torch**, 2012. Oil on panel, 48 x 60 inches. Jordan Schnitzer Museum of Art, University of Oregon: Acquired with the assistance of The Ford Family Foundation, through a special grant program managed by the Oregon Arts Commission, and the Van Duyn Acquisition Endowment; 2015:9.1.

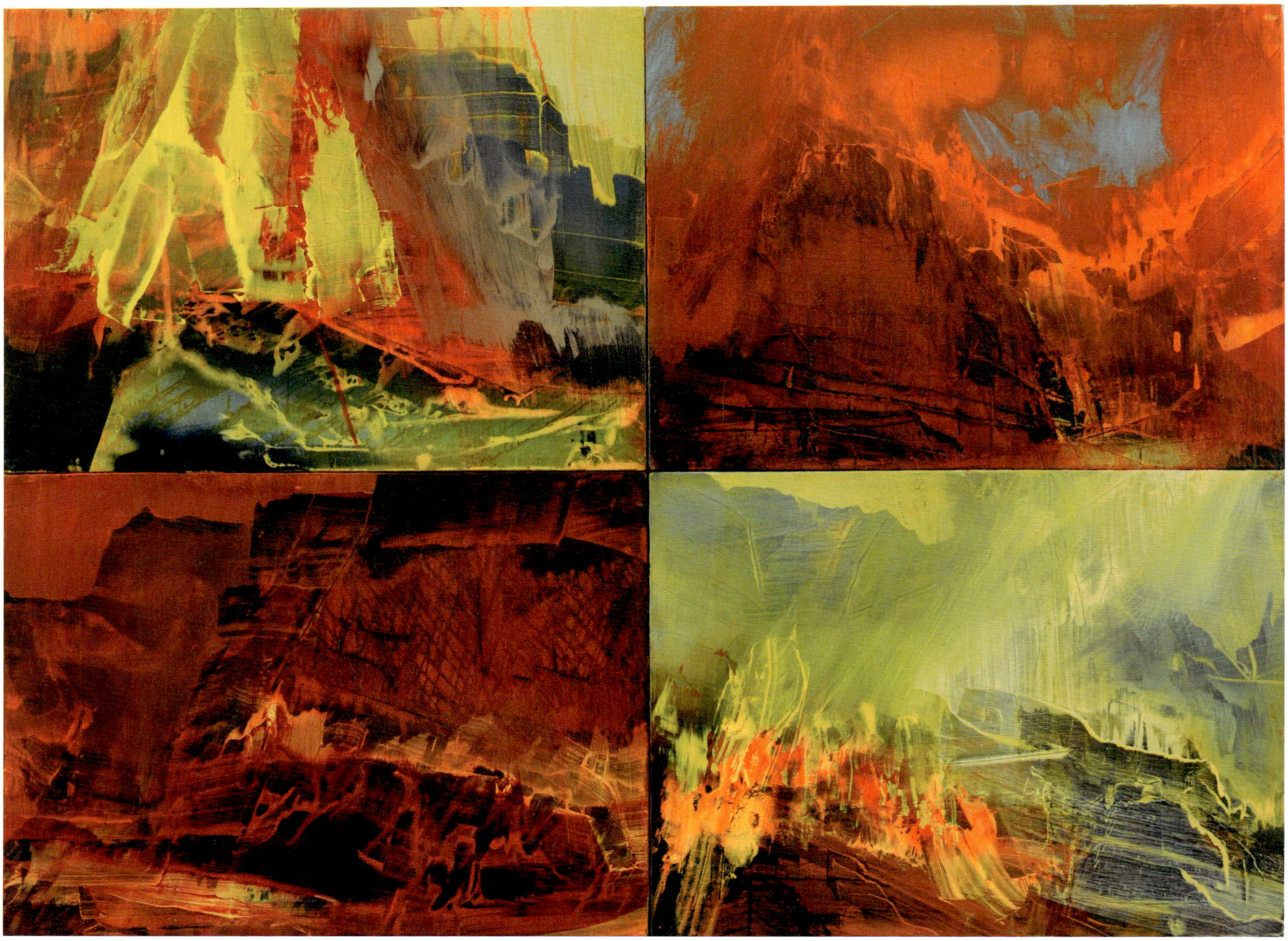

Plate 20: **Out of Range**, 2013. Oil on panel, 36 x 48 x 2 inches. Crystal Bridges Museum of American Art, Bentonville, Arkansas, 2021.42.

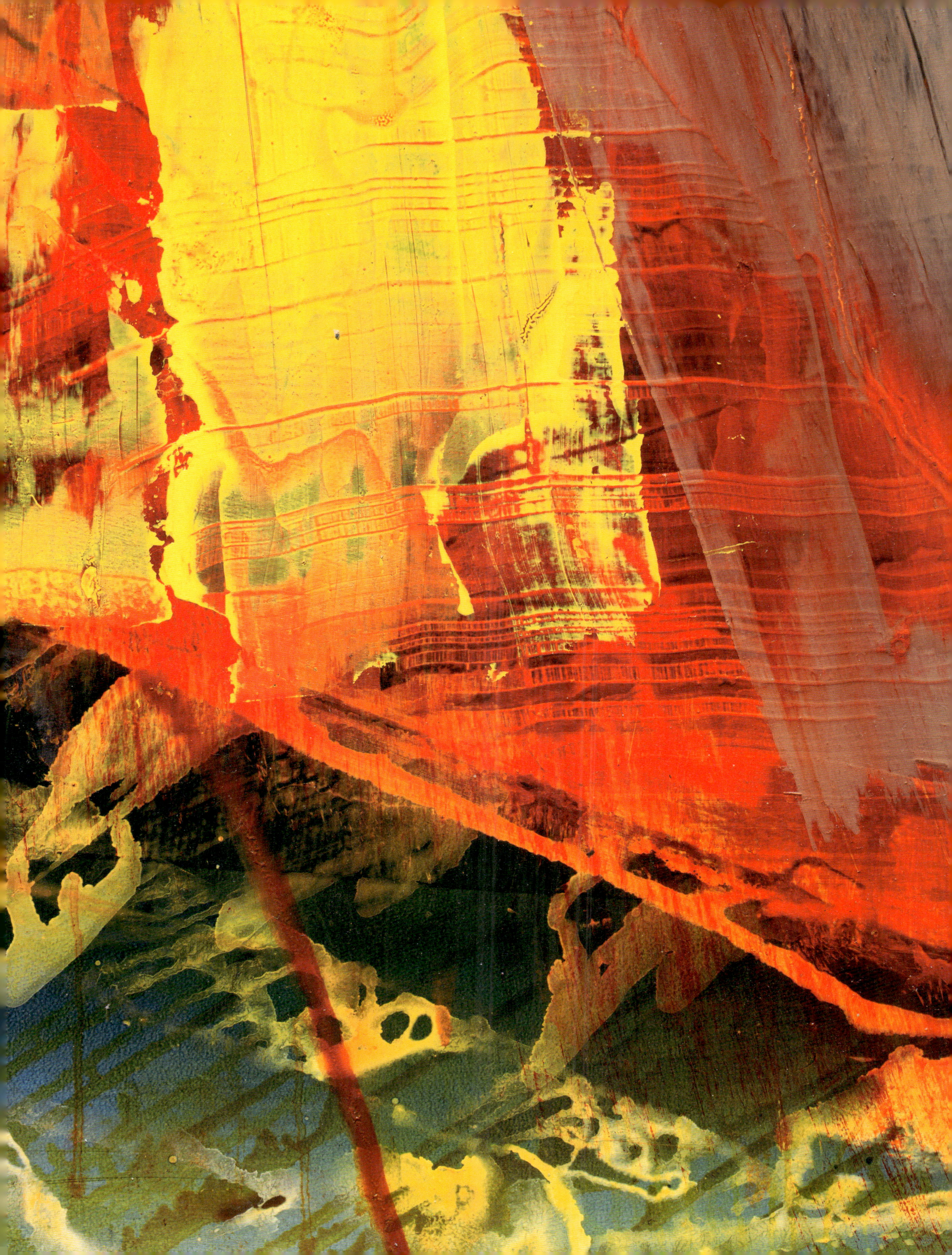

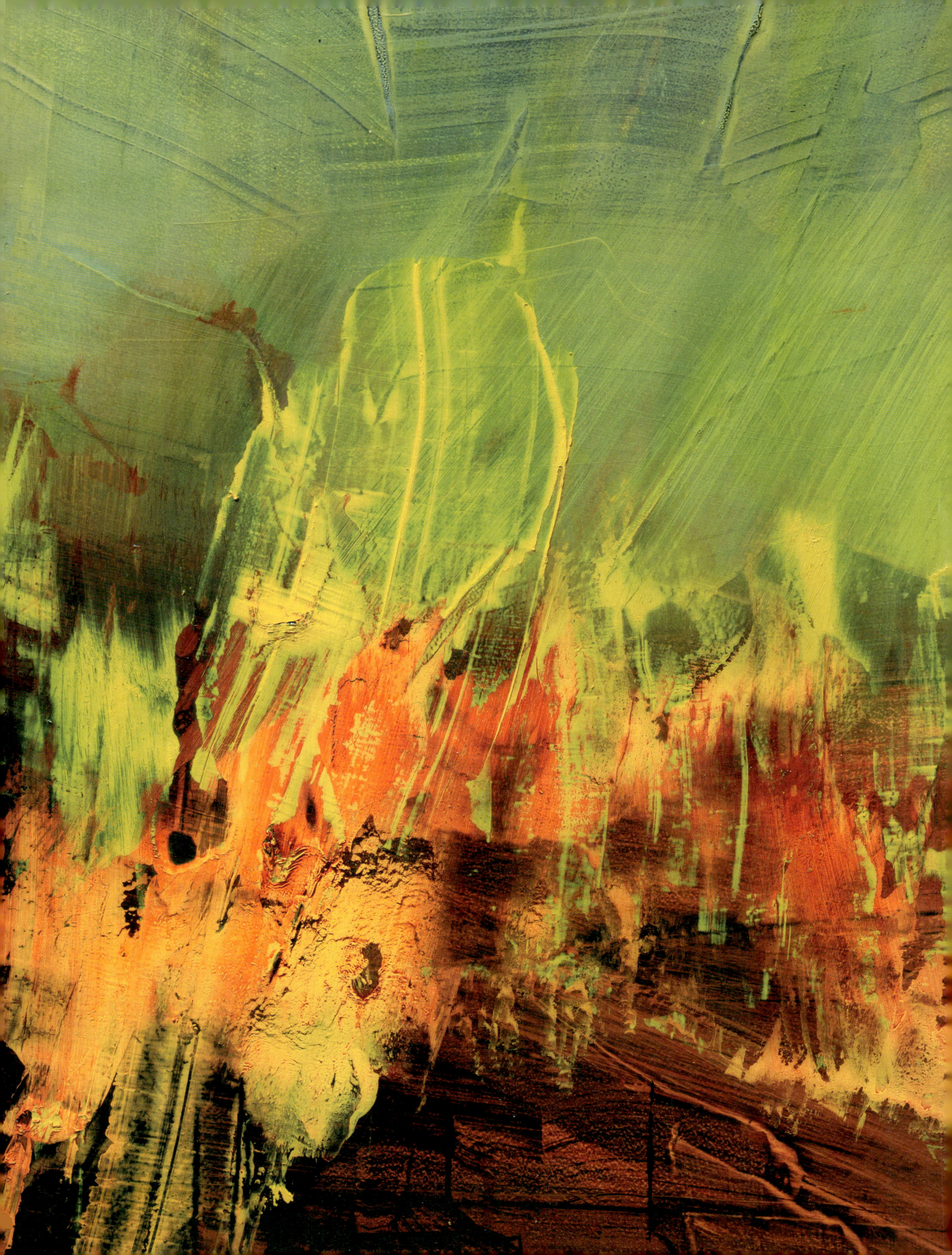

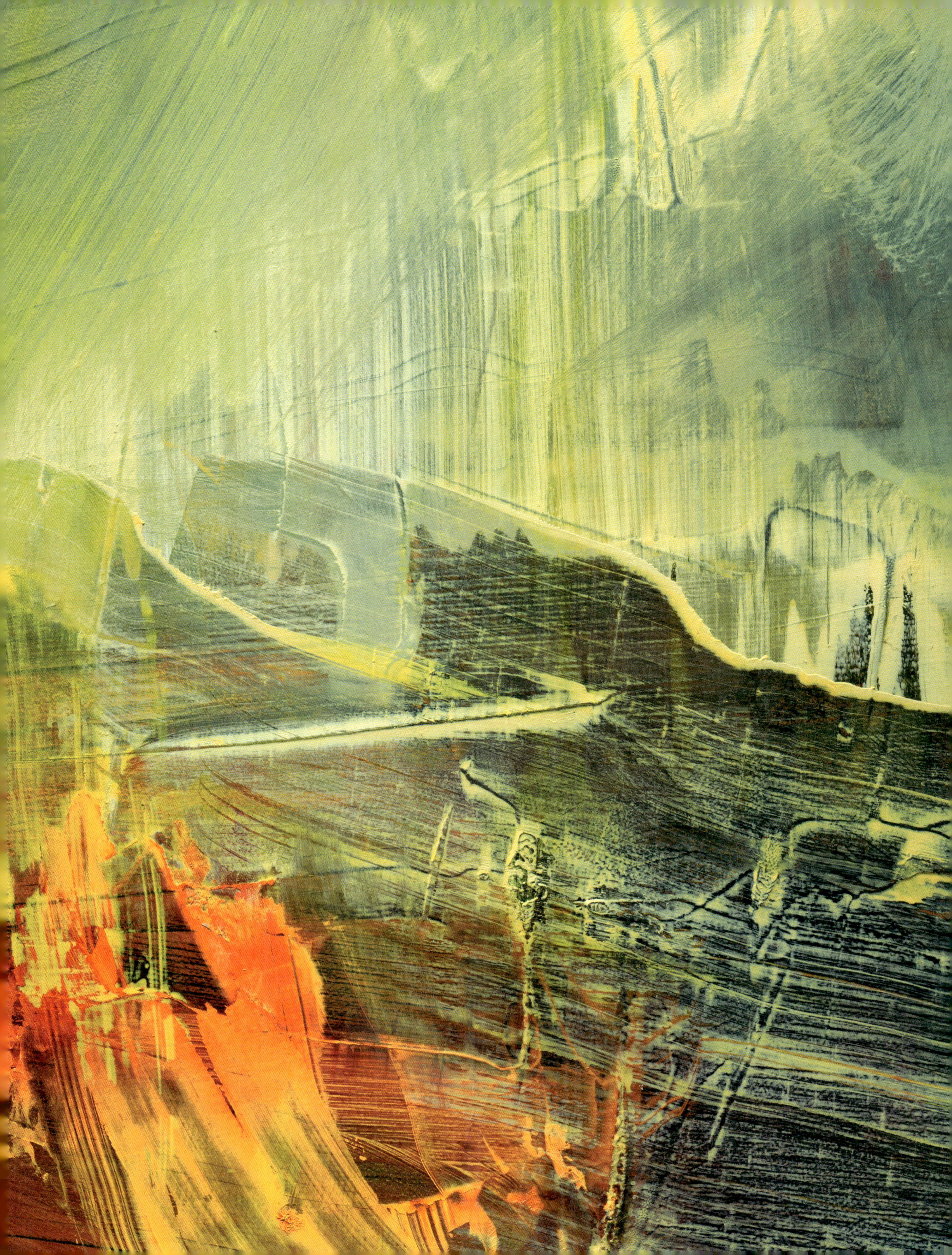

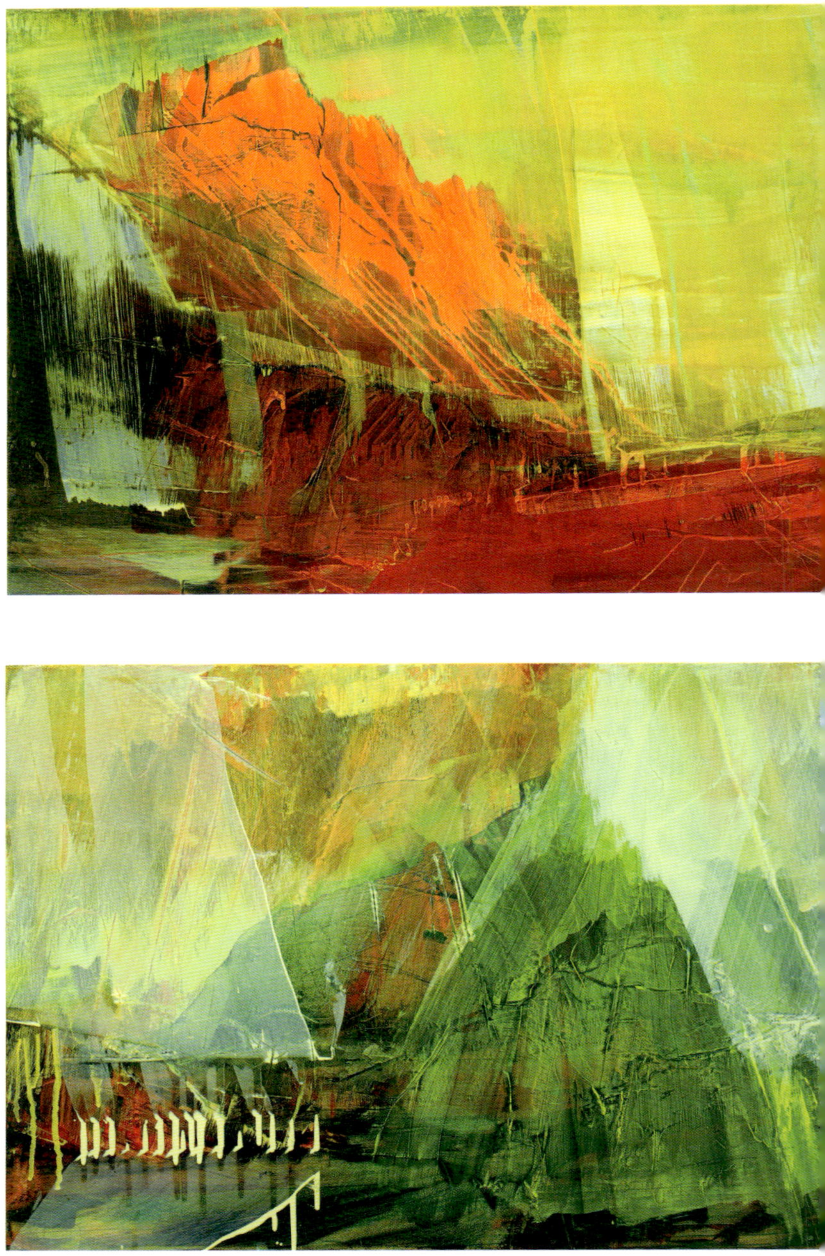

Plate 21: **Land of Origin**, 2015. Oil on panel, 39 x 78 inches. Jane and Spencer Beebe Family Trust.

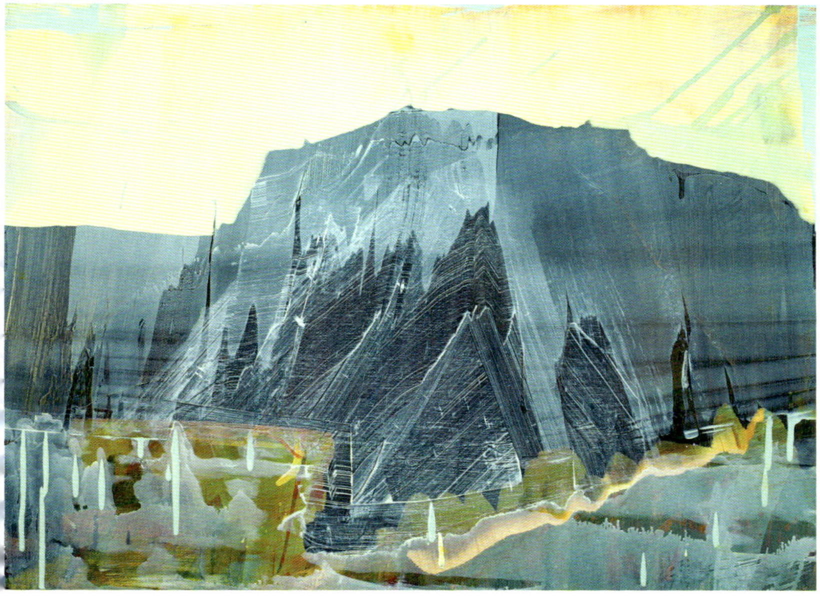
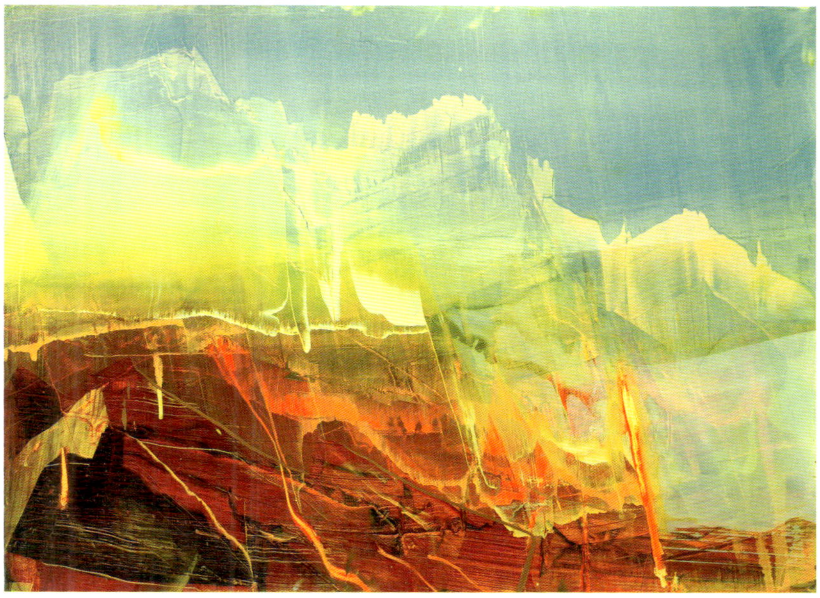
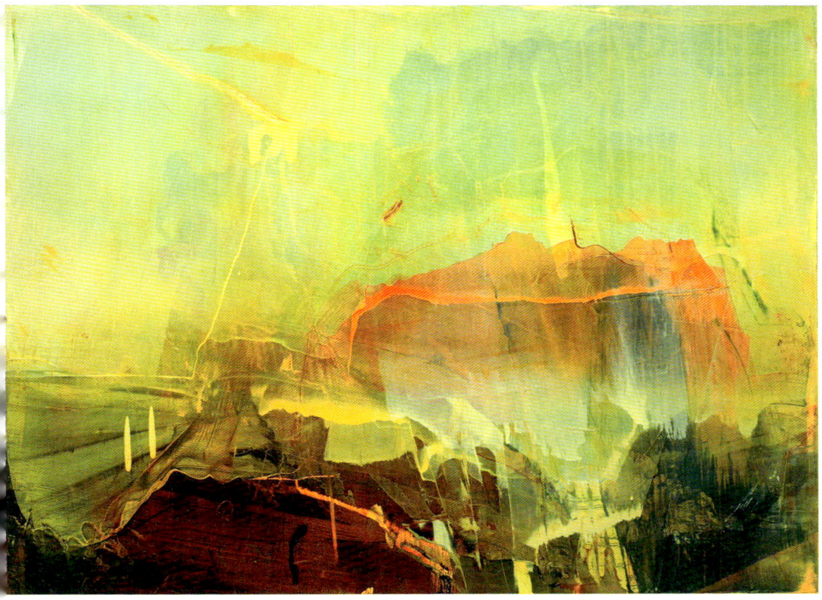
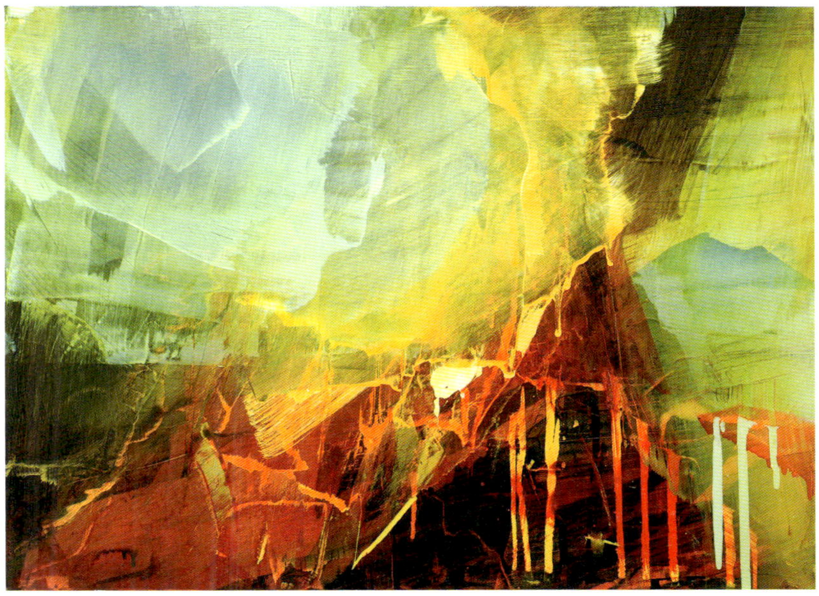

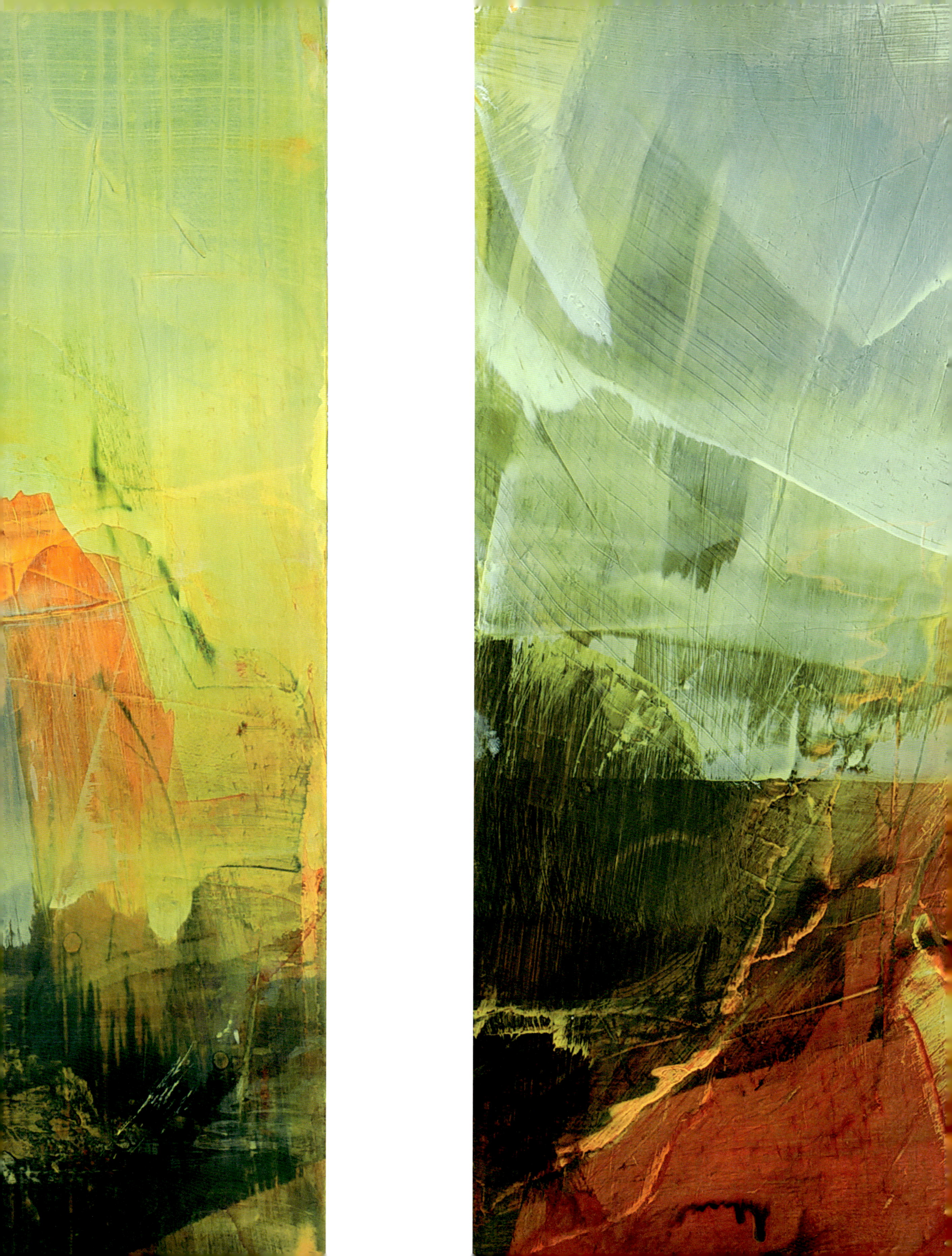

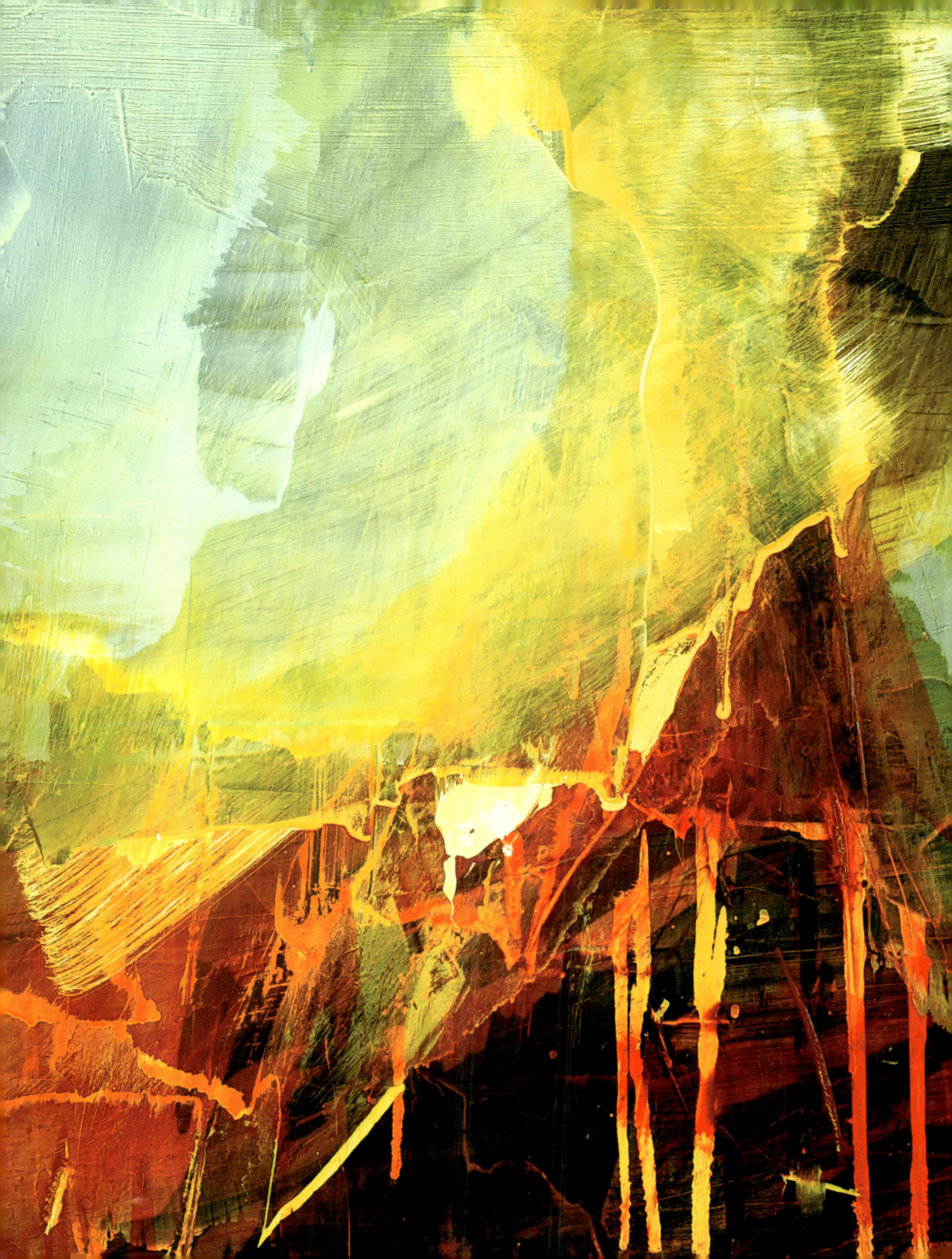

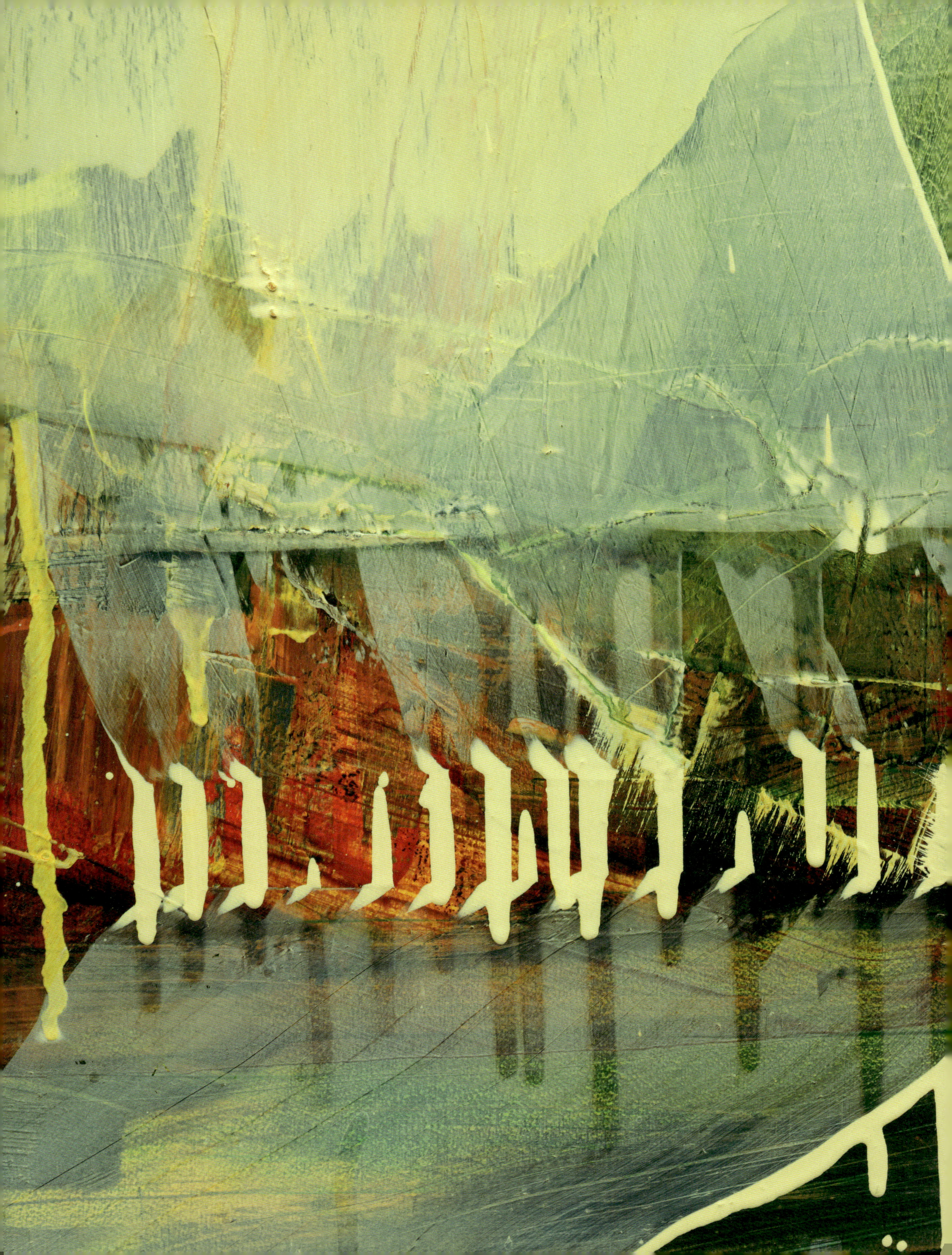

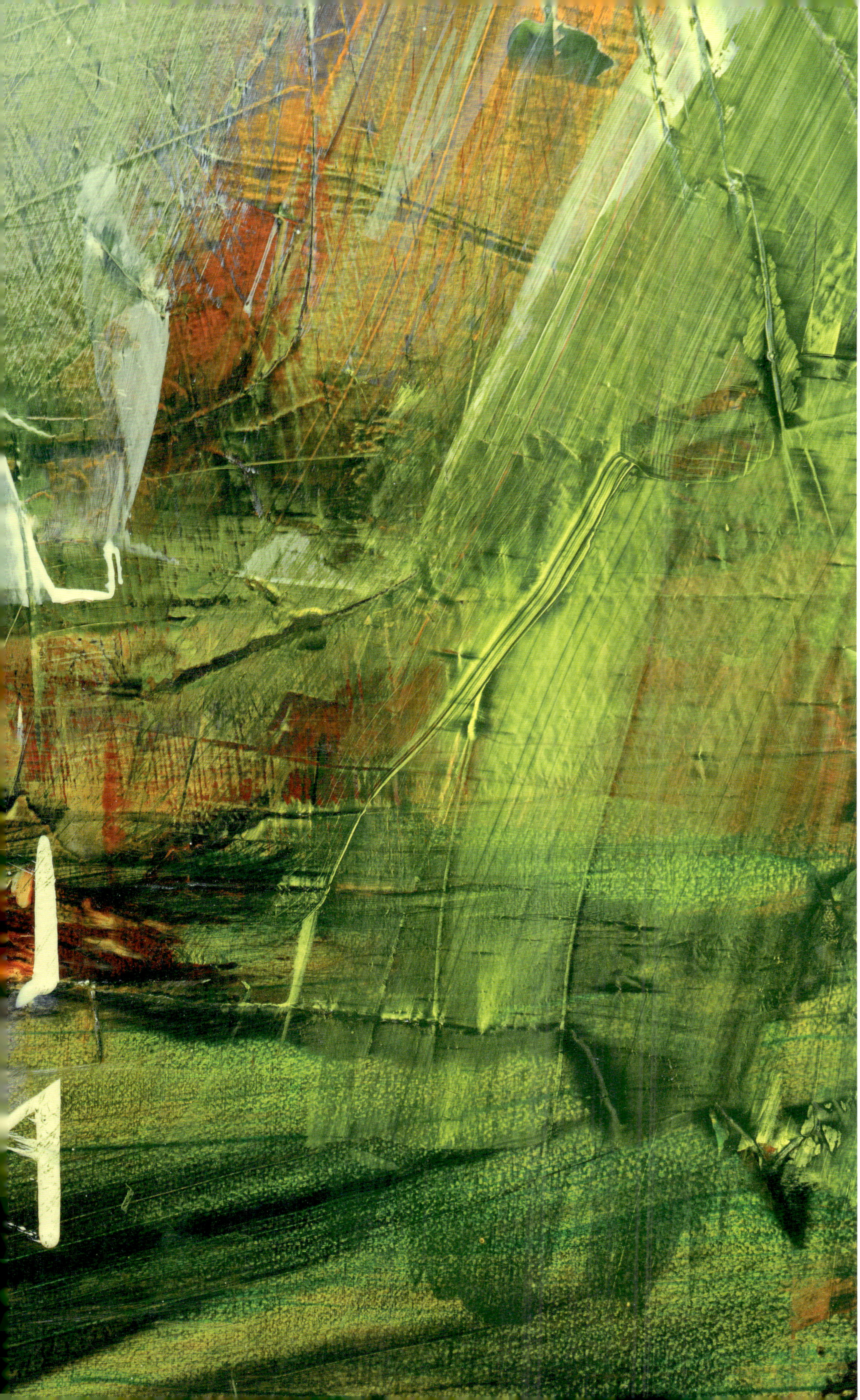

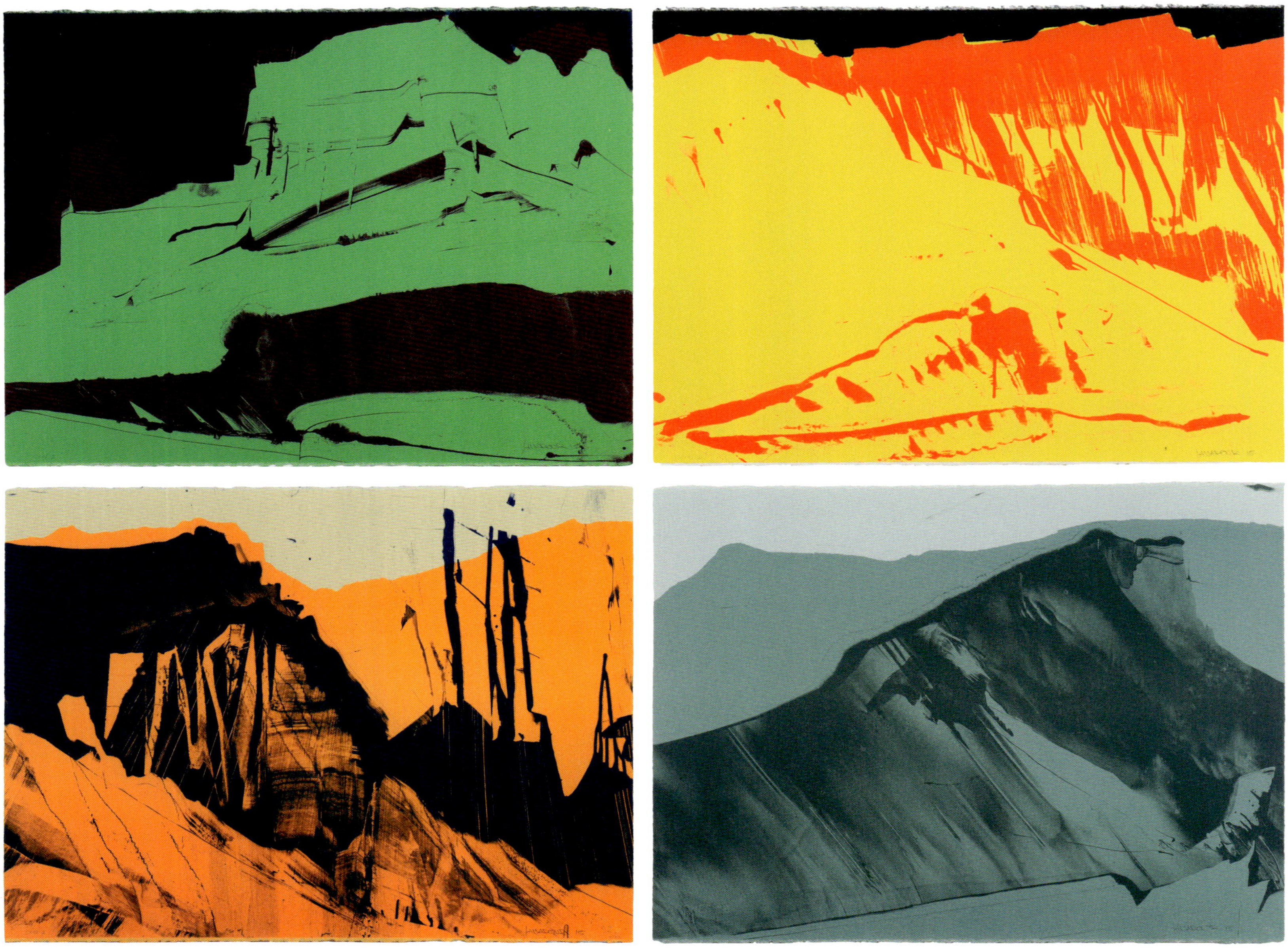

Plate 22: **Land of Origin**, ed. 2/18, 2015. Lithograph, 45 x 60½ inches. Published at Crow's Shadow Institute of the Arts. Collaborating Master Printer: Frank Janzen. Crow's Shadow Institute of the Arts Archive, Hallie Ford Museum of Art, Willamette University.

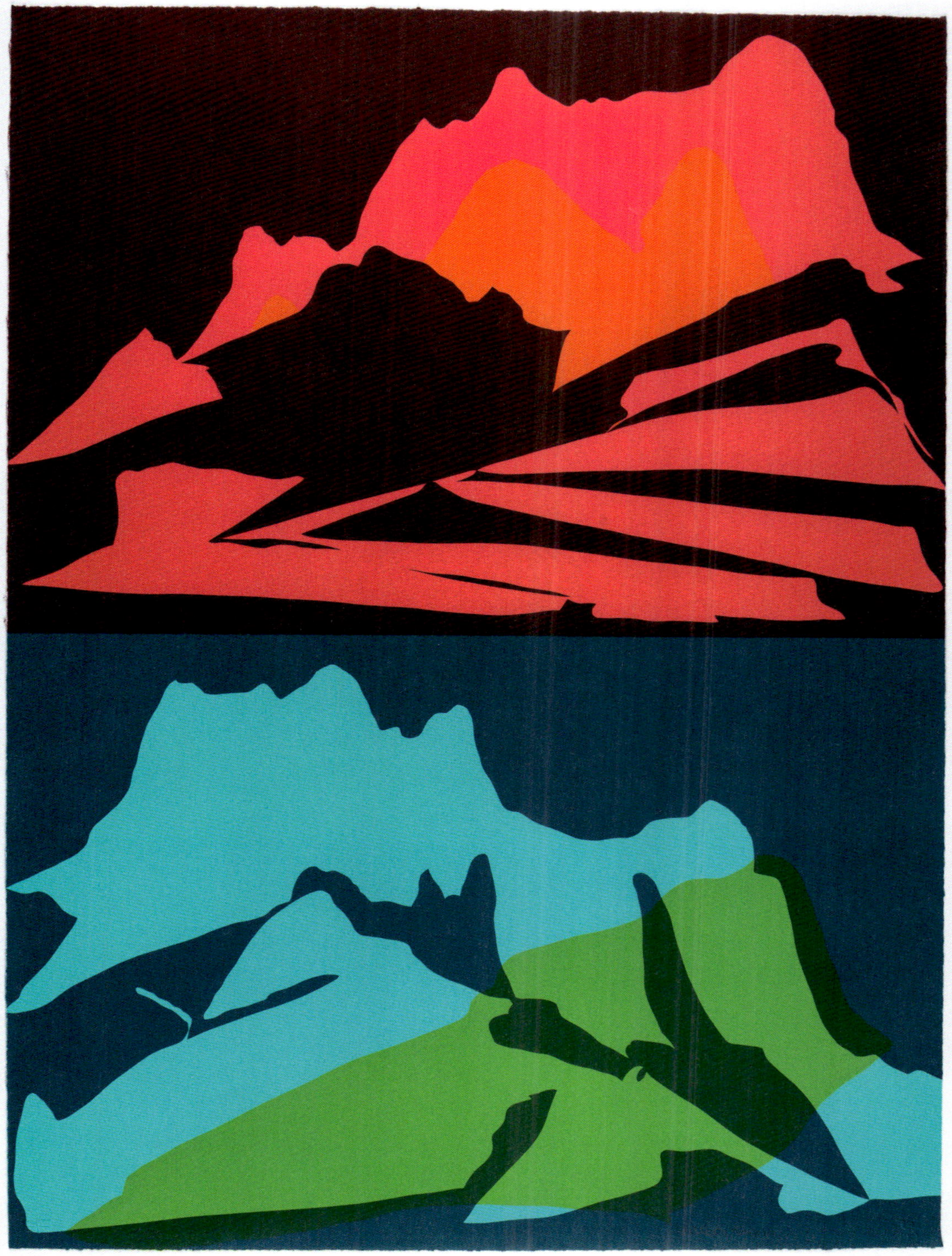

Plate 23: **Summer**, ed. 8/30, 2018-19. Six color lithograph on Somerset Satin White, 30 x 22 inches. Published at Crow's Shadow Institute of the Arts. Collaborating Master Printer: Judith Baumann. Jordan Schnitzer Museum of Art, University of Oregon: Purchased with funds from the William A. Haseltine Endowment for Pacific Northwest Art.

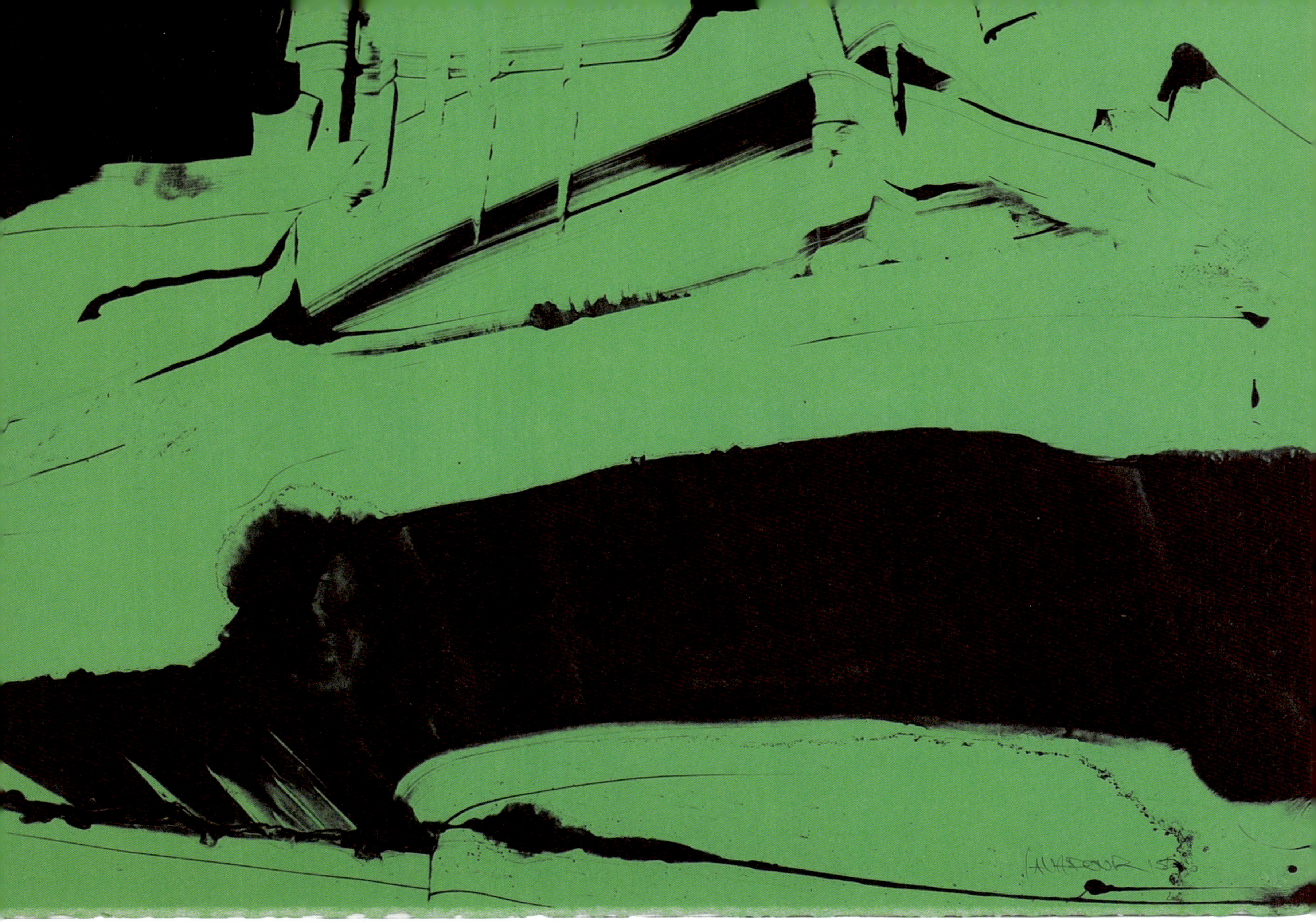

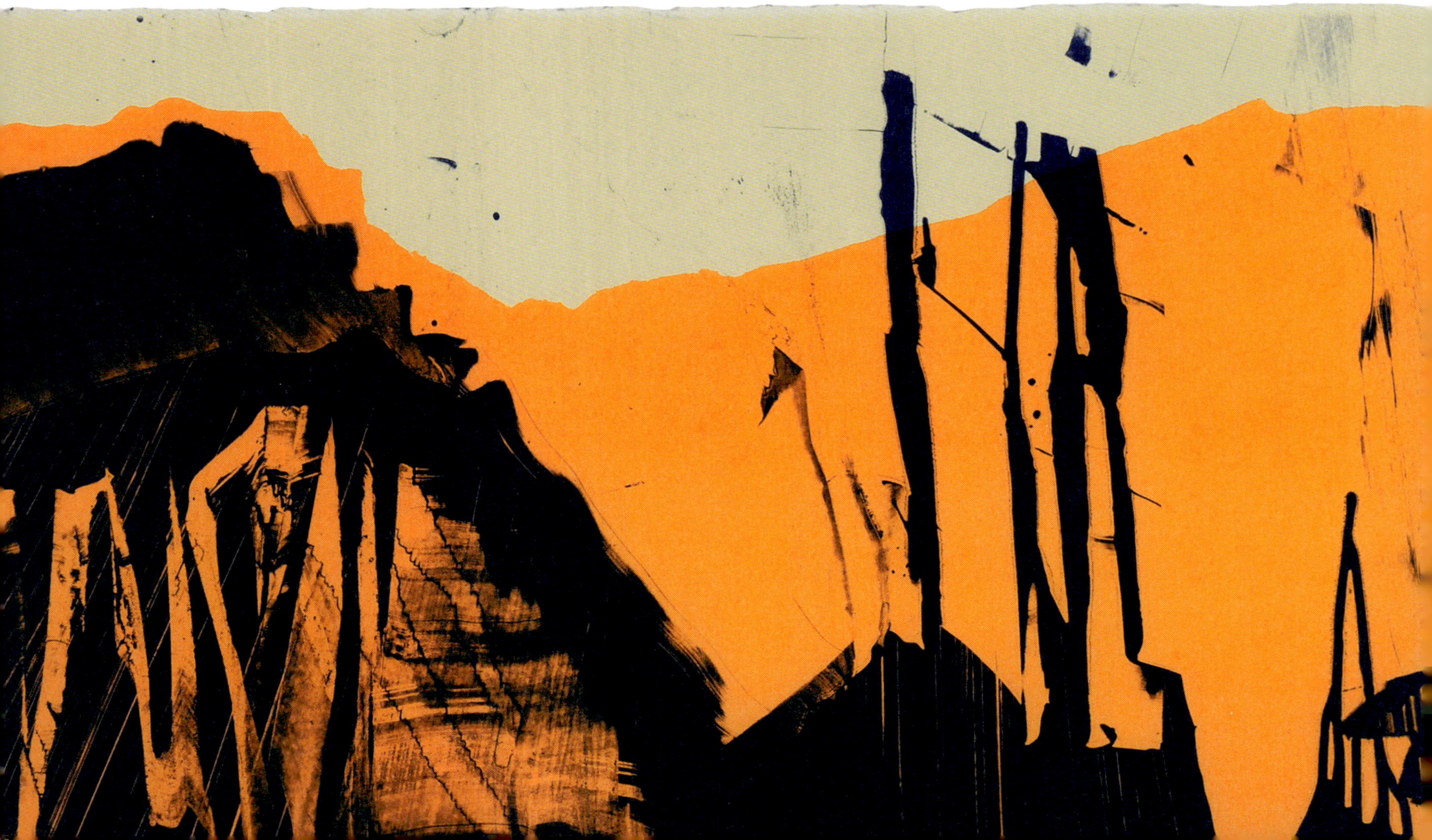

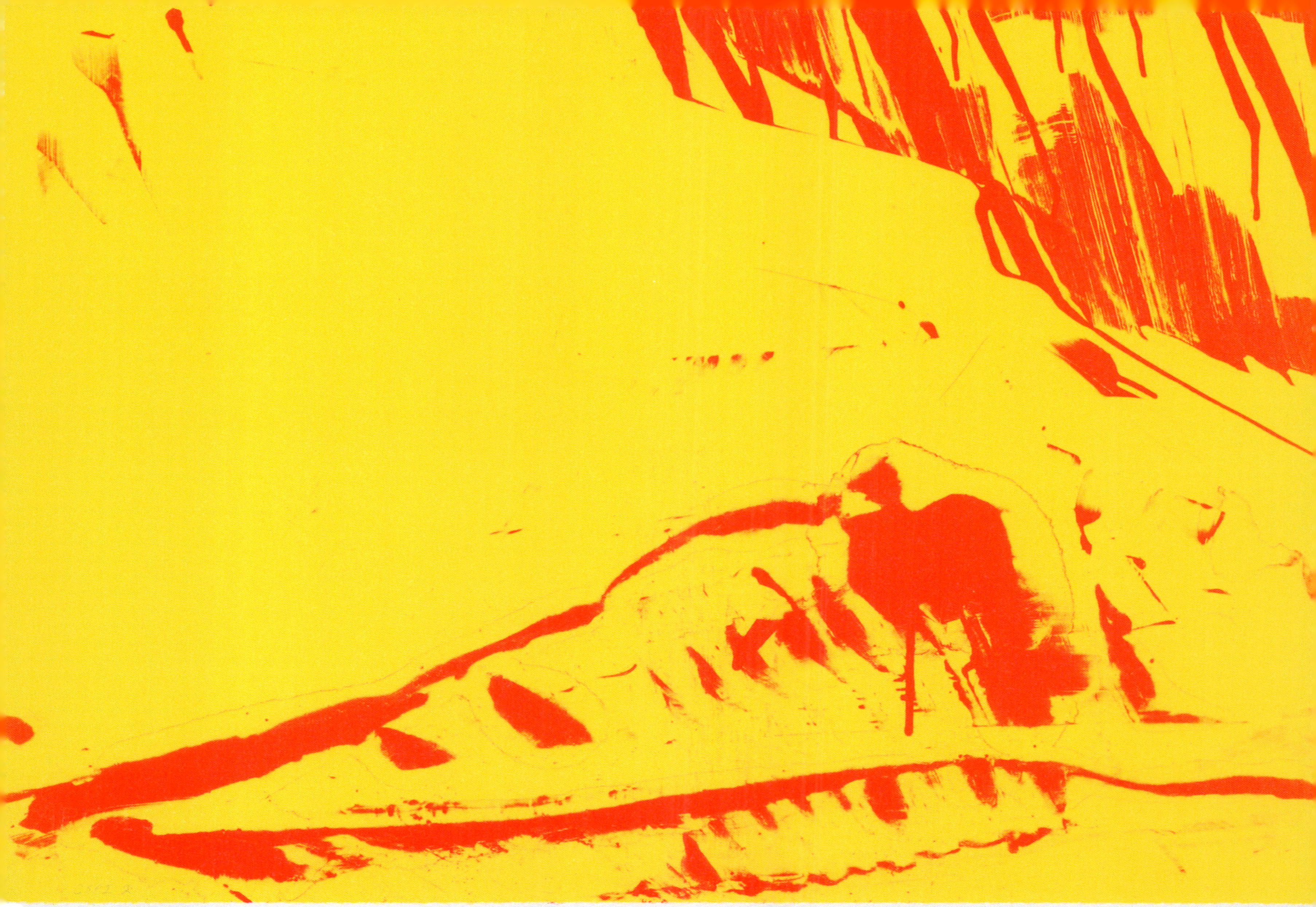

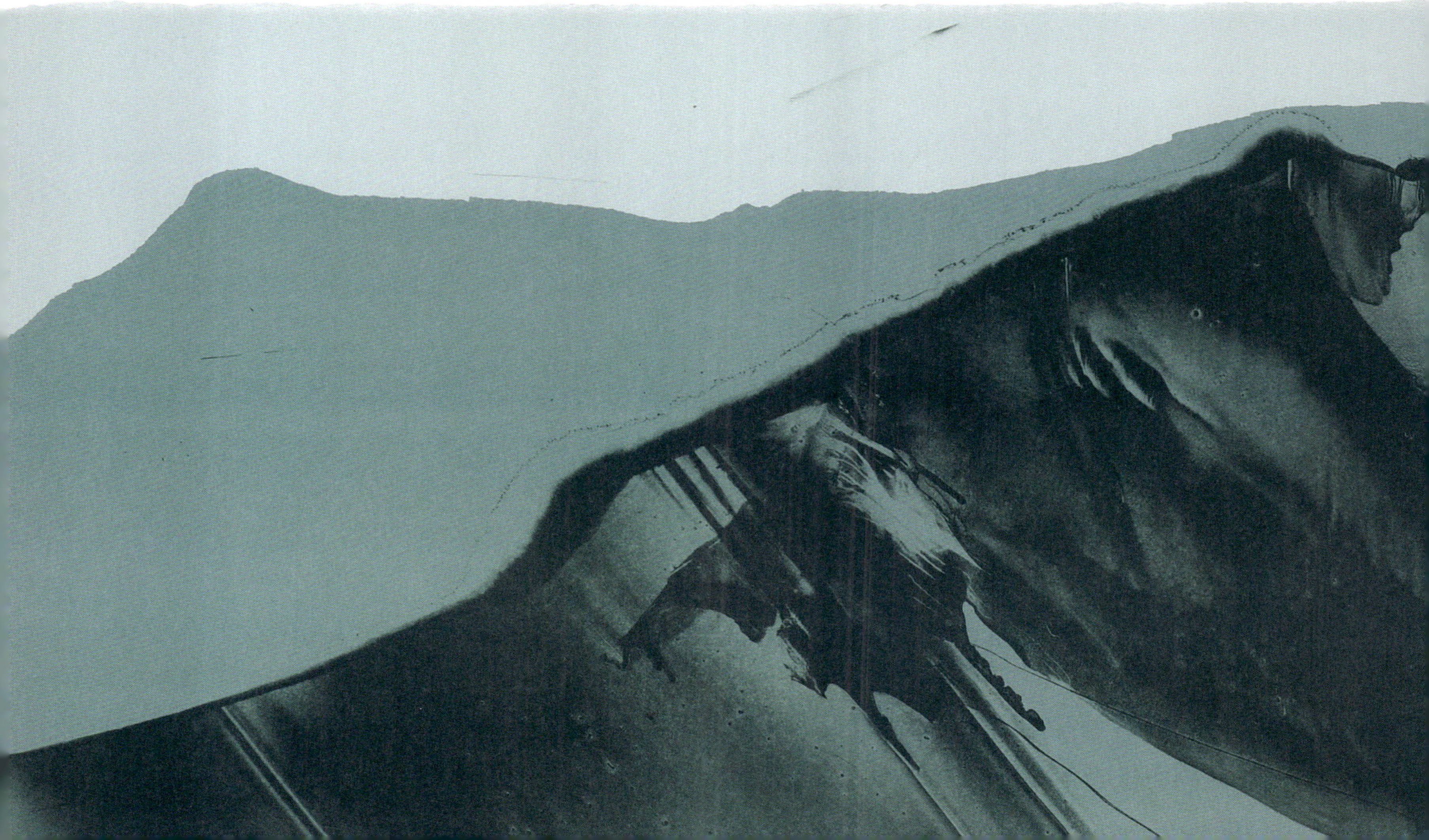

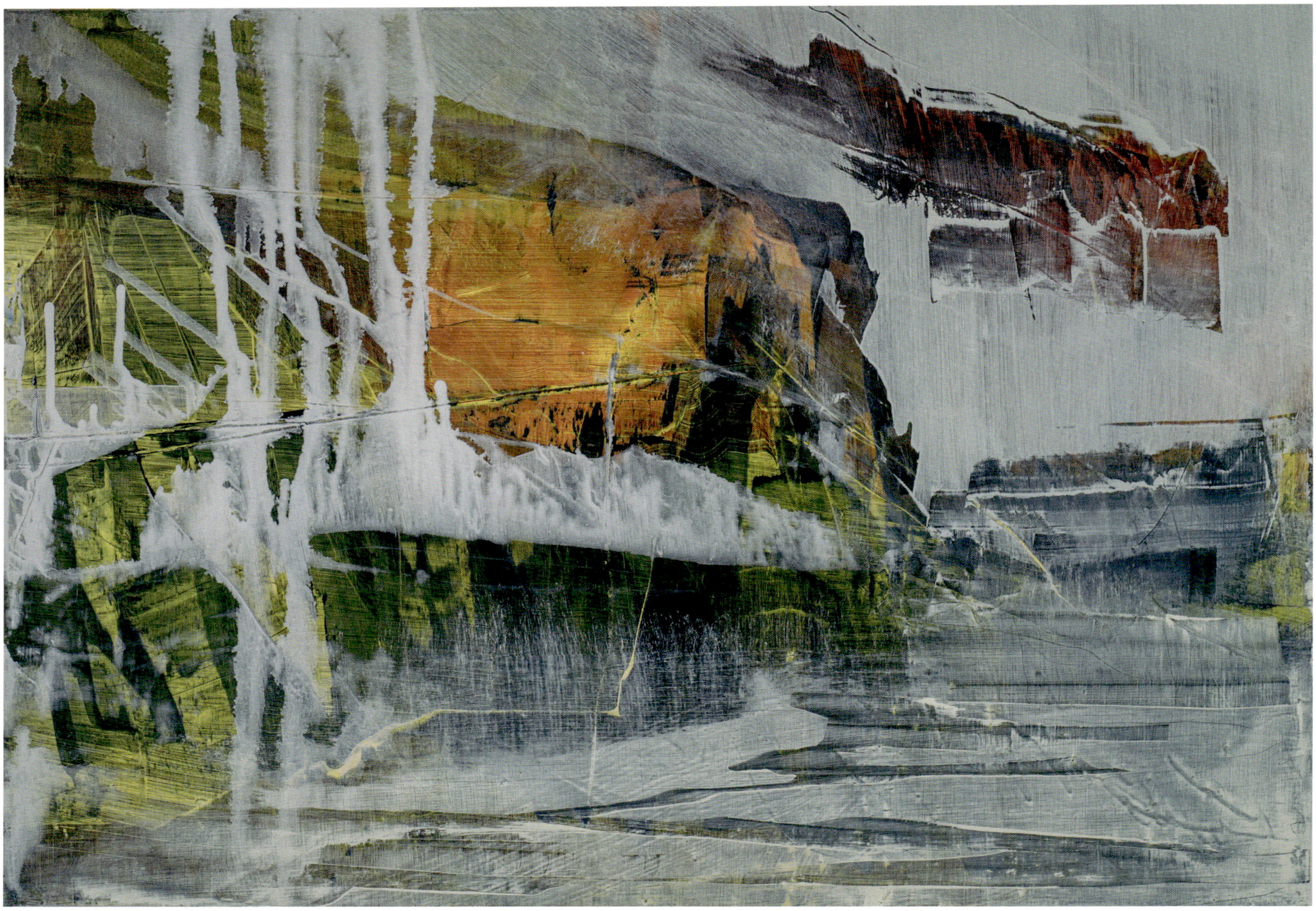

Plate 24: **River Miles I**, 2020. Oil on paper, 20 x 28 inches. Collection of the Regional Arts and Culture Council, Portland, OR.

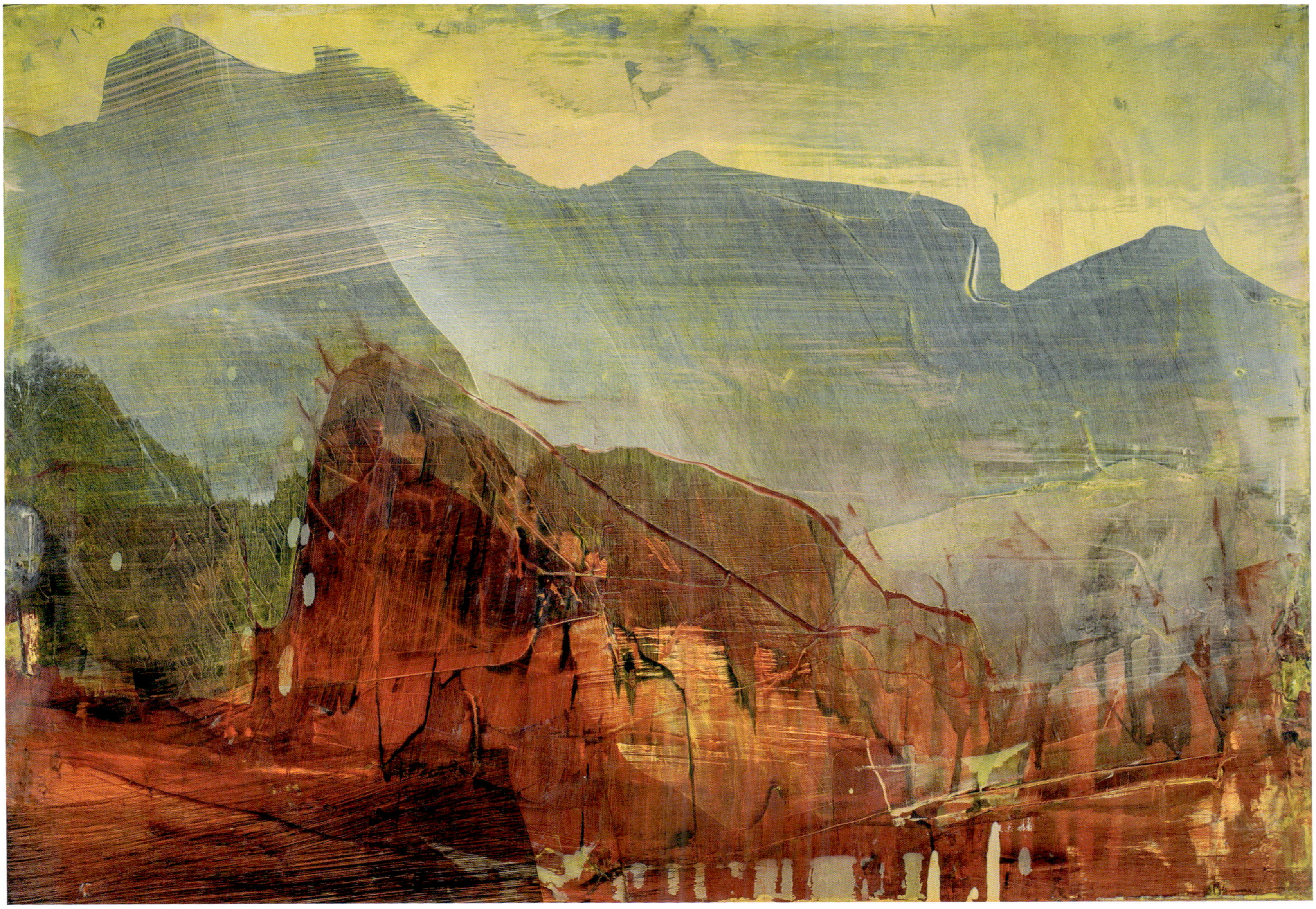

Plate 25: **River Miles II**, 2020. Oil on paper, 20 x 28 inches. Collection of the Regional Arts and Culture Council, Portland, OR.

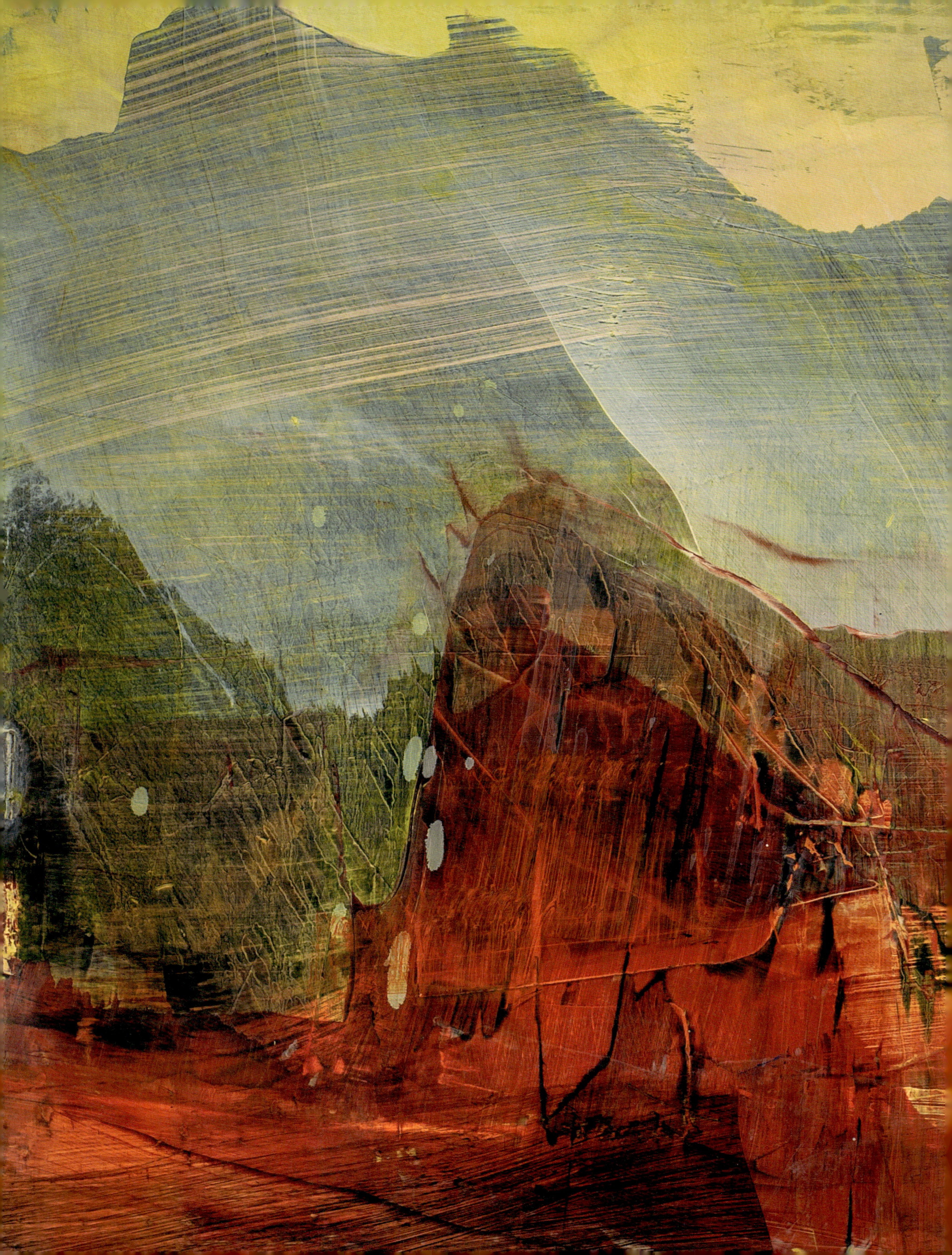

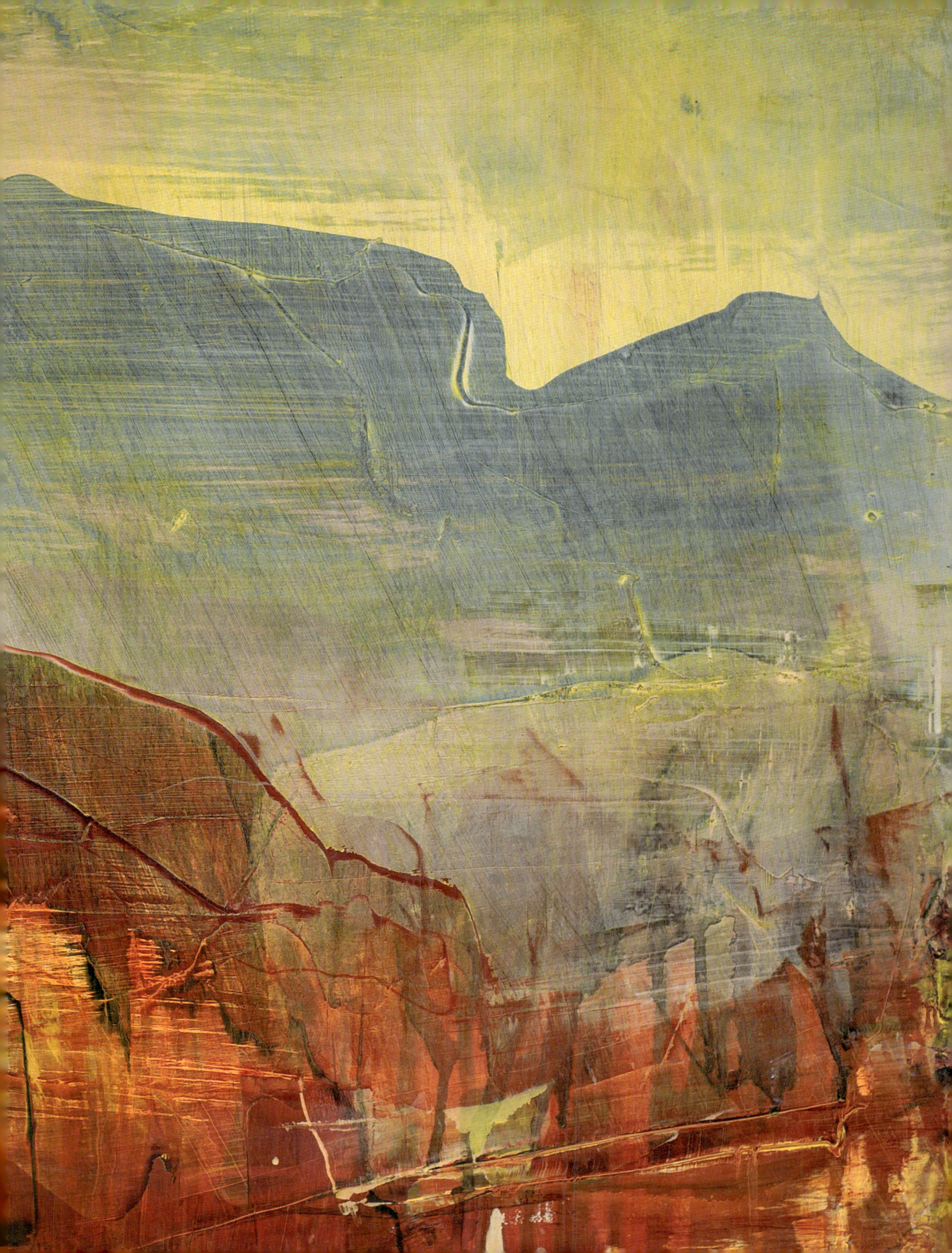

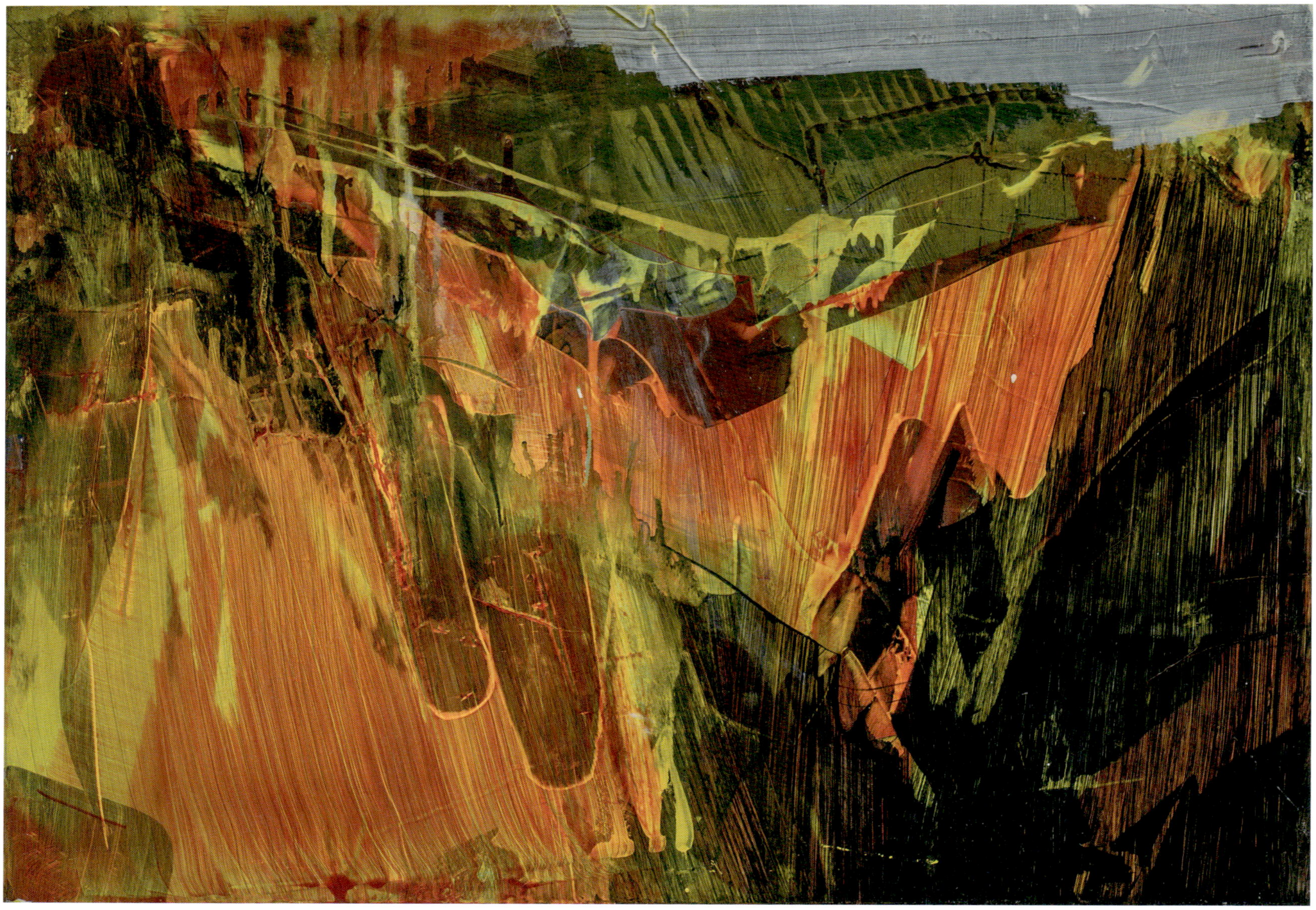

Plate 26: **River Miles III**, 2020. Oil on paper, 20 x 28 inches. Collection of the Regional Arts and Culture Council, Portland, OR.

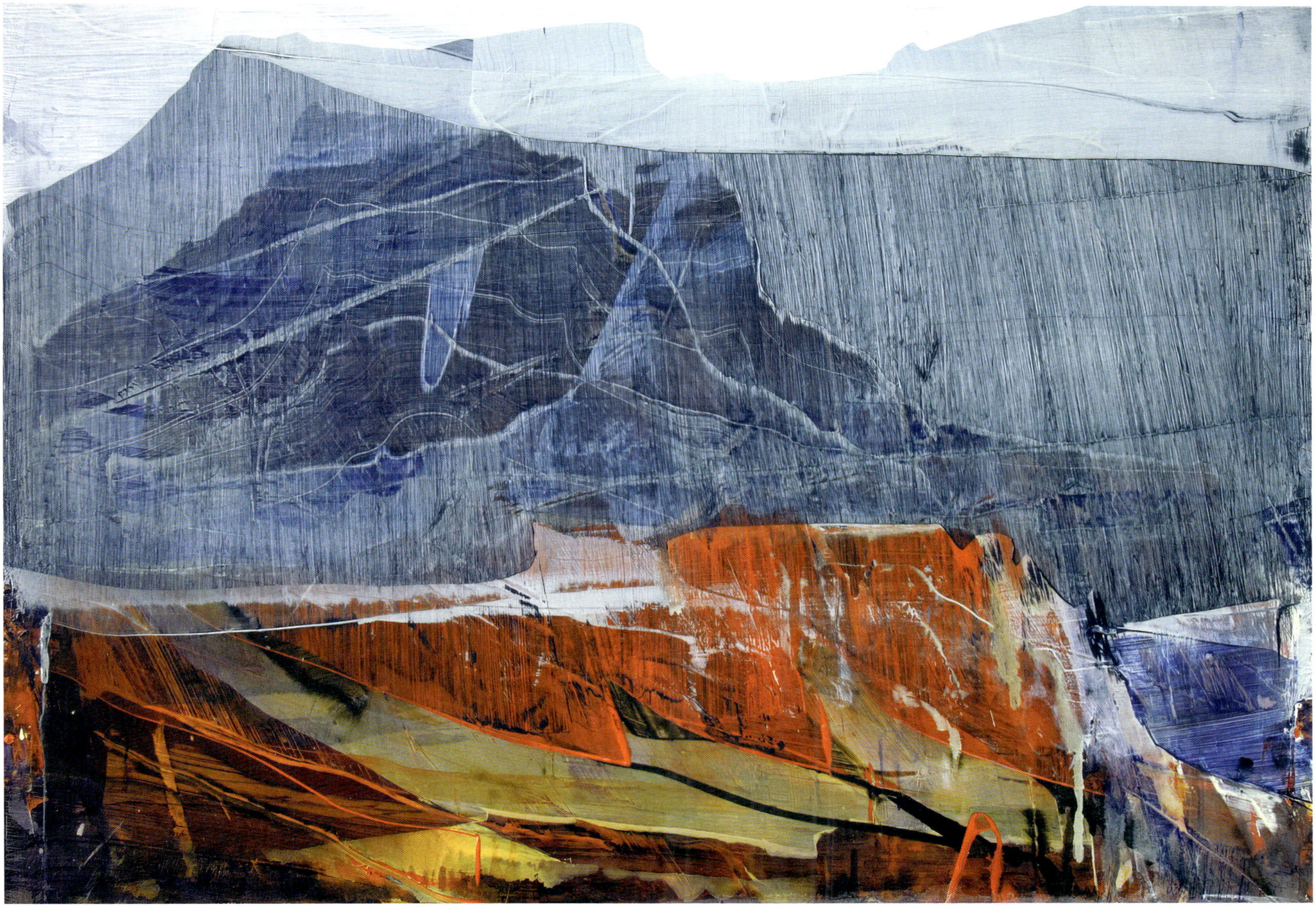

Plate 27: **River Miles VI**, 2020. Oil on paper, 20 x 28 inches. Collection of the Regional Arts and Culture Council, Portland, OR.

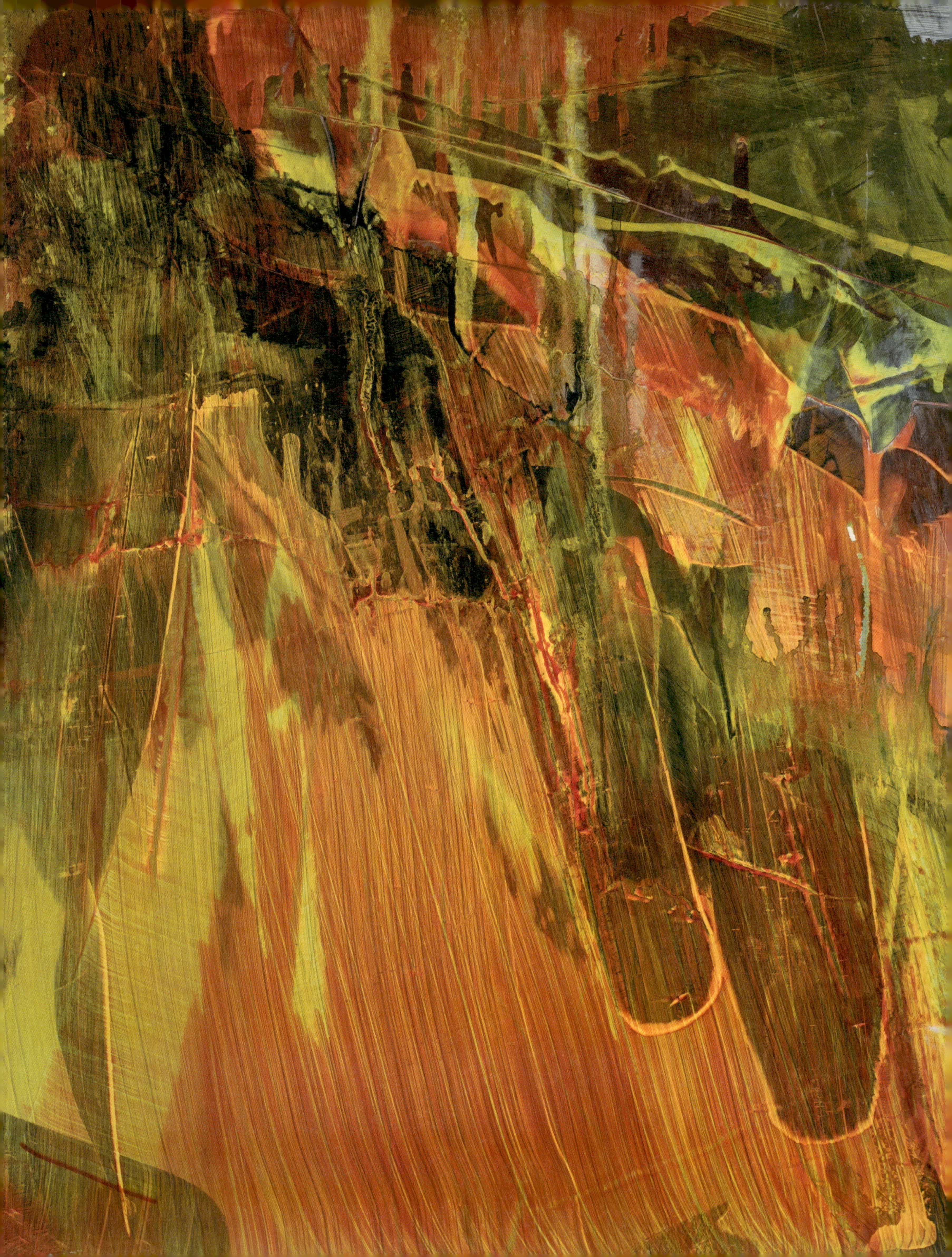

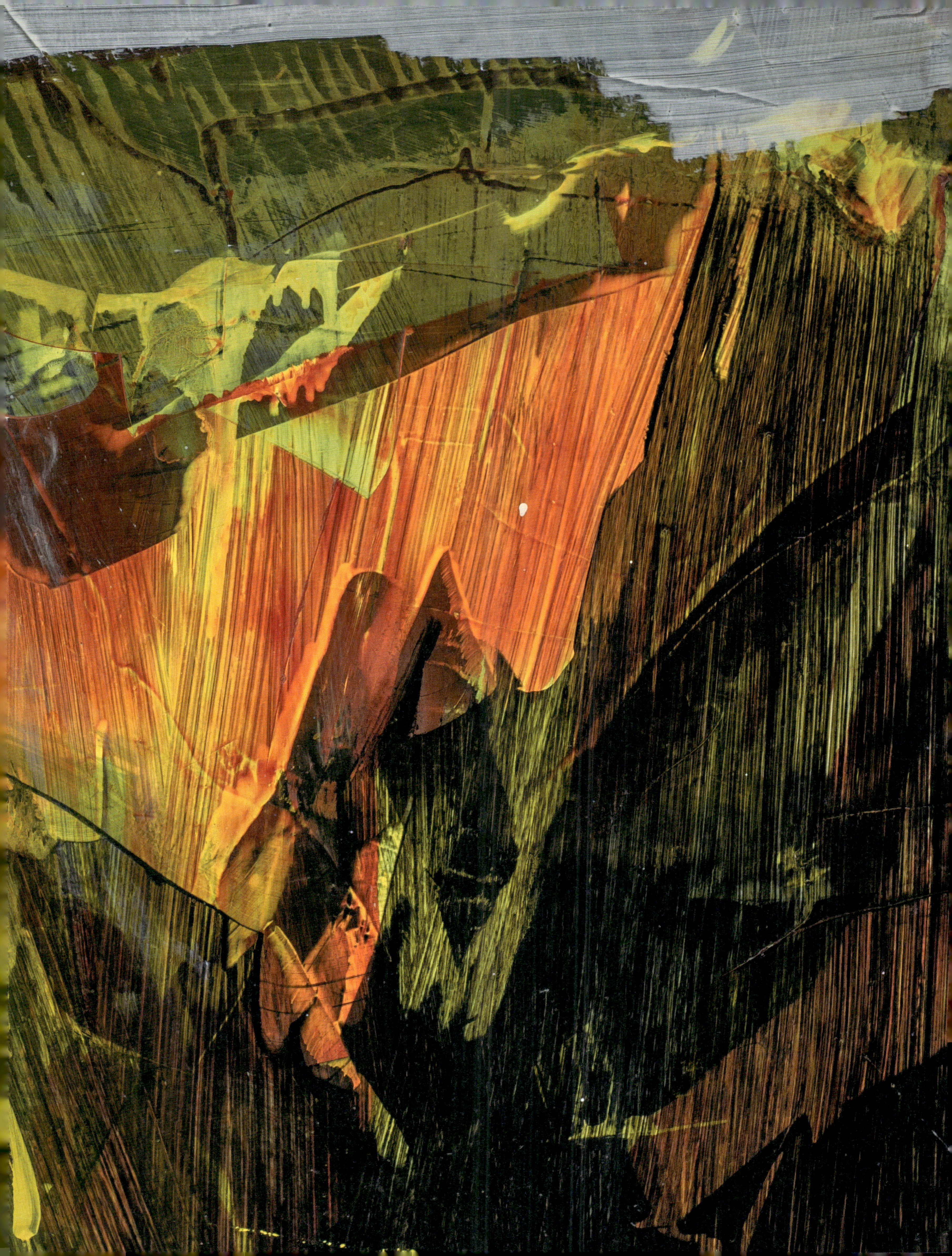

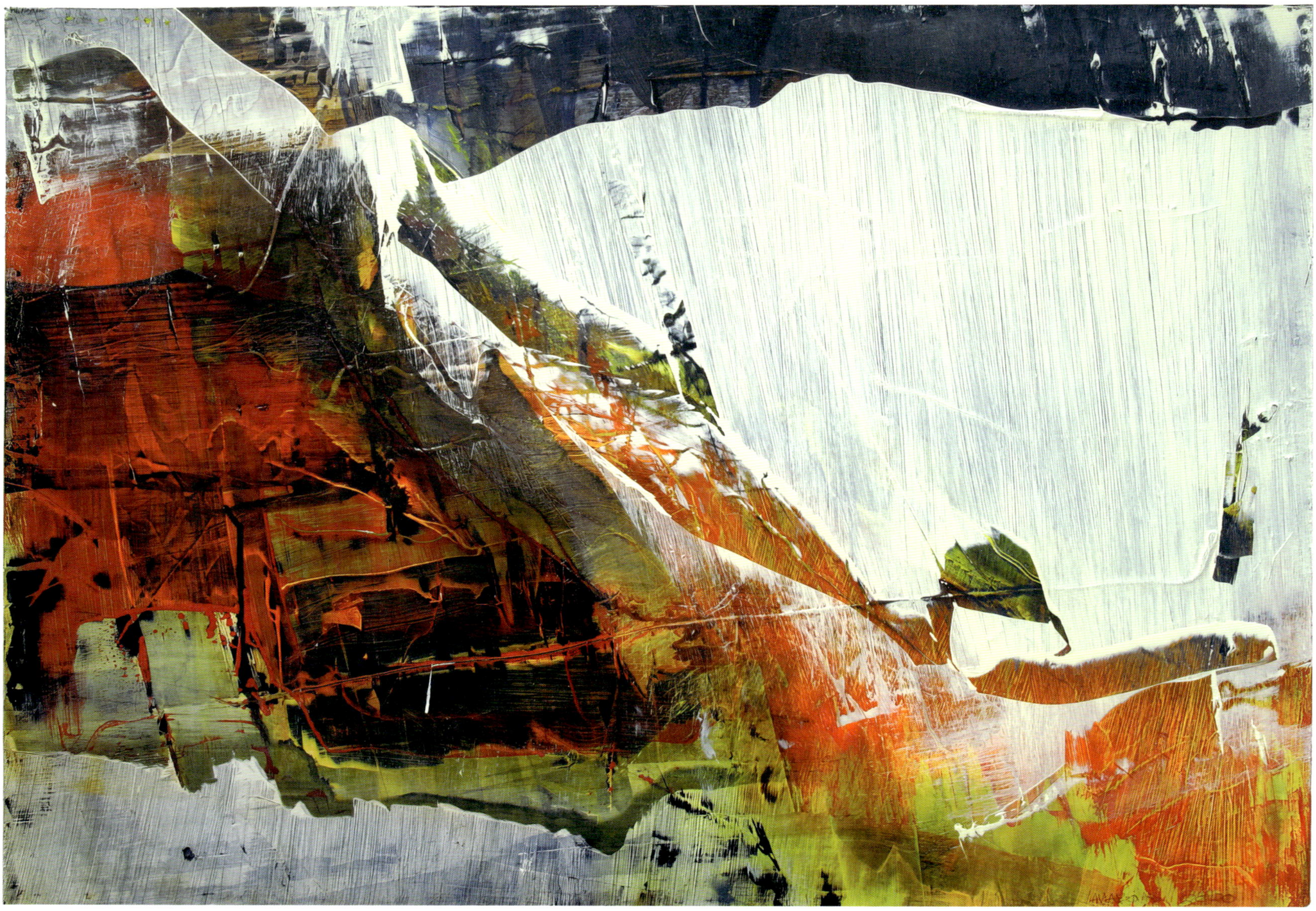

Plate 28: **River Miles VII**, 2020. Oil on paper, 20 x 28 inches. Collection of the Regional Arts and Culture Council, Portland, OR.

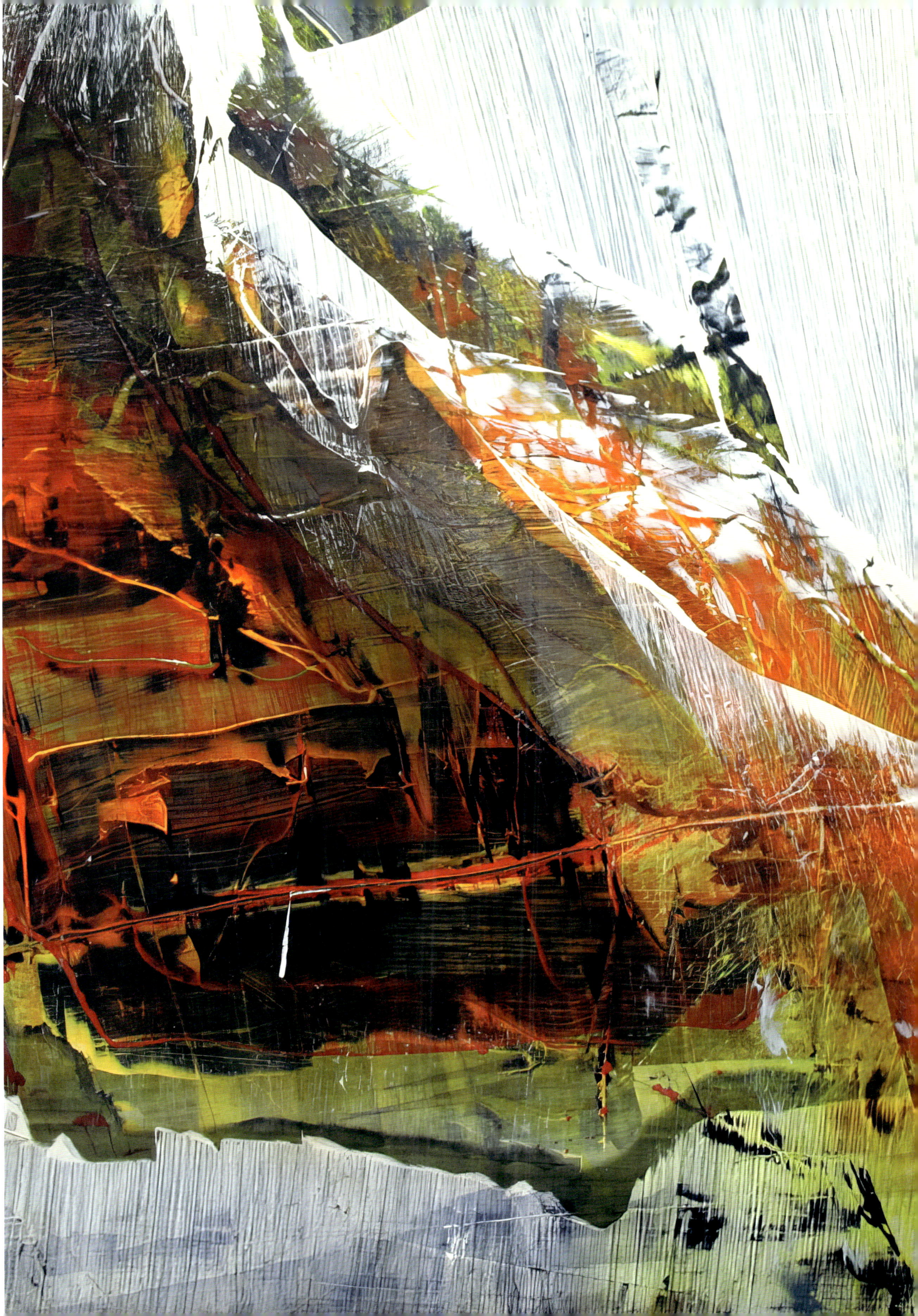

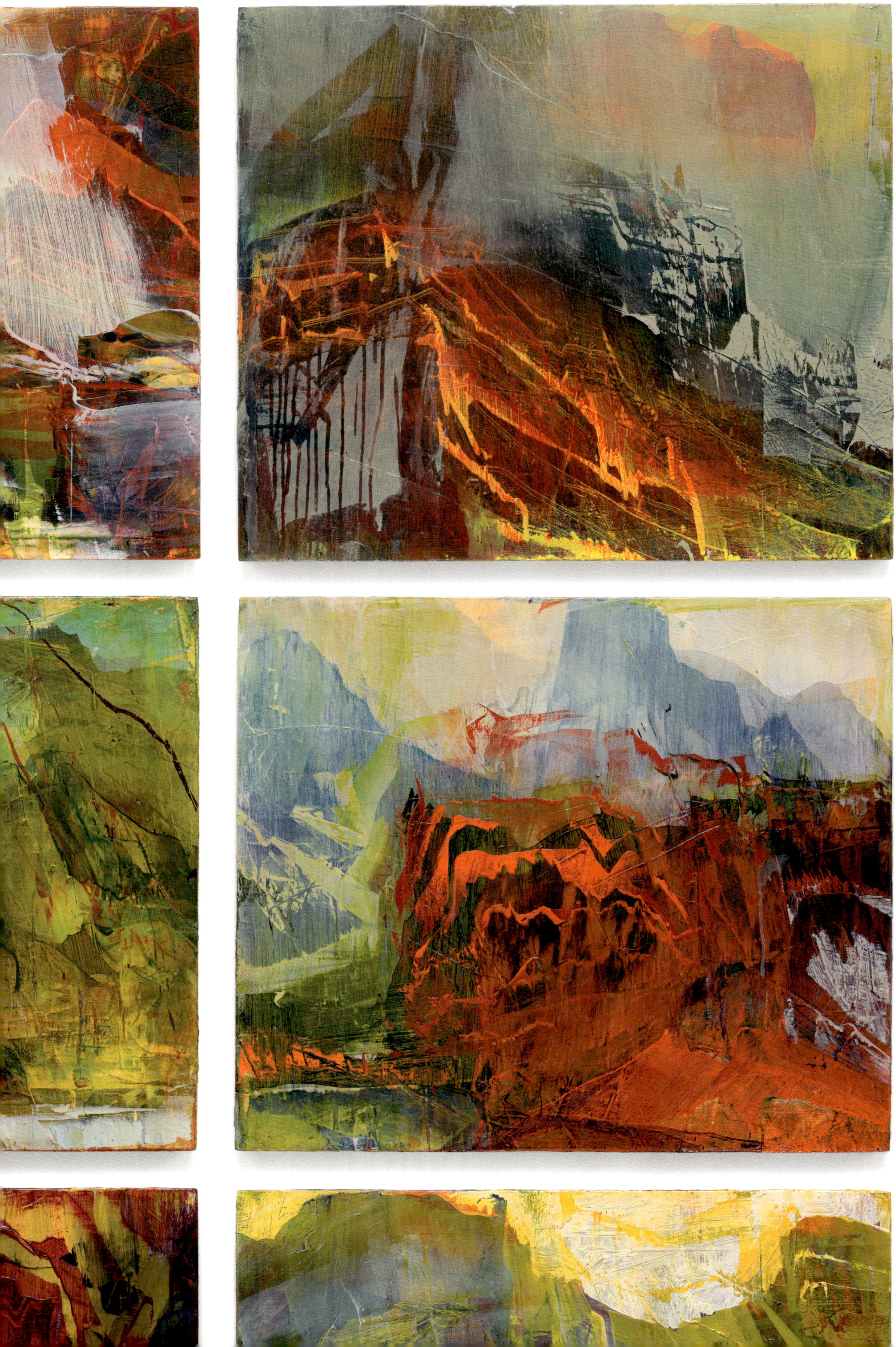

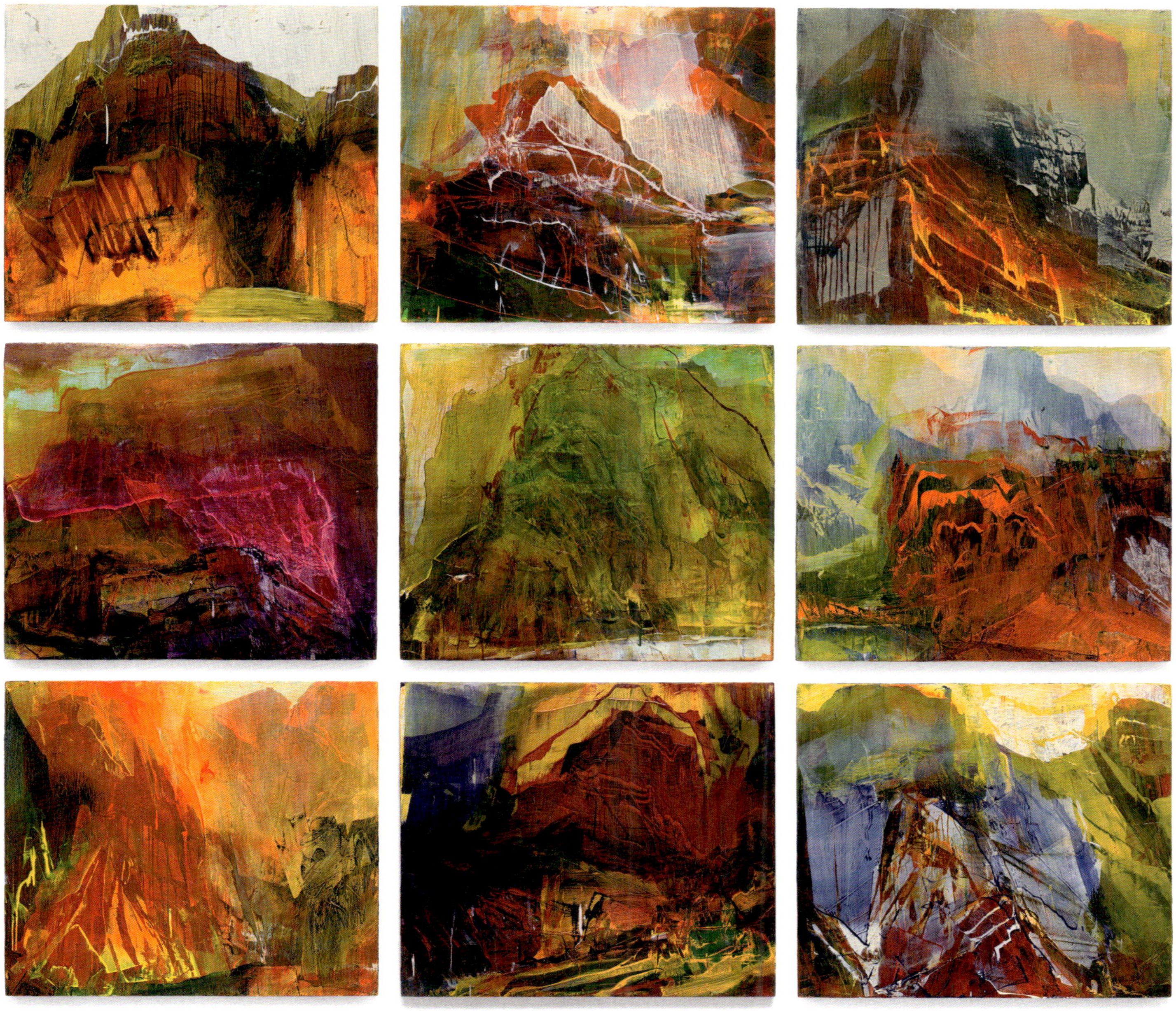

Plate 29: **The New Ghosts of Ceded Boundaries**, 2021. Oil on panel, 90 x 102 x 2 inches. Courtesy of the artist and PDX CONTEMPORARY ART.

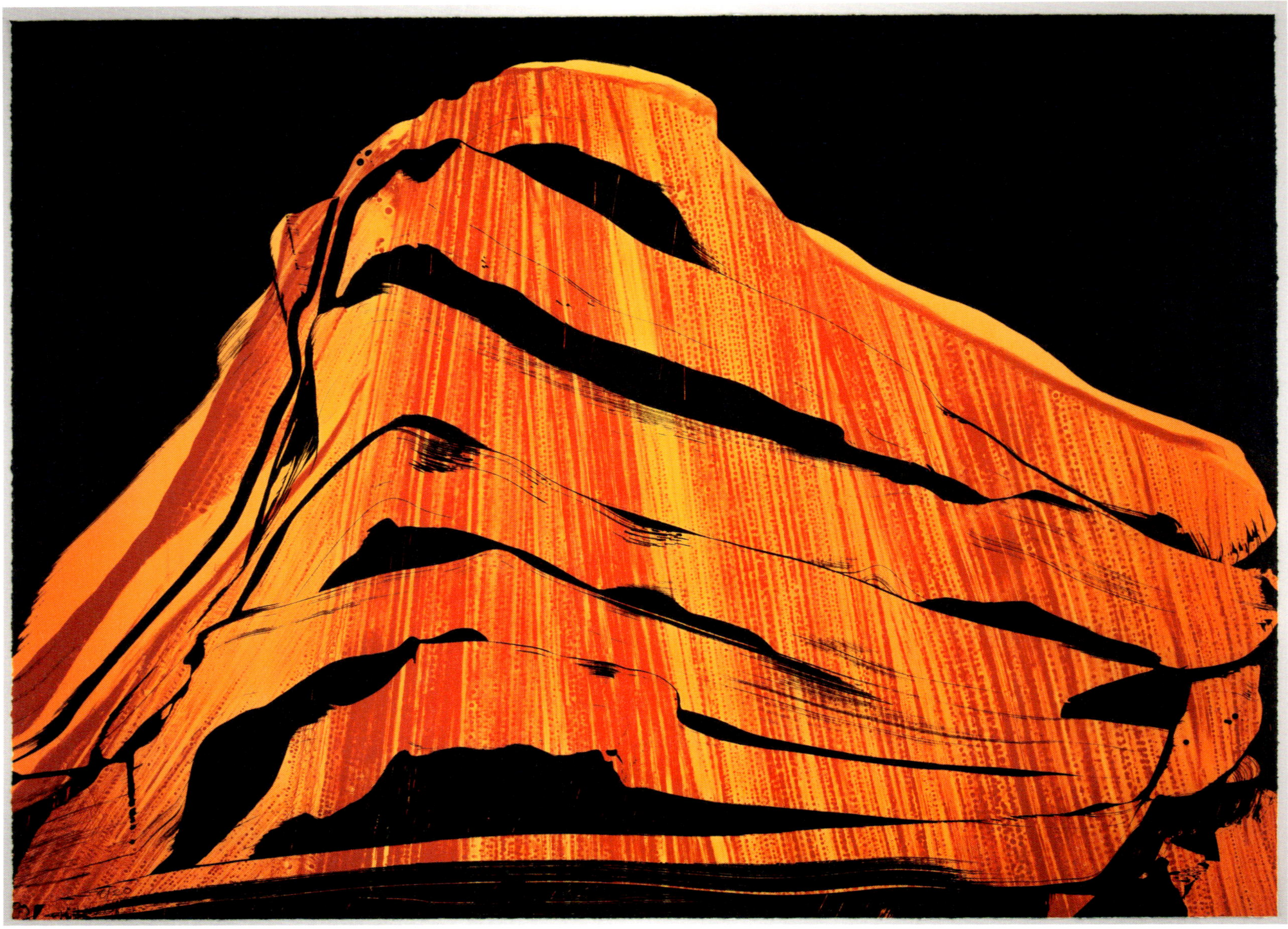

Plate 30: **Winter**, ed. 8/20, 2023. Five color lithograph on Somerset Satin White, 25 x 34 inches. Published at CSIA, January 2024. Collaborating Master Printer: Judith Baumann. Jordan Schnitzer Museum of Art, University of Oregon: Purchased with funds from the William A. Haseltine Endowment for Pacific Northwest Art.

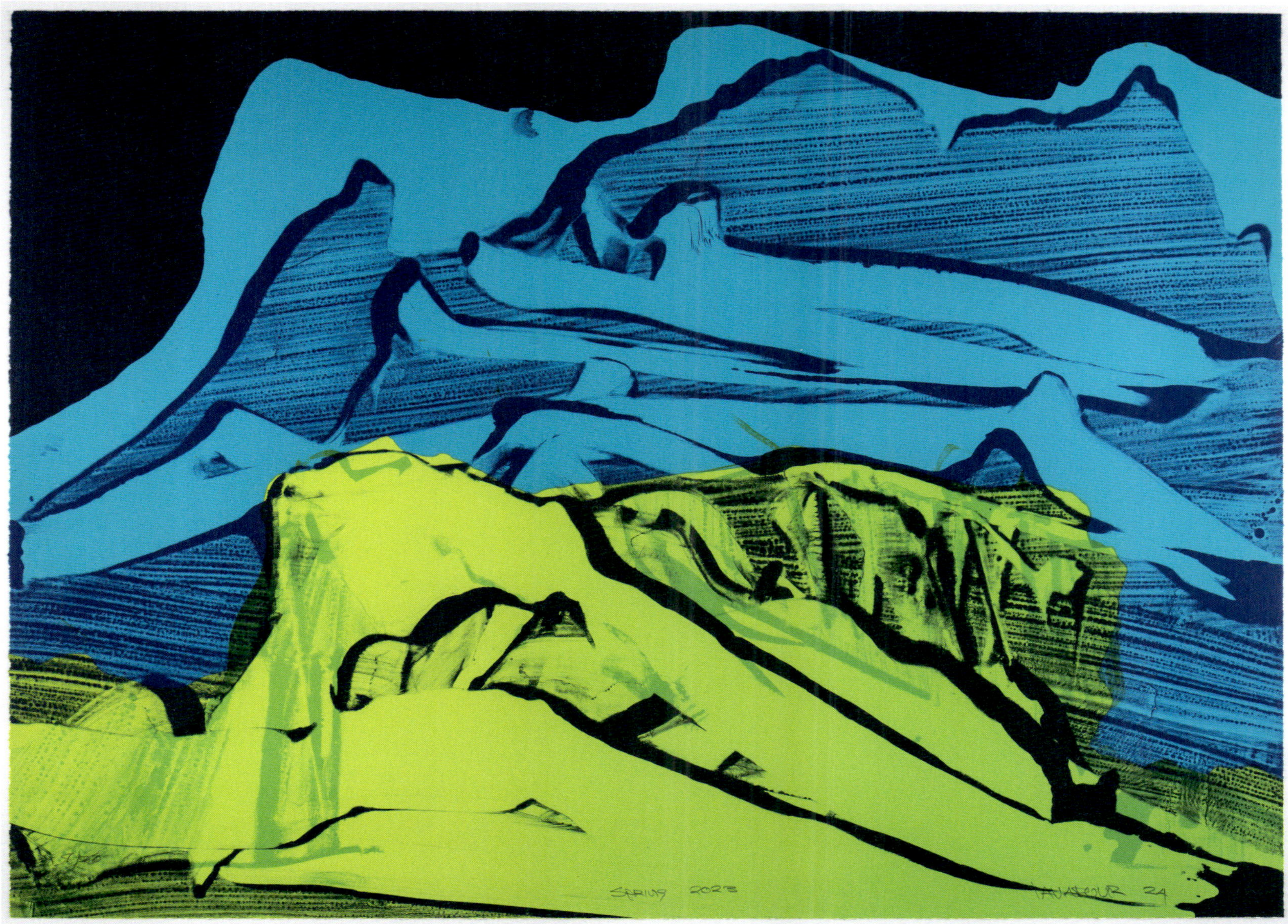

Plate 31: **Spring**, ed. 8/20, 2023. Seven color lithograph on Somerset Satin White, 25 x 34 inches. Published at CSIA, January 2024. Collaborating Master Printer: Judith Baumann. Jordan Schnitzer Museum of Art, University of Oregon: Purchased with funds from the William A. Haseltine Endowment for Pacific Northwest Art.

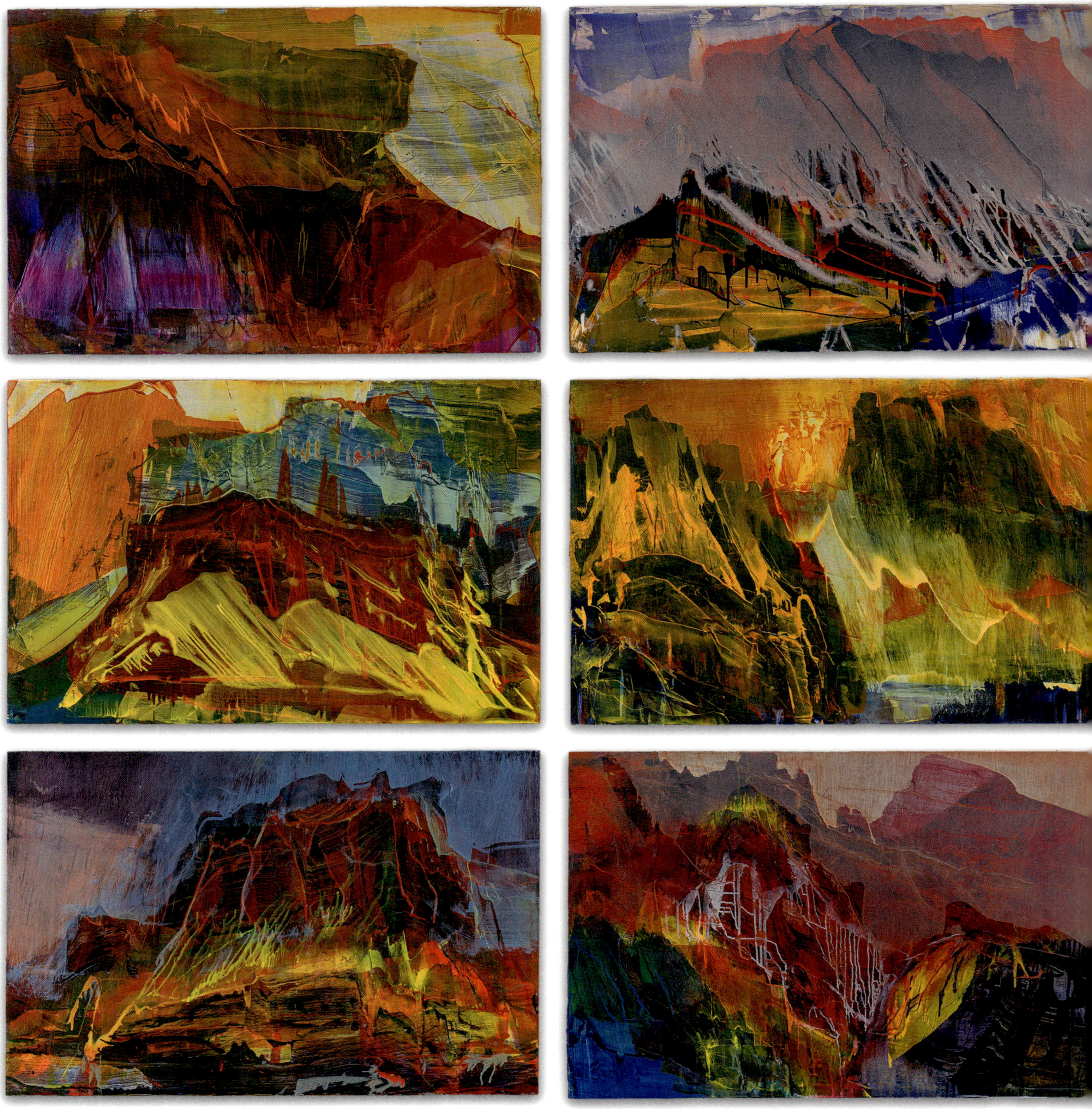

Plate 32: **The Ghosts of Many Things**, 2023. Oil on panel, 76 x 112 x 2 inches. Art Bridges.

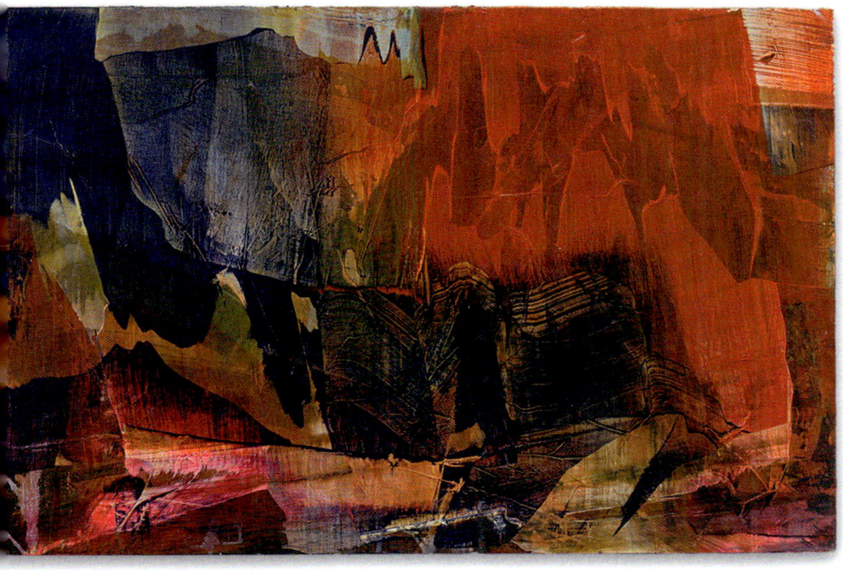

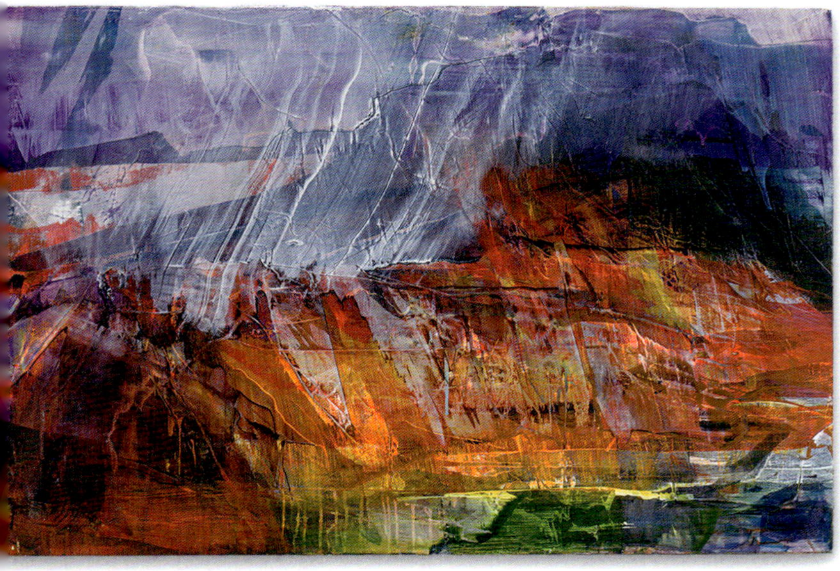

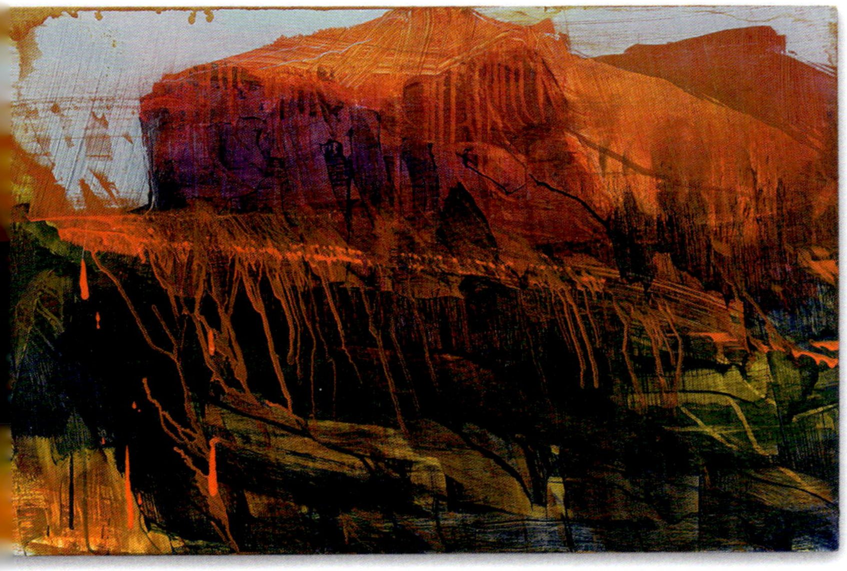

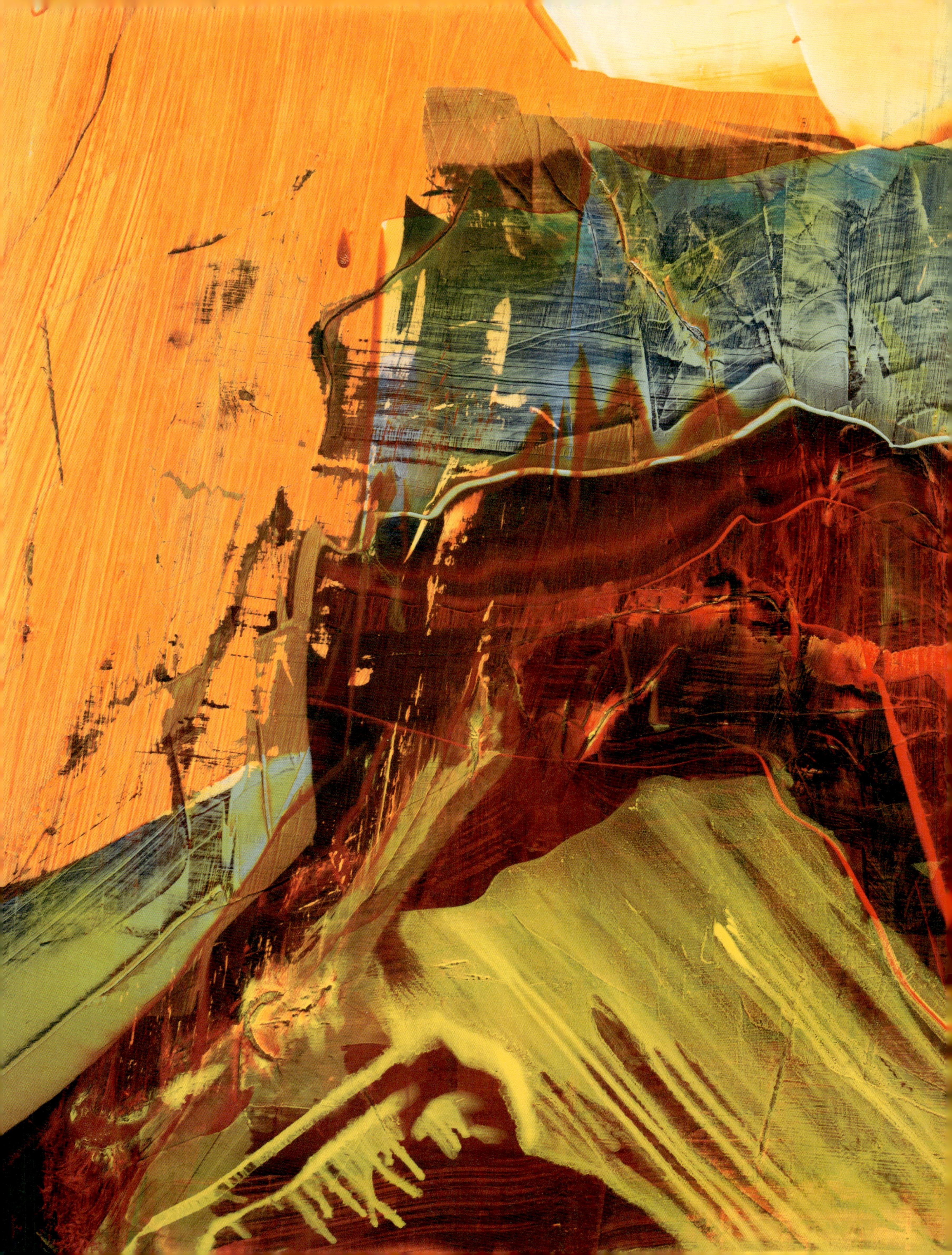

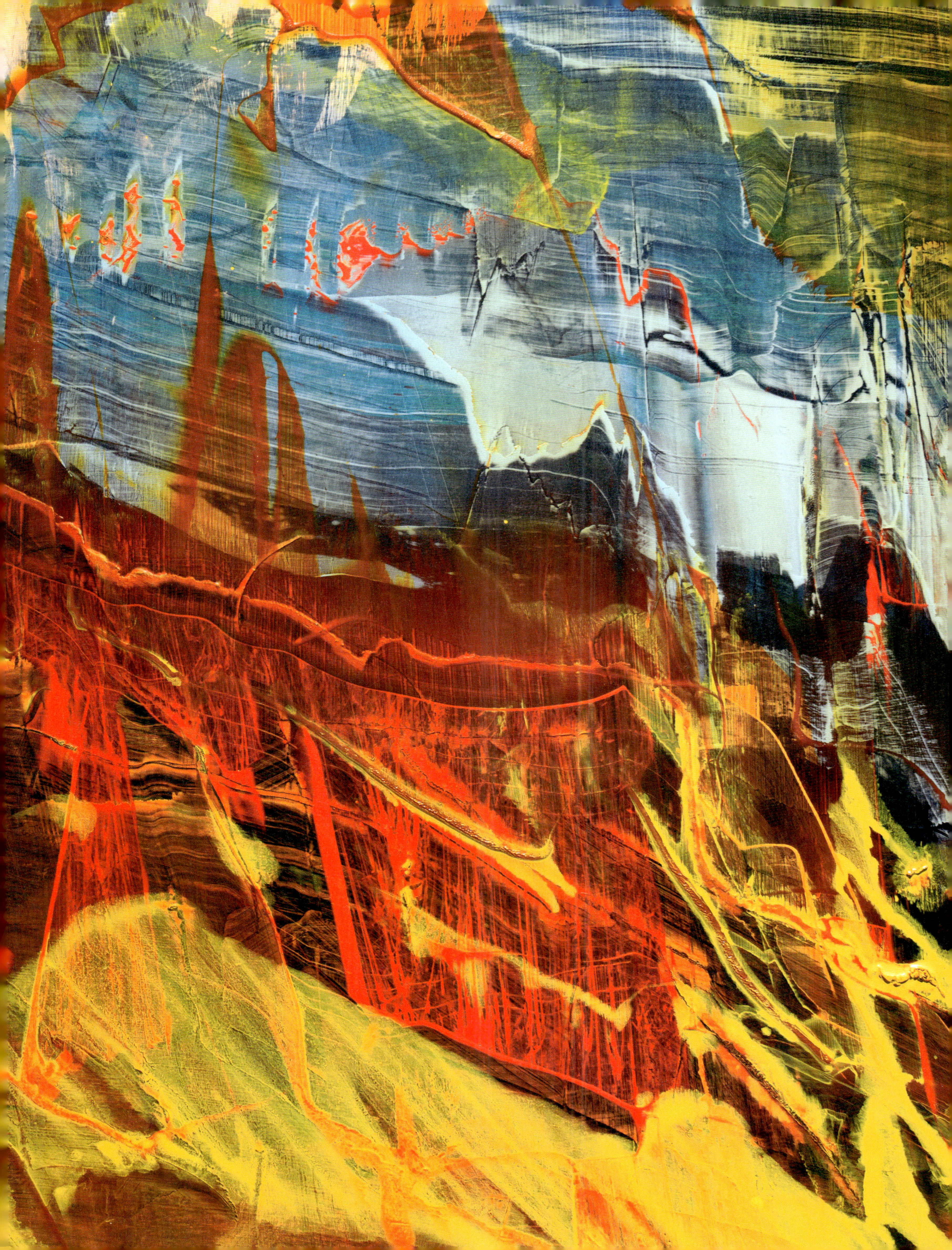

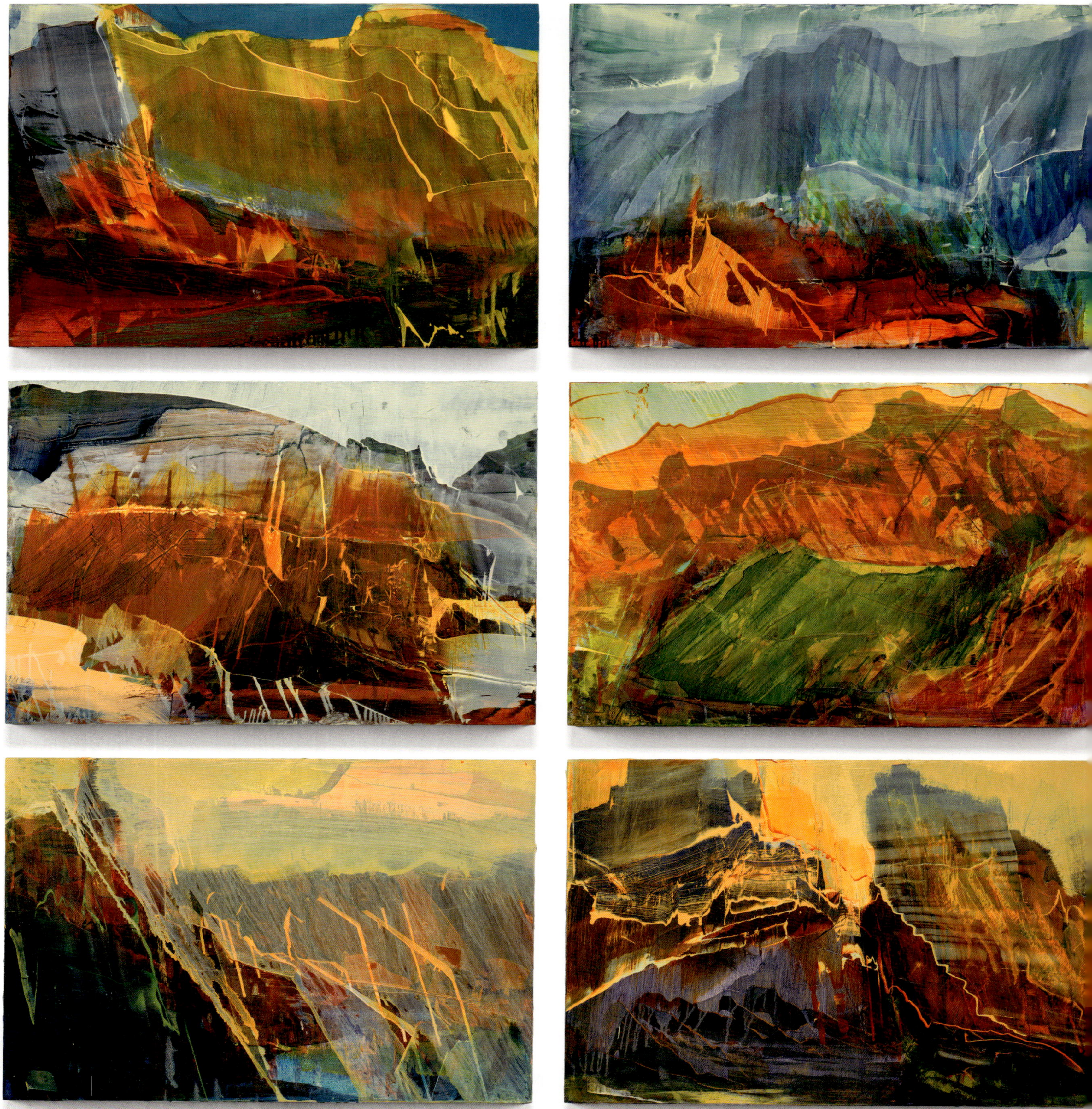

Plate 33: **Lucky Star**, 2024. Oil on wood, 74 x 145 inches. Collection of the Jordan Schnitzer Family Foundation.

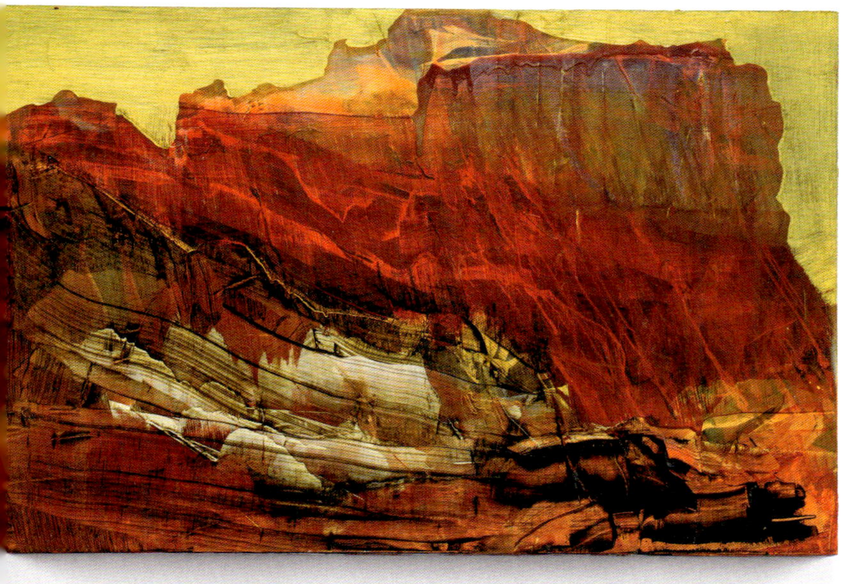
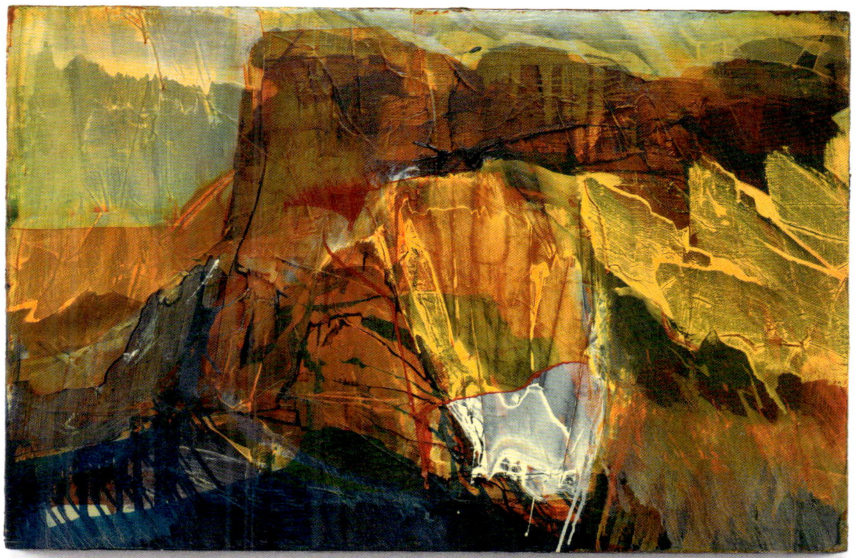
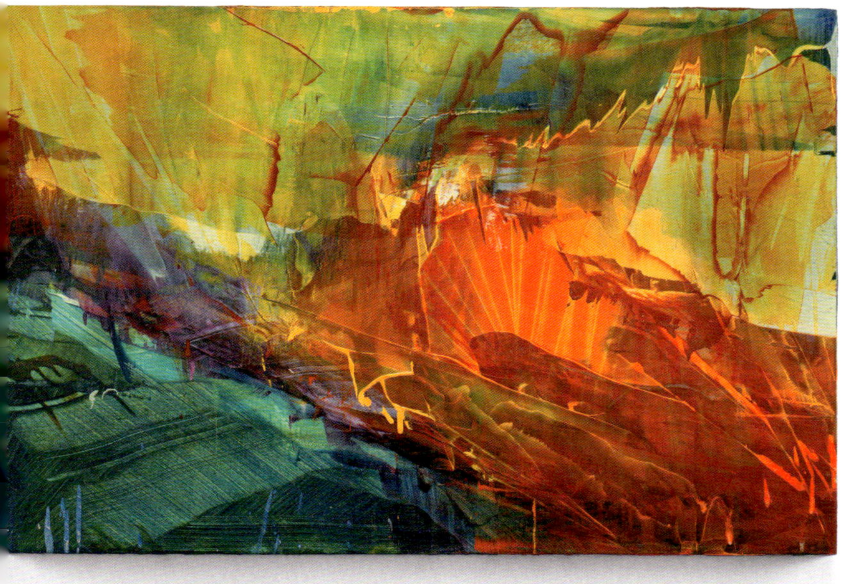
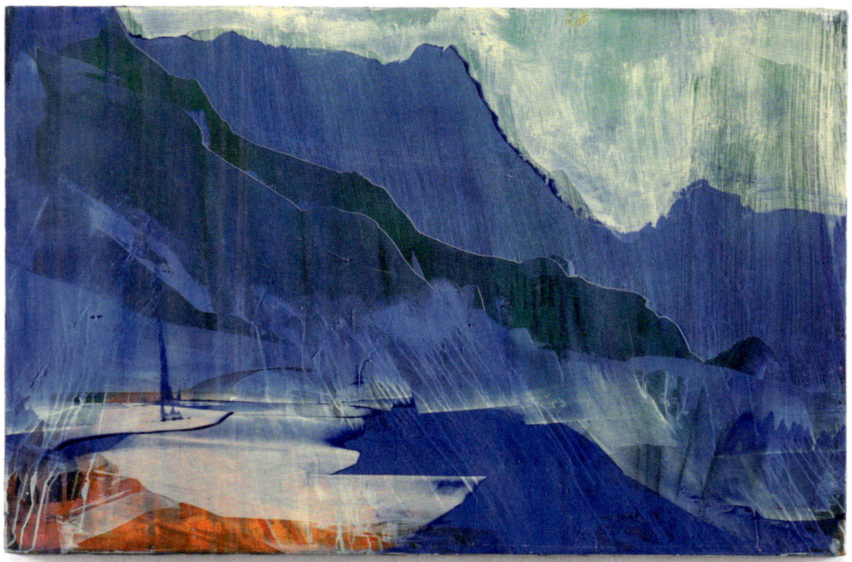
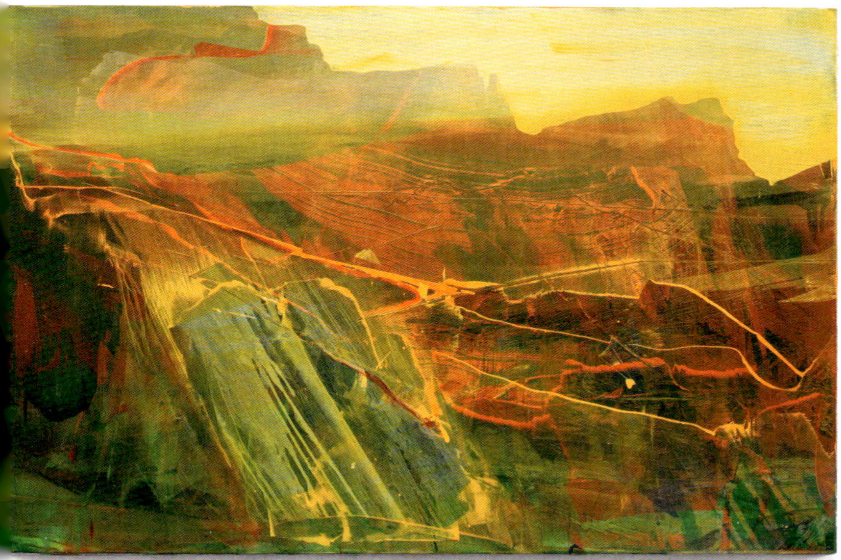
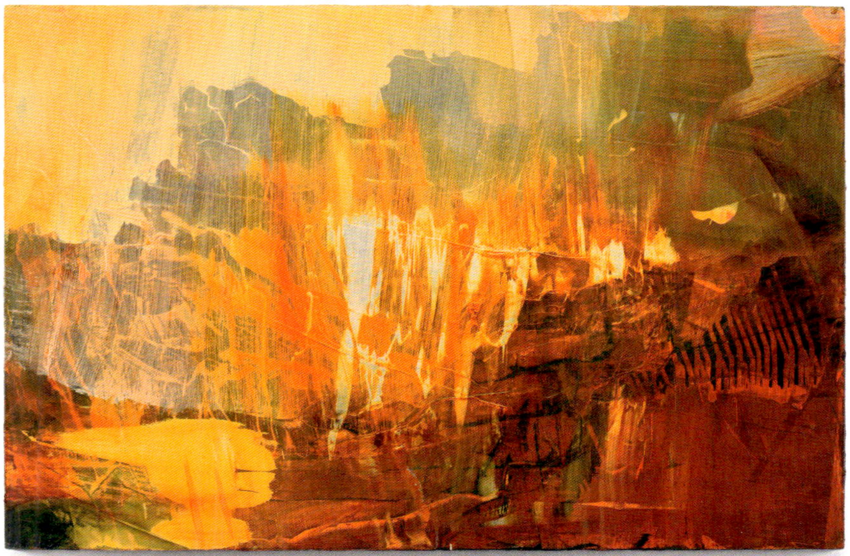

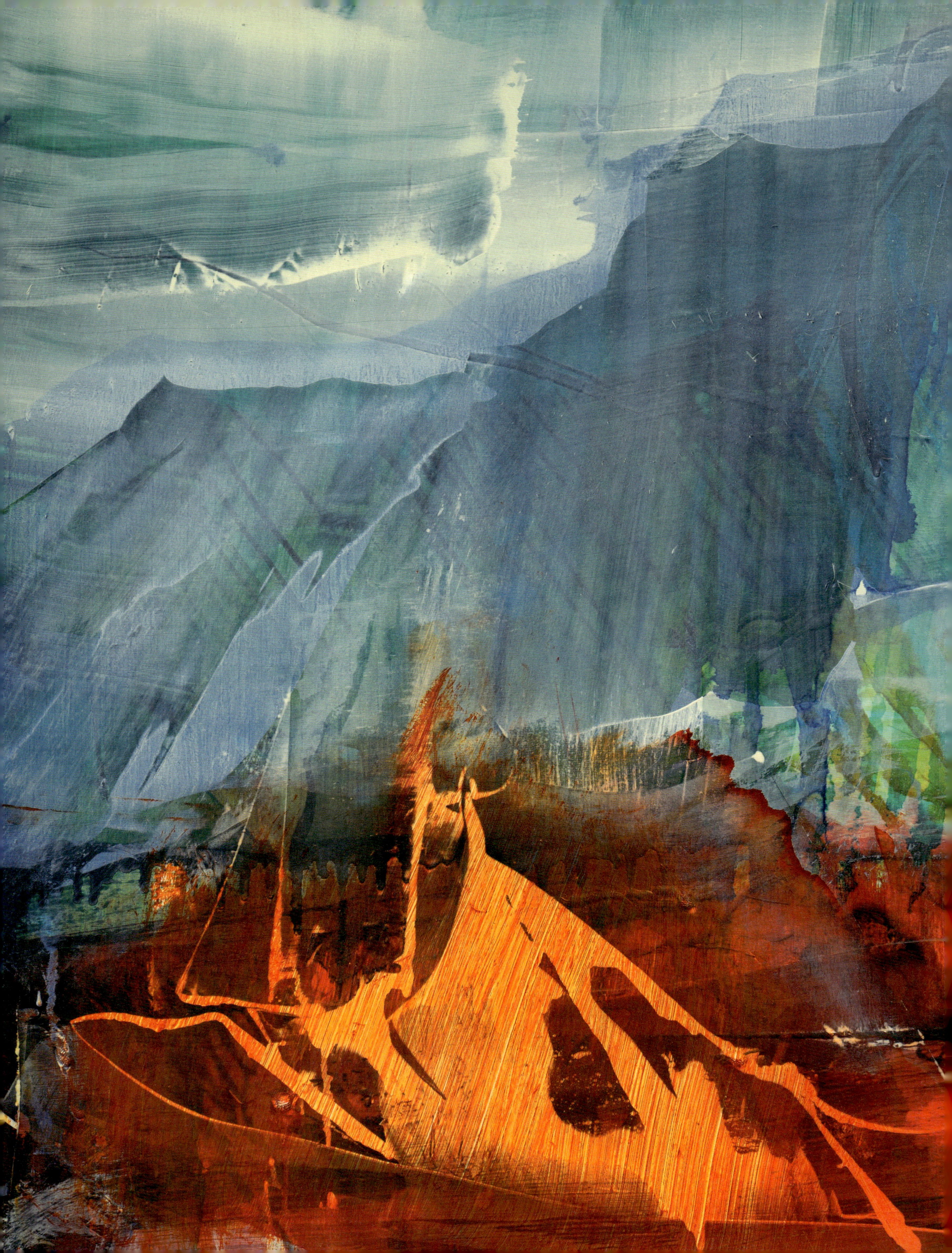

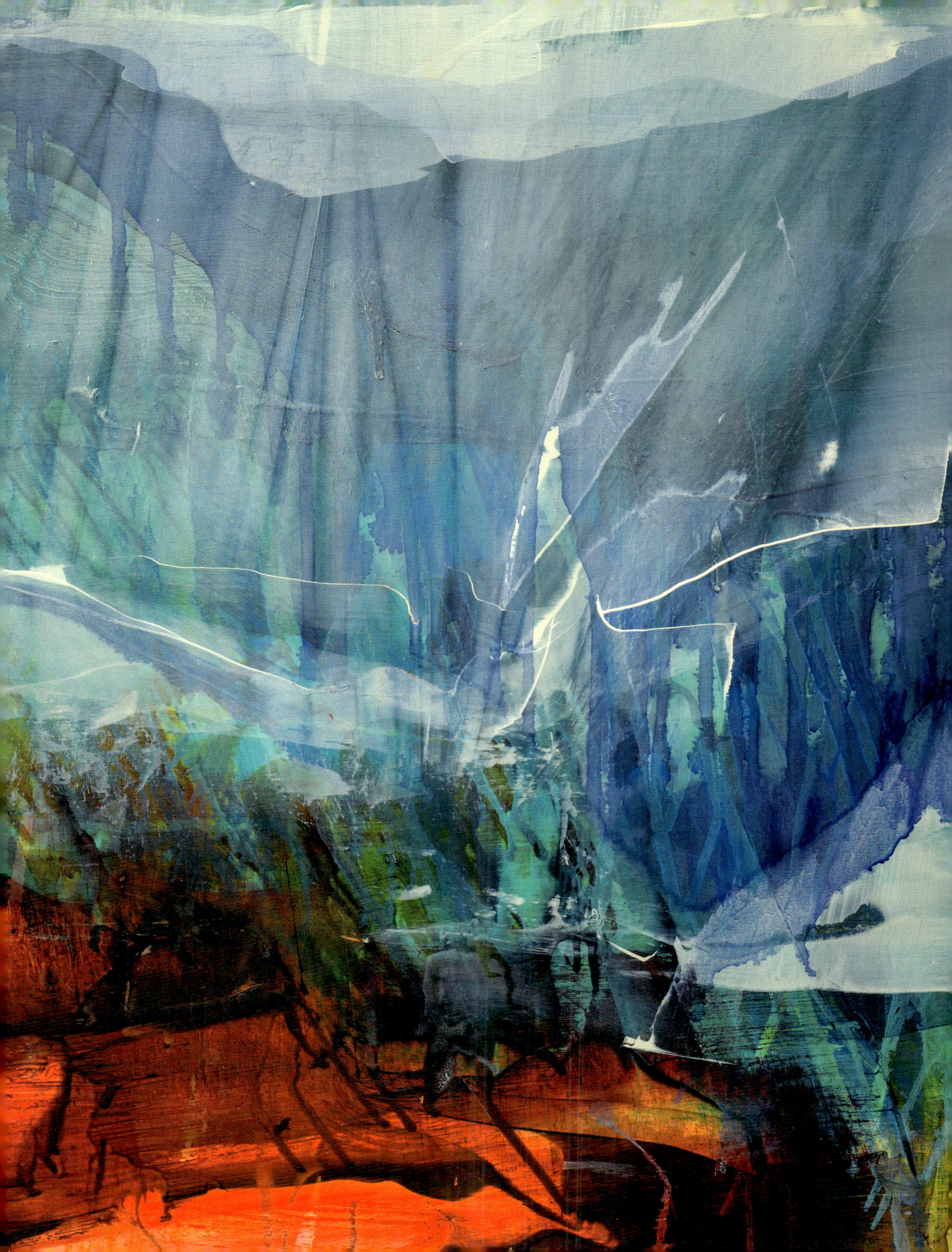

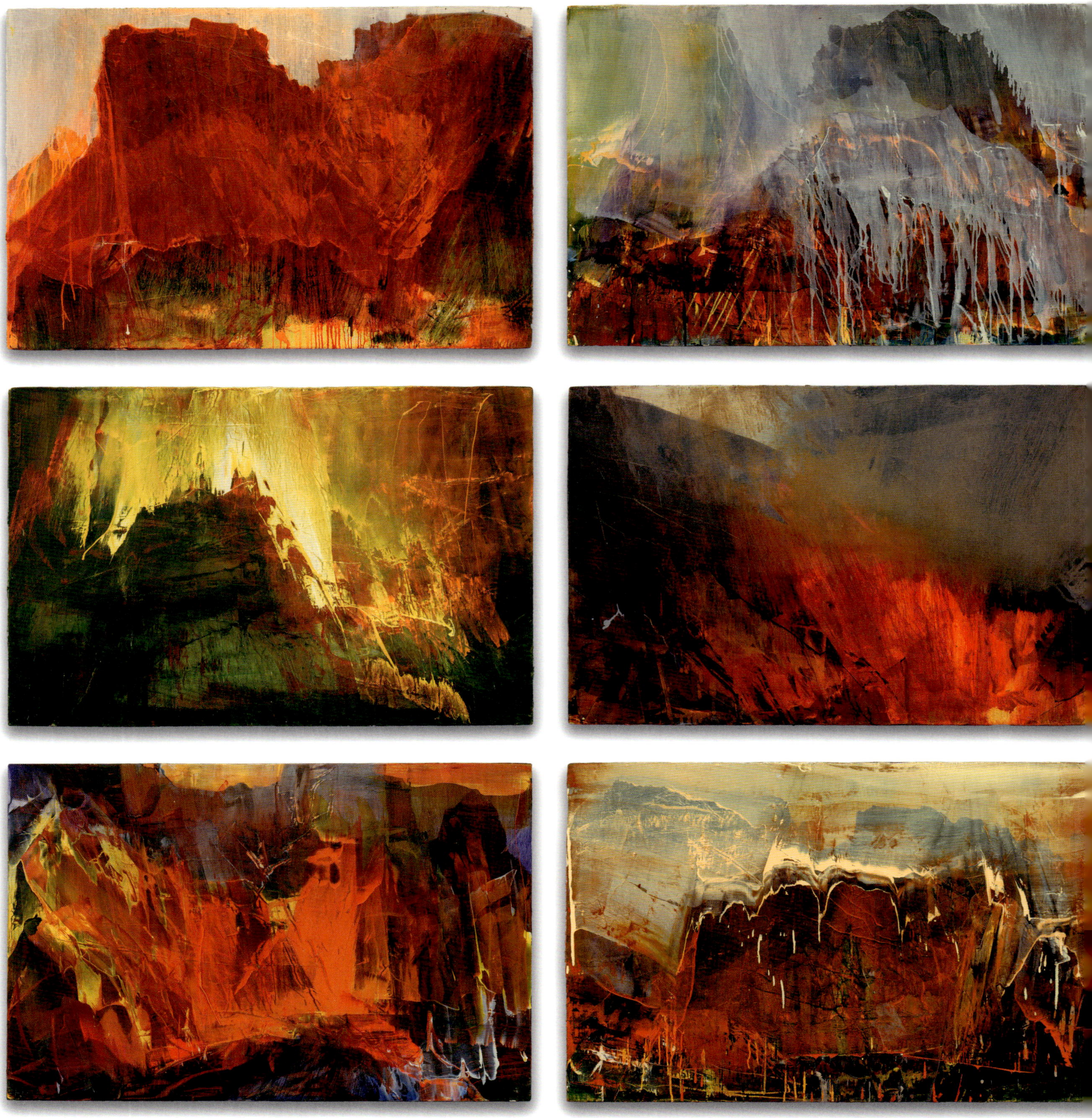

Plate 34: **Bold as Love**, 2024. Oil on wood, 96 x 144 inches. Collection of Bill and Leslie Cornog.

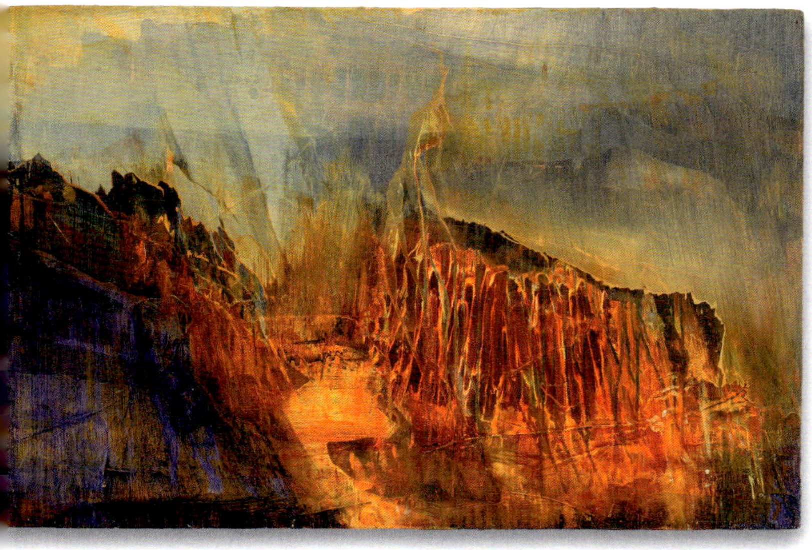
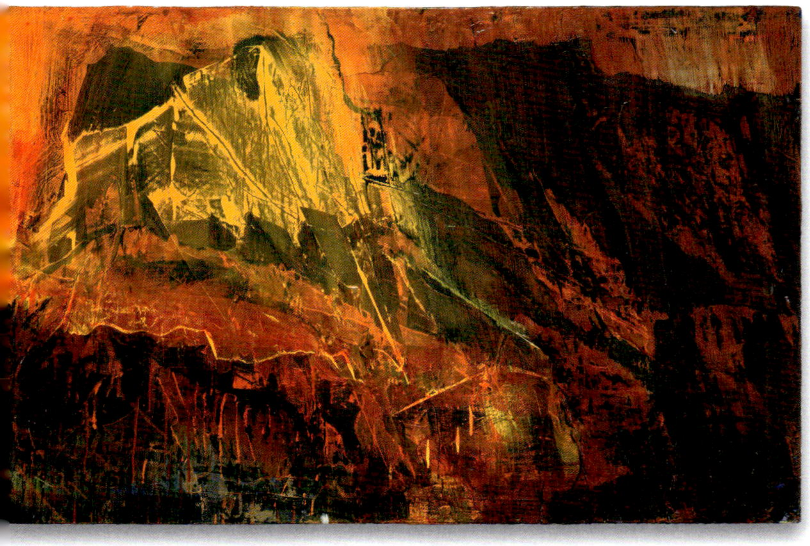
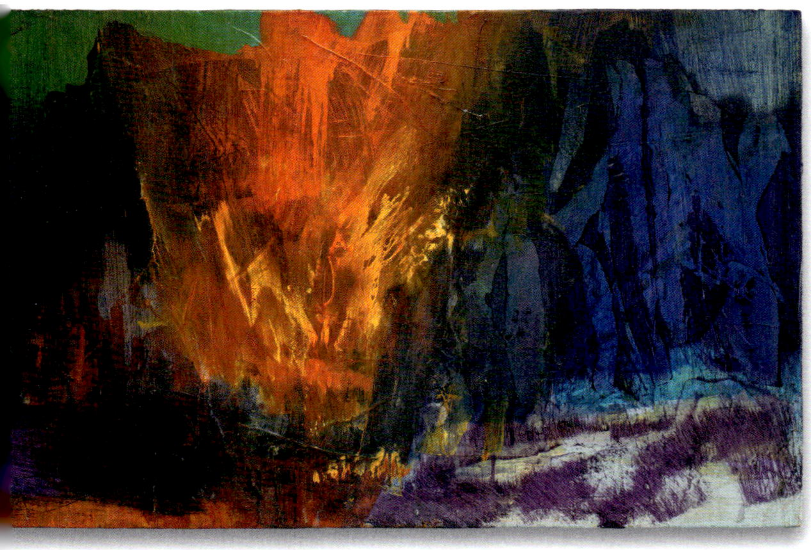

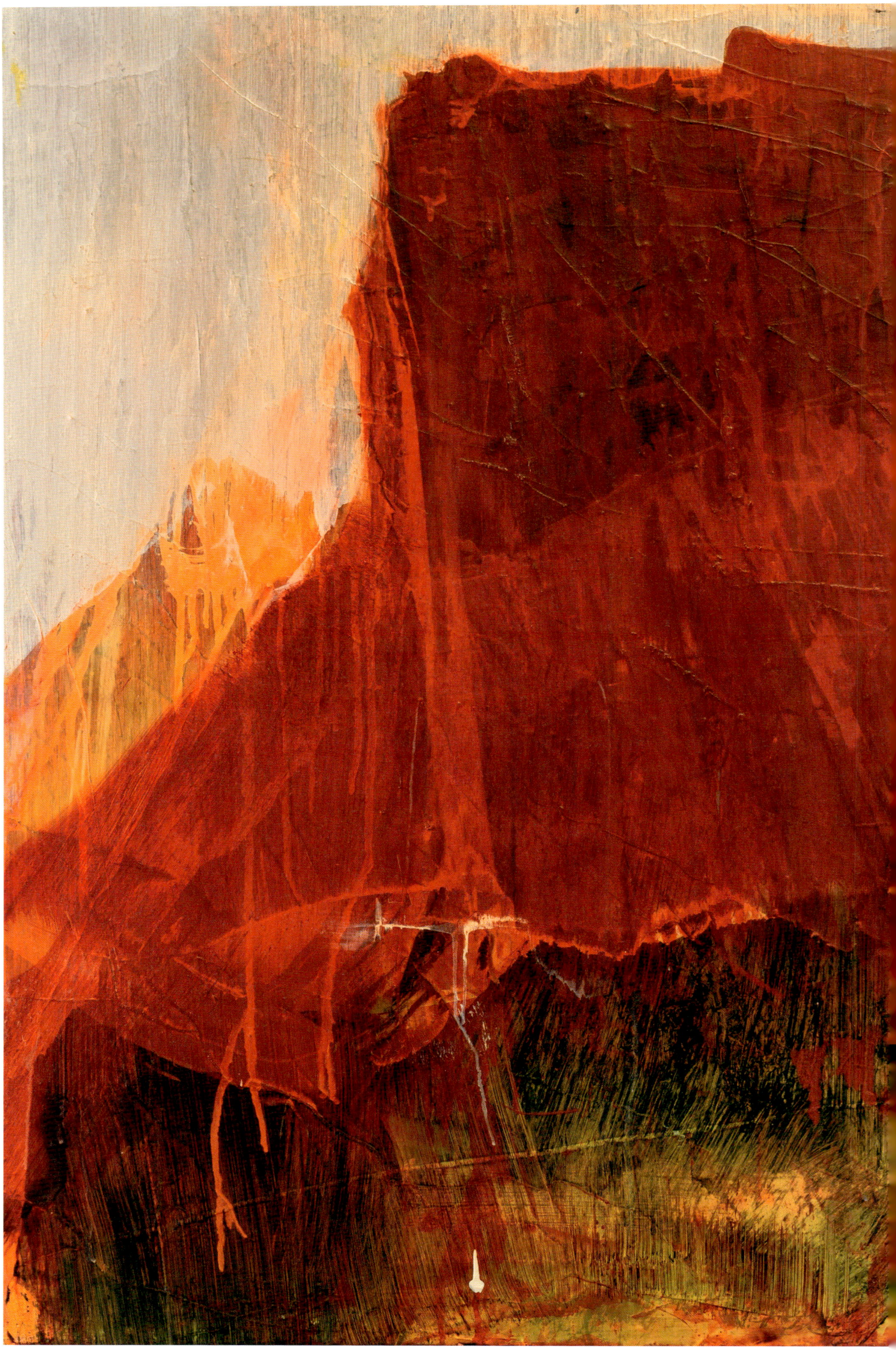

Bold as Love detail 1

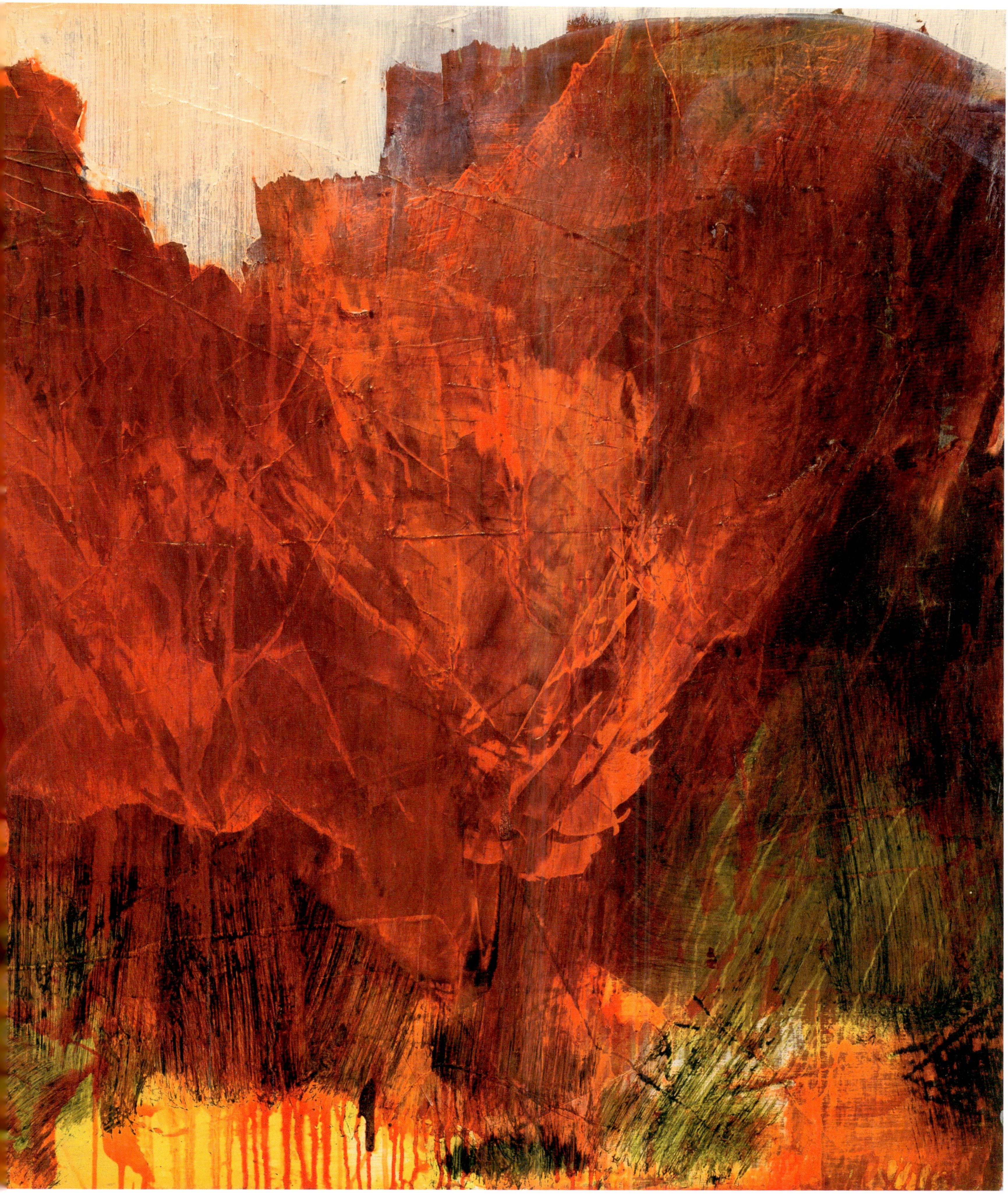

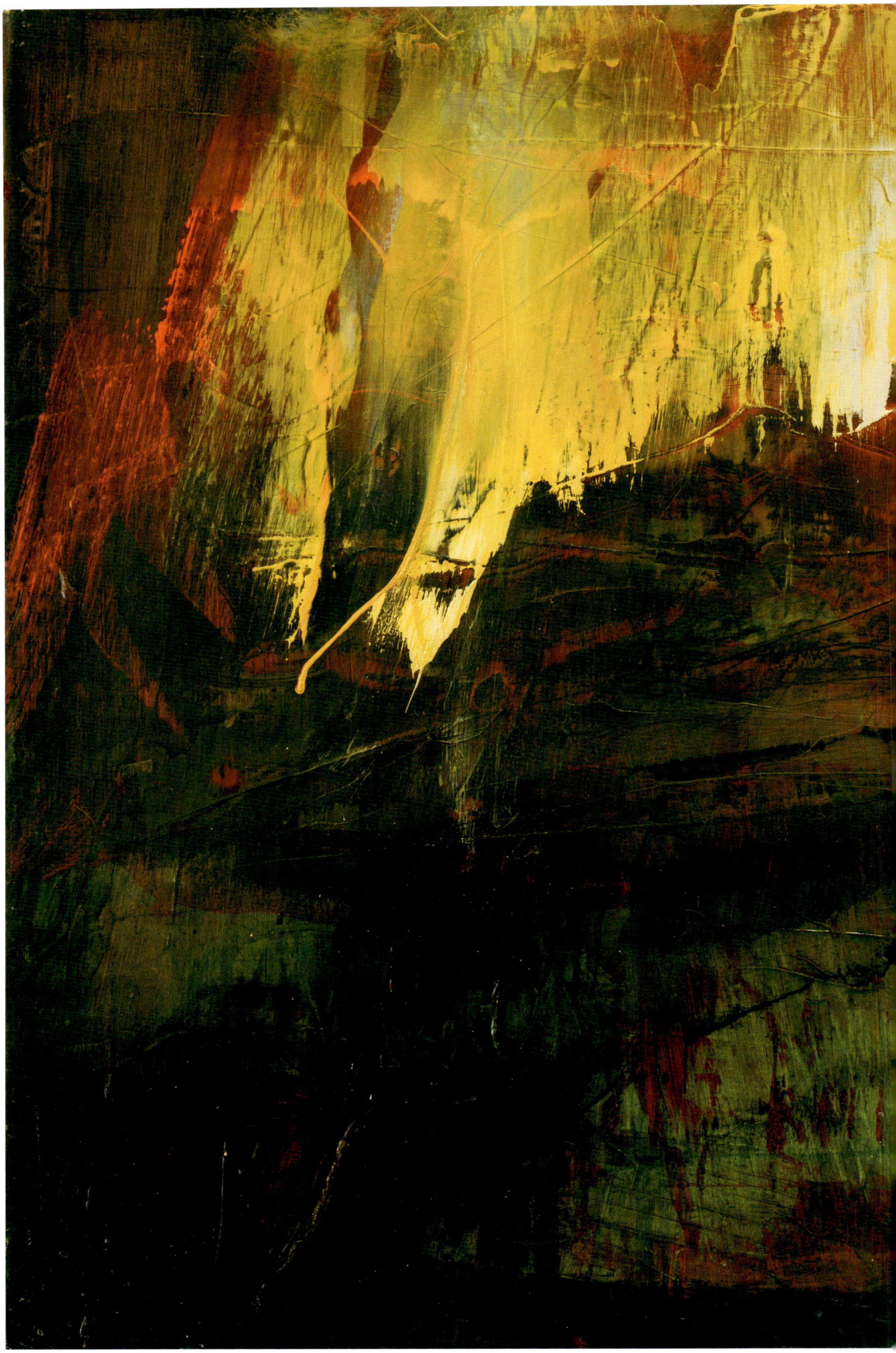

Bold as Love detail 2

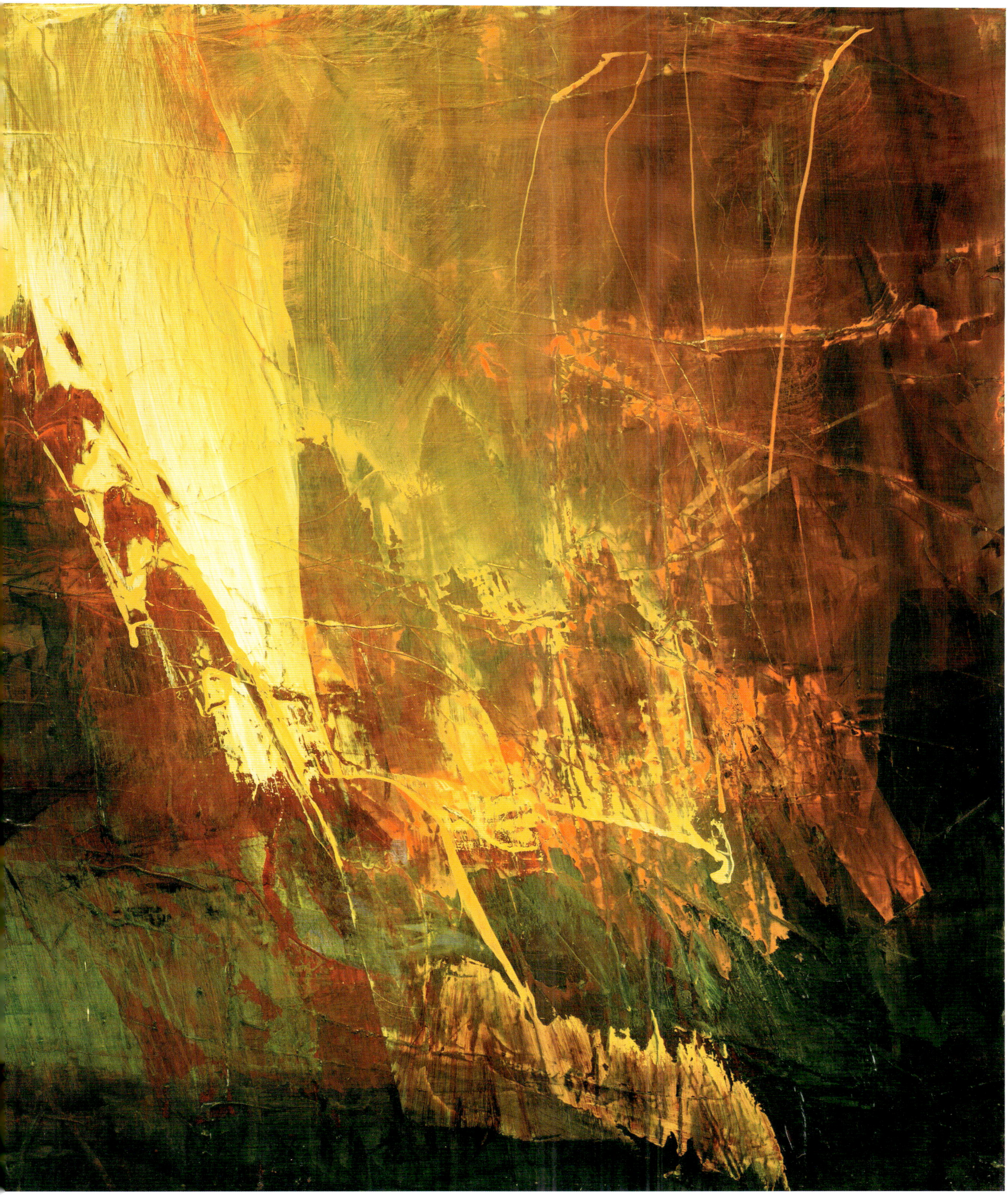

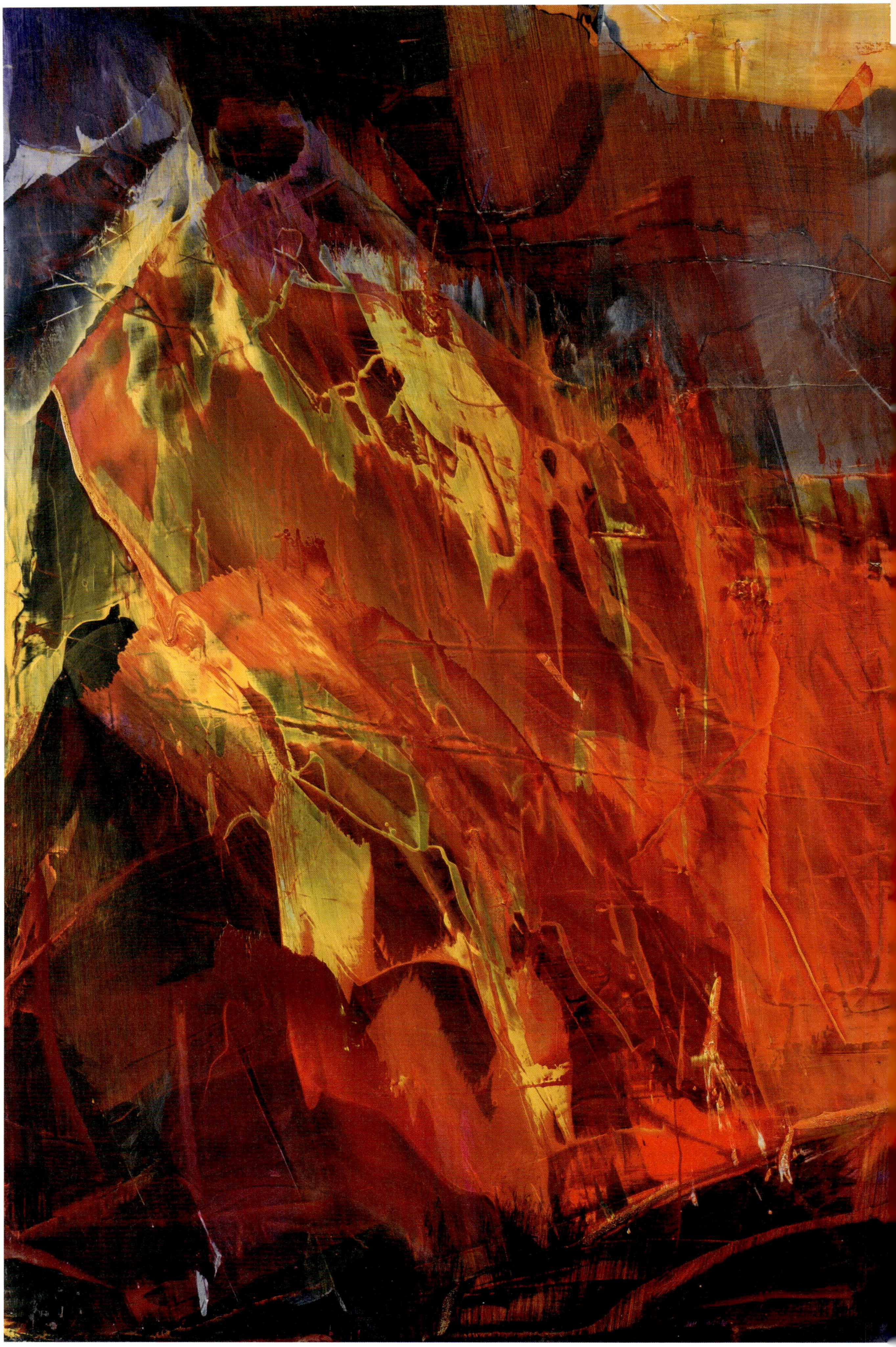

Bold as Love detail 3

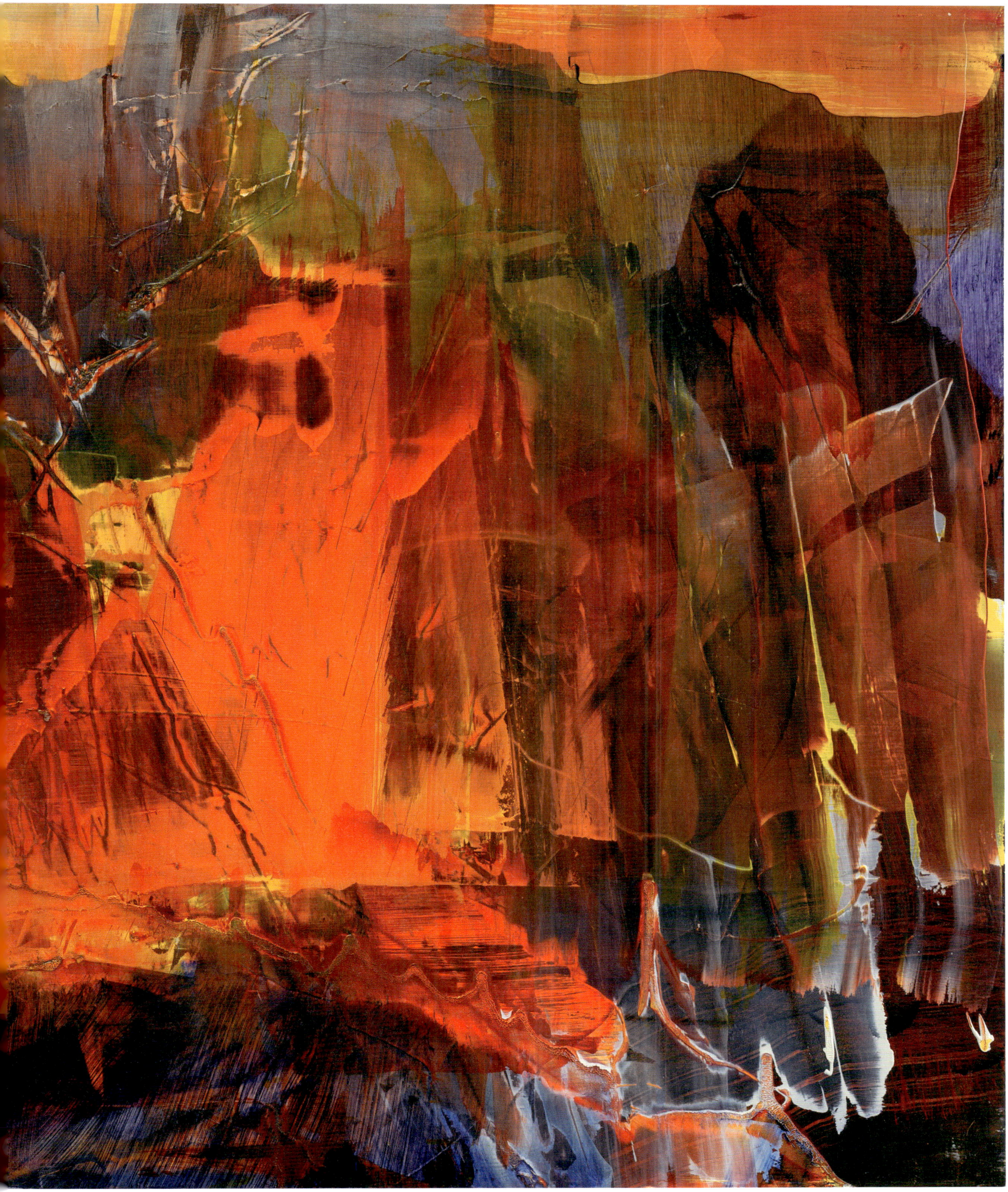

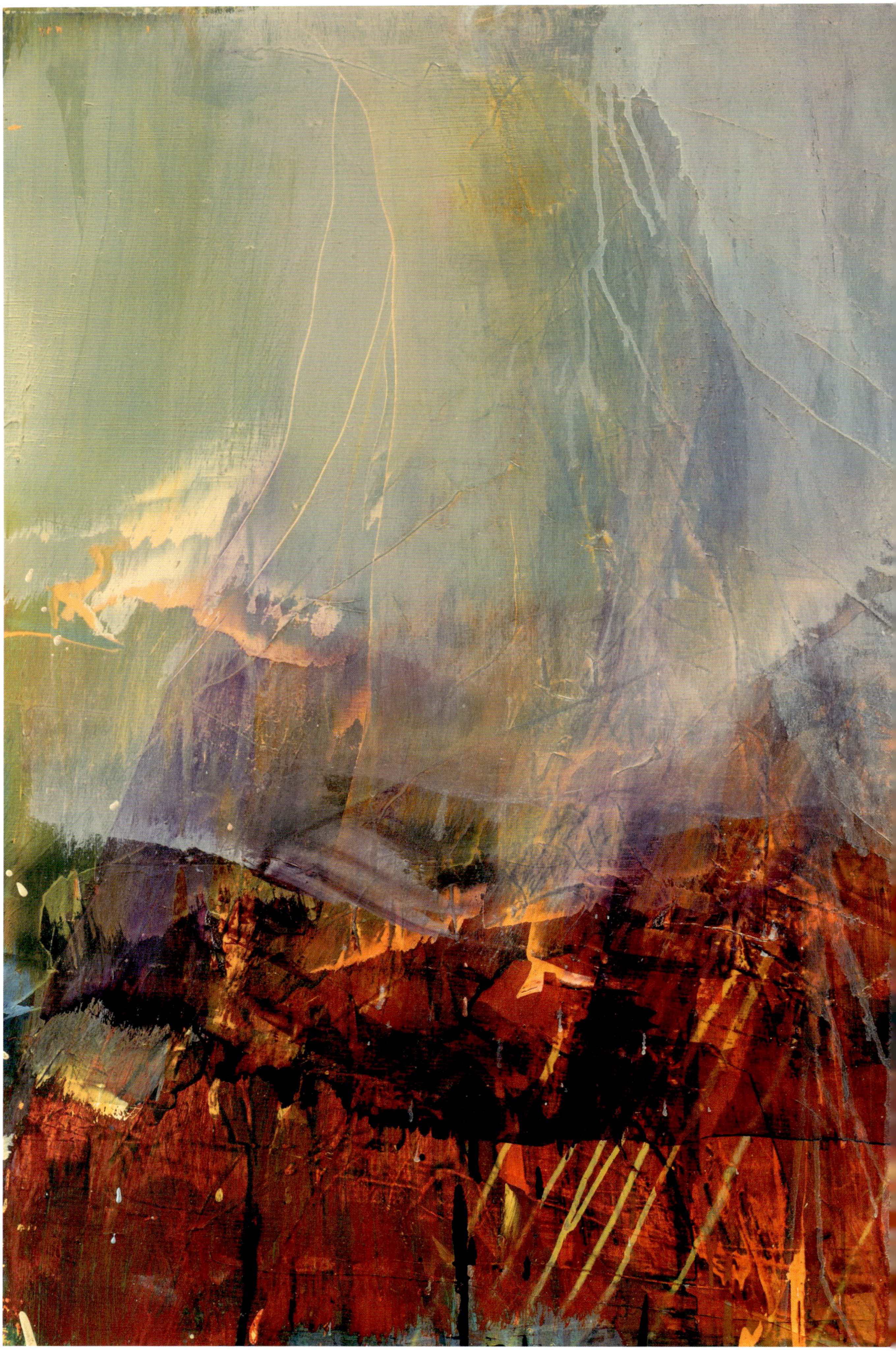

Bold as Love detail 4

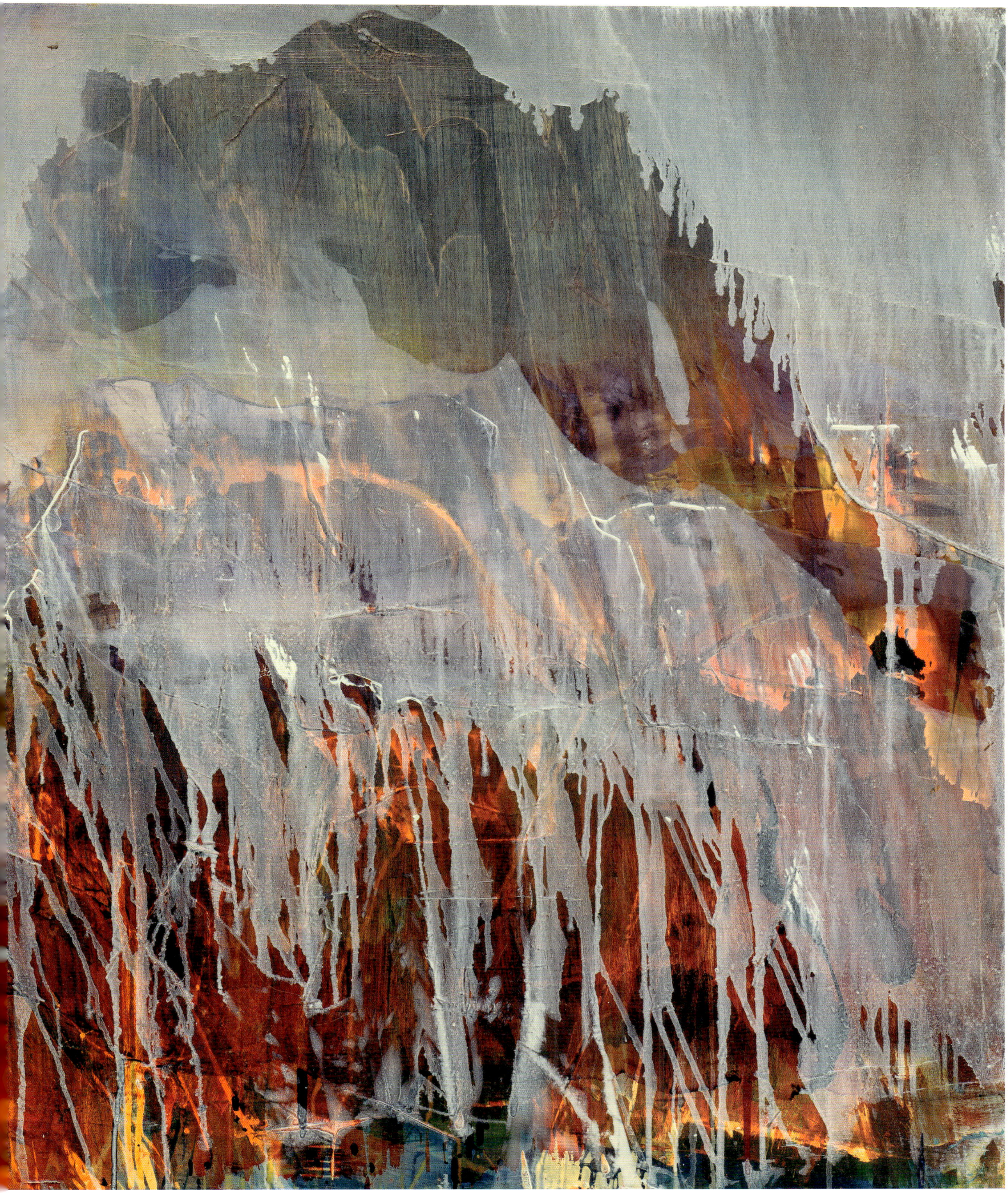

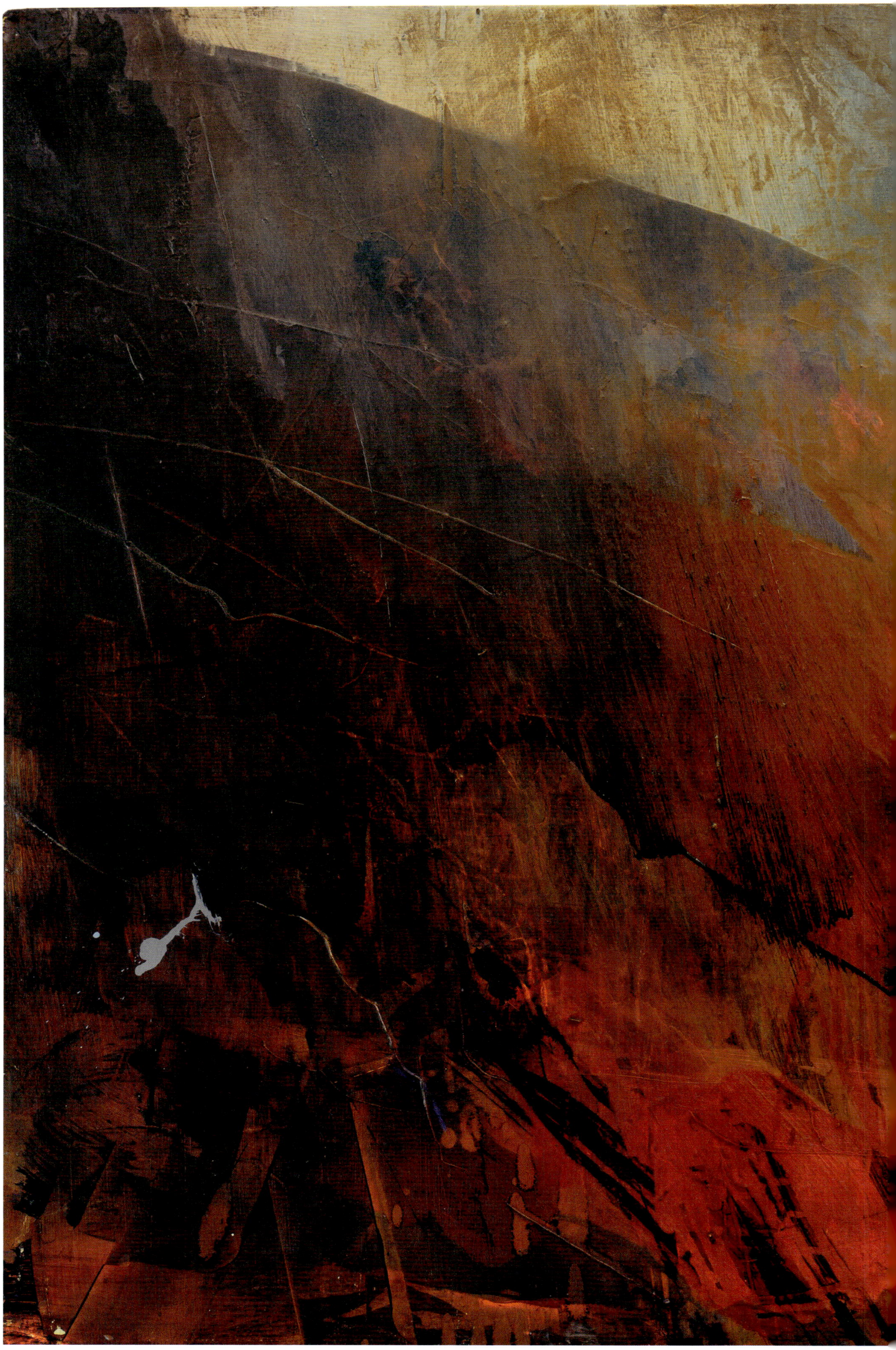

Bold as Love detail 5

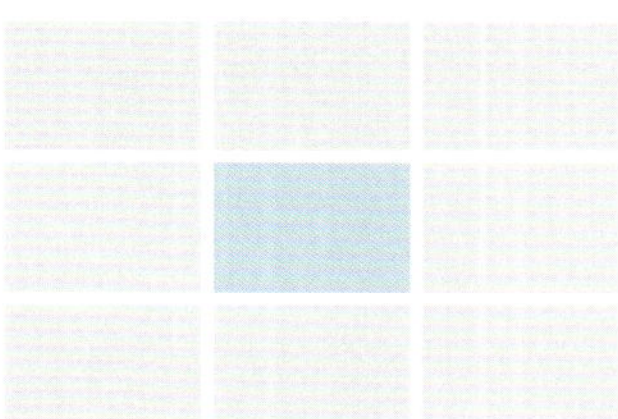

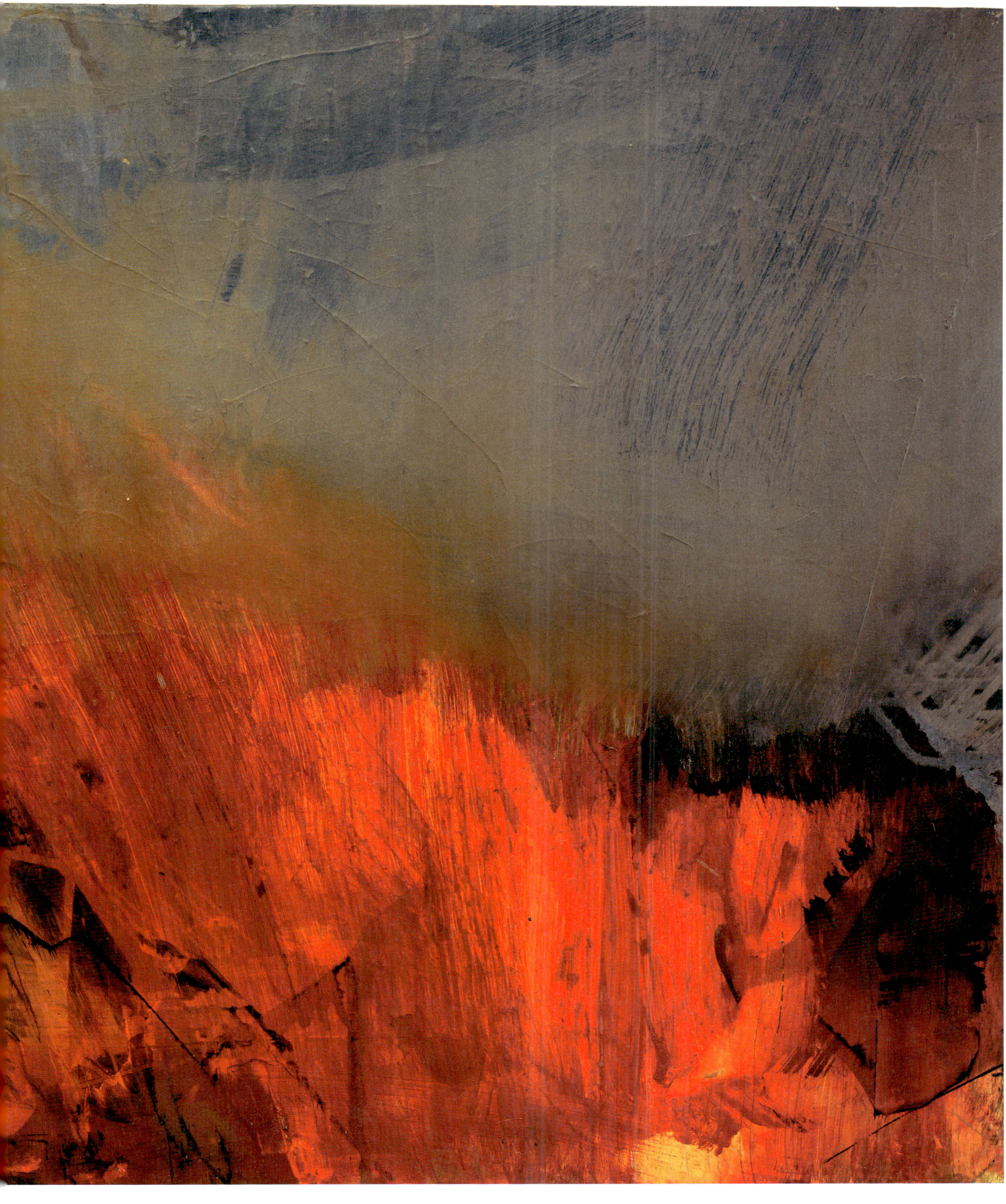

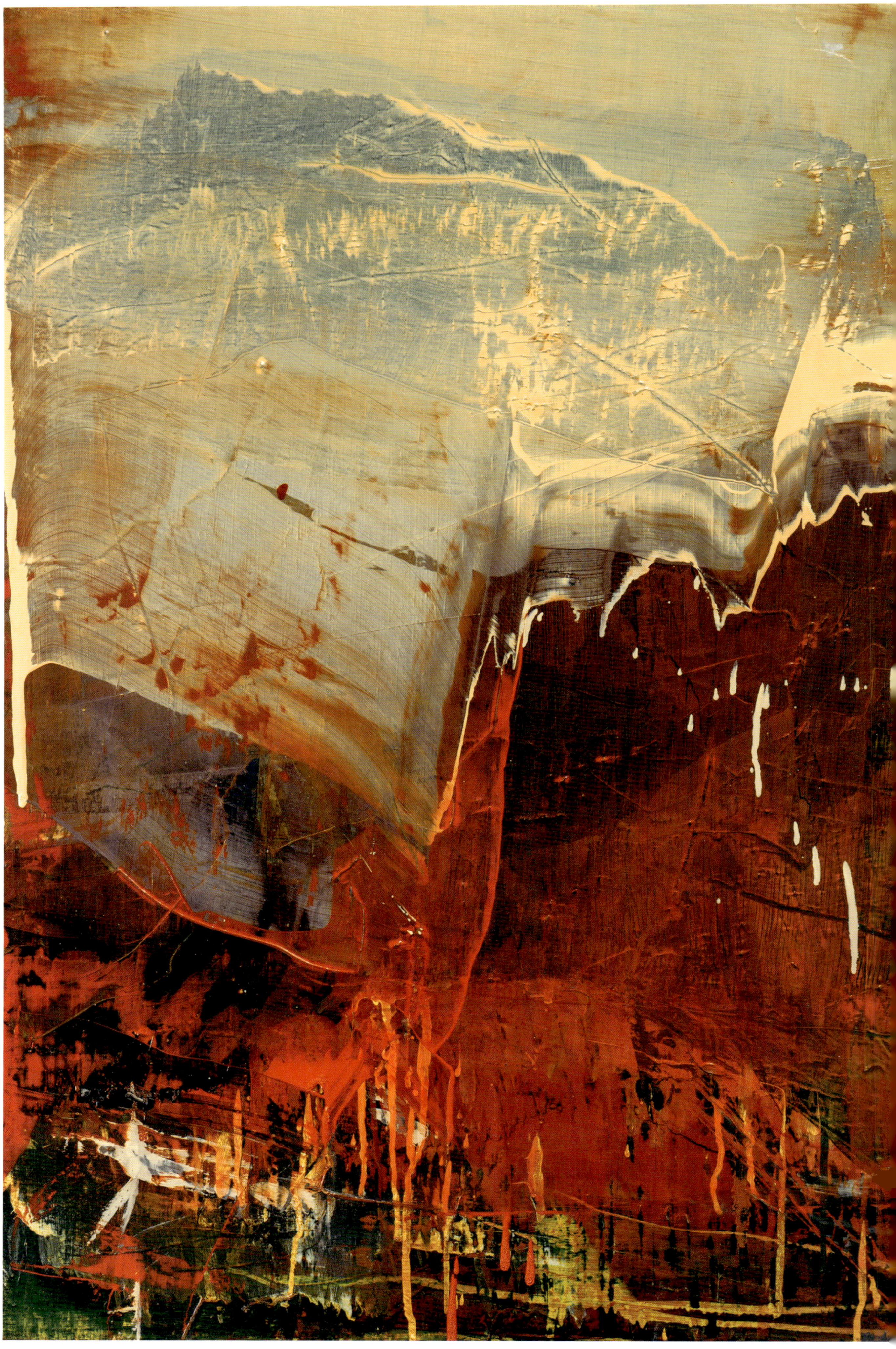

Bold as Love detail 6

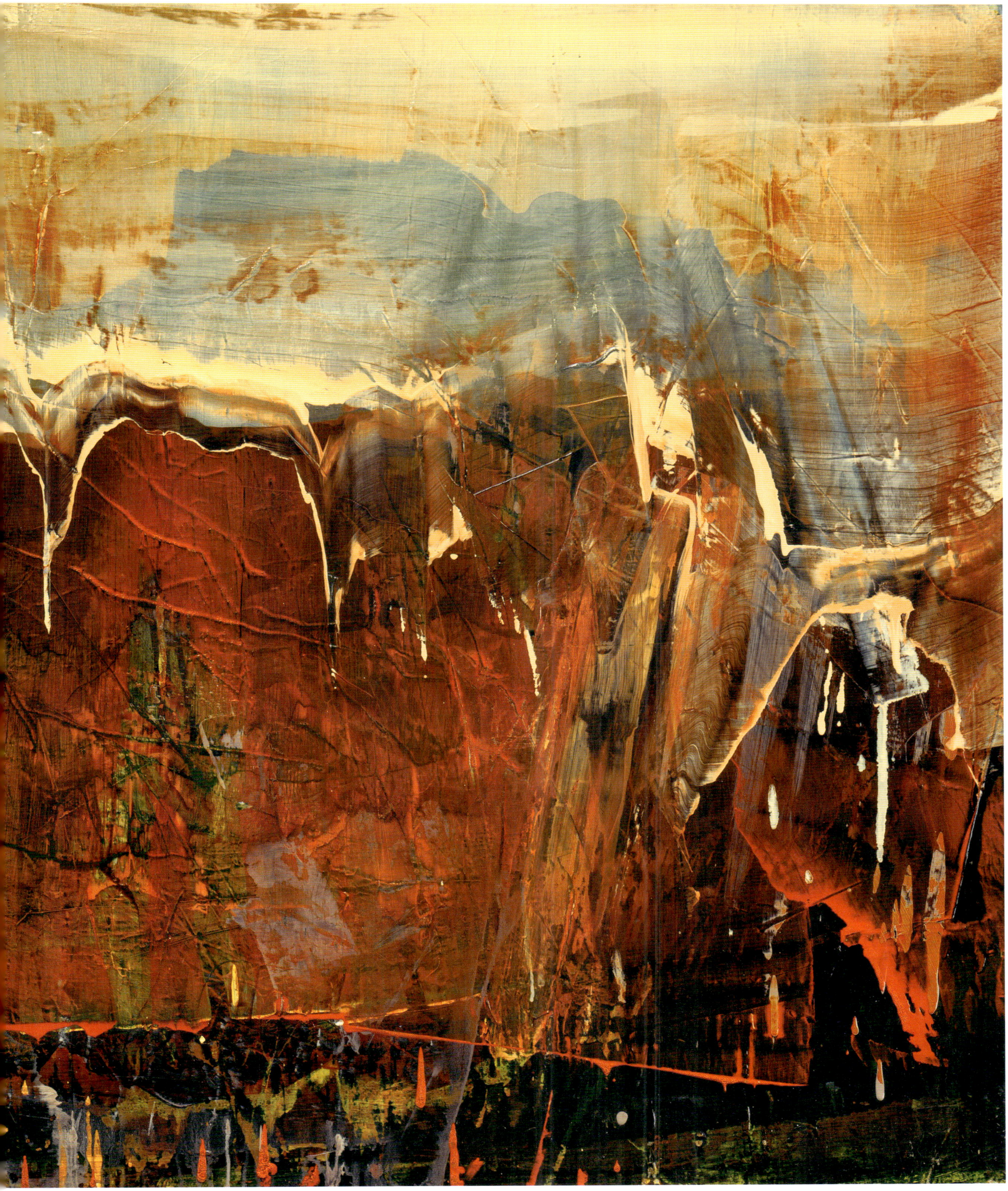

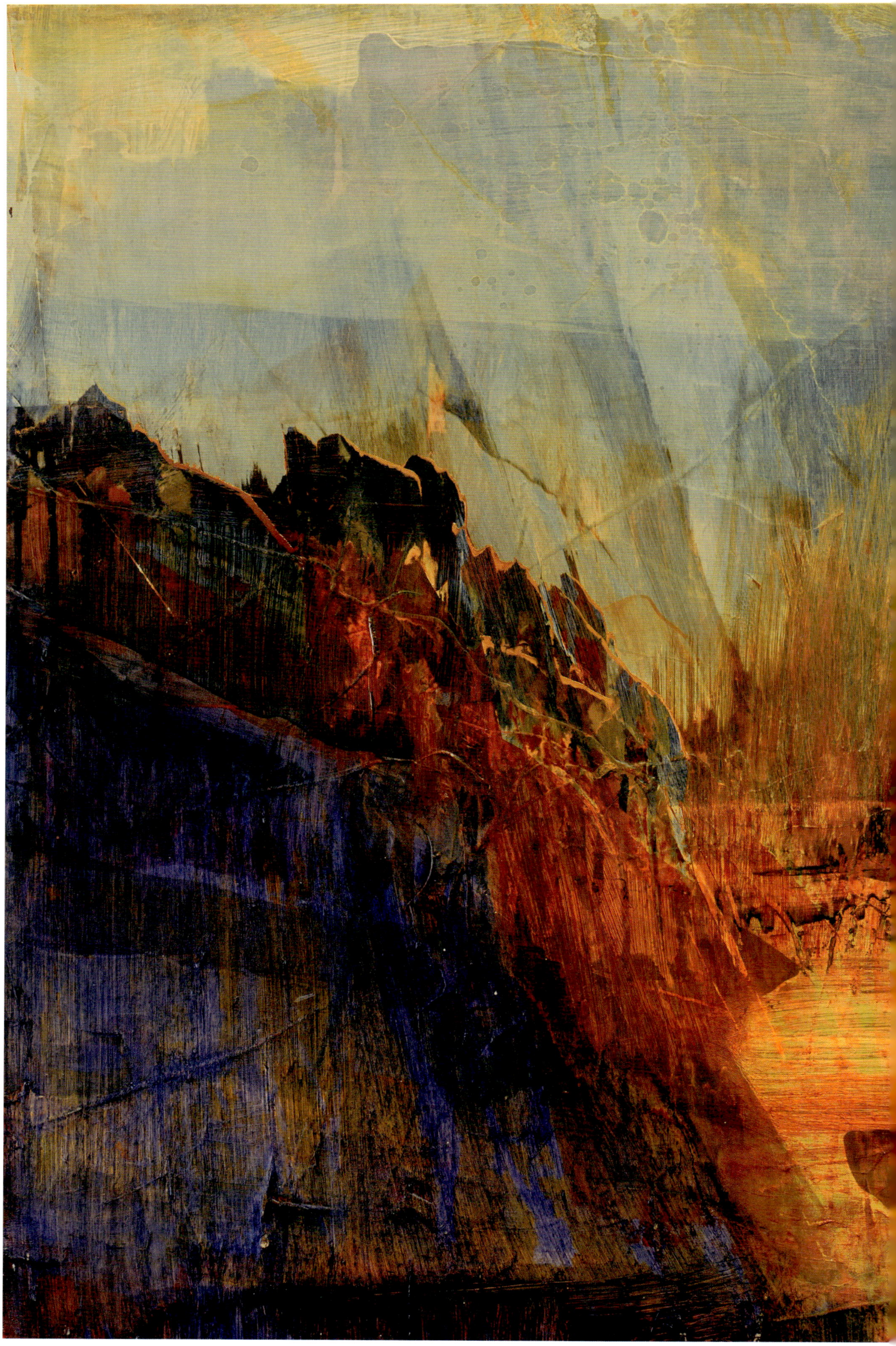

Bold as Love detail 7

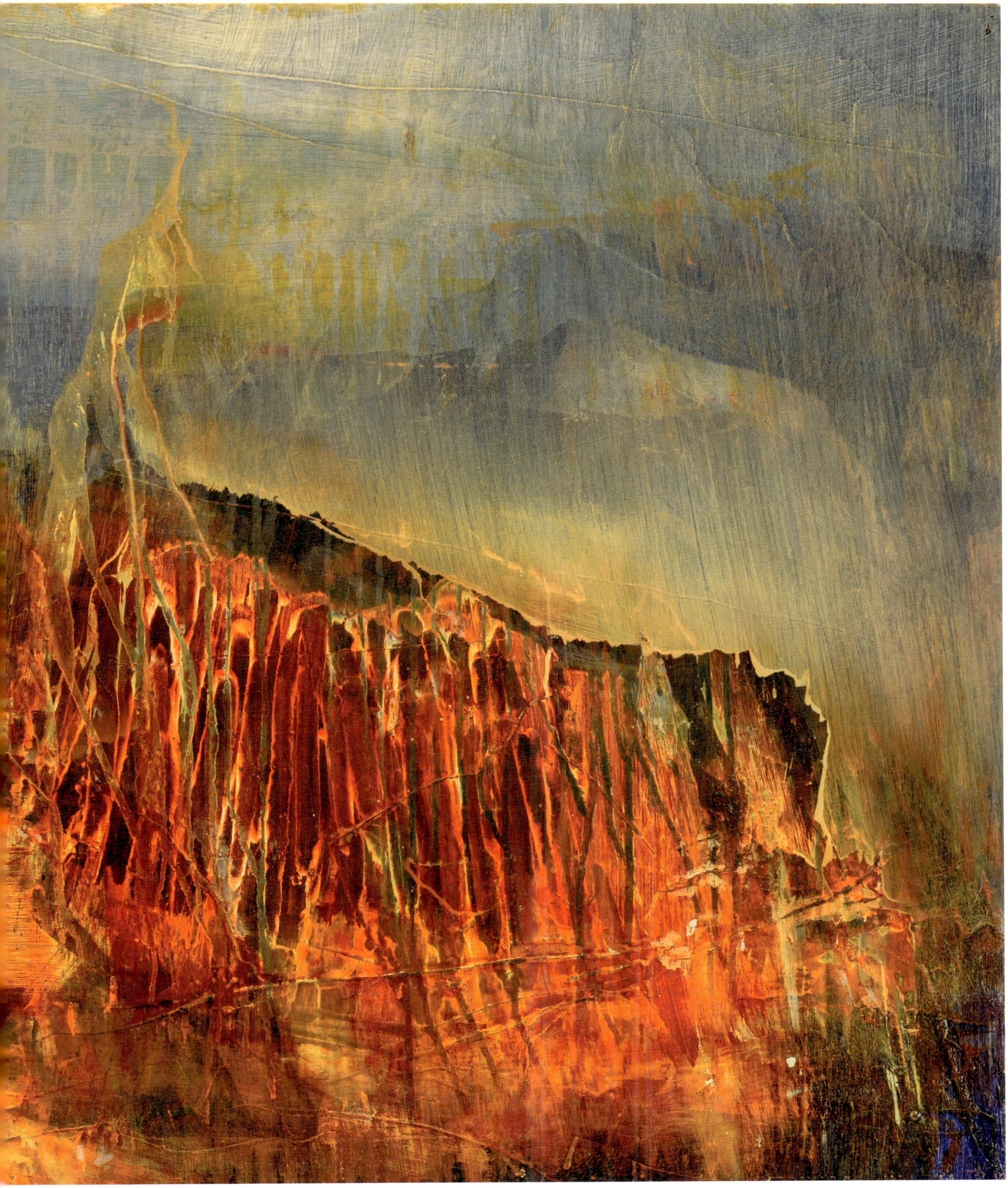

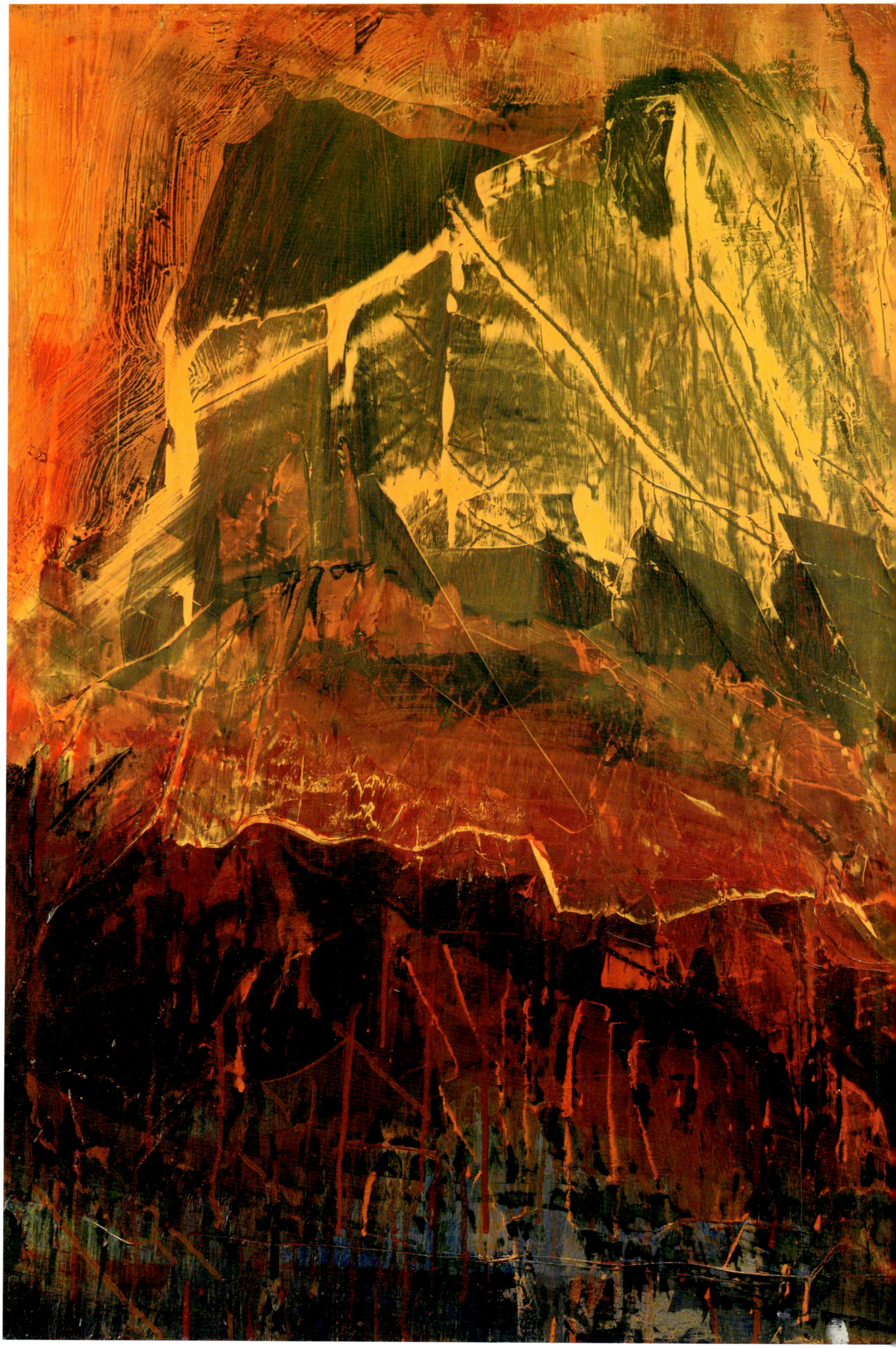

Bold as Love detail 8

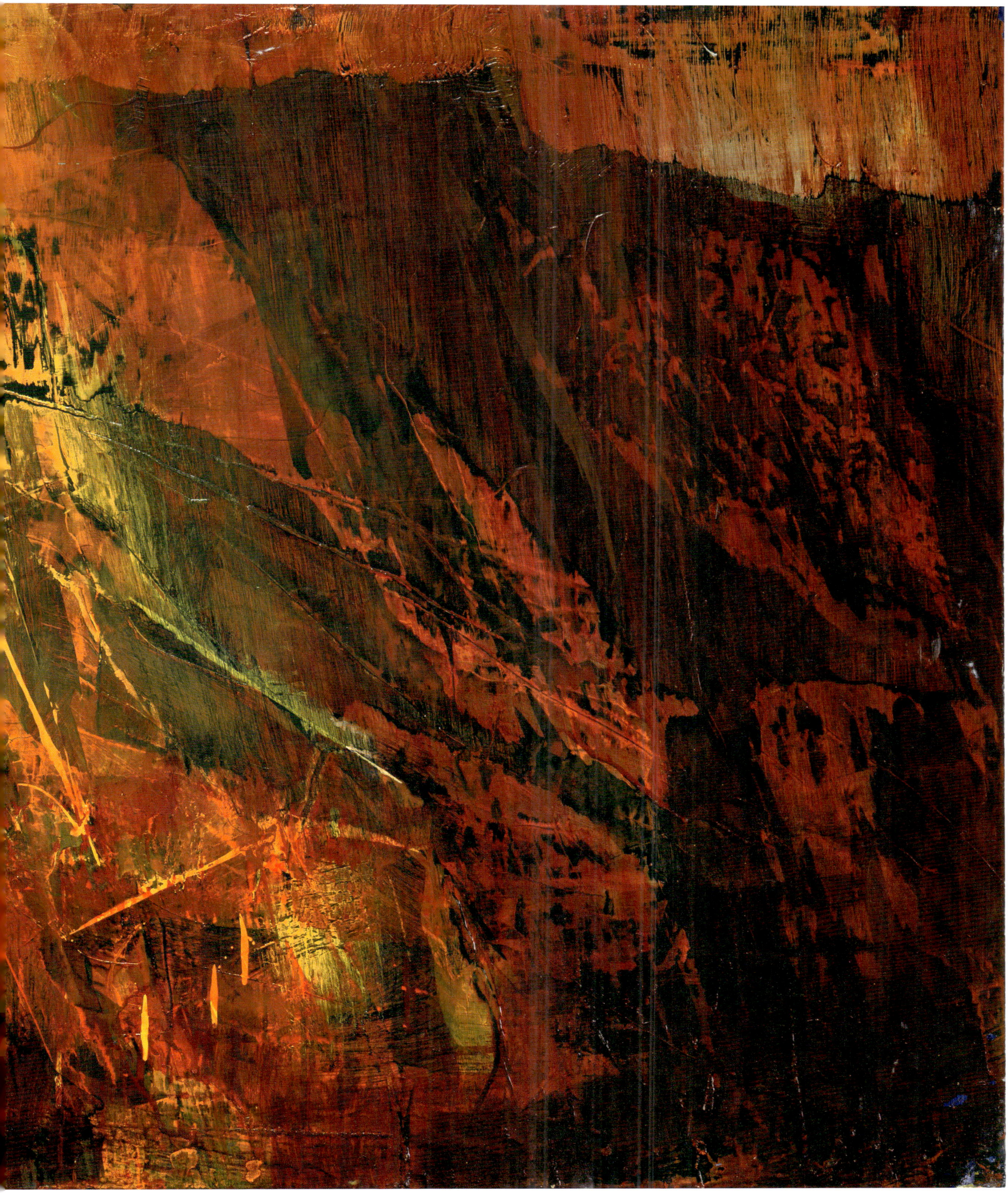

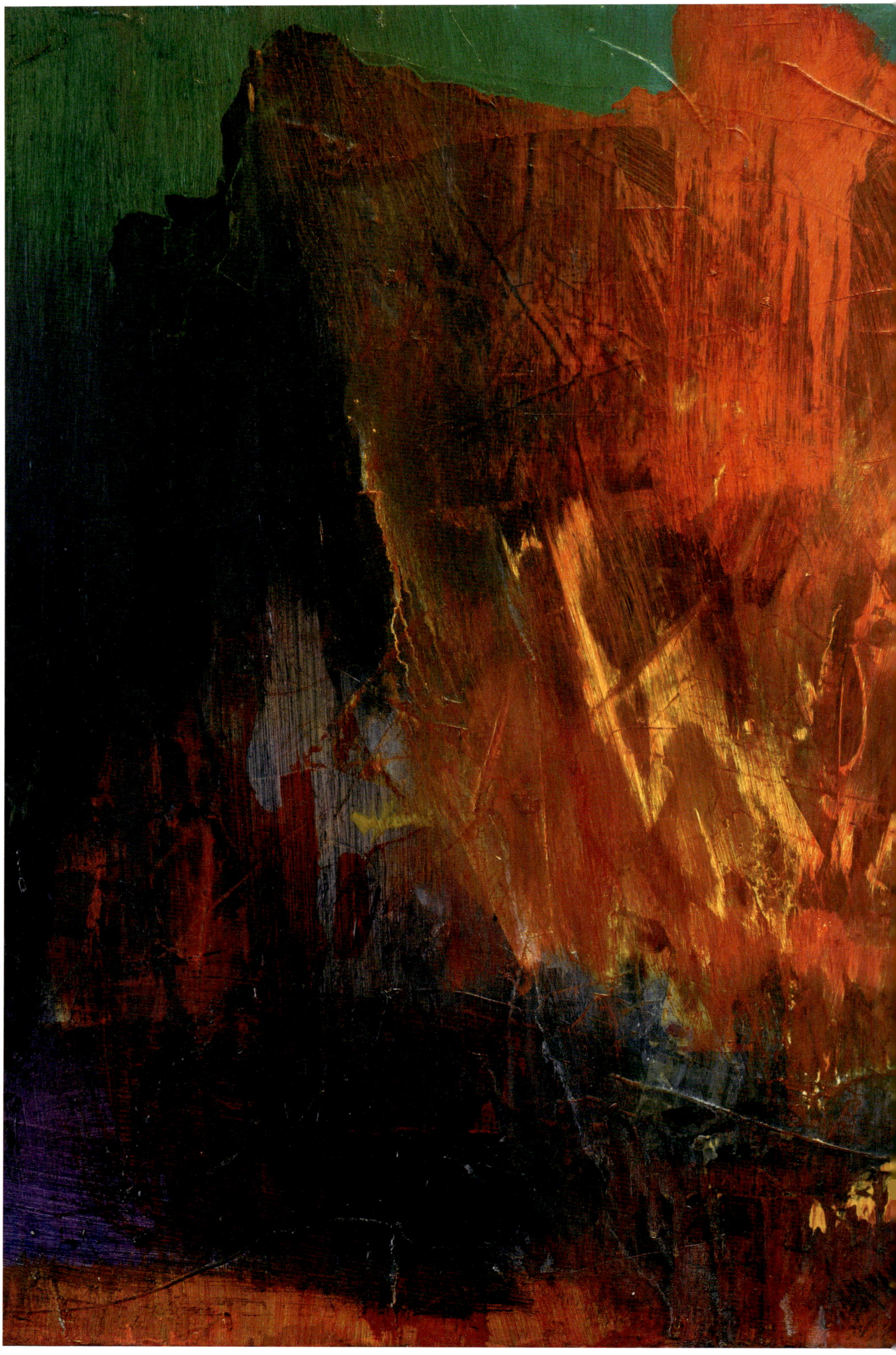

Bold as Love detail 9

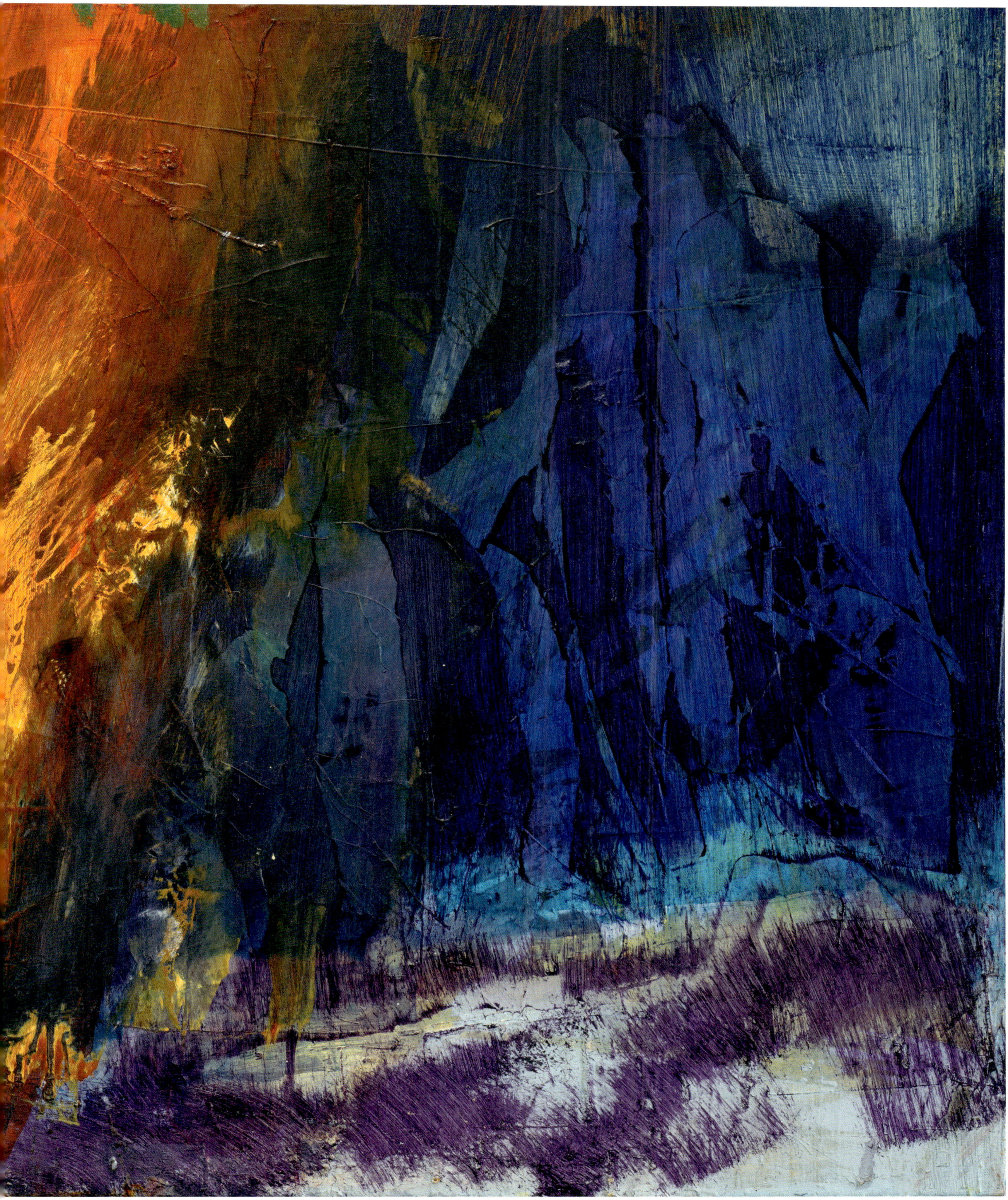

James Lavadour: Land of Origin exhibition checklist

James Lavadour (American, Walla Walla, b. 1951)

Paintings

Crow's Shadow, 1987. Oil on canvas, 48 ¾ x 34 ¾ inches. Lazar-Stock Collection.

The Seven Valleys and The Five Valleys, 1988. Oil on canvas, 55 x 96 inches. Whitney Museum of American Art, New York; Gift of Ida Cole; 2018.107a-l.

Boom!, 1988. Oil on canvas, 74 x 72 inches. Denver Art Museum: Native Arts acquisition funds, 2015.538A-B. © James Lavadour.

Fire and Bones, 1990-91. Oil on linen, 31 x 62 inches. Boise Art Museum Permanent Collection.

Release the Sun, 1990-91. Oil on linen, 83 x 83 inches. Tacoma Art Museum, Gift of Rebecca and Alexander C. Stewart.

Nest of Suns, 1998. Oil on panel, 72 x 96 inches. Courtesy of the Northwest Museum of Arts and Culture, Museum purchase, 2003 (4041.1).

Flag, 2000. Oil on panel, 80 x 80 inches. Tacoma Art Museum, Anonymous gift, 2022.1.

Untitled, 2000. Oil on paper, 27 x 35 inches. Courtesy of the artist.

Bridge, 2001. Oil on panel, 54 x 72 inches. Courtesy of the artist.

Point, 2003. Oil on plywood, 78 x 60 inches. Boise Art Museum Permanent Collection; Gift of Driek and Michael Zirinsky.

Ice, 2007. Oil on panel, 48 x 60 inches. Collection of the Hallie Ford Museum of Art, Willamette University, purchased with funds from an endowment gift from the Confederated Tribes of Grand Ronde, through their Spirit Mountain Community Fund.

Straight Ahead, 2010. Oil on panel, 76 x 158 inches. Collection of Overmeyer-Dougher Family.

Lift, 2011. Oil on panel, 50 x 94 inches. Private Collection.

Torch, 2012. Oil on panel, 48 x 60 inches. Jordan Schnitzer Museum of Art, University of Oregon: Acquired with the assistance of The Ford Family Foundation, through a special grant program managed by the Oregon Arts Commission, and the Van Duyn Acquisition Endowment; 2015:9.1.

Out of Range, 2013. Oil on panel, 36 x 48 x 2 inches. Crystal Bridges Museum of American Art, Bentonville, Arkansas, 2021.42.

Land of Origin, 2015. Oil on panel, 39 x 78 inches. Jane and Spencer Beebe Family Trust.

River Miles I, 2020. Oil on paper, 20 x 28 inches. Collection of the Regional Arts and Culture Council, Portland, OR.

River Miles II, 2020. Oil on paper, 20 x 28 inches. Collection of the Regional Arts and Culture Council, Portland, OR.

River Miles III, 2020. Oil on paper, 20 x 28 inches. Collection of the Regional Arts and Culture Council, Portland, OR.

River Miles VI, 2020. Oil on paper, 20 x 28 inches. Collection of the Regional Arts and Culture Council, Portland, OR.

River Miles VII, 2020. Oil on paper, 20 x 28 inches. Collection of the Regional Arts and Culture Council, Portland, OR.

The New Ghosts of Ceded Boundaries, 2021. Oil on panel, 90 x 102 x 2 inches. Courtesy of the artist and PDX CONTEMPORARY ART.

The Ghosts of Many Things, 2023. Oil on panel, 76 x 112 x 2 inches. Art Bridges.

Lucky Star, 2024. Oil on wood, 74 x 145 inches. Collection of the Jordan Schnitzer Family Foundation.

Bold as Love, 2024. Oil on wood, 96 x 144 inches. Collection of Bill and Leslie Cornog.

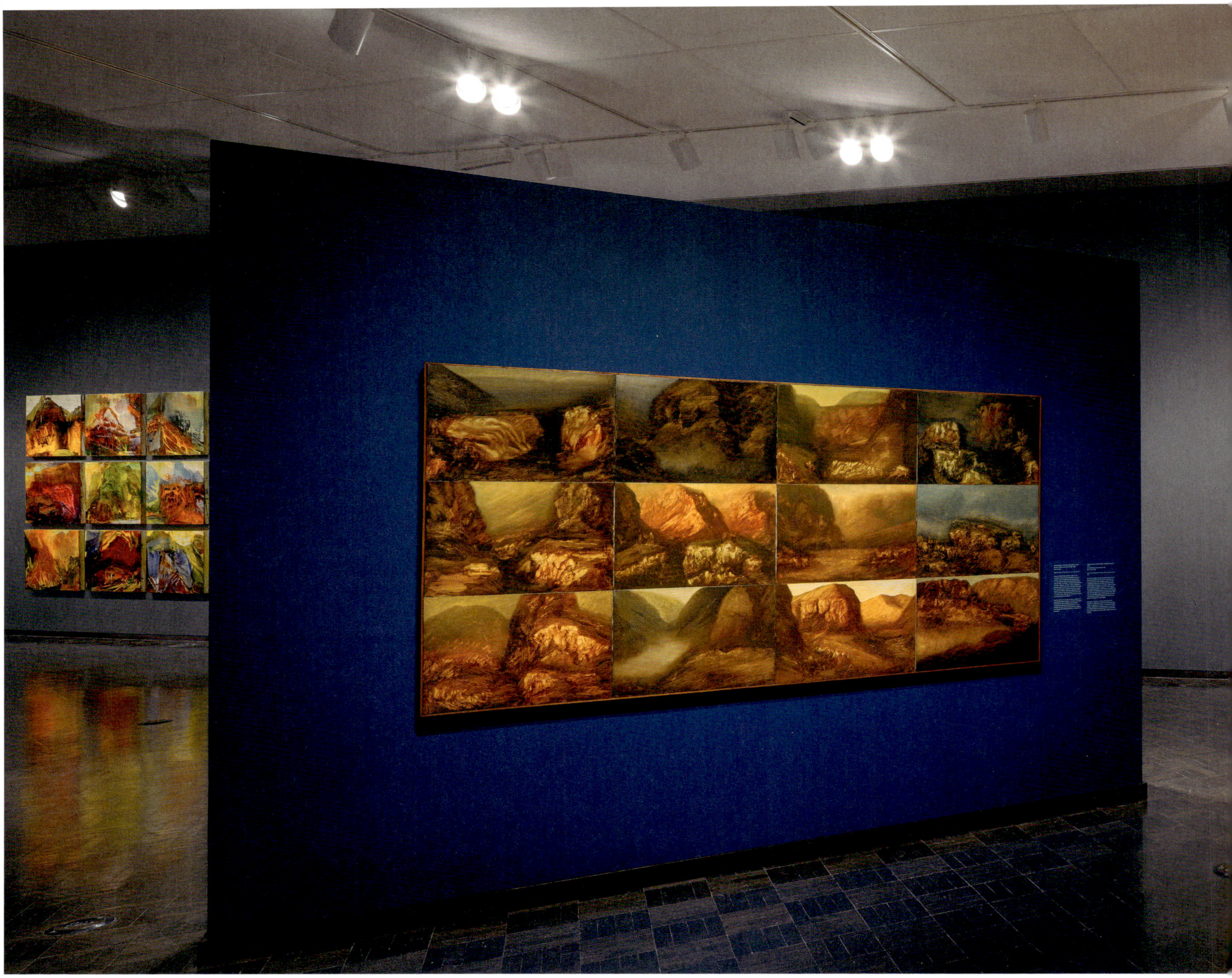

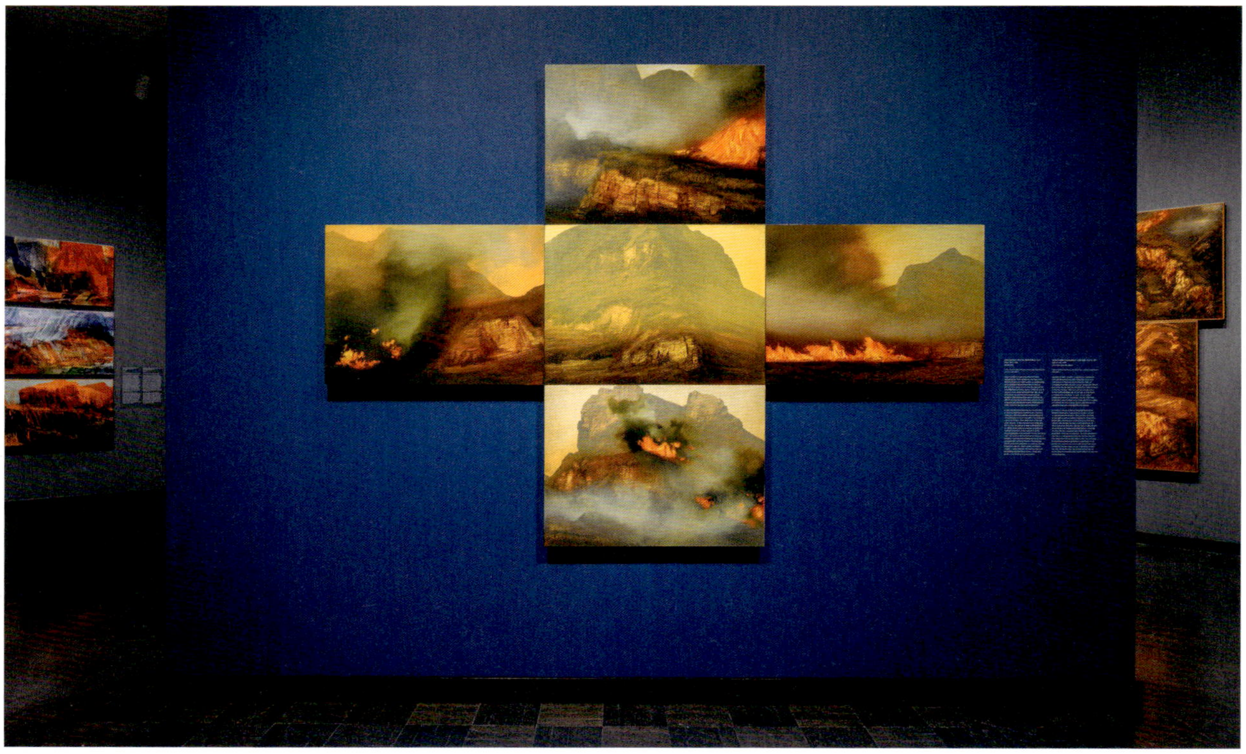

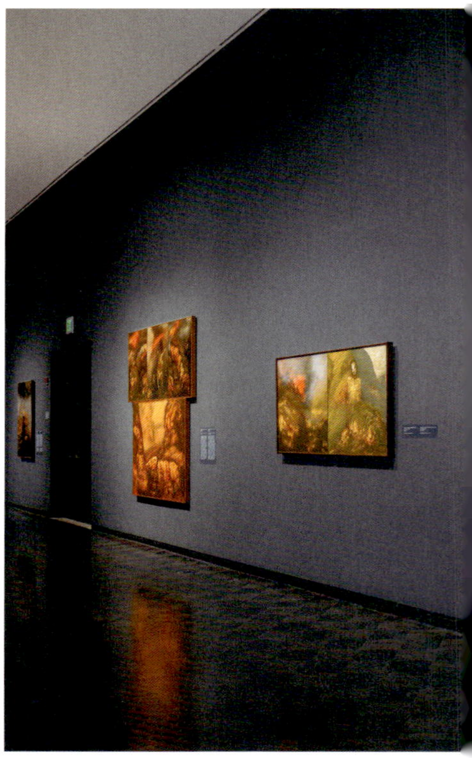

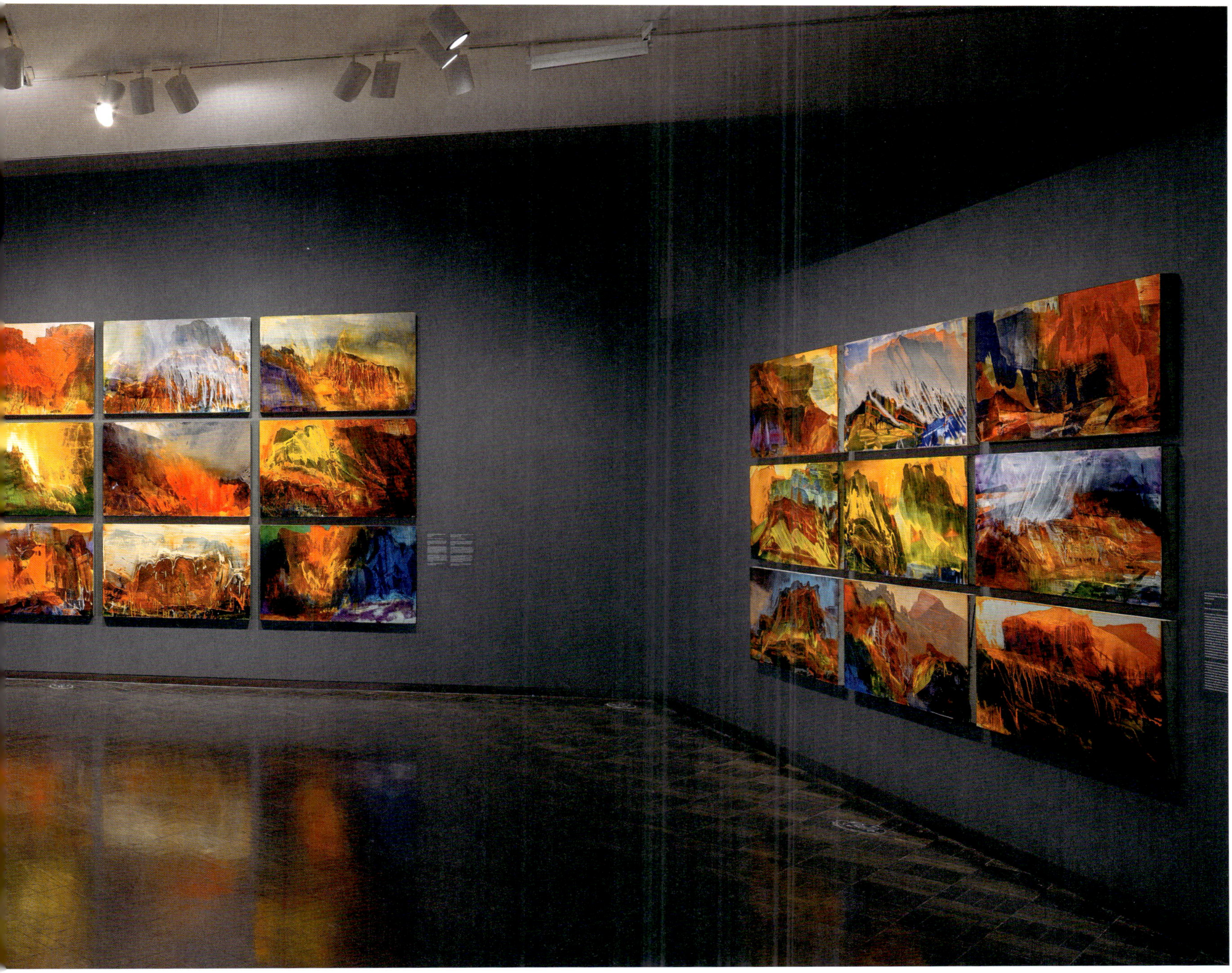

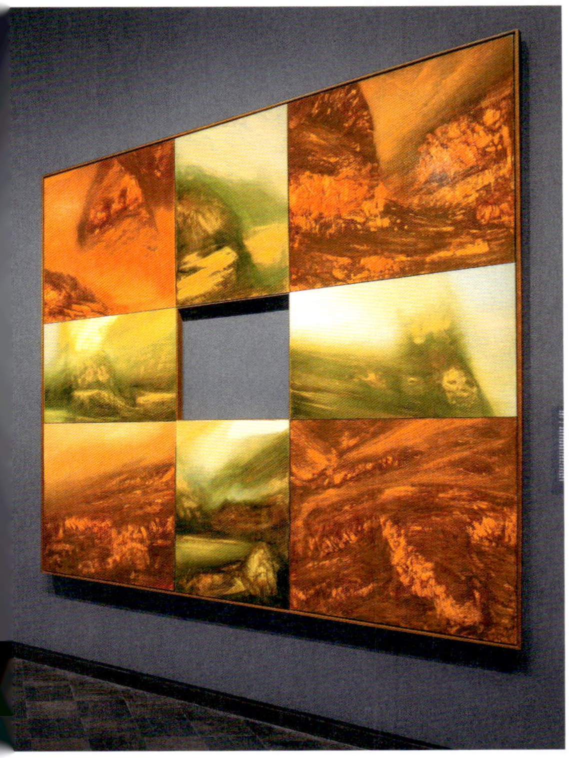

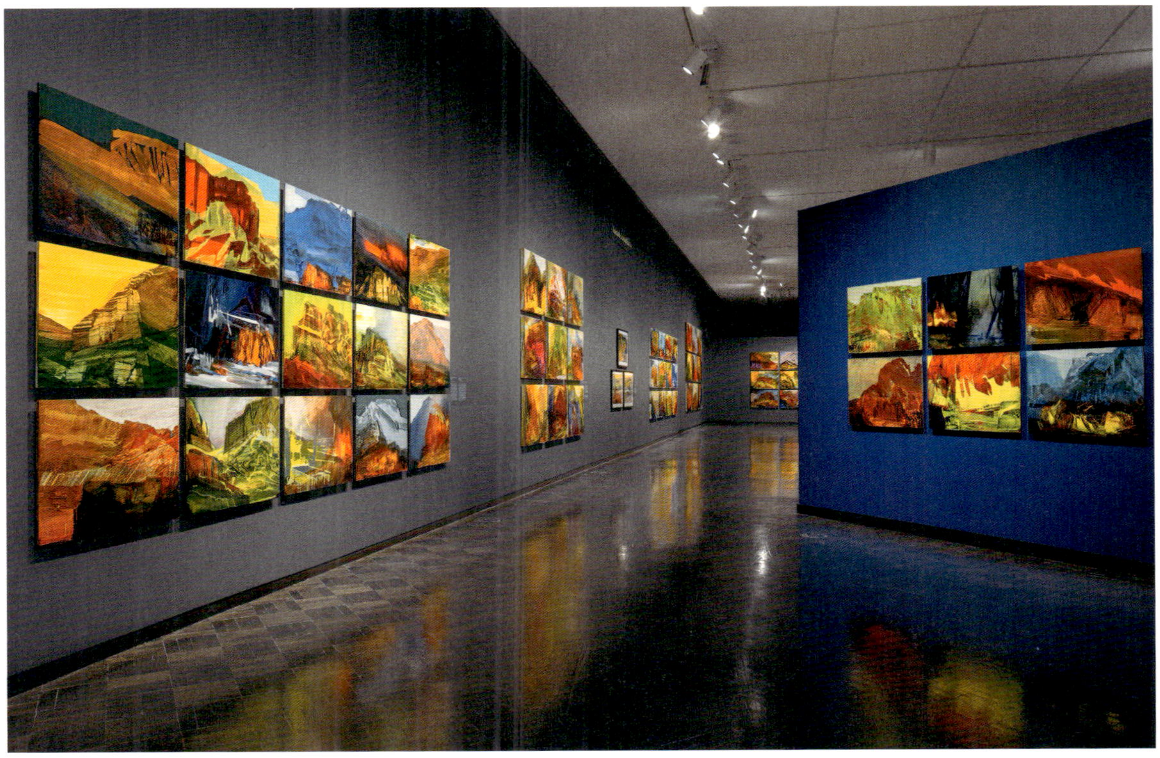

Prints

Man and Woman, ed. 66/100, 1994. Woodblock print in the *ukiyo-e* tradition (printed by Tadashi Toda [Japanese, 1936–2000]), 24 ¼ x 31 inches. Published by the Mokuhanga Project Space, Walla Walla, Washington, April 1994. Courtesy of the artist.

Dreaming of Whirlwinds, T/P, 1994. Color aquatint, soap ground etching, and drypoint, 35 x 46 inches. Published by Beta Press, Seattle. Collaborating Master Printer: Marcia Bartholme. Courtesy of the artist.

Dreaming of Whirlwinds, A/P 3, 1994. Color aquatint, soap ground etching, and drypoint, 35 x 46 inches. Published by Beta Press, Seattle. Collaborating Master Printer: Marcia Bartholme. Private collection.

Untitled, T/P, 1997. Waterless lithograph, 18 x 21 inches. Published by 21 Steps Studio. Collaborating Master Printer: Jeff Ryan. Courtesy of the artist.

Untitled, ed. 18/18, 2002. Lithograph, 42 x 51 inches. Published by the Brodsky Center at PAFA. Collaborating Master Printer: Eileen M. Foti. Courtesy of the artist.

Land of Origin, ed. 2/18, 2015. Lithograph, 45 x 60 ½ inches. Published at Crow's Shadow Institute of the Arts. Collaborating Master Printer: Frank Janzen. Crow's Shadow Institute of the Arts Archive, Hallie Ford Museum of Art, Willamette University.

Summer, ed. 8/30, 2018-19. Six color lithograph on Somerset Satin White, 30 x 22 inches. Published at Crow's Shadow Institute of the Arts. Collaborating Master Printer: Judith Baumann. Jordan Schnitzer Museum of Art, University of Oregon: Purchased with funds from the William A. Haseltine Endowment for Pacific Northwest Art.

Winter, ed. 8/20, 2023. Five color lithograph on Somerset Satin White, 25 x 34 inches. Published at Crow's Shadow Institute of the Arts, January 2024. Collaborating Master Printer: Judith Baumann. Jordan Schnitzer Museum of Art, University of Oregon: Purchased with funds from the William A. Haseltine Endowment for Pacific Northwest Art.

Spring, ed. 8/20, 2023. Seven color lithograph on Somerset Satin White, 25 x 34 inches. Published at Crow's Shadow Institute of the Arts, January 2024. Collaborating Master Printer: Judith Baumann. Jordan Schnitzer Museum of Art, University of Oregon: Purchased with funds from the William A. Haseltine Endowment for Pacific Northwest Art.

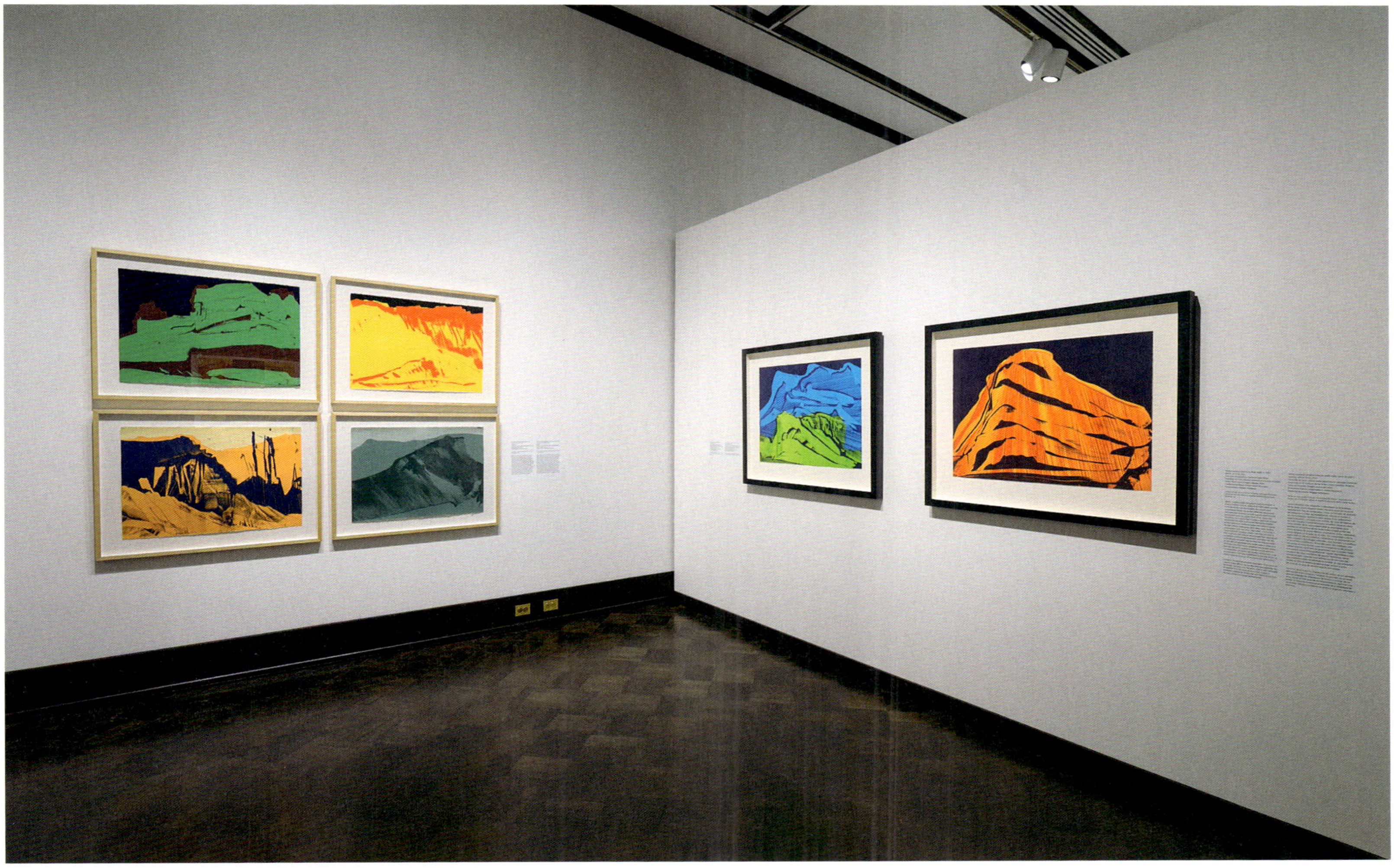

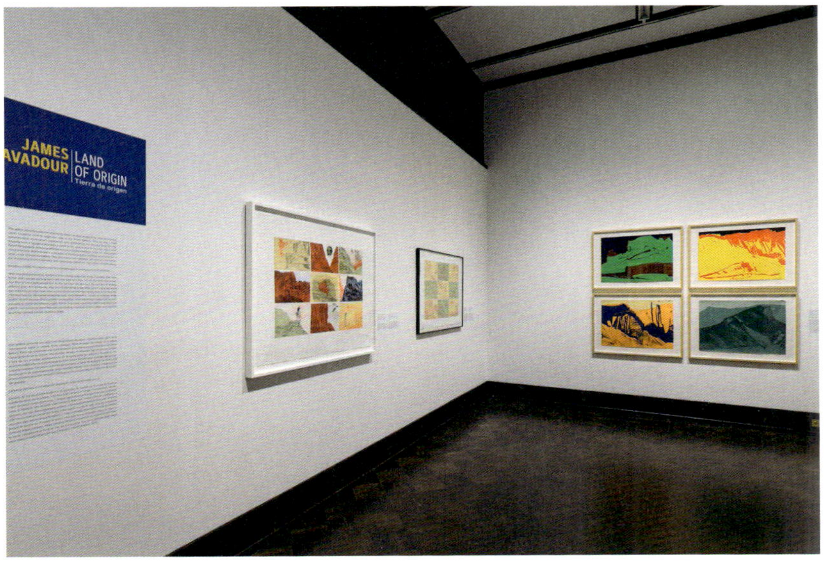
JAMES
AVADOUR
LAND
OF ORIGIN
Tierra de origen

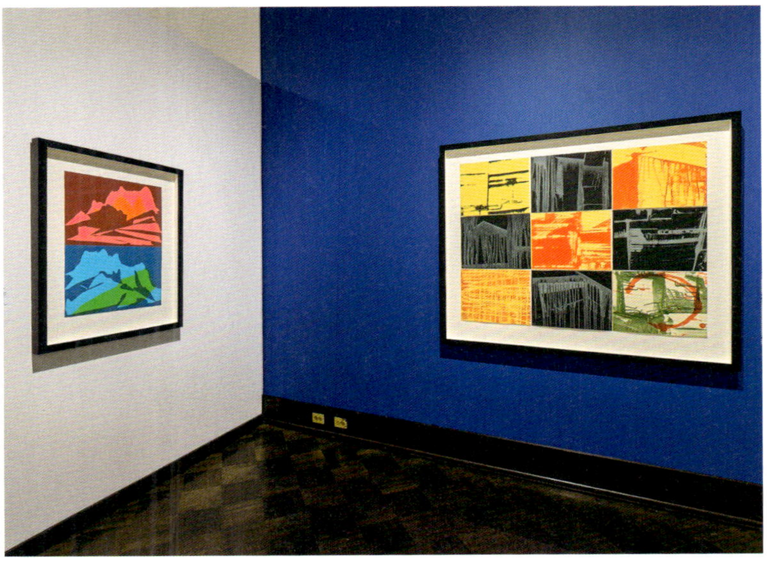

Artist's Curriculum Vitae

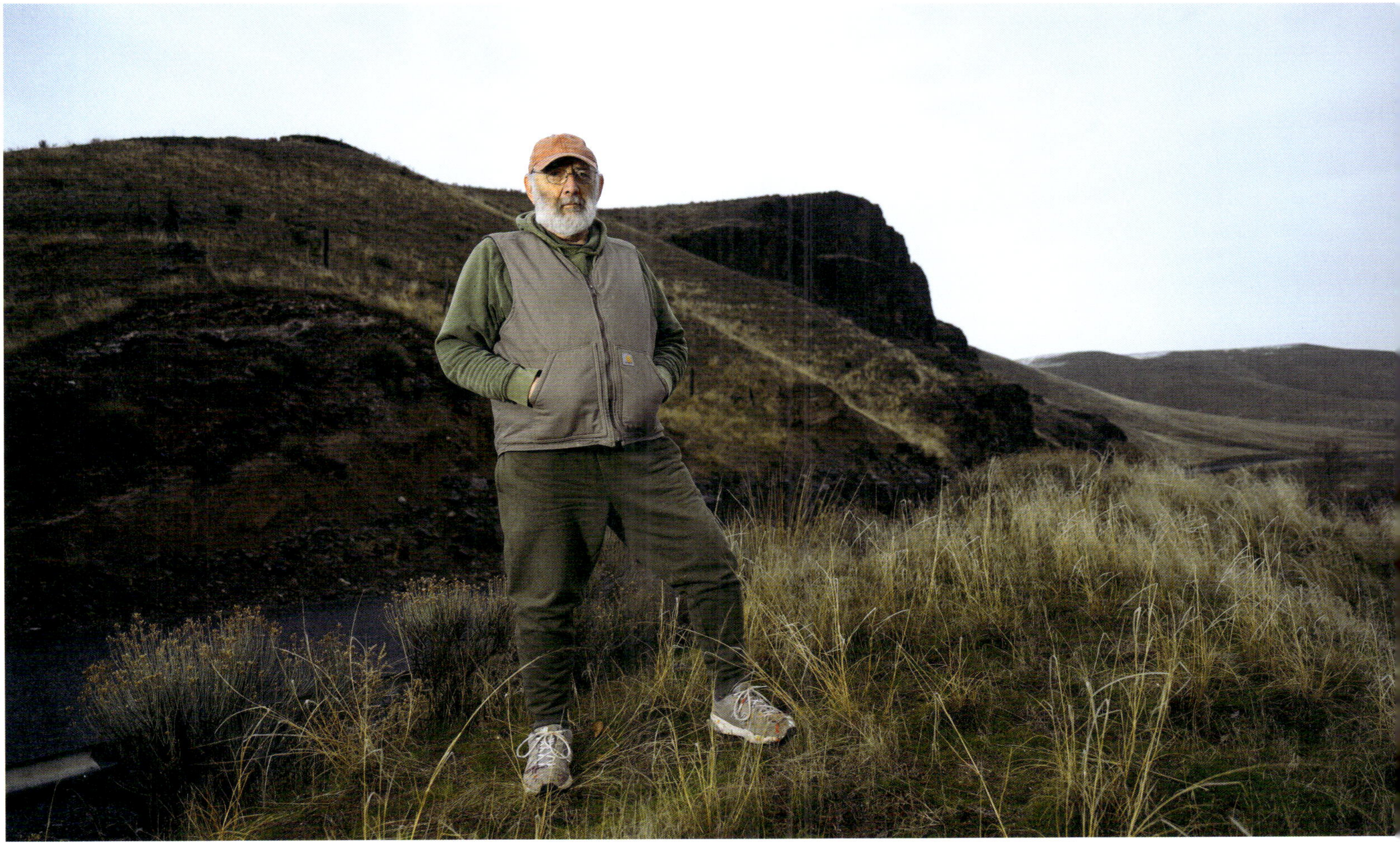

SELECTED SOLO EXHIBITIONS

2025-2029	*James Lavadour: Land of Origin,* Jordan Schnitzer Museum of Art, University of Oregon, Eugene, OR (traveling retrospective): Northwest Museum of Arts and Culture, Spokane, WA; Boise Art Museum, Boise, ID; Whatcom Museum, Bellingham, WA; Heard Museum, Phoenix, AZ; and Missoula Art Museum, Missoula, MT. Tour made possible by Art Bridges.
2025	*HOME GROUND,* PDX CONTEMPORARY ART, Portland, OR
	Oregon Origins Project VI: The Birth of Cascadia, Stelo Arts, Portland, OR
2023	*Planet Waves*, PDX CONTEMPORARY ART, Portland, OR
2022	*Calling Invisible Doctors*, PDX CONTEMPORARY ART, Portland, OR
2020	*EXPECTING RAIN,* PDX CONTEMPORARY ART, Portland, OR
2018	*All that I can see from here,* PDX CONTEMPORARY ART, Portland, OR
	Land of Origin, Foundry Vineyards, Walla Walla, WA
2017	*Recent Findings,* Cumberland Gallery, Nashville, TN
2016	*Ledger of Days,* PDX CONTEMPORARY ART, Portland, OR
2015	*James Lavadour: Land of Origin,* MAC Gallery, Wenatchee Valley College, Wenatchee, WA
2014	*Fingering Instabilities,* PDX CONTEMPORARY ART, Portland, OR
2012	*The Interior,* PDX CONTEMPORARY ART, Portland, OR
2011	Paintings, Grover/Thurston Gallery, Seattle, WA
2010	*Geographies of the Same Stone: for TT*, PDX CONTEMPORARY ART, Portland, OR
2009	Grover/Thurston Gallery, Seattle, WA
2008	*The Properties of Paint,* Hallie Ford Museum of Art, Willamette University, Salem, OR (traveling exhibition): venues included Tamástslikt Cultural Institute, Pendleton, OR; and Schneider Museum of Art, Southern Oregon University, Ashland, OR
	Close to the Ground, PDX CONTEMPORARY ART, Portland, OR
2007	Grover/Thurston Gallery, Seattle, WA
2006	*Sun Spots*, PDX CONTEMPORARY ART, Portland, OR
	Rain, Cumberland Gallery, Nashville, TN
	Magic Valley, Gail Severn Gallery, Ketchum, ID
2005	Grover/Thurston Gallery, Seattle, WA
	Walk, PDX CONTEMPORARY ART, Portland, OR (shown at 219 NW 12th)
2004	Cumberland Gallery, Nashville, TN
2003	*Romantic Landscapes*, PDX CONTEMPORARY ART, Portland, OR
	New Camp, Grover/Thurston Gallery, Seattle, WA
	Gail Severn Gallery, Ketchum, ID

2002	*Intersections II*, PDX CONTEMPORARY ART, Portland, OR
	Intersections, Maryhill Museum of Art, Goldendale, WA
2001	*James Lavadour: Landscapes*, Northwest Museum of Arts & Culture, Spokane, WA
	Grover/Thurston Gallery, Seattle, WA
2000	*Abstracts*, PDX CONTEMPORARY ART, Portland, OR
	Grover/Thurston Gallery, Seattle, WA
1999	*My Body's Edge*, PDX CONTEMPORARY ART, Portland, OR
	Grover/Thurston Gallery, Seattle, WA
1998	PDX CONTEMPORARY ART, Portland, OR
	Sacred Circle Gallery, Seattle, WA
	Philip Feldman Gallery, Pacific Northwest College of Art, Portland, OR
1997	*Honey Tongue*, PDX CONTEMPORARY ART, Portland, OR
	Grover/Thurston Gallery, Seattle, WA
1996	*Works on Paper*, PDX CONTEMPORARY ART, Portland, OR
1995	Elizabeth Leach Gallery, Portland, OR
1993	Greg Kucera Gallery, Seattle, WA
1992	Elizabeth Leach Gallery, Portland, OR
1991	Wentz Gallery, Pacific Northwest College of Art, Portland, OR
	Elizabeth Leach Gallery, Portland, OR
1990	Elaine Horwitch Gallery, Scottsdale, AZ
	Cliff Michel Gallery, Seattle, WA
	Northwest Viewpoints: James Lavadour, Portland Art Museum, Portland, OR
	Elizabeth Leach Gallery, Portland, OR
	Boise Art Museum, Boise, ID
1988	Elizabeth Leach Gallery, Portland, OR
1986	C.N. Gorman Museum, University of California, Davis, CA
1984	Carnegie Center for the Arts, Walla Walla, WA
	James Lavadour: Landscapes and Interiors, University of Oregon Museum of Art, Eugene, OR
1983	Sacred Circle Gallery, Seattle, WA
1982	Oregon State Governors Office, Salem, OR
	Visual Arts Resources/University of Oregon Museum of Art, University of Oregon, Eugene, OR
1981-1983	*Landscapes and Interiors: James Lavadour,* traveling exhibition organized by the Visual Arts Resources, University of Oregon Museum of Art, Eugene, OR

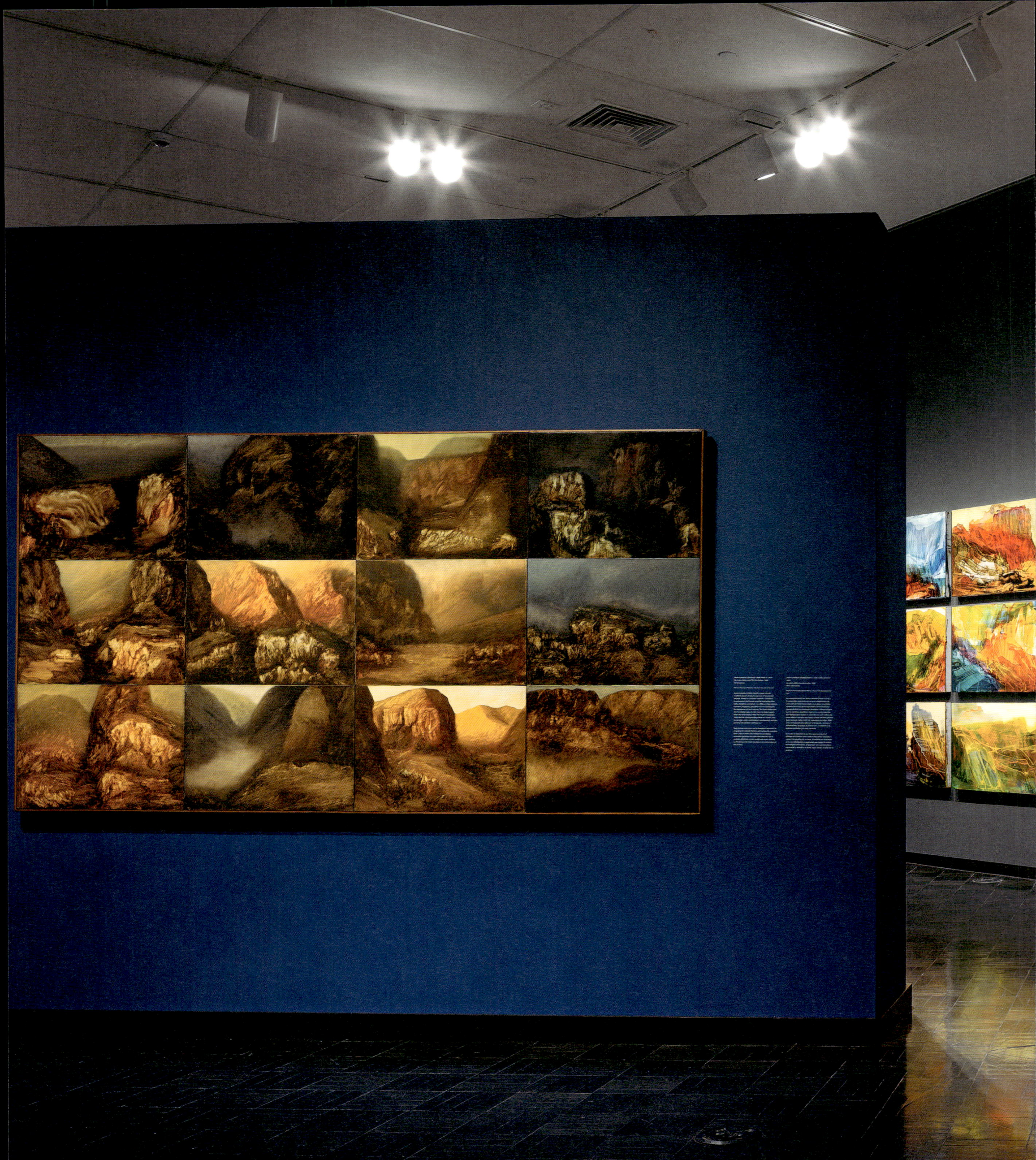

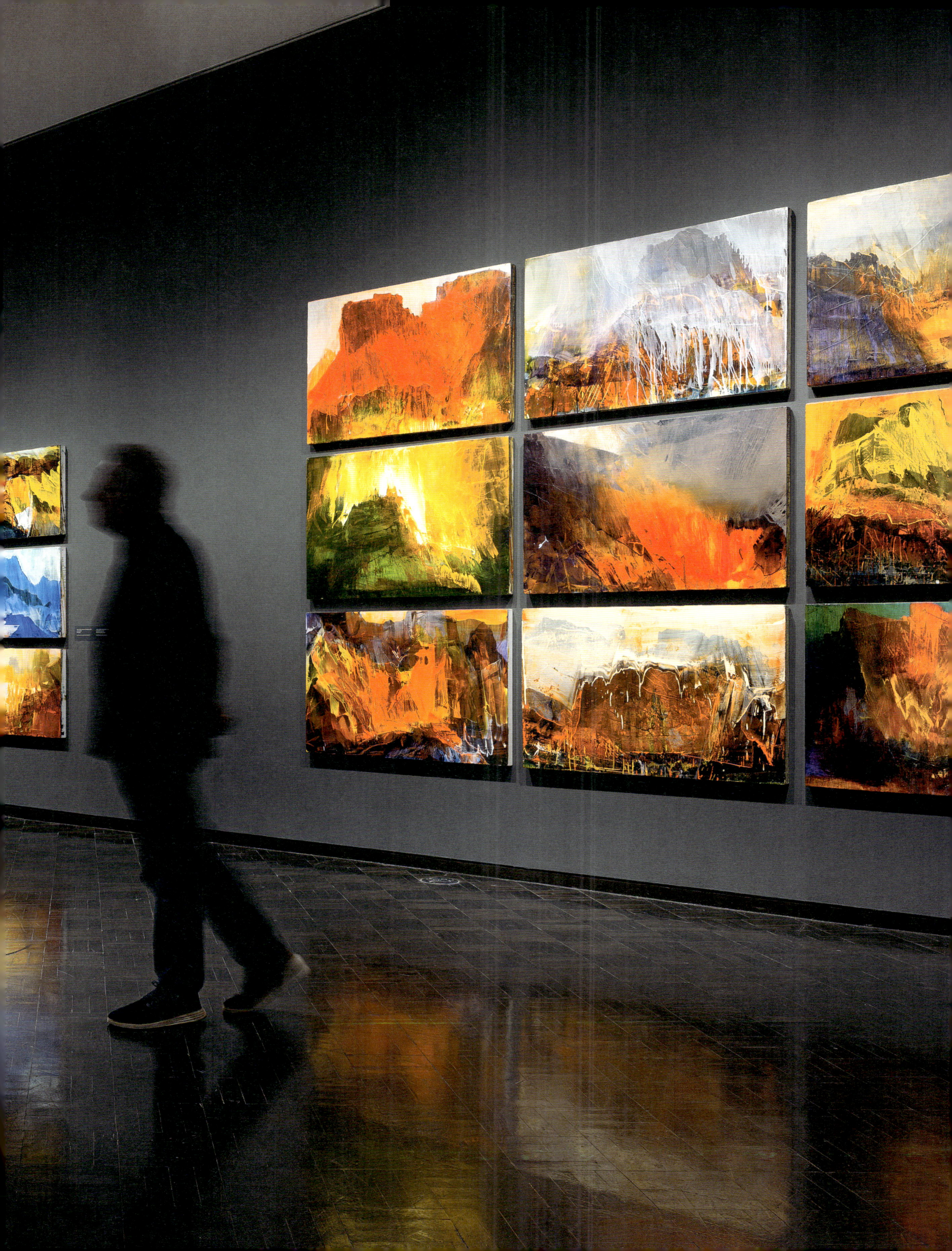

SELECTED GROUP EXHIBITIONS

2025	*Indigenous Identities: Here, Now, and Always*, curated by Jaune Quick-to-See Smith for the Zimmerli Art Museum, Rutgers University, New Brunswick, NJ
	Color Outside the Lines: From the Collections of Jordan D. Schnitzer and His Family Foundation, Jordan Schnitzer Museum of Art, Washington State University, Pullman, WA
2024	*Color Outside the Lines: From the Collections of Jordan D. Schnitzer and His Family Foundation,* Jordan Schnitzer Museum of Art, Portland State University, Portland, OR
2024	*Picturing Family: Métis Life in the Walla Walla Valley*, Whitman College, Walla Walla, WA
	Reframing the 19th Century, Gertrude Bernoudy Gallery, Mildred Lane Kemper Art Museum, St, Louis, MO
	Summer Ritual, PDX CONTEMPORARY ART, Portland, OR
	Super-Natural, Oregon State University President's Residence, Corvallis, OR
2023	*WE ARE THE REVOLUTION*, Converge 45, Curated by Christian Viveros-Faune and William Morrow, Jordan Schnitzer Family Foundation
	Super Natural, Oregon State University, President's Residence, Corvallis, Oregon
	Strange Weather: From the Collections of Jordan D. Schnitzer and His Family Foundation, Jordan Schnitzer Museum of Art, University of Oregon, Eugene, OR; and Bellevue Arts Museum, Bellevue, WA
	The Land Carries Our Ancestors: Contemporary Art by Native Americans, curated by Jaune Quick-to-See Smith for the National Gallery of Art, Washington, D.C
	Treasures from the Vault, Tamástslikt Cultural Institute, Pendleton, OR
	In Bloom, Bellagio Gallery of Fine Art, Las Vegas, NV
	Many Wests: Artists Shape an American Idea, Smithsonian American Art Museum, Washington D.C. and Utah Museum of Fine Arts, University of Utah, Salt Lake City, UT
	OUTSIDE: In, Cummer Museum, Jacksonville, FL
2022	*Giving VOICE: Native American Printmaking*, Fine Arts Center. Dorothy Uber Bryan Gallery, Bowling Green, OH
	Strange Weather: From the Collections of Jordan D. Schnitzer and His Family Foundation, Institute of the Arts and Sciences - UC Santa Cruz, Santa Cruz, CA
	Many Wests: Artists Shape an American Idea, Jordan Schnitzer Museum of Art, University of Oregon, Eugene, OR and Whatcom Museum, Bellingham, WA
	Order / Reorder: Experiments in Collections, Hudson River Muesum, Yonkers, NY
	Hallie Ford Fellows in the Visual Arts 2017-2019, Oregon Contemporary, Portland, OR.
2021	*Time in Place: Northwest Art from the Permanent Collection*, Hallie Ford Museum of Art, Willamette University, Salem, OR
	Untrammeled: At Wilderness' Edge, Sun Valley Museum of Art, Ketchum, ID
	Walking, PDX CONTEMPORARY ART, Portland, OR
	Many Wests: Artists Shape an American Idea, Boise Art Museum, Boise, ID
	Crow's Shadow Institute of the Arts Biennial, Hallie Ford Museum of Art, Salem, OR
	Painting Deconstructed: Selections from the Northwest Collection, Tacoma Art Museum, Tacoma, WA
2020	*Hallie Ford Fellows in the Visual Arts 2017-19*, Jordan Schnitzer Museum of Art, University of Oregon, Eugene, OR
2019	*Stretching the Canvas: Eighty Years of Native Painting, National* Museum of the American Indian, New York, NY
	Crow's Shadow Institute of the Arts at 25, Boise Art Museum, Boise, ID
	Expanded Views: Native American Art in Focus, Toledo Museum of Art, Toledo, OH
	The Western Sublime, Tucson Museum of Art and Historic Block, Tucson, AZ
	Visual Magic: An Oregon Invitational, Jordan Schnitzer Museum of Art, University of Oregon, Eugene, OR

2018	*Art for a New Understanding: Native Voices, 1950s to Now*, Crystal Bridges Museum of American Art, Bentonville, AR
	Ascent: Climbing Explored, The High Desert Museum, Bend, OR
	Along the Edge, PDX CONTEMPORARY ART, Portland, OR
2017	*Native Art Now!*, Eiteljorg Museum of American Indians and Western Art, Indianapolis, IN
	State of the Art: Discovering American Art Now, Frist Center for the Visual Arts, Nashville, TN
	Painted Landscapes: Contemporary Views, Heritage Museum & Gardens, Sandwich, MA
	Conversations in the Round House: Roots, Roads and Remembrances, Jordan Schnitzer Museum of Art, University of Oregon, Eugene, OR
2016	*Artists Select*, Cumberland Gallery, Nashville, TN
2014	*State of the Art: Discovering American Art Now*, Crystal Bridges Museum of American Art, Bentonville, AR
2013	*Personal Structures*, Palazzo Bembo, Venice Biennale, Venice, Italy
	Range, PDX CONTEMPORARY ART, Portland, OR
2011	*The New American Landscape*, Kahnaway Art & Ecology, Washougal, WA
	oomph, PDX CONTEMPORARY ART, Portland, OR
	2011, PDX CONTEMPORARY ART, Portland, OR
2010	*Vantage Point: The Contemporary Native Art Collection*, Smithsonian Institute National Museum of the American Indian, Washington, DC
2009	*Catch-All*, PDX CONTEMPORARY ART, Portland, OR
2007	*Off-the-Map: Landscape in the Native Imagination*, Smithsonian Institute National Museum of the American Indian, New York, NY
	18 Painters, Mt. Hood Community College, Gresham, OR
2005	*Into the Fray*, Eiteljorg Museum of American Indians and Western Art, Indianapolis, IN
	Next, PDX CONTEMPORARY ART, Portland, OR
	Site Unseen: A Contemporary Look at Landscape, Savannah Gallery, Savannah College of Art and Design, Savannah, GA
	A Sense of Place: Selections from the Tacoma Art Museum Collection, Tacoma Art Museum, Tacoma, WA
	New Tradition, Archer Gallery, Clark College, Vancouver, WA
	Native Views: Influences of Modern Culture, Art Train USA, Ann Arbor, MI (traveling USA by rail)
2004	*Wood Work*, J.G. Contemporary, New York, NY
	Seattle Perspective, Seattle Convention Center, City of Seattle Portable Works Collection, Seattle, WA
	The Grand View: Bierstadt to Brophy, Museum of Northwest Art, La Conner, WA
	Clatsop Community College, Astoria, OR
2003	*2003 Oregon Biennial*, Portland Art Museum, Portland, OR
	Extreme Landscape, Hunterdon Museum of Art, Clinton, NJ
	Earth, Wind, Fire and Water, Boise Art Museum, Boise, ID
	Selections from the Elwood Collection, Archer Gallery, Clark College, Vancouver, WA
	Northwest Masters, City Space, City of Seattle Portable Works Collection, Seattle, WA
2001	*The Beta Press Collection: A Decade in the Northwest*, Tacoma Art Museum, Tacoma, WA
	Indian Time Millennial Project, Institute of American Indian Art, Santa Fe, NM
	From Benton to Bartlet: Recent Acquisitions, Washington State University Museum of Art, Pullman, WA

2000	*Physical Manifestations,* PDX CONTEMPORARY ART, Portland, OR
1999	*Indian Time Millennial Project,* Institute of American Indian Art, Santa Fe, NM
	Circle of Friends: Distant Voices, Bush Barn Gallery, Salem, OR Whatcom Museum, Bellingham, WA
	From Benton to Bartlet: Recent Acquisitions, Washington State University Museum of Art, Pullman, WA
1998	*Contemplating Eternity,* Seattle Art Museum, Seattle, WA
	Redefining Tradition: First Nations Artists and Their Work, Whatcom Museum, Bellingham, WA
	Gathered Into Earth: Contemporary Landscape Painting, Sheehan Gallery, Whitman College, Walla Walla, WA
	Gerald Peters Gallery, Santa Fe, NM
	THE LABYRINTH: Visions and Interpretations of the Eternal Myth in Contemporary Art, 2nd International Triennial of Graphic Art Inter-Kontakt-Grafik Prague '98, Prague, Czech Republic
	Twentieth Anniversary of the Betty Bowen Artist Award, Washington State Convention Center, Seattle, WA
	Rediscovering the Landscape of the Americas, Gerald Peters Gallery, Santa Fe, NM
	A Common Thread, Gail Severn Gallery, Sun Valley, ID
1997	*Rising from Tradition*, The High Desert Museum, Bend, OR
1996	*Rediscovering the Landscape of the Americas,* Gerald Peters Gallery, Santa Fe, NM (traveling exhibition): Tucson Museum of Art, Tucson, AZ; The Art Museum of South Texas, Corpus Christi, TX; Western Art Gallery, Western Washington University, Bellingham, WA; Memorial Art Gallery, University of Rochester, Rochester, NY; Gibbes Museum of Art, Charleston, SC.
1995	*Shared Visions: Native American Painters and Sculptors in the Twentieth Century,* organized by The Heard Museum, Phoenix, AZ (traveling exhibition): Museum of New Zealand, Wellington, New Zealand; Sarjeant Gallery, Wanganni, New Zealand; Auckland City Art Gallery, Auckland, New Zealand; Robert McDougall Art Gallery, Christchurch, New Zealand; Wailato Museum of Art and History, Hamilton, New Zealand
	Romance of the Land: Native Northwest Visions, The Bellevue Art Museum, Bellevue, WA
	Twenty-five American Print Artists: La Jeune Gravure, Mairie du Sixieme Arrondissement de Paris, Pairs, France
	Native Papers: Joe Fedderson, James Lavadour, Kay WalkingStick, Phil Young, Gallery 210, University of Missouri, St. Louis, MO
	Recent Northwest Acquisitions, Seattle Art Museum, Seattle, WA
	Print and Paper Projects from the Rutgers Center for Print and Paper, The Printmaking Council of New Jersey, North Branch Station, Branchburg, NJ
	Recent Acquisitions from the Rutgers Center for Print and Paper, Zimmerli Art Museum, Rutgers University, New Brunswick, NJ
	Gail Severn Gallery, Ketchum, ID
1995	Grover/Thurston Gallery, Seattle, WA
1994	*From The Earth X,* American Indian Contemporary Arts, San Francisco, CA
1993	*The Sacred and the Profane,* Jan Baum Gallery, Los Angeles, CA
1993	*Biennial,* Portland Art Museum, Portland, OR
1992	*Land, Spirit, Power: First Nations at the National Gallery of Canada,* National Gallery of Canada, Ottawa, Canada (traveling exhibition): Mackenzie Art Gallery, Regina, Saskatchewan, Canada; The Contemporary Arts Museum, Houston, TX; Nickle Arts Museum, Calgary, Alberta, Canada; The Print Club, Philadelphia, PA
	Crossing Over/Changing Places: Artists and Collaborators, Anderson Gallery, Virginia Commonwealth University, Richmond, VA
	Decolonizing of the Mind, Center on Contemporary Art, Seattle, WA
	The Betty Bowen Legacy: Fourteen Years of Award Winning Art, Security Pacific Gallery, Seattle, WA

	MASTER PRINTS from the Rutgers Center for Innovative Printmaking: The First Five Years, The Gallery at Bristol-Meyers Squibb, Princeton, NJ
1991	*Shared Visions: Native American Painters and Sculptors in the Twentieth Century,* The Heard Museum, Phoenix, AZ (traveling exhibition): The Eiteljorg Museum of American History and Western Art, Indianapolis, IN; Thomas Gilcrease Institute of the American History and Art, Tulsa, OK; Portland Art Museum, Portland, OR; Smithsonian Institute National Museum of the American Indian, Washington, DC; The Customs House, New York, NY
	Northwest Tales: Contemporary Narrative Painting, Anchorage Museum of History and Art, Anchorage, AK
1990	*The Undiminished Landscape,* Security Pacific Corp. Gallery, San Francisco, CA
	NORTHWEST x SOUTHWEST: PAINTED FICTIONS, Museum of the Desert, Palm Springs, CA (traveling exhibition): Yellowstone Art Center, Billings, MT; Western Gallery, Western Washington University, Bellingham, WA; Sarah Campbell Blaffer Gallery, University of Houston, Houston, TX
	Celebrated Selections, The Heard Museum, Phoenix, AZ
	Tradition and Spirit: Contemporary Native American Art, Maryhill Museum of Art, Goldendale, WA Windhorse Gallery, Seattle, WA
	Printed in America, Walters Hall Gallery, Rutgers University, New Brunswick, NJ
1989	*Figurative Show,* Elizabeth Leach Gallery, Portland, OR
1988	*Roll on Columbia: Historic and Contemporary Landscapes of the Columbia River Gorge*, Maryhill Museum, Goldendale, WA
	Crossed Cultures: Five Contemporary Native Northwest Artists, Seattle Art Museum, Seattle, WA
	Artists of the Blue Mountains: 1910-1988, Sheehan Gallery, Whitman College, Walla Walla, WA Non-Objective Landscape, Marylhurst College, Marylhurst, OR
1987	Seattle Art Museum, Seattle, WA
	Recent Generations: Native American Art 1910-1987, The Heard Museum, Phoenix, AZ
	New Directions Northwest: Contemporary Native American Art, Portland Art Museum, Portland, OR
	Beyond Blue Mountains: A Traveling Collection of Contemporary Native American Artworks, Washington State Arts Commission, Olympia, WA
	Contemporary Visions: Fifteen Native American Artists, Read/Stremmel Gallery, San Antonio, TX
	Native American Art: Our Contemporary Visions, Stremmel Galleries, Reno, NV
1986	*The Artist Interprets the Landscape,* Blackfish Gallery, Portland, OR
	Oregon Artist Exhibition, Oregon Pavilion, Expo '86, Vancouver, B.C., Canada
	Artist of Eastern Oregon on Tour, Eastern Oregon State College, La Grande, OR (traveling exhibition): Tacoma Art Museum, Tacoma, WA; Oregon Artists Show, Sacred Circle Gallery, Seattle, WA
1984	*Seattle Urban League: Minority Artist Show,* Seattle Center House, Seattle, WA
	No Beads No Trinkets: An Exhibition of Contemporary American Indian Artists, Palais de Nations, Geneva, Switzerland
	Elizabeth Leach Gallery, Portland, OR
	Contemporary Native American Art, Touchstone Gallery, Spokane, WA
	Innovations: New Expression in Native American Painting, The Heard Museum, Phoenix, AZ
1983	*1983 Oregon Biennial,* Portland Art Museum, Portland, OR
	Indian Artists of the 1980's, Sacred Circle Gallery, Seattle, WA

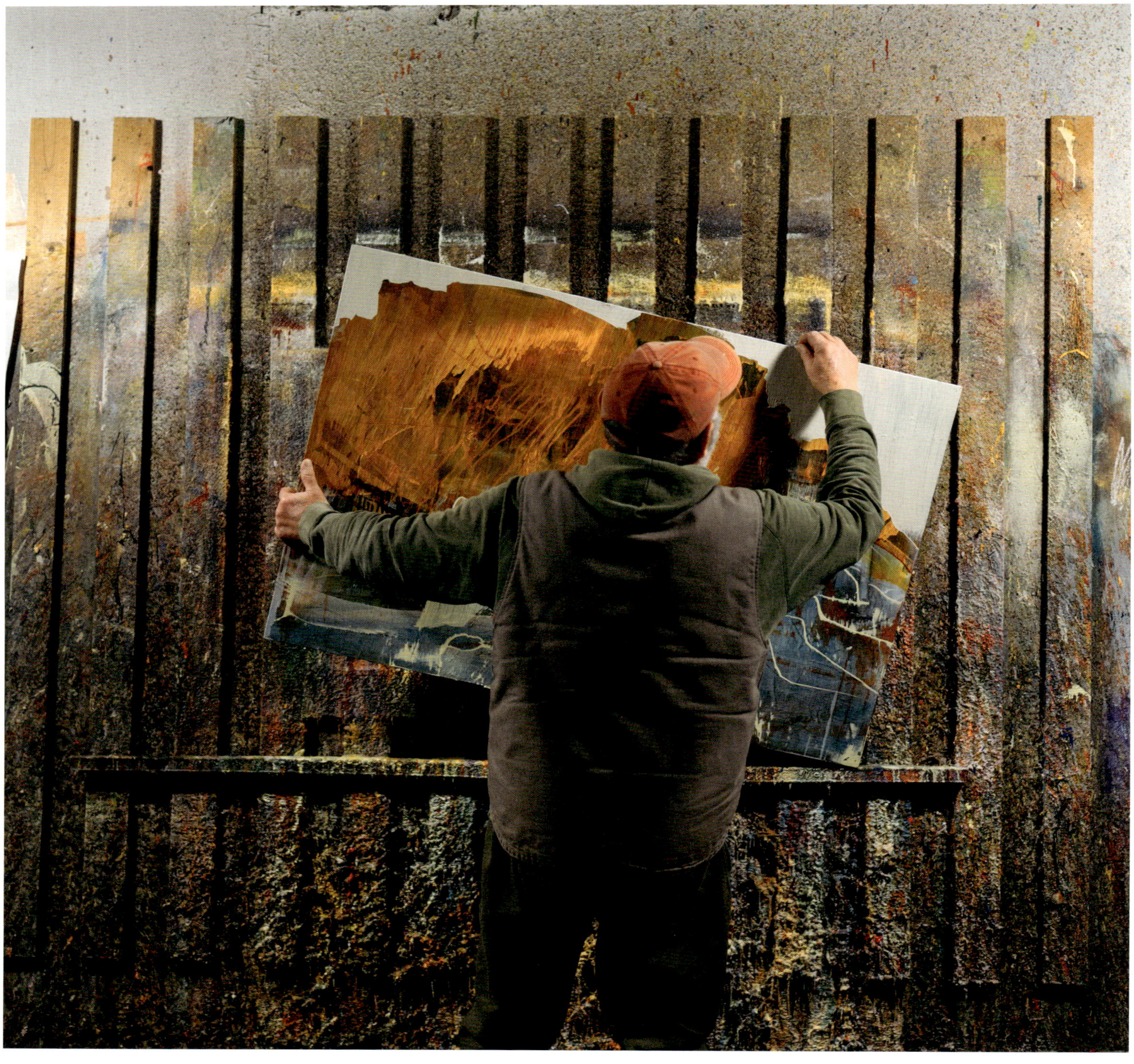

SELECTED AWARDS, FELLOWSHIPS, AND COMMISSIONS

2025	Commission, Portland International Airport (PDX) in collaboration with the Port of Portland the Regional Arts & Culture Council (RACC), Portland, OR
2019	Hallie Ford Fellowship in the Visual Arts, The Ford Family Foundation, Roseburg, OR
2013	Commission, Oregon Department of Transportation, Salem, OR
2005	Fellowship for Native American Fine Art, Eiteljorg Museum of American Indians and Western Art, Indianapolis, IN
	Commission, Ashforth Pacific Inc., Portland, OR
2004	Award for Visual Arts, Flintridge Foundation, Pasadena, CA
	Commission, Bellevue Community College Library, Bellevue, WA
2002	Commission, Southern Oregon University Library, Oregon Arts Commission, Ashland, OR
2001	Commission, Eastern Oregon University Science Building, Oregon Arts Commissions, La Grande, OR
2000	Commission, North Capitol Mall Office Building, Oregon Arts Commission, Salem, OR
1999	Honorary Doctorate of Human Letters, Eastern Oregon University, La Grande, OR
	Commission, Washington State Football/Soccer Stadium and Exhibition Center Project, Seattle, WA
	Commission, Qwest Field, Seahawk Stadium, Seattle, WA
1998	Joan Mitchell Painters & Sculptors Grant, Joan Mitchell Foundation, New York, NY
1995	Fellowship, Rutgers Center for Innovative Print and Paper, Rutgers University, New Brunswick, NJ
1994	Oregon Governor's Arts Award, Oregon Arts Commission, Salem, OR
1991	Betty Bowen Memorial Recognition Award, Seattle Art Museum, Seattle, WA
1990	Fellowship to the Rutgers Center for the Innovative Print and Paper, Rutgers University, New Brunswick, NJ
1989	Northwest Major Works Award, Seattle Arts Commission, Seattle, Washington
1987	Commission, Art in Public Places, Washington State Arts Commission, Olympia, WA
1986	Oregon Arts Fellowship, Oregon Arts Commission, Salem, OR
1985	Commission, Art in Public Places, Washington State Arts Commission, Olympia, WA
	Commission, Artist Advocate Project, Pendleton Arts Council, Pendleton, OR
1983	Commission, Art in Public Places, Seattle Arts Commission, Seattle, WA
1982	Commission, Washington State Arts Commission, Olympia, WA
1981	Artist in Schools Program, Eastern Oregon Regional Art Council, La Grande, OR
1980	Artist-in-Residence, Confederated Tribes of the Umatilla Indian Reservation, Pendleton, OR

SELECTED COLLECTIONS

Bank of America Corporation, San Francisco, CA Boise Art Museum, Boise, ID
Cheney Cowles Museum, Spokane, WA
Confederated Tribes of the Umatilla Indian Reservation, Pendleton, OR
Crocker Art Museum, Sacramento, CA
Crystal Bridges Museum of American Art, Bentonville, AR
Eastern Oregon University, La Grande, OR
Eiteljorg Museum of American Indians and Western Art, Indianapolis, IN
Federal Reserve Bank, San Francisco, CA
Fort Dalles Readiness Center, The Dalles, OR
Frank Russell & Company, Tacoma, WA
Hallie Ford Museum of Art, Willamette University, Salem, OR
Heathman Management Corporation, Portland, OR
The Heard Museum, Phoenix, AZ High Desert Museum, Bend, OR
The Hood Museum, Dartmouth College, Hanover, NH
Hilton Corporation, Portland, OR
Jordan Schnitzer Family Foundation, Portland, OR
Jordan Schnitzer Museum of Art, University of Oregon, Eugene, OR
Microsoft Corporation, Redmond, WA
Montclair Art Museum, Montclair, NJ
Northern Arizona University, Flagstaff, AZ
Northwest Museum of Arts and Culture, Spokane, WA
Oregon Arts Commission, Salem, OR
Oregon Department of Transportation, Salem, OR
Oregon Health and Science University, Portland, OR
Oregon State Capitol Art Collection, Salem, OR
Oregon State University, Corvallis, OR
OZ Art NWA, Bentonville, AR
Pacific Northwest Bell Corporation, Seattle, WA
Perkins Coie, Seattle, WA
Portland Art Museum, Portland, OR
Portland International Airport (PDX), Portland, OR
Regional Arts and Culture Council, Portable Works Collection, Multnomah County, OR
Seattle Arts Commission, Seattle, WA
Seattle Art Museum, Seattle, WA
Seattle Convention Center, Seattle, WA
Seattle Seahawks Stadium, Seattle, WA
Seattle University, Seattle, WA
Smithsonian Institute National Museum of the American Indian, Washington, D.C.
Southern Oregon University, Ashland, OR
Tacoma Art Museum, Tacoma, WA
The Tia Collection, Santa Fe, NM
Trimet, Portland, OR
Washington State Arts Commission, Olympia, WA
Washington State University, Pullman, WA
Western Heritage Savings and Loan, Pendleton, OR
West One Bank Corporation, Portland, OR
Whitney Museum of American Art, New York, NY
University of Oregon, Eugene, OR
University of Washington Medical Center, Seattle, WA
U.S. Department of Interior, Indian Arts and Crafts Board, Washington, D.C.
U.S. State Department, Embassy of Islamabad, Pakistan
Zimmerli Art Museum, Rutgers University, New Brunswick, NJ

COMMUNITY ART SERVICES

1990-2024 Crow's Shadow Institute of the Arts, Confederated Tribes of the Umatilla Indian Reservation: Founder, past president and board member

SELECTED EXHIBITION CATALOGS AND BOOKS

2020 *James Lavadour: 2019 Hallie Ford Fellow in the Visual Arts.* Essay by Emily Zimmerman. The Ford Family Foundation: Roseburg, OR, 2020.

2019 Morris, Kate. *Shifting Grounds: Landscape in Contemporary Native American Art.* University of Washington Press, 2019.

Knapp, Danielle M. *Visual Magic: An Oregon Invitational.* Jordan Schnitzer Museum of Art, University of Oregon. Eugene, OR, 2019.

2014 Bacigalupi, Don. *State of the Art: Discovering American Art Now.* Crystal Bridges Museum of American Art. Bentonville, AR, 2014.

2013 Della Monica, Lauren P. *Painted Landscapes: Contemporary Views.* Schiffer Publishing, Ltd. Atglen, PA, 2013.

Personal Structures: Culture, Mind, Becoming. Essay by Meagan Atiyeh. Global Art Affairs Foundation. Leiden, Netherlands, 2013.

2008 Dobkins, Rebecca. *James Lavadour: The Properties of Paint.* Hallie Ford Museum of Art, Willamette University. Salem, OR, 2008.

2007 *Off the Map: Landscape in the Native Imagination*. National Museum of the American Indian, Smithsonian Institution. New York, NY, 2007.

2005 *Into the Fray: The Eiteljorg Fellowship for Native American Fine Art*. Eiteljorg Museum of American Indians and Western Art, in Association with the University of Washington Press. Seattle, WA, 2005.

2004 Rinder, Lawrence. Awards for Visual Arts 2003/2004 Flintridge Foundation. Pasadena, CA, 2004.

2001 Halper, Vicki. *James Lavadour: Landscapes.* Northwest Museum of Art & Culture. Spokane, WA, 2001.

1997 Sayre, Henry M. *A World of Art.* Edition: 2, Prentice-Hall Inc., Simon & Schuster Co. New York, NY, 1997.

1996 Zevitas, Steven T. *New American Paintings: a quarterly exhibition*. Open Studios Press, Vol. 1, No. VI, Spring 1996. Boston, MA, 1996.

1995 Allen, Lois. *Contemporary Art in the Northwest.* Craftsman House G + B Arts International. Sydney, Australia, 1995.

Spanbauer, Tom. *L'homme qui tomba amoureux de la lune/The Man Who Fell in Love With the Moon,* (cover). STOCK (ĀDITIONS). Paris, France, 1995.

Sayre, Henry M. *A World of Art,* Prentice-Hall Inc., Simon & Schuster Co. New York, NY, 1995.

1994 Penney, David and George Longfish. *Native American Art*. Hugh Lauter Levin Associates, Inc. New York, NY, 1994.

Hansen, Trudy V., Patricia Cudd, and Maggie Patrick. *The RUTGERS ARCHIVES FOR PRINTMAKING STUDIOS: A Catalogue of the Acquisitions 1991-1993.* Library of Congress Catalogue Card No. 94-77603, 1994.

1992 Brodsky, Judith. *Master Prints from the Rutgers Center for Creative Printmaking: The First 5 Years.* The Gallery at Bristol-Meyers Squibb. Princeton, NJ, 1992.

Nemelroff, Diane. *Land, Spirit, Power: First Nations at the National Gallery of Canada.* National Gallery of Canada, Ottawa, 1992.

Farmer, Jane, and Charlotte Townsend-Gault. *Crossing Over/Changing Places: An Exhibition of Collaborative Print Projects and Paperworks.* The Print Club. Philadelphia, PA, 1992.

Rynd, Chase W. *The Betty Bowen Legacy: Fourteen Years of Award-Winning Art.* Security Pacific Gallery. Seattle, WA, 1992.

1991 Archuleta, Margaret. *Shared Visions: Native American Painters and Sculptors in the 20th Century*. The Heard Museum. Phoenix, AZ, 1991.

1990 Chelette, Iona, et al. *NORTHWEST X SOUTHWEST: PAINTED FICTIONS.* Palm Springs Desert Museum. Palm Springs, CA, 1990.

Evens, Linda E. *The Undiminished Landscape*. Security Pacific Gallery. San Francisco, CA, 1990.

Roberts, Prudence. *Northwest Viewpoints: James Lavadour.* Portland Art Museum. Portland, OR, 1990.

1989 Sims, Patterson. *Crossed Cultures: Five Contemporary Native Northwest Artists.* Seattle Art Museum. Seattle, WA, 1989.

1988 Mautz, Roger. *St. James Guide to Native North American Artists.* St. James Press, 1988.

1987 Longfish, George, et al. *New Directions Northwest.* Portland Art Museum. Portland, OR, 1987.

Index of images

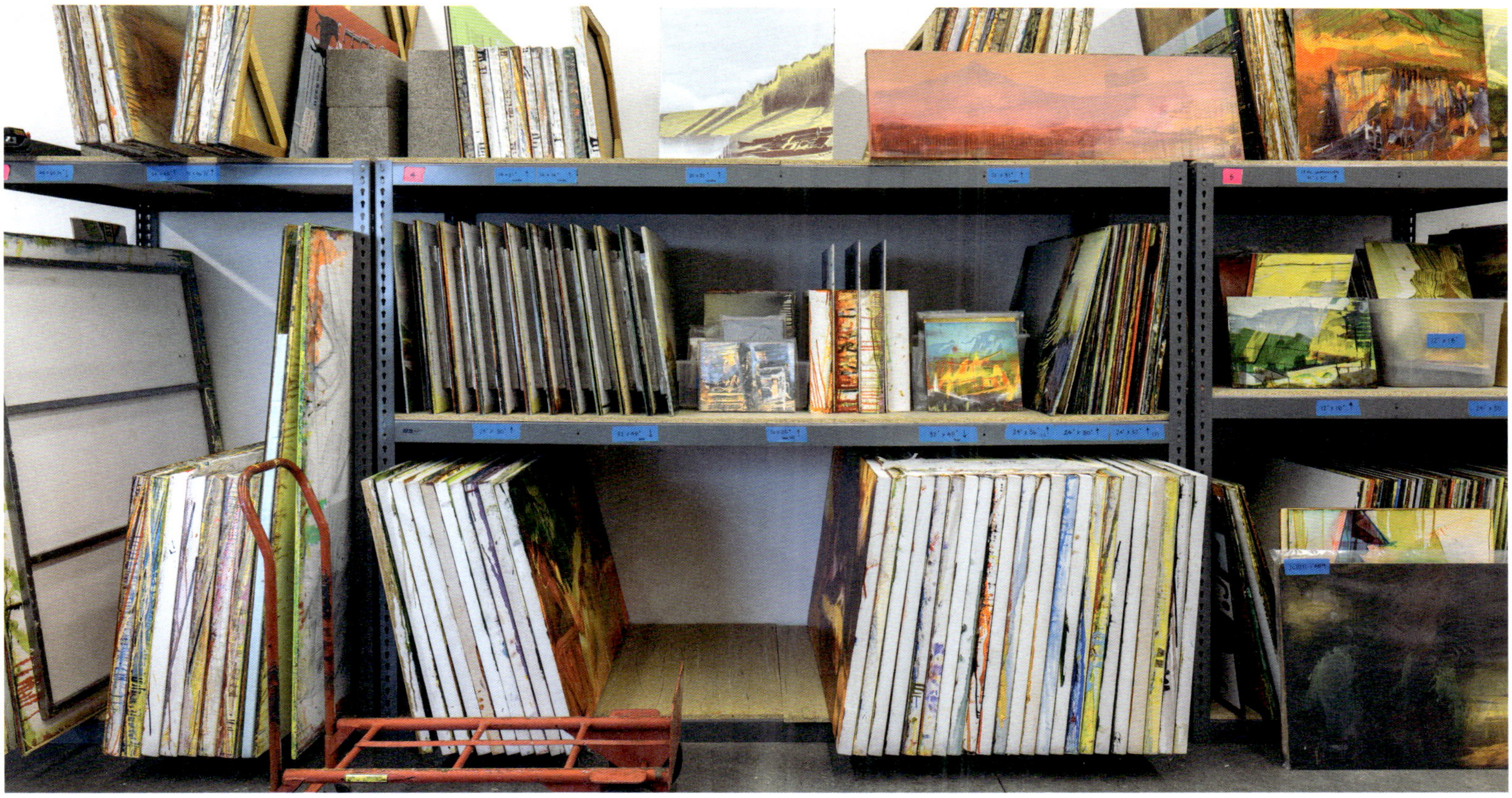

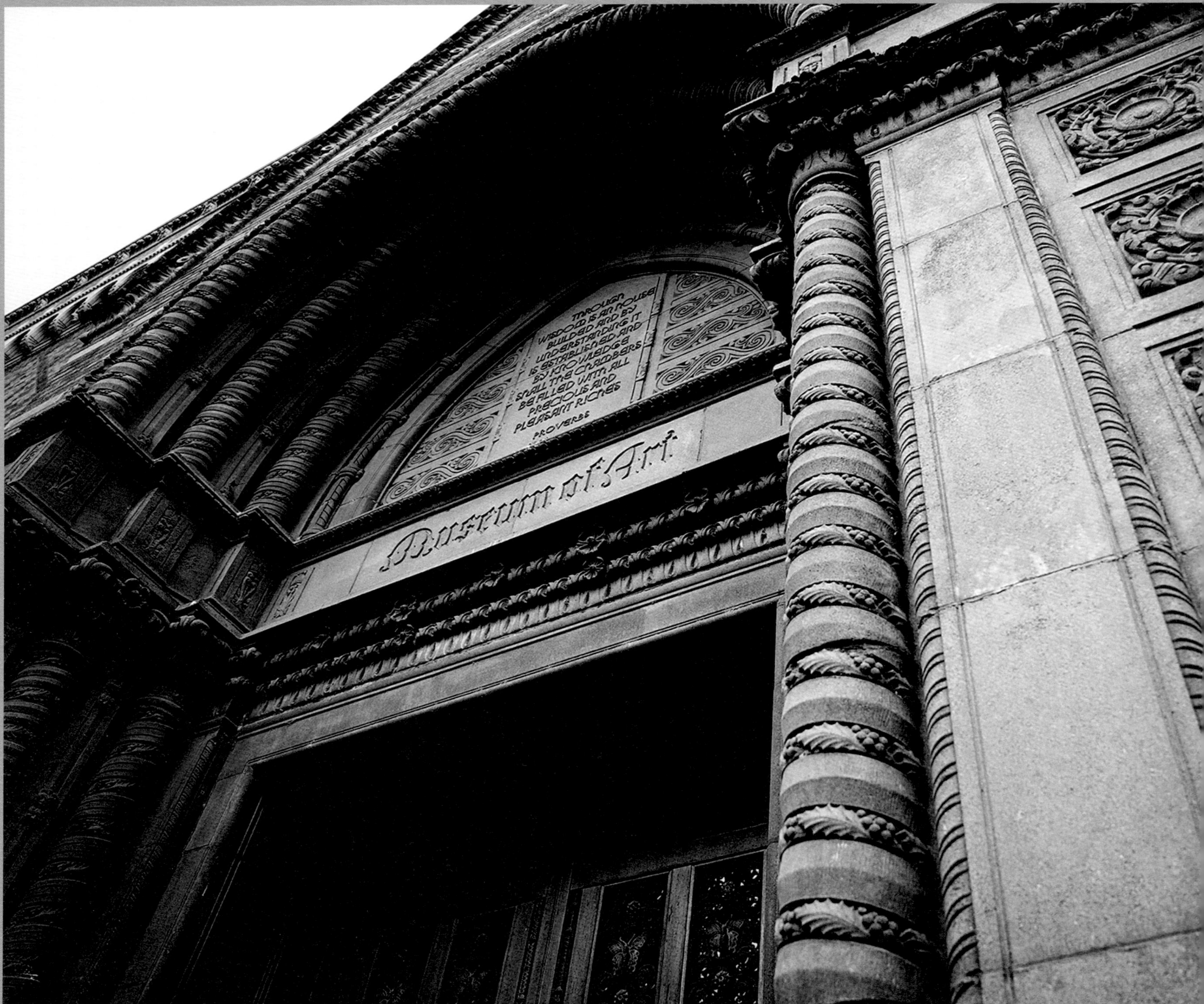

JORDAN SCHNITZER **MUSEUM OF ART**

University of Oregon

The only academic art museum in Oregon accredited by the American Alliance of Museums, the University of Oregon's Jordan Schnitzer Museum of Art (JSMA) features engaging exhibitions, significant collections of historic and contemporary art, and exciting educational programs that support the university's academic mission and the diverse interests of its off-campus communities. The JSMA's collections galleries present selections from its extensive holdings of Chinese, Japanese, Korean and American art. Special exhibitions galleries display works from the collection and on loan, representing many cultures of the world, past and present. The JSMA continues a long tradition of bridging international cultures and offers a welcoming destination for discovery and education centered on artistic expression that deepens the appreciation and understanding of the human condition.

JSMA Staff

Executive Office and Administration
Olivia Miller, Executive Director
Kurt Neugebauer, Associate Director of Administration & Exhibitions
Michele Renee, Administrative Support
Lesley Williams, Executive Assistant

Curatorial
Anne Rose Kitagawa, Chief Curator of Collections, Asian Art, and Academic Support
Heejung Chang, Korea Foundation Global Challengers Museum Intern
Yan Geng, Curator of Contemporary and Traditional Chinese Art
Soojin Jeong, Post-Grad Museum Fellow in East Asian Art
Danielle Knapp, McCosh Curator
Katie Loney, Post-Grad Museum Fellow in European & American Art
Adriana Miramontes Olivas, Curator of Academic Programs and Latin American & Caribbean Art
Thom Sempere, Associate Curator of Photography

Collections and Installation
Chris White, Collections Manager
Joey Capadona, Exhibition Designer and Head Preparator
Melissa Dawn, Associate Registrar
Anthony Edwards, Preparator
Alexander Ellis, Head Registrar & Shared Visions Manager
Noah Greene, Preparator
Elizabeth Larew, Assistant Collections Manager
Mark O'Harra, Preparator-Carpenter
Beth Robinson, Preparator-Conservator
Jonathan Smith, Collections Database Coordinator & Photographer

Communications and Design
Mike Bragg, Museum Design Services Manager
Debbie Williamson Smith, Communications Manager

Development
Peggy Whalen, Sr. Associate Director of Development
John Rustik, Development Program Manager

Education
Lisa Abia-Smith, Director of Education
Gabrielle Miller, Museum Educator
Rosemarie Oakman, Museum Program Manager for Well-being and Community Engagement

Events
Will Kingscott, Event Production Manager
Haley Davis, Scheduling Coordinator

Security and Facilities
Scott Fellman, Facilities & Security Administrator
Dawn Davey, Museum Security Officer
Kim Diaz, Museum Security Officer
Ben Dippy, Museum Security Officer
Jamis Gully, Building Services Assistant
Tyler Johnson, Museum Security Officer
Javi Martinez, Museum Security Officer
Justin Stuck, Facilities Services Coordinator

Visitor Services
Jamie Leaf, Visitor Services & Store Manager
Asha Logan, Visitor Services Assistant

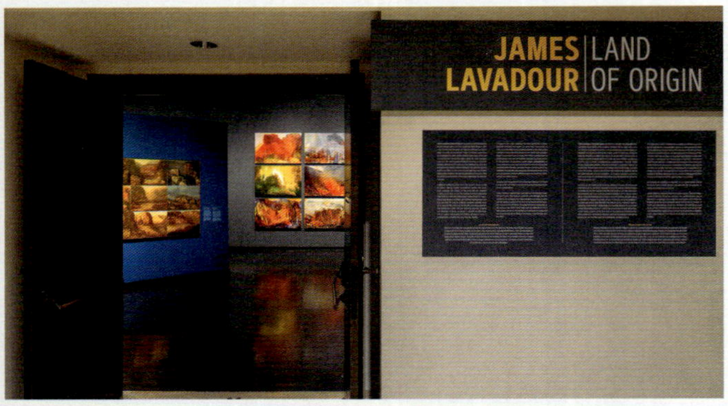

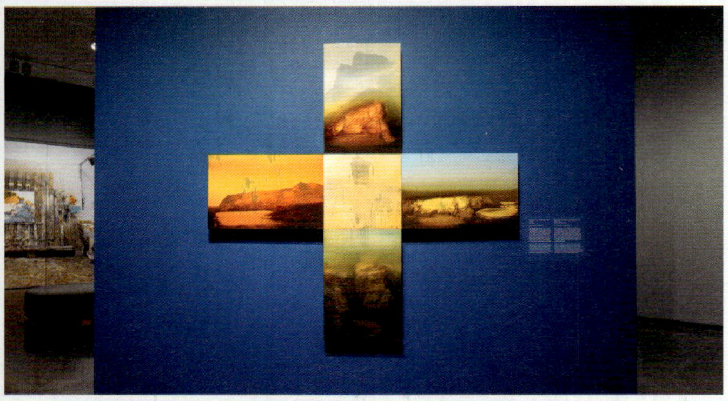

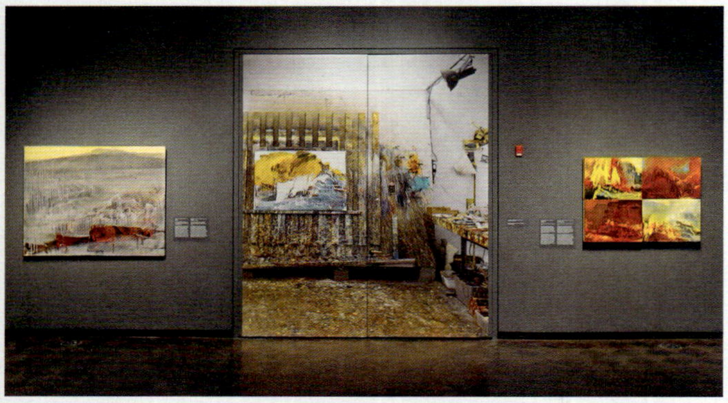

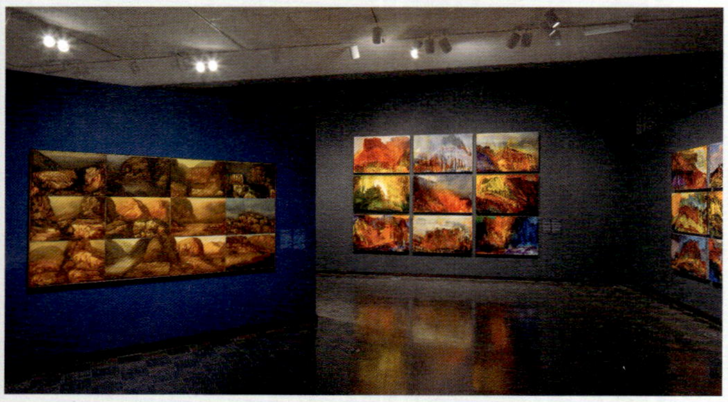

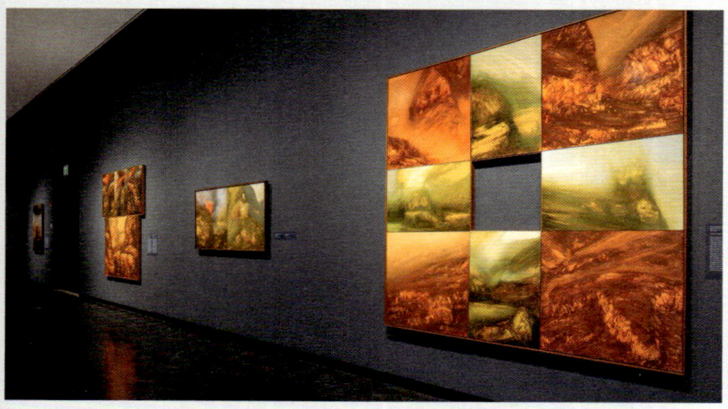

Installation views, Barker Gallery,
Jordan Schnitzer Museum of Art, October 2025
James Lavadour: Land of Origin exhibition design and layout
by Joey Capadona

Published by the Jordan Schnitzer Museum of Art, University of Oregon

James Lavadour: Land of Origin was organized by Danielle M. Knapp, JSMA McCosh Curator. The museum gratefully acknowledges that the exhibition, its catalogue, and related programs are made possible with the generous support of The Ford Family Foundation in Oregon, the Coeta and Donald Barker Changing Exhibitions Endowment at the museum, the JSMA's Hartz FUNd for Contemporary Art, and the JSMA Patron Circle and museum members. Learning and Engagement programming made possible with support from Art Bridges. Additional support for this catalogue was provided by an Exhibition Documentation and Support grant from The Ford Family Foundation, Bill & Leslie Cornog, and PDX CONTEMPORARY ART. The exhibition's national tour is supported and organized by Art Bridges, in partnership with JSMA.

ISBN 978-1-7379136-4-1

Photography, unless otherwise noted Courtesy James Lavadour
and PDX CONTEMPORARY ART.
Pages 1, 12-13, 190, 142-143: Mike Bragg.
Pages 6-11, 72-73, 170-171, 178-179, 192: Brian Davies.
Pages 17-18, 33, 36-39, 58, 60-64, 68-71, 175, 184, 189, and additional Exhibition Plates:
Mario Gallucci.
Page 23: Courtesy Portland Art Museum.
Page 24-25: courtesy Eiteljorg Museum of American Indians and Western Art.
Page 27: Photo by NMAI Photo Services.
Pages 32, 34-35: John S. Weber.
Page 43: Danielle Knapp.
Pages 44-48, 50, 100-101, 122, 124: Courtesy Hallie Ford Museum of Art
Page 47: Photo by Dale Peterson as noted.
Pages 48, 78, 80-83, 86-87, 92-93, 97, 99, 100, 102-103, 110-111, 123, 131, 134, 138-139:
Jonathan B. Smith
Page 49: Courtesy Crow's Shadow Institute of the Arts
Page 53: Photo by Pat Walters.
Pages 76-77: Courtesy Whitney Museum of American Art.
Pages 79-80: Courtesy Denver Art Museum.
Pages 80-81, 99: Courtesy Boise Art Museum.
Pages 82-83, 92-93: Courtesy Tacoma Art Museum.
Pages 90-91: Courtesy Northwest Museum of Arts and Culture.
© Dean Davis Photography.
Pages 112-123: Courtesy Crystal Bridges Museum of American Art.
Pages 140-141: Courtesy Art Bridges.
Page 173: Josie Brown.

Designed by Mike Bragg.
Edited by Danielle M. Knapp, John S. Weber, and Katie Loney.
Copyedited by Susan Mannheimer, Katie Loney, and Debbie Williamson Smith.
Joey Capadona, The *James Lavadour: Land of Origin* exhibition design and layout.

Cover image:
Lucky Star (detail), 2024. Oil on wood, 74 x 145 inches.
Collection of the Jordan Schnitzer Family Foundation.

Printed by Trifolio in 2026

UNIVERSITY OF OREGON

JORDAN SCHNITZER
MUSEUM OF ART